Life-Span Development and Behavior

VOLUME 3

Life-Span Development and Behavior

VOLUME 3

Edited by

Paul B. Baltes

College of Human Development
The Pennsylvania State University
University Park, Pennsylvania

and

Orville G. Brim, Jr.

Foundation for Child Development
New York, New York

1980

Academic Press

A Subsidiary of Harcourt Brace Jovanovich, Publishers

New York London Toronto Sydney San Francisco

ACADEMIC PRESS, INC.
111 Fifth Avenue, New York, New York 10003

United Kingdom Edition published by
ACADEMIC PRESS, INC. (LONDON) LTD.
24/28 Oval Road, London NW1 7DX

LIBRARY OF CONGRESS CATALOG CARD NUMBER: 77–0531

ISBN 0–12–431803–7

PRINTED IN THE UNITED STATES OF AMERICA

80 81 82 83   9 8 7 6 5 4 3 2 1

Dedicated to Guenther Reinert

1928–1979

Guenther Reinert has been one of the second-generation pioneers who contributed much to the recent growth of the life-span movement in psychology, both as a scholar and mentor. His premature and unexpected death due to heart failure shocked us and deprived us of an esteemed friend and visionary colleague. Reinert's rich professional life included many additional dimensions including the founding of the Department of Psychology at the University of Trier and of Germany's Center for Documentation in Psychology located at that same institution.

Contents

The Development of Wisdom across the Life Span: A Reexamination of an Ancient Topic

Vivian P. Clayton and James E. Birren

Aging and Parenthood in the Middle Years

Alice S. Rossi

Female Sexuality through the Life Span

Judith Long Laws

On the Properties of Life Events

Orville G. Brim, Jr., and Carol D. Ryff

List of Contributors

Numbers in parentheses indicate the pages on which authors' contributions begin.

Ronald P. Abeles[1] (307), American Institute for Research in the Behavioral Sciences, Palo Alto, California 94305

Toni C. Antonucci (253), Department of Family Practice and Institute for Social Research, The University of Michigan, Ann Arbor, Michigan 48106

James E. Birren (103), Andrus Gerontology Center, University of Southern California, Los Angeles, California 90007

Orville G. Brim, Jr. (367), Foundation for Child Development, New York, New York 10017

Vivian P. Clayton (103), Department of Applied Human Development and Guidance, Teachers College of Columbia University, New York, New York 10027

Paul T. Costa, Jr. (65), National Institute on Aging, Gerontology Research Center, Baltimore City Hospitals, Baltimore, Maryland 21224

Steven J. Danish (339), College of Human Development, The Pennsylvania State University, University Park, Pennsylvania 16802

Kenneth J. Gergen (31), Department of Psychology, Swarthmore College, Swarthmore, Pennsylvania 19081

Robert L. Kahn (253), Survey Research Center, Institute for Social Research, The University of Michigan, Ann Arbor, Michigan 48106

Judith Long Laws (207), Sociology Department, Syracuse University, Syracuse, New York 13210

Robert R. McCrae (65), National Institute on Aging, Gerontology Research Center, Baltimore City Hospitals, Baltimore, Maryland 21224

[1] Present address: Social and Behavioral Research, National Institute on Aging, Bethesda, Maryland 20205.

Carol A. Nowak (339), College of Human Development, The Pennsylvania State University (Altoona Campus), Altoona, Pennsylvania 16603

David W. Plath (287), Department of Anthropology, University of Illinois at Urbana-Champaign, Urbana, Illinois 61801

Guenther Reinert[2] (1), Department of Psychology, University of Trier, Trier, West Germany

Alice S. Rossi (137), Department of Sociology, University of Massachusetts, Amherst, Massachusetts 01002

Carol D. Ryff (367), Department of Psychology, Fordham University, Bronx, New York 10458

Michael A. Smyer (339), College of Human Development, The Pennsylvania State University, University Park, Pennsylvania 16802

Laurie Steel (307), American Institute for Research in the Behavioral Sciences, Palo Alto, California 94302

Lauress S. Wise (307), American Institute for Research in the Behavioral Sciences, Palo Alto, California 94302

---

[2] Deceased. A detailed obituary has been published in *Psychologische Rundschau,* 1979, *30,* 310–311.

Preface

The annual serial publication, *Life-Span Development and Behavior,* is aimed at reviewing life-span research and theory in the behavioral and social sciences, with a particular focus on contributions by psychologists and sociologists. The prefaces to the two preceding volumes stated the purposes of introducing more empirical research into the field of life-span development and of increasing the interdisciplinary character of work in this new field. These two purposes are reaffirmed in the current volume and, we believe, fulfilled to a somewhat greater degree by the chapters presented here than was true for past volumes. At the same time, our commitment to a stronger dose of empirical work needs to remain at a high level of awareness.

As editors, we are making little attempt to organize each volume around a particular topic or theme. Rather, we solicit manuscripts from investigators who are either conducting programmatic research on current problems or are interested in refining particular theoretical positions. Occasionally, authors are invited to identify new areas of concern worthy of theoretical articulation or exploration.

Life-span research on human development contributes to a variety of intellectual positions. Some of them deserve particular elaboration at this time. First, in the past few years, research and theory in life-span development have given increased attention to the issue of constancy and change in human development. The assumption that the experiences of infancy and early childhood have a lasting effect on adulthood and personality is under increasing challenge by careful studies of the effects of early experiences, the results of which have not been entirely supportive of the traditional view. Second, life-span development scholars are more sensitive to the restrictive consequences of studying only specific age periods such as old age, infancy, or adolescence. A life-span development view encourages each scholar to relate the facts about one age group to similar facts in other age groups, and to move toward the study of transformation of characteristics over the life span. A third issue of high salience in current life-span research is the effect on human development of growing up in different historical eras. The course of history influences the life patterns of different birth cohorts, and we see that each birth cohort has features of uniqueness because it shares the experience of certain events and conditions at the same age as it moves through its lifetime. These three perspectives are evident in the chapters in this volume and are likely to be reflected in future volumes of the series as well.

The editors wish to acknowledge with gratitude and respect the contributions of many colleagues, who assisted in making the volume what it is. They deserve much of the credit and none of the blame. In addition to the wise counsel of our advisory editors, a number of ad hoc reviewers provided valuable comments to the contributors before final chapters were prepared:

Patricia K. Arlin	Nannerl O. Keohane
Diana Baumrind	Janet L. Lachman
Sandor B. Brent	Roy Lachman
Richard T. Campbell	Richard M. Lerner
David A. Chiriboga	Howard A. Moss
Elizabeth Douvan	Carol D. Ryff
Seymour Epstein	Irwin G. Sarason
David L. Featherman	Martin E. P. Seligman
Donald H. Ford	Ilene C. Siegler
Frank F. Furstenberg	M. Brewster Smith
Gunhild Hagestad	Graham B. Spanier
E. Mavis Hetherington	Lillian E. Troll
Jerome Kagan	

Our special thanks go to Steven W. Cornelius and Manfred Schmitt, who provided expert help in translating Guenther Reinert's (to whom this volume is dedicated) chapter into English; to Rosie Ammerman for her superb secretarial work; and to Ellen Skinner for her reliable editorial assistance and incisive, substantive comments on several chapters.

Contents of Previous Volumes

Life-Span Development and Behavior

VOLUME 3

Educational Psychology
in the Context of the Human Life Span

Guenther Reinert

UNIVERSITY OF TRIER

TRIER, WEST GERMANY

Abstract

Educational psychology is viewed from a life-span developmental perspective. Traditional viewpoints in educational psychology are too restricted in their primary focus on children and youth as the targets of educational efforts, adults as educators, school and family settings as primary educational arenas, and with its general disregard for the sociohistorical cultural context influencing education. A conceptual model for a life-span educational psychology is introduced and elaborated. The target persons in the model include individuals of all ages interacting with one another in the dual roles of educators and individuals being educated. A systems formulation of the ecological contexts in which education occurs is developed; with immediate environments, combinations of them, and metaenvironments identified. Target persons and ecological environments are interactively linked together in the model, with ontogenetic, historical, and nonnormative components exhibiting proximal and distal temporal relations. The task of a life-span educational psychology is aimed at the optimization of human development through prevention and, less importantly, through correction (secondary prevention). Responsible intervention necessitates an understanding of the relationships among educators and individuals being educated in the interactive ecological systems they experience. The design of educational intervention to actively create optimal developmental paths may be desirable because significant influences on development are often unknown. This intervention approach emphasizes the modifiability, multidirectionality, and interactive nature of behavioral development; it is counter to educational intervention models that assume passive or simply reactive individuals following fixed or invariant developmental paths.

LIFE-SPAN DEVELOPMENT
AND BEHAVIOR, VOL. 3

1

I. Introduction

More than 50 years ago, Aloys Fischer (1917, p. 5) deemed it "worth-while" to more "carefully analyze how educational psychology is actually conceptualized and how it should be conceptualized if it claims the right to be called a special discipline" (translation by author). It seems appropriate to ask this question again as the conceptualization of a scientific discipline guides scientific training and behavior.

Research on, teaching in, and the application of educational psychology depends largely on educational psychologists' understanding of "the concept and task" of their discipline. It is beyond the scope of this chapter to discuss the self-understood meaning of educational psychology as extensively as Aloys Fischer did. Rather, educational psychology will be examined from just one—yet a particularly revealing—viewpoint: What target persons are the predominant focus of educational psychology, what target persons should be its focus, and what tasks and problems stem from its orientation?[1]

II. The Traditional Concept of Educational Psychology

If one tries to obtain an overview of contemporary conceptualizations of educational psychology by an examination of the contents of some dozens of handbooks, textbooks, and other readings published in the last two decades, one will be surprised by the variability of conceptualizations that are offered. One will realize that the representatives of educational psychology lack even a minimal consensus about their discipline. In addition, one will also form the impression that *Homo sapiens* is a species composed of individuals who have completed their development by the end of childhood and adolescence—having been guided only a little by their mothers and, more importantly, having been taught by professional educators. One will find only a few authors who either conceive of educational psychology as also dealing with adults (e.g., Smith & Hudgins, 1964; Weinert, 1968), with humans of all ages (e.g., Weinert, 1974), or include at

---

[1] Educational psychology in German, "Pädagogische Psychologie," has a broader meaning than in English (particularly in the United States). Educational psychology is used here to refer to educational activities associated with formal institutions (e.g., schools, continuing education programs, professional and vocational training programs), informal institutions (e.g., child-rearing practices, intra- and extrafamilial socialization, etc.), and professional intervention (e.g., human development intervention, especially preventive intervention). An extended discussion and definition of life-span educational psychology is offered in Section IV.

Note also that some of the evaluative comments offered are strongly influenced by the author's familiarity with the situation of education and educational psychology in German-speaking countries and German universities.

least some brief chapters about adults and senior citizens in their texts (e.g., Hetzer, 1959; Hillebrand, 1974; Pressey, Robinson, & Horrocks, 1959).

Apparently, Herbart's (1835) opinion that adults are no longer "educable" and therefore "not reachable by the educator's effort" is still dominant within educational psychology. This view overshadows Aloys Fischer's belief that "educating and being educated does not only exist for children and adolescents" because "both are a lifelong reality" (1917, p. 10, translation by author). Will Herbart's restrictive opinion continue to be influential in the future? There are at least some indicators that support this impression. For example, there are Gagné and Rohwer's (1969) widely accepted definition of "educational psychology" as "instructional psychology" and Gage's demand, as reported by Weinert (1974, p. 50), "that educational psychology should increasingly examine the processes of teaching and instruction, whereas the focus on developmental, educational, and policy-related questions should be decreased" (translation by author).

III. The Beginning of a New Conceptualization of Educational Psychology

Usually, the questions asked within a scientific discipline are not generated "in a systematic way that follows logically from a clear conception of the total of tasks; rather, actual needs of daily life [and] stimulation from adjacent disciplines . . . contribute" (Krueger, 1915, p. 126, translation by author) to their formulation. Krueger's apparently valid comment does not support the potential expectation that programs designed by individual scientists could substantially and permanently influence the development of a scientific discipline. Rather, the other two conditions mentioned by Krueger seem to play a significant role in the development of science and—if the picture is not completely wrong—in the further development of educational psychology. Practical needs of daily life as represented throughout the world by new ideas in educational policies and, in addition, recent initiatives for innovation manifested in the adjacent discipline of developmental psychology can be considered significant determinants of the definition of "new" tasks faced by contemporary educational psychology.

A. LIFELONG EDUCATION

Discussions of educational policies during the last decade were dominated by a magical phrase: lifelong education. The basis of this concept is the idea that education is a process that encompasses the entire human life span. The idea dates back at least to the classical educational theorists of the eighteenth century (e.g., Comenius; cf. Condorcet, 1792; Helvetius, 1784; Tschizewskij, 1960).

Without being based on this historical tradition, related ideas are apparently represented in the educational systems of twentieth-century Western societies as adult education. At least Lengrand (1970) believed that the concept of lifelong education originated from the idea of adult education (which formerly was termed "volksbildung" [education for the masses] in Germany and is often called "weiterbildung" [continuous education] now). According to Suchodolski (1976), Yeaxlee (1929) made the concept of lifelong education popular among representatives of adult education, and it continues to be a preferred concept among them (cf. Knoll, 1974; Lange & Raapke, 1976; Picht, Edding *et al.,* 1972). Likewise, "lifelong education" (also labeled in English: "permanent education," "lifetime education," "continuous education," as well as concepts that use "learning" instead of "education"; in French: *éducation permanente;* in German: *permanente erziehung, lebenslanges lernen*) is a concept that is as dazzling as "adult education."

Although it is a slight simplification, one can say that the differences among the shades of meaning of these concepts signify two major postures: "learning to be" (*leben lernen; apprendre à être*), on the one hand, and "recurrent" or "continuing education" (*Weiterlernen; éducation continue*), on the other hand. The second posture refers to the necessity for continuously learning and developing new skills, even after the formal education of the first 20 years has been passed, to ensure an appropriate life style in a world that is changing at an increasing speed. This view focuses on the improvement of the quality of adults' lives. The first posture is mainly based on the ideas of "educating man as a whole" (Faure, Herrera, Kaddoura, Lopes, Petrovski, Rahnema, & Ward, 1972), which means enabling him to manage the private, scholastic, professional, and public aspects of his life in an independent and self-actualizing manner. This orientation is concerned with the optimization of the quality of life of the developing generations from early childhood to death. For both postures, their educational efforts are aimed at equal opportunity in school and profession, social maturity, civic involvement, and the development of a creative life.

The idea of permanent education received a chance of being implemented on a worldwide basis in the early 1960s. Especially under the guidance of Bertrand Schwartz, the director of the "Institut National pour la Formation des Adults" in Nancy (cf. Schwartz, 1967), the idea was forwarded to the French Department of Educational Affairs (headed by Edgar Faure at that time). From there, it was transmitted to the European Council, the United Nations Scientific and Cultural Organizations (UNESCO), and the Organization for Economic Cooperation and Development. UNESCO declared "éducation permanente" to be one of the primary goals during the process of preparing the "International Year of Education 1970," and Faure *et al.* (1972) presented a report referring to it. Thereafter, "lifelong education" was quickly adopted in reports and initiatives of educational innovators with various ideological backgrounds (cf., e.g., Knoll, 1974). It seems that the general tendency for innovation in the 1970s was not the only reason that the concept of lifelong education was adopted. Rather, it seems the basic reason for its acceptance, not only in Western societies, but also in socialist countries (cf. Darinskij, 1977; Filipovic, 1968), and in countries of the third world (cf. Brest *et al.*, 1972; Skander, 1972) is that the concept is open to interpretation instead of having specific or limited connotations.

It is unclear whether the concept of permanent education only has "significance as an agent for change" or whether it is even a signal of a "kind of Copernican turning point in education" (Hausmann, 1972, pp. 13, 14, respectively; translation by author). It seems certain, however, that the concept implies some kind of action (Husén, 1974). This implication has been accepted by most, though not all, educational experts (cf. Dauber & Verne, 1976; Illich, 1971).

The concept has received relatively little attention in psychology except for some authors who should be mentioned. Léon (1971) used the concept as a starting point for an educational psychology of adulthood. Dubin (1972, 1974) questioned the use of the concept in relation to efforts to overcome professional obsolescence. Cropley (1973, 1976) attempted to provide a psychological basis for the concept. Jones (1975) called "continuing education" a challenge for psychology. However, as indicated by the few attempts to deal with the concept, psychology as a discipline was not prepared for such a challenge. This is understandable for at least four reasons. First, because the concept has such a molar connotation, a discipline that emphasizes empirical research as much as psychology does is more likely to react in a surprised rather than a supportive way. Second, psychologists are traditionally rather reserved when it comes to education and educational policy. Third, some excessive formulations of a pure "learning society" that have been associated with the concept (e.g., Husén, 1974; cf. Bednarik, 1966) or exaggerated demands that have sometimes been imposed on universities on the basis of the idea of lifelong education ("lifelong university"; cf. Hesburgh, Miller, & Wharton, 1973) may have scared psychologists instead of encouraging them to adopt the concept. The fourth reason seems to be at least equally important. Psychology is only beginning to rediscover *Homo sapiens* as a biological organism that develops ontogenetically as well as phylogenetically. Of course, psychologists that favor this model of human beings included the idea of lifelong education in their theoretical formulations (Baltes & Willis, 1979; Brandtstädter, Fischer, Kluwe, Lohmann, Schneewind, & Wiedl, 1974; Brandtstädter, Fischer, Lohmann, Reinert, Schneewind, & Wiedl, 1976). However, they avoid the vague ideological attitude or naive organizational conclusions that are often associated with the idea.

B. LIFE-SPAN DEVELOPMENTAL PSYCHOLOGY

Considering the many different research activities in developmental psychology during the last decade, it is unjust to say that the field has been equally dominated by a magical concept. However, *one* perspective in developmental psychology has become increasingly prominent—the perspective of life-span developmental psychology. The realization that individual development is not complete by the end of adolescence but must be understood as a process that spans the entire life course is not new (e.g., Baltes, 1979; Carus, 1808; Groffmann, 1970; Quetelet, 1838; Reinert, 1976, 1979; Tetens, 1777). It reappeared without any reference to its historical foundation at the beginning of the 1930s (Bühler, 1933; Hollingworth, 1927). Life-span developmental psychology has become actively pursued, especially in the United States (Baltes & Schaie, 1973: Datan & Ginsberg, 1975; Datan & Reese, 1977; Goulet & Baltes, 1970; Nesselroade & Reese, 1973).

A conceptualization of human development from a life-span viewpoint is advisable if one wants to avoid invalid conclusions about the laws of ontogenetic development. If one focuses only on single segments of the life span, as do specific developmental theories that deal with particular age segments of the life span (e.g., child, adolescent, adult, gerontological psychology) even today, one runs the risk of generalizing laws found in one part of the life span to other parts or even to all of ontogenetic development. During the first half of the twentieth century, developmental psychology was primarily concerned with childhood and adolescence. Stage theories were dominant in Europe (cf. Kroh, 1928, 1932), whereas Gesell's (1928, 1946, 1957) maturational theory of development was of major importance in the United States. These two theoretical orientations receive widespread acceptance even today among laymen. Even scientists propagate their basic formulations (McCall, 1977). In general agreement with Baltes and Willis (1979), this developmental model can be described as normative–universal (interindividually invariant), unidirectional (directed toward a maximal end state), and dealing primarily with intraorganismic determinants (dependent on functional maturation). Apparently, this model is the framework for many other conceptualizations of the course of human development, such as Bromley's (1966) normative concept of behavioral change in old age as being oriented toward reversal or decline (directed toward the minimal level; dependent on biological decline). A normative model has been suggested especially by developmentally oriented research on intelligence. In childhood and adolescence, an almost linear increase of intelligence has been the normative course of development. In the realm of gerontological psychology, continuous decline has been the normative course of intellectual development.

These process models have been criticized and revised in many theoretical positions in psychology. During recent years, they have received stronger and more explicit attention than previously in life-span developmental psychology. Life-span developmental psychology assumes nonnormative characteristics (interindividually variable), multidirectionality (directed toward various states), and interactional determinants (dependent on organism–environment interaction) are necessary to describe the process of ontogenetic behavioral change across the life span. Chronological age is accorded a very different status in this model. The model implies both large intraindividual plasticity and large interindividual variability in developmental processes. Further, it is assumed that only some behavioral changes occur over the entire life span (i.e., some start late and some end early). Consequently, each individual's life course is characterized by a pattern of multiple change processes. A heuristic concept of interaction between biological and environmental determinants is presumed in life-span developmental psychology (Baltes & Willis, 1979) to explain ontogenetic behavioral changes. Three major antecedents influence change processes in an interactive way: Influences that are associated with culturally defined age groups (they covary with chronological age), cohort-related influences (they covary with historical and cultural changes), and nonnormative influences (Dohrenwend & Dohrenwend, 1974) such as war, illness, unemployment, and loss of a partner.

Life-span developmental psychology inherently emphasizes the modification of developmental processes through intervention. This emphasis is related to both the generation and application of knowledge. Thus far, the approach of life-span developmental psychology has been explicated in the area of cognitive and especially intellectual development (e.g., Baltes & Labouvie, 1973; Baltes & Schaie, 1976). Intervention has been considered in the areas of the elderly (Baltes, 1973), childhood education (Montada & Filipp, 1976), as well as social and educational policy (Baltes & Willis, 1979). In connection with the last consideration, the approach of life-span developmental psychology has been linked to the idea of "permanent education."

The fruitfulness of the life-span view of human development can hardly be overestimated. The course of life is a biological reality for all organisms.

If one understands this "reality," it is clear that no better framework can be found for developmental psychological investigations of the human being. The life-span framework is broad enough to incorporate even a large number of special developmental topics (e.g., questions concerning childhood, periods of the life span, or single events). The new life-span developmental psychology may be credited with bringing developmental psychological thinking back to this framework. This articulation facilitates the recognition that educational concepts separating the life span into segments are inappropriate (such as "andragogy" and "gerontogogy," cf. Ruprecht, 1974). The current model of life-span developmental psychology, although it clearly needs further specification (Thomae, 1978, 1979), has the advantage of being heuristically open. It is useful for describing various currently known developmental psychological phenomena more realistically than has been possible heretofore. Importantly, it demands the explanation of behavioral change processes. Constructs representing events occurring before the individuals under investigation were born (historical influences) as well as constructs that refer to events in the future (and beyond) of such individuals (aspect of prevention) may be included in efforts to explain behavioral change processes. Use of constructs of the first kind may reinforce the historical consciousness in psychology. Consideration of constructs of the second type may lead psychology to a higher level of experimental methodology.

The life-span view of development is of vital interest for educational psychology. Educators depend very much on being protected from false assumptions because their educational efforts are directed toward ideal states that they hope to attain for their clients. Therefore, it is important to search for educationally useful developmental laws that are valid for more than just one short period of the life span. Many educators have turned to developmental psychology in attempts to determine whether a certain educational activity is appropriate for their clients' age. This question "about the correct 'timing' of education" is much too simple (Weinert, 1974; cf. Nickel, 1973). It does not imply that there is a desirable course of development that is inherently modifiable. Rather, it assumes that there is a law of development that is independent of education. Further, it considers "something emerging from the inside of the child" (Kohlberg & Mayer, 1972, p. 451) as the most important aspect of development. Meumann's (1911) comments continue to be applicable. He warned that it was necessary to be careful because it is possible "to show that the laws of development may not be simple," and therefore, "it is justified to be suspicious of all formulations [prescriptions] that simplify a very complicated fact" (p. 666, translation by author). To illustrate this, one has to acknowledge only that all age changes are the joint product of ontogeny and education. Finding "pure" developmental laws, therefore, is always difficult. In some regards, developmental psychology has made remarkable progress since Meumann. However, even today it cannot offer a better answer to the question of what law is the basis of ontogenetic development. Cooperation between developmental and educational psychology could accelerate the process of finding an answer to this question. This cooperation would require an integration of developmental and educational psychological thinking.

IV. The Concept of a Life-Span Educational Psychology

If both the concept of lifelong education and the concept of life-span developmental psychology are simultaneously considered, this consideration provides a fertile basis for the growth and survival of a life-span educational psychology. Advocates of permanent education have adopted an open attitude toward a life-span educational psychology, and representatives of life-span developmental psychology have at least provided a framework for conducting research in life-span educational psychology. Because the fact that both concepts are not just being presented at the present time but are also receiving acceptance (in addition to other signs pointing in the same direction) may indicate that the time has arrived for conceptualizing educational psychology in the context of the life span.

A. GENERAL DEFINITION

It is not easy to describe the meaning of an educational psychology framed in the context of the life span. A definition is offered initially to avoid an a priori misunderstanding (cf. Brandtstädter, Fischer, Kluwe, Lohmann, Schneewind, & Wiedl, 1974, 1976): *Educational psychology means the generation (research aspect), transmission (teaching aspect), and application (practical aspect) of psychological knowledge with the goal of optimizing the behavioral development of individuals through planned educative intervention.*

The adjective "psychological" demarcates educational psychology from other disciplines and fields dealing with optimization in the field of education. Knowledge refers to substance as well as to methodology. Behavior is a broad concept—also encompassing emotions and phenomenological experiences (i.e., both overt and covert behaviors are included). Behavioral development refers to behavioral change processes during the life course. The development of behavior can be classified into various categories (e.g., according to the functional components of behavior and/or the complexity of behavior), and it can be viewed in terms of a number of indices such as direction, speed, and intensity.

Optimization means the improvement of behavioral change processes. Optimization is required when existing developmental states are judged to be undesirable, and if it is believed that these states are dysfunctional for the development of desirable states in the future. There are two strategies for optimizing developmental processes. One strategy, corrective intervention, is applied to counteract those influences that disturb the course of development or prevent it from being optimal. The second strategy, preventive intervention, is applied to create the conditions necessary for an optimal development that is free of disturbing influences. "Educative influence" is a construct that consists of educational behavior (e.g., instruction) exhibited by other individuals, impersonal influences existing in an individual's environment, and the interaction between individuals and their environment. These personal, as well as impersonal, factors comprising the educational influence cannot be known in advance. At best, one can hypothesize or make a guess about them. Afterward, however, these factors can be estimated on the basis of knowledge about the interrelations among the hypothesized antecedents, on the one hand, and the developmental consequences, on the other hand.

B. EXPANDING THE TARGET POPULATION

An extension of educational psychology to the entire life span means, in essence, expanding the population of its target persons. Today an attitude about education that conceives of education only as the adults' influence on the developing generations still prevails: Educational psychology is assumed to deal with adults (parents, professional educators) only as educators and with children and adolescents as the only educational recipients (i.e., persons that have to be educated).

A life-span educational psychology, however, presumes that all people— children, adolescents, adults, and senior citizens—are potential students and have to be educated. Of course, the division into these age groups is only done to order the target population in a natural way. For special purposes, a division could be made somewhat differently. Such a differentiation is not meant to suggest qualitatively different developmental stages. Nor should it reintroduce chronological age as an "independent psychological variable" after Carus had already "denied" chronological age that status as early as 1808. On the other hand, this classification corresponds to the psychological reality that the human life span is stratified in every culture in one way or another according to chronological age. Age, so to speak, is a basic life-span dimension that is assigned behavioral implications.

As noted, the population of target persons is expanded with respect to both educators and students or learners.[2] Advocates of life-span education have focused almost exclusively on the second group. Their main criticism (cf., among many others, Birren & Woodruff, 1973; Cropley, 1976; Eklund, 1969) is directed against the present educational system that is based on an ideology dichotomizing the human life span into two major periods. The first period, during which individuals attend schools and various training institutions, is reserved for the acquisition of knowledge and skills that then are to be applied during the second period of the life course. The "inocculation model of education" (Birren & Woodruff, 1973) is not suited to an epoch characterized by rapid societal, scientific, and technological change because most adults and senior citizens are forced to acquire knowledge and skills that they could not have learned at school (i.e., during the first period of their lives).

In principle, this modern insight corresponds to the long-known wisdom attributed to Seneca (A.D. 1–65): "Unfortunately, we do not learn for our lives but for the school." Meanwhile, this old wisdom becomes especially obvious in contemporary industrialized societies. The effects of accelerated change in science and technology as well as the change in the age structure of the population are becoming increasingly visible (the percentage of old people increases relative to children and adolescents because of declining birth rates and changing mortality patterns).

These effects demonstrate at the same time both the possibilities of and problems in educating adults and old people. Some examples will clarify this statement. Usually, requirements in today's professions change rapidly, and many adults are forced to continuously change their professional skills to satisfy these changing requirements. If a profession becomes obsolete, very often the professional has no other choice but to learn a new profession. Furthermore, retirement age is decreasing compared with previous decades and, at the same time, the average life expectancy has been increasing. Due to these two phenomena, more leisure time is available today. For some older adults, it is a problem to occupy this free time, especially if they are unprepared. Others, however, use this free time to assume responsibility for new tasks. In addition, because of the higher life expectancy (lower mortality rate), the average length of marriage has increased considerably during the last century. At the same time, the

---

[2] The German version of the chapter consistently uses the contrast between the Latin-derived terms "educator" and "educandus" to identify the roles of a teacher versus a student, respectively. In the following, educandus is variously translated as individual to be educated, student, or learner.

reproductive period has become increasingly concentrated in the first years of marriage. These two effects combined with a relatively young age of first marriage have lengthened substantially the time of the "empty nest" (the time from the youngest child moving away from the parents to the death of one spouse) and, thereby, opened a new period of educability. Divorce and remarriage (without significantly diminishing the general trend toward increasing length of marriage) yield additional needs for adults to be educated, as well as, for instance, the increasing parental insecurity about their children's education.

There has also been an increased need to provide education for very old people because of a general tendency to relocate them to new living environments (e.g., homes for the elderly, nursing homes). At the other end of the age continuum, advocates of lifelong education "discovered" (Hunt, 1961) the kindergarten child. Early childhood is seen neither as a period of passive maturation occurring independently of the environment nor as "waiting time" before school entrance (Cropley, 1976). Rather, it is considered a period during which the environment has a potential influence on the child and a time for the development of basic requisites for later development, in general, and adaptability to the environment, in particular. Of course, life-span educational psychology supports the important role of childhood. This does not mean, however, that the proper strategy for early childhood education is highly formalized preschool programs delivered in regular school settings.

The life-span education movement proposes to enlarge the scope of educators and broaden the educational potential that adults provide (e.g., the use of adult educators, other than parents and professionals). Yet, the use of adolescents to educate children or same-aged peers is well known from models applied by many youth organizations. In this vein, Faure *et al.* (1972) recommended that students act as instructors for their peers. A life-span educational psychology goes even further. It considers people of all ages to be potential educators and emphasizes the multidirectionality of educational influences (especially in the sense of positive and negative reinforcement and modeling). Older people educate younger people (adolescents influence children; adults influence children and adolescents; and, senior citizens influence adults, adolescents, and children). Younger people educate older people (adults influence senior citizens; adolescents influence adults and senior citizens; and, children influence adolescents, adults, and senior citizens). Peers educate peers (children influence children; adolescents influence adolescents; adults influence adults; and, senior citizens influence senior citizens). This emphasis on the multidirectionality of education through the life span is not intended to question the special significance of the education of children and adolescents by adults but to place it into perspective. Several demographic changes just mentioned have implications not only for the persons that are being educated but for the educators as well. In contrast with earlier decades, parents, on the average, are younger than they have been, and the same situation is true for grandparents. As a whole, there are more generations living simultaneously. "A bride of today cannot only expect to see her daughter becoming married but also her grandchild entering school" (Feichtinger, 1978, p. 152, translation by author).

C. EXPANDING THE ECOLOGY OF EDUCATION

If educational psychology expands the population of its target persons, it also must enlarge the environment in which educators and their clients act and interact. There are many ways to structure the educational environment for the sake of a life-span educational psychology. Especially the areas of environmental or ecological psychology (cf. Kaminski, 1976), mainly based on Lewin's (1935, 1936) ideas, indicate possibilities of providing a structure for the organization of the educational environment.

A particularly promising structure has been proposed by Bronfenbrenner (1977). Based on an approach formulated by Brim (1975), Bronfenbrenner distinguishes among four environmental systems located at different levels: a *microsystem* (the immediate environment of a developing person; for example, the home, the school, the professional setting); *mesosystem* (an enlarged system containing two or more microsystems), *exosystem* (an influence system containing microsystems and mesosystems at a local level; for example, influences of the transportation system, medical, social, and administrative institutions), and *macrosystem* (a molar system of explicit and implicit rules, regulations, and ideologies imposed by society). Bronfenbrenner conceptualized these four systems as influencing the entire development of individuals. It is important for life-span educational psychology to recognize those segments of Bronfenbrenner's four systems that are related to the educational development of individuals (i.e., the development of educators as well as of individuals that are to be educated). The author does not intend to propose a final structure of the environmental systems that are relevant to education. Rather, using Bronfenbrenner's conceptualizations, in the following sections, some aspects of an environmental structure that seem to be most important for educational action are exemplified.

First, it is important to understand educational ecology in systems terms. The elements of these systems are interrelated in a complex fashion. They act upon and react with each other. The microsystem composed of the immediate environment of educators and individuals being educated can be divided into two main groups of elements: (*a*) personal elements in the microsystem exerting educational influence; and (*b*) physical elements that influence the individuals within the system. Parts of these personal and physical elements operate as immediate and direct influences. For example, unidirectional educational influences of an adult upon a child or of an adolescent upon an adult are direct and immediate (personal elements). Similarly, some of the physical elements (e.g., the work setting in the home, literature, and media) influence individuals in the system in a direct and immediate way.

However, a large number of the elements can be conceptualized as indirect and mediating influences. Personal influences are usually embedded in a pattern of complex and subtle interrelations. They may be observable, but often the individuals involved do not consciously recognize them. For example, research, especially in sociological socialization theory (Hartmann, 1974) and developmental psychology oriented to social learning theory (Ahammer, 1973; Gewirtz & Boyd, 1976), has recently demonstrated the reciprocity of influences in dyads (particularly in mother–child dyads). In addition, reciprocal personal influences "beyond the ones within dyads" (Bronfenbrenner, 1977) can be expected, although they have hardly been studied thus far. Within families, multidirectional personal influences can consist of interactions among the members of a triad (e.g., mother, father, child) or among more than three family members (e.g., mother, father, child A, and sibling of child A).

Indirect influences of physical elements in the environment on educational development have hardly been investigated either. Such influences are called indirect if they alter the pattern of interactions among the personal elements and, thereby, affect indirectly the behavior of educators and individuals being educated. Bronfenbrenner (1977) demonstrated the indirect influence of physical elements using an example of noise in the home and television-viewing behavior. An obvious example of indirect influence is the design of a home (especially size and groundplan) and its influence on educators and individuals being educated.

The modifiability of microsystems, finally, is a particularly important aspect that facilitates an understanding of the influence of microsystems on educational development. Especially, the enrichment and diminution of the number of personal and physical elements of the system can significantly influence educators and students or learners. For example, in the educational environment of the home, the birth of a sibling or death of a family member illustrates personal enlargement and diminution, respectively. Similarly, enlargement and/or diminution of physical elements may occur as a consequence of residential relocation. Some changes of the elements (especially of personal elements) may affect the significance of the environment to such an extent that it assumes the character of a new environment relative to its state before the change. For example, divorce represents a significant change of this type in the home environment. Similarly, the basic character of the school environment may be significantly altered if a class receives a new teacher.

The relation between the life span and *microsystems* as immediate educational environments is obvious. Individuals in Western cultures pass from one educational setting into another during their development—beginning in the delivery room and ending in the death bed. Between these two end points, there is an almost prototypical sequence of educational environments: the parents' home, preschool, grade school, high school, professional training (both academic and nonacademic), first professional environment, one's residence independent of the family of origin, one's residence in the family of procreation, extended or new family environments, extended or new professional environments, the environments of the reduced family and part-time job, and the home for the elderly. Less typical environments include, for example, foster care homes, orphanages, boarding schools, correction homes, juvenile detention houses, juvenile divisions of jails, environments during the military service, adult jails, and nursing homes.

However, the less typical environments are also age-specific. Even most of the environments that are topologically less clearly structured (e.g., youth groups, groups of friends, groups of people spending their leisure time or vacation periods together, continuous education groups, senior citizen's groups, political and religious groups) are age-stratified—at least insofar as their internal significance is concerned. Although these environments overlap each other, they are largely confined to the sequence of different segments of the life span. This phenomenon indicates a cultural requirement insured to make the life course more efficient (in the sense of simplifying it). Thus, culture is designed to arrange for individuals of equal or similar ages to encounter and experience specific environments for a certain length of time. Thereby, individuals can use a simple and easily understandable reference scale (i.e., their age group) to orient their behavior and simultaneously protect themselves from overindividualization.

Society offers not only age-similar environments, but also settings that are more age-disparate, especially settings containing older age groups (compared with a group's own age), and settings that are not defined in terms of age but composed of individuals of all ages. Hence, individuals can compare not only behaviors that are typical for their age but also can anticipate behaviors that will be typical for them in the future. Thus, culture guarantees its own continuity. From a developmental psychological viewpoint, this culturally determined age-stratification of environments generates age-related patterns of expectations and behaviors. During early parts of the life span (childhood and adolescence), age-related stratification of environmental fields is particularly strong and closely convergent with age-related constraints associated with maturation (anatomical, physiological, and neurological).

The interaction among specific educational environments during the life course is important for a fuller understanding of the nature of ontogenetic development. Bronfenbrenner (1977) correctly emphasized that the same individuals simultaneously belong to several microsystems (i.e., a combination of microsystems). Bronfenbrenner labeled the combination of microsystems a mesosystem. Some examples of typical combinations of educational microsystems at a *mesosystem* level are as follows: Children may simultaneously belong to a combination of the two microsystems of the home and day-care center, the home and preschool, or a combination of the microsystems of the home, grade school, and a group of peers. In adolescence, combinations of microsystems include the home, high school, professional schools, youth groups, groups of friends, or a group of peers spending their leisure time together. Adults usually belong to a mesosystem containing their home, the professional setting, and the environment in which they typically spend their free time. Finally, most senior citizens have a reduced mesosystem consisting of their reduced family environment and the environment where they typically spend leisure time.

Consequently, an important task for life-span developmental psychology is to recognize and investigate these interactions among microsystems at the mesosystem level across the entire life span vis-à-vis personal, impersonal, direct, and indirect interactive influences. Obviously, educational influences in one microsystem can modify (either enhance or inhibit) educational influences in a different microsystem. Single case studies that illustrate these positive and negative interactive effects are known well enough so that it is unnecessary to describe them here. However, because relevant research has not yet been conducted, systematic knowledge is unavailable about the relations between the combination of educational environments, on the one hand, and the life-span development of educators and learners, on the other hand.

A specific but limited way to generate the systematic knowledge about educational goals and environments currently lacking could be provided by a combination of Bronfenbrenner's (1977) ideas with Havighurst's (1972) approach. Havighurst tried to assemble developmental tasks that are typical of the human life span. For example, some "developmental tasks of human life" are learning to speak (early childhood) and read (middle childhood), becoming independent of adults (adolescence), choosing a mate and raising children (early adulthood), helping teens to grow up (middle adulthood), and adapting to retirement (late adulthood). As a whole, Havighurst's developmental tasks provide a useful descriptive framework. In a formal sense, they are a kind of culturally specific guidance system, and their contents specify "the qualitative elements of the human life span that are typical for specific cultures" (Oerter, 1978b, p. 67, translation by author).

Focusing on the dynamics of development, it is important to realize that Havighurst's (1972) developmental tasks operate as forces (pushes and pulls) for changing behavior across the life span. Learning to speak and read, becoming independent of adults, raising children, and other tasks similar to these represent goals for the developing individual that must be pursued more or less actively. During the pursuance of developmental goals, individuals must adapt to both biological capabilities and biocultural requirements imposed on them. But why do individuals "pursue these goals?" Havighurst's general statements about the origin of developmental tasks (physical maturation, cultural pressure, personal values, and aspirations) do not answer this question. However, Havighurst realized that educational environments—usually multiple ones in joint action—contribute to the process of solving developmental tasks. For instance, he roughly described the impact of the family, school, peer groups, as well as other environments on the solution of developmental tasks imposed on children and adolescents. Yet, Havighurst's focus was on the educational support for solving these developmental tasks that individuals may receive from one or another person in the educational environments. He did not ask which general environmental conditions facilitate the motivation to solve developmental tasks—what environmental properties trigger the tendency of individuals to solve developmental tasks.

Perhaps Bronfenbrenner's (1977) research approach would be helpful at this point. Bronfenbrenner does not discuss developmental tasks and goals but, instead, searches for environmental conditions that are responsible for behavioral changes over the life course. The basic hypothesis implied by his approach assumes that ontogenetic development can essentially be understood as a function of influences encountered by the individual as he or she passes through the various environmental systems during the life course. Bronfenbrenner considers "ecological transitions" (i.e., successive environmental changes in the sense of entering new environments and/or encountering changes in the internal structure of environments) to be particularly important for the formal and substantive aspects of human development. Apparently, specific experiences due to successive ecological transitions and, more precisely, the direct and indirect educational incentives of the environmental elements are significant factors in the regulation and control of developmental tasks. That is, environmental transitions may be characterized as driving forces for the identification and mastery of developmental tasks. Thereby, they trigger behavioral changes over the life course in educators as well as in individuals being educated.

The educational environments and their combinations discussed so far are systems of influence that have similar relevance for an explanatory life-span educational psychology as does the age-related system of influences described by Baltes and Willis (1979) in their model. Bronfenbrenner's two higher-order systems (i.e., the exosystem and the macrosystem) parallel the history-related system of influences described by Baltes and Willis (1979). It is interesting to note that traditional viewpoints (e.g., Herbart, 1835; Roth, 1959) considered historical influences on individual development to be rather troublesome and to reduce the value of empirical findings. However, from life-span educational and developmental viewpoints, they are important empirical resources in the study of lifelong processes of behavioral change. If these historical influences are considered, one realizes that the human being "is a changing organism in a changing world" (Riegel, 1978, p. 288, translation by author).

Bronfenbrenner (1977) did not define exosystems and macrosystems very clearly—at least he did not draw an exact boundary between them. Therefore, these concepts cannot be used for the present purpose without some modification. Also, apparently it is sufficient for a life-span educational psychology to postulate just one higher-order system incorporating period-typical educational influences that are relevant for explaining life-span behavioral changes. One could label this external system an educational macrosystem or an educational metaenvironment. For example, the various basic values and propositions of education dominant during different historical periods of cultural development are condensed into a higher-order educational environment. This higher-order educational environment can be conceptualized as a source from which the previously mentioned "cultural requirements" are derived. Cultural requirements reflected in the educational metaenvironment become particularly explicit in federal and community laws and prescriptions that are significant to the educational process. Further indicators of the existence of such an educational metaenvironment are prescriptions and suggestions of religious as well as secular institutions and recommendations made by science and popular science. Implicitly, this educational metaenvironment is expressed in behavioral dispositions that educators and learners have as a function of the historical period they are living in.

The educational metaenvironment is a culturally specific source of variation that gives structure to immediate educational environments (microsystems). Thus, because there are historical changes in metaenvironments, microsystems and their combination (i.e., the mesosystems) change as well, owing to internal changes in the macrosystem. Therefore, both educators and individuals being educated who live during different historical periods

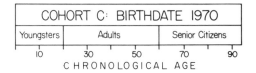

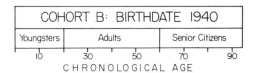

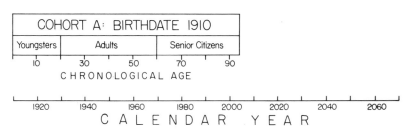

Fig. 1. The life span of individuals belonging to different birth cohorts occurs in different historical periods. Depending on the historical time, same-aged individuals of different birth cohorts are exposed to different educational influences. Further explanations are in the text. The figure is similar to one used in Riley and Foner (1968, p. 2).

are exposed to influences of different educational environments at several levels of analysis. Time of birth becomes significant for the course of their educational development. Figure 1, which has been adapted from Riley and Foner (1968) and used in a similar way by Baltes and Willis (1979; also see Baltes, 1979) is intended to illustrate this interactive situation.

For example, imagine how significantly the educational influences of the mesosystem home–preschool differ for 3–6-year-old preschool children from Cohort A (during the calendar years 1913–1916) compared with preschool children of Cohort B (1943–1946) and preschool children of Cohort C (1973–1976). Also, imagine how differently the mesosystem of family–work–leisure will influence the educational behavior of 30-year-old fathers in 1940 (Cohort A) versus 1970 (Cohort B) versus 2000 (Cohort C). Further, consider the effects of changes in the educational metaenvironment on interpersonal relations, such as dyadic, triadic, or even more complex interactions among members of different cohorts within one family (e.g., 10-, 40-, and 70-year-old family members), and how different these social relationships would be for members of a typical three-generation family living in 1980 compared with a family living in 1880. Finally, consider how the incentives to solve developmental tasks offered within educational environments and during transitions from one educational environment to another one differ for same-aged educators and learners who belong to different birth cohorts.

These examples are sufficient for broadening the reader's view and emphasizing the fact that education does not occur in a stable environment. They illustrate the effects of short- and long-term historical changes in the educational metaenvironment on the immediate educational environments and their combination, and, thereby, on the development of educators and learners.

D. SPECIFIC IMPLICATIONS

Based on the foregoing general discussion, tasks of educational psychology in the context of the human life span can be described in more detail.

The educational psychologist faces a complex area of tasks (see Fig. 2). The target persons of educational action are not only seen in their roles of educators but also in the roles of individuals being educated (educandi). Children, adolescents, adults, and senior citizens, for example, are seen as educators if they function as educational influences and as individuals being educated if they are the target of educational influences. (Thus, if educators are exposed to educational influences—in the larger sense of "education of educators"—then they also assume the status of individuals being educated.)

At the same time, the educational psychologist recognizes that in-

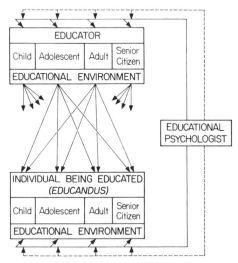

Fig. 2. Area of tasks of the educational psychologist in the context of a life-span educational psychology. More detailed explanations are in the text.

dividuals are part of multiple environmental systems; some are concurrently existing, others existed at an earlier time. At the time of an investigation or intervention, therefore, individuals (i.e., the target persons of educational psychology) have reached certain points in their lives as indicated by their chronological ages (5, 10, 15 years of age). Depending on their age, learners belong to certain educational environments and combinations of them that are influenced by the larger educational metaenvironment. At the same time, they have passed through a variety of educational environments and combinations of them in the past, which had also been determined by metaenvironments. These earlier metaenvironments may differ from the present one and have been superseded more or less by more recent educational metaenvironments.

The basic task for the educational psychologist is to estimate the educational influences that both past and present environments and their combinations have had and currently have on target persons. In particular, it is important to examine which specific influences of educators were and are directed toward the learners and how their behavioral development has been altered (arrows in the middle of Fig. 2) by them. This task is quite complex mainly because educators and learners (*a*) usually live in different educational environments at all levels of Bronfenbrenner's (1977) analysis; (*b*) partially act and interact in environments that are topographically similar but psychologically different; and (*c*) are exposed to some immediate educational environments that not only differ but may exhibit interactions as well.

It follows from this disparity between educator and learner in educational environments that the optimization tasks of the educational psychologist show similar complexity. For corrective intervention, the task of the educational psychologist is to eliminate or minimize environmental influences known to interfere with the development of individuals being educated. Depending on where these negative influences occur in the environmental system, the corrective efforts may be concentrated in the educational environment of educators and/or the educational environments of individuals being educated (arrows of the broken lines in Fig. 2). The types of intervention strategies considered by the educational psychologist and their successful application depend largely on the interventionist's understanding and knowledge of the interrelations among past and present educational environments. If intervention is successful, this is a prerequisite for the further constructive development of individuals being educated. This is why corrective intervention can also be labeled secondary preventive intervention.

In primary preventive intervention, the educational psychologist is faced with an even more difficult task: preventing negative influences due to environmental impact on the development of the individual being educated. Similar to corrective (secondary preventive) intervention, educational psychologists direct their efforts toward the educational environment of the educator and/or the individual being educated (arrows of the solid lines in Fig. 2). Again, this decision depends on where the disturbing influences have been located in the environmental matrix. Compared with corrective intervention, preventive intervention not only must consider the influences of present and past environments but also must estimate the influences of prospective educational environments. Of course, these estimates will decrease in precision as the period of the life span on which the preventive effort is focused is farther removed in time (distal). Therefore, it is easier to plan and implement preventive efforts for adults concerning issues that become relevant in old age than to do so for children regarding their development for the entire remainder of their lives.

As long as the laws of lifelong development are still unknown and the hypotheses about critical or sensitive periods of development remain hypotheses, the question about the best period of the life span for preventive intervention will remain unanswered. Consequently, educational psychologists engaged in preventive intervention from a life-span educational perspective will not favor any particular age period of the life span. Instead, they will need to attend to the entire life span. Pragmatically, they may concentrate on periods of the life span. However, the program of educational prevention will make every effort to consider the interconnectedness of the life course and apply preventive educational measures that are temporally distributed across the entire life span (cf. Baltes & Willis, 1979; Huston-Stein & Baltes, 1976; Montada & Filipp, 1976).

V. Prospects and Problems
of a Life-Span Educational Psychology

It seems appropriate to list some implications (e.g., concerning research, instruction, applied efforts) of life-span educational psychology because past educational psychology has paid so little attention to a life-span view of education and human development. However, problems in meeting the posture of a life-span educational psychology will also become apparent.

The major objection to the intervention approach aimed at optimizing the behavioral development of individuals in the context of the entire life span through the application of educational measures consists of two criticisms. First, it is objected that research in developmental psychology so far has provided only a rough and incomplete system of knowledge for describing behavioral change. Second, it is argued that research both in education and in educational psychology has provided hardly any knowledge about the effects of specific educational influences on behavioral development. However, responsible attempts to optimize ontogenetic development through educational efforts would require a sufficient knowledge base about both life-span development and educational impact.

This objection is justified. Hence, one is left with the question of how it can become possible to gather that knowledge (i.e., how to identify the still unknown educational antecedents of developmental consequences). One answer to this question is straightforward. Research in educational psychology should no longer assume that life-span processes of behavioral change are passively embedded in the natural context of the life course. On the contrary, such research should attempt to actively create experimental contexts and, thereby, investigate the possible effects of larger environmental variations on individual development (cf. Baltes, 1973; Baltes & Willis, 1977; Labouvie, 1973). In a broad sense, this answer reflects the idea of working on an experimental basis even with complex systems. Campbell and Stanley (1963) refer to this work as "quasi-experimental." In a narrow sense, this idea corresponds to suggestions offered by Soviet educational psychologists (child psychologists) "to change the conditions of life via educational and instructional reforms" (Nepomnjaschtschaja, 1977, p. 44, translation by author) or to develop "experimental models of psychological development" (Petrowski, 1977b, p. 24, translation by author). Bronfenbrenner (1977) explicitly described this experimental approach as "change experiments" and "ecological experiments." Only such experiments can help to identify educational antecedents of developmental consequences and, thereby, provide the information needed for responsible educational planning aimed at the optimization of developmental changes. On the other hand, planning these experiments and applying optimization measure in a responsible manner requires thorough considerations of and detailed decisions about educational goals and societal values. The possibilities and problems of the latter issue have been discussed in a particularly comprehensive fashion by Brandtstädter (1976, 1979).

For the professional application of educational optimization efforts by educational psychologists, it is correct to highlight the danger of initiatives that are too pragmatically oriented and hasty in view of the present state of research knowledge. In a similar context, Looft (1973) emphasized the need for psychologists to carefully consider the consequences of their behavior before joining the "cult of interventionism." Similarly, Labouvie (1973) argued that psychologists should not formulate intervention strategies before research has provided the appropriate and necessary prerequisites. These warnings must be taken seriously. However, it is important to recognize that decisions about educational interventions affecting development are always being made in daily life, both in immediate educational environments (e.g., family, school, correction home) and educational metaenvironments (e.g., in the form of official reforms). Often, these decisions are so "successful" that psychologists are busy trying to correct the effects of those interventions. Furthermore, a large number of educational psychologists, in fact, have increasingly turned toward preventive intervention work (e.g., training parents and professional educators, or supervising and evaluating educational reform programs). Considering these facts, the questions of whether educational psychologists should try to optimize development based on the present state of research has to be reformulated and substituted by another question. How should the training of educational psychologists be designed to enhance their competence in optimizing development in the context of the life span? This new question addresses the issue of teaching and professional training (also see Danish, Smyer, & Nowak, Chapter 9, this volume).

Currently, only a few university programs in educational psychology offered in German-speaking countries are designed to meet the requirements of a life-span view of educational psychology. Most training programs in education and psychology still appear to be committed to Herbart's (1835) misunderstanding that practical philosophy (today called "education") is in charge of setting the goals of education, whereas psychology should provide the necessary means and techniques for attaining these goals. In addition, most programs in German-speaking countries seem to teach a methodological attitude that hinders students from thinking in systems terms. Brandtstädter (1976) argued that students learn to think in terms of "paradigms of single causal relations" (p. 231, translation by author) and learn to "cut the interrelations within systems apart" (p. 231, translation by author) because traditional courses in experimental design are committed to the classical experiment. Bronfenbrenner (1977) has made a similar argument. In contrast to this tendency in education and educational psychology, most programs in developmental psychology offered by universities in German-speaking countries seem to be moving toward a life-span view of development giving increasing attention to explanatory approaches to behavioral change processes. One can only hope that this trend in developmental psychology has an impact on the further development of educational psychology in German-speaking countries. This would require that educational psychology disengage itself from Herbart's (1835) restrictive perspective and commit iself to the broad conception that Aloys Fischer had already argued for in 1917.

Acknowledgments

A similar version of this chapter is published in German as "Pädagogische Psychologie im Kontext der menschlichen Lebensspanne," in J. Brandtstädter, G. Reinert, and K. A. Schneewind (Eds.), *Pädagogische Psychologie: Probleme und Perspektiven*. Stuttgart, West Germany: Klett-Cotta, 1979.

The editors would like to acknowledge the valuable contributions of Steven W. Cornelius and Manfred J. Schmitt in the translation and editorial revision of this chapter for publication in this series. The author, to whom this volume is dedicated, met an untimely death before the translation and editorial revision were completed.

References

Ahammer, I. M. Social-learning theory as a framework for the study of adult personality development. In P. B. Baltes & K. W. Schaie (Eds.), *Life-span developmental psychology: Personality and socialization*. New York: Academic Press, 1973.

Baltes, P. B. (Ed.). Strategies for psychological intervention in old age: A symposium. *Gerontologist*, 1973, **13**, 3–38.

Baltes, P. B. Life-span developmental psychology: Some converging observations on history and theory. In P. B. Baltes & O. G. Brim, Jr. (Eds.), *Life-span development and behavior* (Vol. 2). New York: Academic Press, 1979.

Baltes, P. B., & Labouvie, G. V. Adult development of intellectual performance: Description, explanation, and modification. In C. Eisdorfer & M. P. Lawton (Eds.), *The psychology of adult development and aging*. Washington, D.C.: American Psychological Association, 1973.

Baltes, P. B., & Schaie, K. W. (Eds.). *Life-span developmental psychology: Personality and socialization*. New York: Academic Press, 1973.

Baltes, P. B., & Schaie, K. W. On the plasticity of intelligence in adulthood and old age: Where Horn and Donaldson fail. *American Psychologist*, 1976, **31**, 720–725.

Baltes, P. B., & Willis, S. L. Toward psychological theories of aging and development. In J. E. Birren & K. W. Schaie (Eds.), *Handbook of the psychology of aging*. New York: Van Nostrand Reinhold, 1977.

Baltes, P. B., & Willis, S. L. Life-span developmental psychology, cognition, and social policy. In M. W. Riley (Ed.), *Aging from birth to death*. Boulder, Colo.: Westview Press, 1979.

Bednarik, K. *Die Lerngesellschaft: Das Kind von heute—der Mensch von morgen*. Wien: Molden, 1966.

Birren, J. E., & Woodruff, D. S. Human development over the life span through education. In P. B. Baltes & K. W. Schaie (Eds.), *Life-span developmental psychology: Personality and socialization*. New York: Academic Press, 1973.

Brandtstädter, J. Zur Bestimmung eines Tabugegenstandes der Psychologie. Bemerkungen zum Problem der "Verbesserung" menschlichen Erlebens und Verhaltens. In G. Eberlein & R. Pieper (Eds.), *Psychologie—Wissenschaft ohne Gegenstand?* Frankfurt a. M.: Campus, 1976.

Brandtstädter, J. Relationship between life-span developmental theory, research, and intervention: A revision of some stereotypes. In R. R. Turner & H. W. Reese (Eds.), *Life-span developmental psychology: Intervention*. New York: Academic Press, 1979.

Brandtstädter, J., Fischer, M., Kluwe, R., Lohmann, J., Schneewind, K. A., & Wiedl, K. H. Entwurf eines heuristisch-taxonomischen Schemas zur Strukturierung von Zielbereichen pädagogisch-psychologischer Forschung und Lehre. *Zeitschrift für Entwicklungspsychologie und Pädagogische Psychologie,* 1974, **6**, 1–18.

Brandtstädter, J., Fischer, M., Lohmann, J., Reinert, G., Schneewind, K. A., & Wiedl, K. H. Zur Entwicklung eines Curriculums für das Hauptfachstudium der Psychologie mit der Spezialisierungsrichtung "Pädagogische Psychologie." *Psychologische Rundschau,* 1976, **27**, 95–117.

Brest, R., DeGilda, L., Pain, A., & Bursilowsky, S. *Lifelong education: An alternative strategy for educational planning.* Buenos Aires: Centro de Investigaciones en Ciencias de la Educacion, 1972.

Brim, O. G., Jr. Macro-structural influences on child development and the need for childhood social indicators. *American Journal of Orthopsychiatry,* 1975, **45**, 516–524.

Bromley, D. B. *The psychology of human aging.* Baltimore: Penguin Books, 1966.

Bronfenbrenner, U. Toward an experimental ecology of human development. *American Psychologist,* 1977, **32**, 513–531.

Bühler, C. *Der menschliche Lebenslauf als psychologisches Problem.* Leipzig: Hirzel, 1933.

Campbell, D. T., & Stanley, J. C. Experimental and quasi-experimental designs for research on teaching. In N. L. Gage (Ed.), *Handbook of research on teaching.* Chicago: Rand McNally, 1963.

Carus, F. A. *Psychologie. Zweiter Teil: Specialpsychologie* (Nachgelassene Werke. Zweiter Teil: *Der Psychologie zweiter Band*). Leipzig: Barth & Kummer, 1808.

Condorcet, A. *Bericht und Entwurf einer Verordnung über die allgemeine Organisation des öffentlichen Unterrichtswesens.* 1792.

Cropley, A. J. *Psychological foundations of lifelong education.* Paris: UNESCO, 1973.

Cropley, A. J. Some psychological reflections on lifelong education. In R. H. Dave (Ed.), *Foundations of lifelong education.* Oxford: Pergamon Press, 1976.

Darinskij, A. V. Lebenslanges Lernen in der USSR. *International Review of Education,* 1977, **23**, 287–303.

Datan, N., & Ginsberg, L. H. (Eds.). *Life-span developmental psychology: Normative life crises.* New York: Academic Press, 1975.

Datan, N., & Reese, H. W. (Eds.). *Life-span developmental psychology: Dialectical perspectives on experimental research.* New York: Academic Press, 1977.

Dauber, H., & Verne, E. (Eds.). *Freiheit zum Lernen. Alternativen zur lebenslänglichen Verschulung. Die Einheit von Leben, Lernen, Arbeiten.* Reinbeck bei Hamburg: Rowolt, 1976.

Dave, R. H. (Ed.). *Foundations of life-long education.* Oxford: Pergamon Press, 1976.

Dohrenwend, B. S., & Dohrenwend, B. P. (Eds.). *Stressful life events.* New York: Wiley, 1974.

Dubin, S. S. Obsolescence or lifelong education: A choice for the professional. *American Psychologist,* 1972, **27**, 486–498.

Dubin, S. S. *The psychology of lifelong learning.* New York: Russell Sage Foundation, 1974.

Eklund, L. Aging and the field of education. In M. W. Riley, J. W. Riley, & M. F. Johnson (Eds.), *Aging and Society* (Vol. 2: Aging and the professions). New York: Russell Sage Foundation, 1969.

Faure, E., Herrera, F., Kaddoura, A.-R., Lopes, H., Petrovski, A. V., Rahnema, M., & Ward, F. C. *Apprendre à être.* Paris: Fayard, 1972.

Feichtinger, G. Altersstrukturen, Lebenserwartung und Familienzyklus. In L. Rosenmayr (Ed.), *Die menschlichen Lebensalter: Kontinuität und Krisen.* München: Piper, 1978.

Filipovic, D. Permanent education and reform of the educational system in Yugoslavia. *Convergence,* 1968, **1**, 42–46.

Fischer, A. Über Begriff und Aufgaben der pädagogischen Psychologie. *Zeitschrift für Pädagogische Psychologie und Experimentelle Pädagogik,* 1917, **18,** 5–13, 109–118.

Gagné, R. M., & Rohwer, W. D. Instructional psychology. *Annual Review of Psychology,* 1969, **20,** 381–418.

Gesell, A. *Infancy and human growth.* New York: Macmillan, 1928.

Gesell, A., & Ilg, F. L. *The child from five to ten.* New York: Macmillan, 1946.

Gesell, A., & Ilg, F. L. *Youth: The years from ten to sixteen.* New York: Macmillan, 1957.

Gewirtz, J. L., & Boyd, E. F. Mother-infant interaction and its study. In H. W. Reese (Ed.), *Advances in child development and behavior* (Vol. 11). New York: Academic Press, 1976.

Goulet, L. R., & Baltes, P. B. (Eds.). *Life-span developmental psychology: Research and theory.* New York: Academic Press, 1970.

Groffmann, K. J. Life-span developmental psychology in Europe: Past and present. In L. R. Goulet & P. B. Baltes (Eds.), *Life-span developmental psychology: Research and theory.* New York: Academic Press, 1970.

Hartmann, H. Die Sozialisation von Erwachsenen als soziales und soziologisches Problem. In O. G. Brim, Jr. & S. Wheeler (Eds.), *Erwachsenen-Sozialisation: Sozialisation nach Abschluss der Kindheit.* Stuttgart: Enke, 1974.

Hausmann, G. Einleitung. In P. Lengrand (Ed.), *Permanente Erziehung. Eine Einführung.* München-Pullach: Verlag für Dokumentation, 1972.

Havighurst, R. J. *Developmental tasks and education* (3rd ed.). New York: McKay, 1972.

Helvetius, M. *De l'homme, de ses facultés intellectuelles et de son éducation* (3 vols.). Deux-Ponts: Sanson, 1784.

Herbart, J. F. *Umriss pädagogischer Vorlesungen* (Pädagogische Schriften in chronologischer Reihenfolge, Band 2). Leipzig: 1835.

Hesburgh, T. M., Miller, P. A., & Wharton, C. R. *Patterns for lifelong learning.* San Francisco: Jossey-Bass, 1973.

Hetzer, H. (Ed.). *Pädagogische Psychologie* (Vol. 3). In K. Gottschaldt, P. Lersch, F. Sander, & H. Thomae (Eds.), *Handbuch der Psychologie in 12 Bänden.* Göttingen: Hogrefe, 1959.

Hillebrand, M. J. *Einführung in die Pädagogische Psychologie.* Darmstadt: Wissenschaftliche Buchgesellschaft, 1974.

Hollingworth, H. L. *Mental growth and decline: A survey of developmental psychology.* New York: Appleton, 1927.

Hunt, J. McV. *Intelligence and experience.* New York: Ronald, 1961.

Husén, T. *The learning society.* London: Methuen, 1974.

Huston-Stein, A., & Baltes, P. B. Theory and method in life-span developmental psychology: Implications for child development. In H. W. Reese (Ed.), *Advances in child development and behavior* (Vol. 11). New York: Academic Press, 1976.

Illich, I. *Deschooling society.* New York: Harper & Row, 1971.

Jones, N. F. Continuing education: A new challenge for psychology. *American Psychologist,* 1975, **30,** 442–447.

Kaminski, G. *Umweltpsychologie: Perspektiven, Probleme, Praxis.* Stuttgart: Klett, 1976.

Knoll, J. H. (Ed.). *Lebenslanges Lernen: Erwachsenenbildung in Theorie und Praxis.* Hamburg: Hoffman & Campe, 1974.

Kohlberg, L., & Mayer, R. Development as the aim of education. *Harvard Educational Review,* 1972, **42,** 449–496.

Kroh, O. *Entwicklungspsychologie des Grundschulkindes.* Langensalza: Beyer, 1928.

Kroh, O. *Psychologie der Oberstufe.* Langensalza: Beyer, 1932.

Krueger, F. *Über Entwicklungspsychologie: Ihre sachliche und geschichtliche Notwendigkeit.* Leipzig: Engelmann, 1915.

Labouvie, G. V. Implications of geropsychological theories for intervention: The challenge for the Seventies. *Gerontologist,* 1973, **13,** 10–14.

Lange, O., & Raapke, H.-D. (Eds.). *Weiterbildung der Erwachsenen. System und Didaktik.* Bad Heilbrunn: Klinkhardt, 1976.

Lengrand, P. *An introduction to lifelong education.* Paris: UNESCO, 1970.

Léon, A. *Psychopédagogie des adultes.* Paris: Presses Universitaires de France, 1971.

Lewin, K. A. *A dynamic theory of personality: Selected papers.* New York: McGraw-Hill, 1935.

Lewin, K. A. *Principles of topological psychology.* New York: McGraw-Hill, 1936.

Looft, W. R. Reflections on intervention in old age: Motives, goals, and assumptions. *Gerontologist,* 1973, **13,** 6–10.

McCall, R. B. Challenges to a science of developmental psychology. *Child Development,* 1977, **48,** 333–355.

Meumann, E. *Vorlesungen zur Einführung in die experimentelle Pädagogik und ihre psychologischen Grundlagen* (Band 1). Leipzig: Engelmann, 1911.

Montada, L., & Filipp, S.-H. Implications of life-span development for childhood education. In H. W. Reese (Eds.), *Advances in child development and behavior* (Vol. 11). New York: Academic Press, 1976.

Nepomnjaschtschaja, N. I. Psychische Entwicklung und Bildung. In A. W. Petrowski (Ed.), *Entwicklungspsychologie und pädagogische Psychologie.* Berlin: Volk und Wissen, 1977.

Nesselroade, J. R., & Reese, H. W. (Eds.). *Life-span developmental psychology: Methodological issues.* New York: Academic Press, 1973.

Nickel, H. Zum Verhältnis von Entwicklungspsychologie und praktischer Pädagogik: Versuch einer Revision und Neuorientierung. In H. Nickel & E. Langhorst (Eds.), *Brennpunkte der Pädagogischen Psychologie.* Stuttgart: Klett, 1973.

Oerter, R. (Ed.). *Entwicklung als lebenslanger Prozess.* Hamburg: Hoffmann & Campe, 1978. (a)

Oerter, R. Zur Dynamik von Entwicklungsaufgaben in menschlichen Lebenslauf. In R. Oerter (Ed.), *Entwicklung als lebenslanger Prozess.* Hamburg: Hoffmann & Campe, 1978. (b)

Petrowski, A. W. (Ed.). *Entwicklungspsychologie und Pädagogische Psychologie.* Berlin: Volk und Wissen, 1977. (a)

Petrowski, A. W. Aus der Geschichte der Entwicklungspsychologie und der pädagogischen Psychologie. In A. W. Petrowski (Ed.), *Entwicklungspsychologie und pädagogische Psychologie.* Berlin: Volk und Wissen, 1977. (b)

Picht, G., Edding, F., *et al. Leitlinien der Erwachsenenbildung: Aufsätze zu Entwicklungstendenzen der Weiterbildung.* Braunschweig: Westermann, 1972.

Pressey, S. L., Robinson, F. P., & Horrocks, J. E. *Psychology in education.* New York: Harper & Row, 1959.

Quetelet, A. *Sur l'homme et le développement de ses facultés.* Paris: Bachelier, 1838.

Reese, H. W. (Ed.). *Advances in child development and behavior* (Vol. 11). New York: Academic Press, 1976.

Reinert, G. Grundzüge einer Geschichte der Human-Entwicklungspsychologie. In H. Balmer (Ed.), *Die europäische Tradition. Tendenzen, Schulen, Entwicklungslinien.* In *Die Psychologie des 20.Jahrhunderts* (Band 1). Zurich: Kindler, 1976.

Reinert, G. Prolegomena to a history of life-span developmental psychology. In P. B. Baltes & O. G. Brim, Jr. (Eds.), *Life-span development and behavior* (Vol. 2). New York: Academic Press, 1979.

Riegel, K. Versuch einer psychologischen Theorie der Zeit. In L. Rosenmayr (Ed.), *Die menschlichen Lebensalter. Kontinuität und Krisen.* München: Piper, 1978.

Riley, M. W., & Foner, A. *Aging and society* (Vol. 1: An inventory of research findings). New York: Russell Sage Foundation, 1968.

Rosenmayr, L. (Ed.). *Die menschlichen Lebensalter: Kontinuität und Krisen.* München: Piper, 1978.

Roth, H. Psychologie und Pädagogik und das Problem einer Pädagogischen Psychologie. In J. Derbolav & H. Roth (Ed.), *Psychologie und Pädagogik: Neue Forschungen und Ergebnisse.* Heidelberg: Quelle & Meyer, 1959.

Ruprecht, H. Lernen für das Älterwerden. In J. H. Knoll (Ed.), *Lebenslanges Lernen: Erwachsenenbildung in Theorie und Praxis.* Hamburg: Hoffmann & Campe, 1974.

Schwartz, B. *Réflexions sur le développement de l'éducation permanente.* Paris: Presses Universitaires de France, 1967.

Skander, O. Strategies for directing existing educational systems towards lifelong education: What the Algerian experience has to contribute. In B. Suchodolski (Ed.), *Lifelong education: Problems, tasks, conditions. Contribution to the interdisciplinary symposium on lifelong education 1972 in Paris.* Paris: UNESCO, 1972.

Smith, L. M., & Hudgins, B. B. *Educational psychology: An application of social and behavioral theory.* New York: Knopf, 1964.

Suchodolski, B. Lifelong education—some philosophical aspects. In R. H. Dave (Ed.), *Foundations of life-long education.* Oxford: Pergamon Press, 1976.

Tetens, J. N. *Philosophische Versuche über die menschliche Natur und ihre Entwicklung* (Band 2). Leipzig: Weidmanns Erben und Reich, 1777.

Thomae, H. Zur Problematik des Entwicklungsbegriffs im mittleren und höheren Lebensalter. In R. Oerter (Ed.), *Entwicklung als lebenslanger Prozess.* Hamburg: Hoffman & Campe, 1978.

Thomae, H. The concept of development and life-span developmental psychology. In P. B. Baltes & O. G. Brim, Jr. (Eds.), *Life-span development and behavior* (Vol. 2). New York: Academic Press, 1979.

Tschizewskij, D. (Ed.). *Pampaedia: Lateinischer Text und deutsche Übersetzung.* In *Pädagogische Forschungen* (Band 5). Heidelberg: Quelle & Meyer, 1960.

Weinert, F. Vorwort. In F. Weinert (Ed.), *Pädagogische Psychologie.* Köln: Kiepenheuer & Witsch, 1968.

Weinert, F. E. Einführung in das Problemgebiet der Pädagogischen Psychologie. In F. E. Weinert, C. F. Graumann, H. Heckhausen, & M. Hofer (Eds.), *Funk-Kolleg Pädagogische Psychologie* (Band 1). Frankfurt a. M.: Fischer, 1974.

Yeaxlee, A. B. *Lifelong education: A sketch of the range and significance of the adult education movement.* London: Cassell, 1929.

The Emerging Crisis
in Life-Span Developmental Theory

Kenneth J. Gergen

SWARTHMORE COLLEGE

SWARTHMORE, PENNSYLVANIA

Abstract

In their fresh reconsideration of developmental study, life-span investigators have raised issues of critical significance to the future of both developmental study and the science of psychology more generally. Two of these issues are of critical importance. First, the view is becoming increasingly widespread within the life-span domain that developmental trajectories are historically situated: Alterations in life patterns are imbedded within sociohistorical circumstances. Second, increasing emphasis is being placed on the capacities of the human organism to act autonomously upon the environment as opposed to being an environmental by-product. To the extent that these views gain hegemony, traditional goals of the science are rendered problematic. In particular, the quest for developmental theory with transhistorical predictive capacity is threatened. Theoretical activity would largely seem limited to descriptions of developmental trajectories within particular cohorts during isolated periods of history. The empirical assessment of theories is also thrown into question, as theoretical validity may be enhanced or reduced depending on one's selection of sociohistorical context. Although such a crisis is thus precipitated with respect to traditional empiricist conceptions of theory and research, one may more optimistically employ the emerging views in the life-span arena to reconstruct the contours of the behavioral sciences themselves. One may view the major function of theory not as that of enhancing prediction and control, but as a means for

31

rendering intelligible and communicable one's experience of the world. Rather than comparing intelligibility systems in terms of empirical corroboration, one may usefully inquire into the particular functions of varying theoretical forms. It is proposed that a primary criterion for theoretical comparison is the extent to which theory is generative; that is, the extent to which it unsettles or challenges prevailing views within the culture and thereby points the way toward alternative solutions to existing problems, elaborates alternative forms of social action, and sustains values otherwise submerged. A premium is thus to be placed in the life-span domain on general theory with generative potential.

I. Introduction

In his 1978 volume, *The Restructuring of Social and Political Theory*, Richard Bernstein explored the contemporary decay of the positivist scaffold undergirding much traditional social science. He described an "emerging new sensibility" to alternatives in the aims, scope, and methods of the sciences. Surely there is ample support for Bernstein's claim within sociology and political science. However, judged by the mass of critical literature, it would also appear that Bernstein has underestimated the boundaries of such reconstructive efforts. General controversy over the aims and potential of the psychological sciences now exceeds that manifested during the 1930s advent of radical behaviorism. For example, contributing to a self-reflective zeitgeist, from which may be emerging a significant restructuring of the field, are Meehl's (1978) critique of traditional hypothesis testing along with the Popperian view of scientific progress, Cronbach's (1975) discouragement with the cumulativeness of experimental findings, Sarbin's (1977) argument for a contextualist science, Neisser's (1976) misgivings over traditional cognitive research, Harre and Secord's (1973) proposal for an ethogenic approach to social understanding, Sampson's (1978) examination of the value base of social psychological theorizing, Buss's (1979) proposal for a dialectic alternative to traditional sciences, along with the present author's arguments for an historically embedded science (Gergen, 1973, 1976).

Even though substantial upheaval may be discerned within the discipline of psychology more generally, the steadfast reconsideration of longstanding tradition is perhaps nowhere more evident than in the domain of life-span study. Within this arena, vigorous debates are encountered at every level of the scientific process, including the metatheoretical (cf. Datan, 1977; Reese & Overton, 1970; Weiss, 1978), the theoretical (cf. Brim & Kagan, 1980; Freedle, 1977), and the methodological (cf. Hultsch & Hickey, 1978; Labouvie, 1975; Nesselroade & Reese, 1973). In part, this querulous condition may be traced to the context of the field's inception, a context of grave doubt over the adequacy of traditional developmental theory to deal with problems of adulthood and aging. If the long-revered theories of development could have led so many for so long to believe that human development was being fully portrayed, then what other traditional premises might be amiss? And, because the field has been vitally concerned with cross-time change, it has captured the interests of dialectical theorists whose orientations oppose that of the traditional empiricist in many significant ways (cf. Riegel, 1975a). Finally, as Baltes and Cornelius (1977) argue, life-span study is unlike other fields in psychology in its focus on long-term change. With such a focus, it often stretches the boundaries of existing assumptions at both the theoretical and methodological levels.

Because of its singularly intense reassessment of tradition, life-span study may possibly serve as a weathervane for future developments within the field of psychology more generally. The enhanced degree of self-consciousness, the openness to fresh alternatives, and the high degree of sensitivity to the metatheoretical bases of the science, suggest that developments within the life-span domain may presage future concerns within the more conservative areas of the discipline. *It is a central thesis of the present chapter that a major crisis in the function of general theory is emerging within life-span study and this crisis will have profound implications for the psychological sciences more generally.* We shall first examine two major lines of investigation that give rise to the crisis. On the empirical level, we shall consider the historical relativity of individual life-span trajectory. In what degree are we dealing with fundamentally replicable phenomena? On the theoretical level, we will examine the evolving image of the individual as autonomously self-determining. In what degree is it appropriate to view human action as mechanically determined? Based on these lines of work, traditional beliefs in both the testability of general theory and the utility of such theory for purposes of prediction and control are thrown into jeopardy. In light of the problems raised with traditional assumptions, we shall inquire into alternative functions of life-span theory. In particular, we shall examine the use of theory for altering action patterns and sustaining value systems.

II. The Historical Relativity of the Developmental Trajectory

During the present century, much American research on the process of human development has been governed by the traditional empiricist assumption that the primary task of the scientist is to develop general theoretical accounts of nature's regularities. For the developmentalist, this mandate is represented in the manifold attempts to document and to account theoretically for the orderly patterns of individual activity occurring across time. From this plethora of systematic investigation, two major types of theoretical accounting may be discerned. The first, termed the *stability account,* is based on the observation of behavioral constancy. The theorist attempts to render an accurate description and explanation of this stability. Such accounts have most frequently looked to the early years of socialization as the critical period in which basic patterns of individual activity are established. This period of early socialization is said to lay the foundations for relatively enduring patterns of adult activity. One may thus anticipate, for example, reasonably stabilized patterns of personal identification, cognitive and emotional processing, interpersonal relating, goal setting, moral decision making, political and ideological commitment, and interpersonal relating for any given individual. This orientation is dominant in psychoanalytic and neoanalytic theory, in forms of learning theory emphasizing the importance of primacy effects, and in the study of long-term continuities in personality (Block, 1971; Epstein, 1977; Kagan & Moss, 1962).

The stability orientation may be contrasted with the *ordered change account,* one that has dominated the past 30 years of developmental inquiry. This form of account typically centers not on stabilized or continuous aspects of human activity, but on those that appear to change over time in systematic and reliable ways. Typically, the individual is seen as passing through a series of predetermined, epigenetic stages, often but not necessarily terminating in late adolescence. Illustrative of this general orientation are the theories of Piaget, Bühler, Werner, Erikson, and Kohlberg.

Many criticisms of both the stability and the ordered change accounts of early development have appeared over the years. In particular, it has been argued, on empiricist grounds, that such accounts are not accurate with respect to the range of available evidence and that their methodologies are often biased in their favor (Brim & Kagan, 1980; Kurtines & Grief, 1974; Mischel, 1968; Runyan, 1978). In part, because of the strength of such criticism, and in part because such accounts have raised few interesting questions concerning conduct over the full life span, we find that investigation into life-span development has not been significantly affected by either approach. Rather, life-span inquiry has been relatively unrestricted in its acceptance of new forms of data, its vigorous pursuit of new methodologies, and its robust development of new theoretical insights. Although the full range of such work defies tidy summarization, one can discern amidst the numerous empirical findings and just beneath the theoretical veneer, an alternative to the stability and the ordered-change accounts of development. This may be termed the *aleatoric account* (Gergen, 1978), an account that calls attention to the flexibility of developmental patterns. The aleatoric account emerges from the study of the broad diversity of developmental patterning. From this perspective, existing patterns appear potentially evanescent, the unstable result of the particular juxtaposition of contemporary historical events. For any individual, the life course seems fundamentally open-ended. Even with full knowledge of the individual's past experience, one can render little more than a probabalistic account of the broad contours of future development. It is useful to touch on several forms of investigation undergirding this view.

First, much interest has been taken in historical accounts of human development in other eras (Borstelmann, 1976; Demos & Demos, 1969; Gadlin, 1978). To the extent that people in earlier periods of history manifested developmental patterns different from those posited by contemporary theories of stability or ordered change, doubt is cast upon such theories, and one must consider the possibility for the historical relativity of developmental trajectories. Particular interest has been taken in childhood development, the period that by most traditional accounts, should demonstrate transhistorical stability. In perhaps the classic investigation of this type, van den Berg (1961) examined the concepts of childhood and maturation across widely disparate time periods. As he demonstrated, from the fifteenth to the seventeenth century, no strong distinction was made in Western culture between the child and the adult. The child was simply viewed as an adult in miniature; distinctions between mental and emotional maturity versus immaturity were virtually absent. Thus, Montaigne wrote placidly of a child who read Greek, Latin, and Hebrew when he was 6 years old and translated Plato into French when he was not yet 8. Girls could typically read the Bible before they were 5; 6-year-olds were often confronted with the most serious discussions of death, sex, and ethics. From the perspective of contemporary theories of cognitive and emotional maturation, such capacities would fall beyond the pale of reason. As van den Berg concluded, contemporary society has essentially "created" the character of today's child and the stages of development that he or she must traverse. Of course, accounts such as these are necessarily anecdotal, but the questions raised by them are of fundamental magnitude.

Much the same message is reiterated in comparative studies of sex-role development. Clear developmental patterns of male as opposed to female behavior over the life-span prove exceedingly difficult to locate. As the literature suggests, males and females can adopt wide-ranging patterns of behavior, and these patterns may be radically transformed at any point in life. As Neugarten (1968) argues from her research, the manner in which the "female personality" unfolds is importantly dependent on existing demands for labor. For example, the proportion of women in the labor force at various stages of adulthood have undergone dramatic differences between 1870 and 1966, with consequent alteration of the adult female life pattern, her needs, and her prevailing dispositions. As Neugarten and Datan (1973) write, "Changes in the life cycle [such as these] have their effects upon personality, and it is likely that the personalities of successive age cohorts will, therefore, be different in measurable ways . . ." (p. 68). Consistent with this theme, David Gutmann (1975) found current sex-role patterns potentially dangerous to the nuclear family, and argued for an alteration in social conditions to reinstate earlier sex-role patterns. Not all investigators are willing to abandon the possibility of ontogenetic sex-role patterning. However, even one of the most reluctant of theorists, Walter Emmerich (1973), concluded, on the basis of his review, that "many ontogenetic changes in sex-role behavior will continue to occur only as long as diffusion of changed sex-role norms to all age-graded environments remains incomplete" (p. 143). In effect, historically contingent role conceptions may overpower whatever ontogenetic proclivities may be discerned.

This emphasis on shifting sociohistorical circumstances is amplified by contemporary studies of mental health over the life span. As Lieberman (1975) maintained, emotional maladjustment appears far less dependent on intrinsic patterns of development than on environmental stressors, wherever they happen to occur in adult life. Explorations of Pearlin (1975) and of Schlegel (1975) into the environmental sources of the often observed differences in depression between males and females reach much the same conclusion. The onset of depressive symptoms in males as opposed to females does not primarily seem to be the result of genetic programming; rather, such patterns seem to depend on the differential configuration of demands placed on men and women in contemporary culture. Klaus Riegel's (1975a) research into people's accounts of their own development extended this conclusion into the domain of normality. As Riegel demonstrated, people typically see change in their lives not as the result of smooth and orderly unfolding, but in terms of crises or disruptions largely stemming from a concatenation of unique circumstances. Additional research has concentrated on potential disruptions or marked deviations in life-span trajectory that may occur at virtually any point in the life cycle. Depending on insinuating circumstances, previous developmental directions may be wholly revised (Baltes & Labouvie, 1973; Birren, 1964; Botwinick, 1970). Or, as the individual is exposed to various training experiences, whether by accident or systematically imposed by social intervention, previous trajectories can be modified, halted, or reversed (cf. Birren & Woodruff, 1973; Hooper, 1973; Montada & Fillipp, 1976). Similarly, life crises may disrupt otherwise stabilized life styles and shift trajectories, sometimes dramatically (Dohrenwend & Dohrenwend, 1974; Riegel, 1975a).

The most systematic support for the aleatoric position has been furnished by the exploration of cohort differences in life-span development. As cohort research indicates, differing developmental trajectories are almost invariably found among cohorts born in different historical eras within the same culture. Depending on the sociohistorical circumstances, differing age-related trajectories are found in value commitments, personality characteristics, mental capabilities, political ideology, communication patterns, and so on (cf. Baltes & Schaie, 1973; Baltes & Reinert, 1969; Huston-Stein & Baltes, 1976; Nesselroade & Baltes, 1974; Woodruff & Birren, 1972). Elder's closely detailed analysis of the life-span effects of growing up in the Great Depression, as opposed to a more stabilized economic period (see Elder, 1974; 1979) does much to elaborate on the many interacting factors that may shape development within a given historical period. As Allan Buss (1974, p. 66) has argued in his review of the literature, "Each new generation interprets reality without the years of commitment of a previous ideology and thereby transforms that reality." Or, as Looft (1973, p. 51) has concluded, "No longer should developmental psychologists focus so exclusively on ontogenetic age functions; each new generation will manifest age trends that are different from those that preceded it, and thus, previous empirical endeavors are reduced to exercises in futility."

The practical implications of such findings have also been disconcerting to investigators attempting to develop dependable programs of social intervention. For example, an educational reform that proves highly serviceable in one generation may lose its potency in the next, only to be discarded at a point when it once again might be effective. As Baltes and Schaie (1973, p. 380) conclude, "it is questionable whether behavioral scientists will ever be able to demonstrate the type of treatment and prevention effects that characterize much of the classical biological and medical sciences."

In summary, the theme that is continuously reiterated in life-span research is that human developmental trajectories may be virtually infinite in their variegation. In contrast to the stability account, we find little in the way of adult behavior pattern that is compellingly fashioned by early experience. And, with respect to ordered change accounts, we find their applicability limited largely to early periods of physiological maturation. Explorations into adult developmental sequences largely support an aleatoric standpoint: Developmental trajectories may be largely traced to the accidental composite of existing circumstances. This does not mean that the social world is essentially chaotic or that continuities may never be found in developmental trajectory. People may ensure that their environment remains reasonably well ordered at any time, and over time they may find a stable behavioral niche. However, precisely what patterns are maintained or changed over time is not recurrent in principle. In the main, we may view developmental trajectories in Meehl's (1978, p. 811) terms: "a human being's life history involves . . . something akin to the stochastic process known as a 'random walk.' At several points that are individually minor but collectively critically determinative, it is an almost 'chance' affair whether a person does A or not A . . . Luck is one of the most important contributors to individual differences in human suffering, satisfaction, illness, achievement, and so on. . . ."

III. The Emergence of Autonomous Self-Direction

Coupled with the emerging view of developmental patterns as historically contingent, one may also discern within life-span study a shift in theoretical conception of human functioning. At base, the conception has its origins in rationalist philosophy, including the words of Kant, Leibniz, Schopenhauer, and Hegel. As Theodore Mischel (1975, pp. 144–145) has described it

> Central to Kant's analysis . . . is his claim that human beings can have a *conception* of what it is they want and what they should do in order to get what they want, and that their conceptions—the meaning which situations and behaviors have for them in virtue of the way they construe them—can make a difference to their actions. Rational beings "have a faculty of taking a rule of reason for the motive of an action"(Kant, 1788/1909, p. 151). They have the capacity to formulate plans, policies, or rules, and they can follow these rules—they have the power to act from the "mere conception" of a rule.

This view of the individual as an active agent may be contrasted with the traditional American empiricist view of individual action as the product of independently observable, environmental inputs. From the empiricist standpoint, individual behavior will bear a lawful relationship to stimulus conditions, and the scientific search is thus for the conditions necessary and sufficient to produce various forms of activity. However, if the individual is viewed as an active agent who may construe the environment in an infinity of ways, he or she remains fundamentally independent of the impinging environment (excepting physical constraints). If the individual conceptually constructs the environment, the environment is essentially the product of the individual, not the determinant of the individual's activity. Stable relations between environment and behavior may be found only as long as the individual's construction of the world remains stable.

Attempts to discredit this analysis by attributing lawful structures or intervening mechanisms to the individual have also failed generally to be sustained. That is, arguments that internal processes represent implanted habits, mental associations, stimulus–response connections, habits of self-reinforcement, conceptual habits and the like, all of which may operate systematically according to antecedent inputs, do not seem fully convincing. In particular, each falls victim to the individual's capacity for reflexive conceptualization. In each case, the individual may turn to review his or her own patterns of thought or feeling with the effect of alteration. As it is argued, any internal tendency, habit, association, or feeling may be critically confronted by the individual and the result may be self-generated curtailment, modification, or accentuation. The internal system may thus continue to operate on itself without benefit from environmental inputs, and may undergo autonomous, internally generated transformation.

One of the most important examinations of life-span development theory relevant to the image of the autonomous organism is that of Reese and Overton (1970; Overton & Reese, 1973). They essentially distinguish between two major models of understanding human beings, the *mechanistic* and the *organismic*. From the former perspective, the dominant metaphor of human functioning is said to be the machine. Here the investigator sets out to identify the individual components or mechanisms; their interrelationships are plotted systematically, and the prediction of any given component is based on knowledge of the antecedent conditions of those components to which it is related. For example, in the case of learning theory, the strength of internal S–R connections may be based on the number of preceding reinforcements; in modeling theory, the tendency to emulate a model is said to be a joint function of the model's attractiveness, power, and outcomes; and in psychoanalytic theory the strength of the superego is believed to depend on the intensity of castration threats. Thus, from the mechanistic perspective, human behavior is held to be fundamentally predictable, and thus subject to highly general descriptive laws. As can be seen, the mechanistic view of human development is largely embedded in the stability orientation discussed earlier; behavior patterns at any given time are based on preceding environmental inputs (e.g., socialization), and such patterns are assumed to remain stable until the individual is exposed to differing stimulus conditions.

This view is contrasted with what Reese and Overton (1970, P. 133) term the organismic model of human functioning. From this standpoint, the individual is seen as "the source of acts, rather than as the collection of acts initiated by external (peripheral) force." In this case, a major emphasis is placed on change, and such change is not itself explicable by efficient, material cause, but by formal cause. That is, organismic change must be traced to the properties or form of the entity itself rather than to antecedent events. For Reese and Overton, this view of the organism is tied to several correlative assumptions. For one, a commitment to wholism as opposed to elementarism is implied; if the organism is autonomously operating as a complex organization, any given action must be seen in relation to the full state of the organization. Thus, for example, a smile as a single action cannot be properly interpreted. The act is subject to a variety of interpretations depending on the total state of the individual's system at the time. The same action may imply pleasure or pain, insight or defensive rigidity, and so on, depending on the full psychological context. A commitment is also made to a structure–function orientation as opposed to one emphasizing antecedents and consequents. The task of the scientist is said to be that of discovering the function or goals of various interacting components of the organismic system rather than of tracing the relationships among componential states. From the organismic standpoint, the individual may be viewed teleologically, as striving toward certain, systemically necessitated ends. It also follows from these assumptions that primary investigatory emphasis should be placed on change in the overall organismic structure as opposed to discrete behavioral acts. One is thus primed to explore qualitative changes in the total organization of the system over time, a view that lends itself to stage theories of development. As Overton and Reese (1973) indicated, the developmental theories of Piaget, Werner, and Erikson all embody essentials of the organismic model. However, many other life-span investigators would generally subscribe to these assumptions as well.

One is inclined at this point to seek a parallel with the earlier association drawn between the mechanistic view and the stability account. If these two are linked, is it not clear that the organismic view is favorable to the ordered-change account? This point deserves closer scrutiny, for it appears that at its root, the organismic model may lend itself to the vision of the autonomous actor (the aleatoric account) as opposed to that emphasizing orderly, preordained change. It is only in Overton and Reese's (1973) elaboration of the collative assumptions that the aleatoric account is obscured. To elaborate, the organismic view is chiefly concerned with the individual as an active participant in social interchange as opposed to a passive respondent. As an active participant, the individual is in motion, continuously changing, and such change can be internally originated. This emphasis is clearly consistent with the previously described image of the autonomous actor. And, as we saw, if the individual is capable of self-direction, and may through symbolization direct his or her activities along an infinity of paths, then the likelihood of universal life-span trajectories is considerably diminished. Reese and Overton (1970, p. 134) are also intrigued with this possibility, as they state, "[the organismic] position results in a denial of the complete predictability of man's behavior." Yet, in adding certain associated corrolaries, the image of the self-directed, unpredictable actor is obscured. In particular, this possibility is diminished when Reese and Overton argued that there are certain necessary or systematic ends to which organisms generally strive, and that these ends are reached through a series of sequential stages. As Looft (1973) pointed out, this final form of the organismic model views the individual as a "closed system." Are these particular corollaries necessary? The point is surely moot. The argument that all self-directed organisms must share a finite set of teleological ends, and that movement toward these ends essentially occurs in stagelike sequence does not presently seem convincing. In any case, the Overton and Reese formulation does much to clarify the contrasting images of the individual as self-directed as opposed to respondent.

The image of the individual as autonomously self-directed also surfaces within many of the dialectic contributions to the life-span literature. The primary emphasis of dialectic theory is cross-time change, usually traced to the ongoing conflict between being and negation, between an entity and its obverse (located either within itself or exogenously). Clearly the dialectic emphasis on ongoing change is antithetical to the mechanistic, stability orientation. And, for many, it is also supportive of the autonomy argument. However, a distinction must be made in the latter case between what may be viewed as a materialistic–deterministic form of dialectic theory and a rationalist–autonomous orientation. In the former case, change over time is viewed in part as the result of material determinants. An interaction is posited between the individual and both the social and material context: The individual both shapes and *is shaped by* the context. For example, Riegel (1972, 1975b) posits an ongoing set of mutually interacting relations among inner–biological, individual–psychological, outer–physical, and cultural–sociological factors. Thus, self-direction is only partial; one is also influenced systematically by external forces. In some instances, dialectitions tend to view the interchanges as being fundamentally lawful. Hook (1957) speaks, for example, of laws of dialectic change, and Reese (1977) has argued for a dialectic theory of discriminative learning that may be subjected to empirical test. In effect, dialectic theory is sometimes treated as a form of the ordered-change orientation.

It is this latter view of a dialectic determinism that has been so roundly criticized by Popper (1959). As he argued, dialectic theories of societal transformation are not fundamentally scientific: Rather, they are fatalistic. They do not admit to conditions under which their premises could be falsified, and are thus nonconditional in their predictions. As we see, the same argument may be applied as well to the closed system of ordered, developmental change.

However, coexisting with this deterministic emphasis in some realms of dialectic theory is a rationalist perspective that lends itself substantially to the image of the self-directing organism. For those who favor the Hegelian form of dialectics, the emphasis is placed on internal processes operating upon themselves; the individual is viewed as self-reflexive and thus capable of autonomous change. What is seen as the objective material world by the more deterministically oriented dialectician is a world that in this instance is subjectively constructed. From this standpoint, inputs into the psychological system from the material, the sociocultural and the biological world are all psychologically constructed by the individual. As these constructions may be altered from within the psychological domain over time, there is no means of developing dialectic principles tied to observables. Thus, "what there is" is primarily a result of psychological construction. If such constructions may be altered from within, as the individual engages in self-reflection, one cannot presume the existence of a stabilized observation base upon which universal, deterministic principles might be based. It is this view of dialectic theory that is favored, for example, in Kvale's (1977) work on memory. As he writes, "The formal structure of the stream of consciousness consists of a *now,* constituted through an impression and joining a train of *retentions* and a horizon of *protentions.* As the retentions refer to the 'just gone,' the immediate memory, the protentions refer to the 'not yet' of the immediate future . . . The flux of consciousness constitutes its own unity" (p. 168). Similarly, Meacham (1977, p. 265) adopts the subjective form of the dialectic orientation in his transactional model of memory. Fundamental to the transactional view, "both the perceiver and the world-as-perceived are products of the processes of perception." From this perspective, then, we are confronted with an organism in the state of conceptually based, self-initiated change.

Finally, in her integrative synthesis of research on the development of individuality, Leona Tyler (1978) lends strong support to the image of the autonomously directed individual. Central in her view of development is the role of active, cognitive processing in the selection of behavioral alternatives. As she argues, people "deal actively with possibilities, recognizing, selecting, combining, organizing the voluminous raw material of experience and incorporating the patterns of individuality . . . More than on anything else, one's individuality depends on the choices one makes" (pp. 204–205). And, reiterating our present theme of open-ended development, Tyler concluded her review by maintaining that, "each individual represents a different sequence of selective acts by means of which only some of the developmental possibilities are chosen and organized. No one individual can ever be considered typical of the human race. . . . As Whitehead [1929, p. 233] pointed out, the fundamental realities are actual occasions in which indeterminate possibilities are transformed into determinate actualities . . . Individuals create themselves."

IV. Historically Situated Self-Direction
and the Conduct of Behavioral Science

Having explored two major developments within the life-span arena, let us consider their implications when viewed in tandem. First, it is becoming increasingly apparent to investigators in this domain that developmental trajectories over the life span are highly malleable; neither with respect to psychological functioning nor overt conduct is there strong evidence of transhistorical generality in life-span trajectory. To be sure, there may be certain psychobehavioral implications of early physiological maturation as well as of biological decline in the later years, and there may be eras of relative stability in which life-span trajectories are similar across groups and across generations. Yet, as is increasingly apparent in more recent treatises, the individual seems fundamentally flexible in most aspects of personal functioning. Significant change in the life course may occur at any time. In effect, few predictions can be made about the course of human development outside those resulting from simple extrapolation from contemporary norms of development: In the same way, an economist may employ present economic patterns and trends to predict outcomes in the following year. An immense panoply of developmental forms seems possible; which particular form emerges may depend on a confluence of particulars, the existence of which is fundamentally unsystematic. Firm prediction would depend on foreknowledge of the concatenation of events unfolding over time.

The emphasis placed on the individual's processes of interpretation are further consistent with arguments for flexibility. One of the major capabilities of the human organism, and that upon which its malleability seems centrally reliant, is that of symbolization. In particular, the possibility for multiple symbolic translations of the same experiential conditions, and for singular translations of multiple and varying conditions, enable the individual to move in any number of directions at any time (or conversely, to remain stable over a variety of seemingly diverse circumstances). Furthermore, the possibility of prediction through assessment of conceptual styles is rendered problematic because of the individual's capability to reconceptualize the styles themselves. Processes of self-reflexive activity may themselves generate alteration in conceptual preferences. We see, then, considerable agreement between arguments for the relativity of developmental trajectory and the capacity for autonomous self-direction.

As important as it may be to examine the shifting views of human development currently taking place within the discipline, far more is at stake in these arguments. If their implications are seriously considered, fundamental questions are raised concerning the function of knowledge-generating processes within the discipline of psychology, along with their broad social utility. Furthermore, such reconsideration may have implications of signal importance for the sociobehavioral sciences more generally. Let us consider briefly two fundamental tenets of the traditional positivist-empiricist model of science, tenets upon which rest the vast share of American behavioral science activity. In particular, let us consider the assumptions of predictive regularity and of empirical validation, both of which are sufficiently central that their elimination would demand a fundamental reshaping of the science.

A. THE ASSUMPTION OF PREDICTIVE UTILITY

From the empiricist perspective, the three major functions of scientific theory are traditionally said to be *understanding, prediction,* and *control.* Scientific understanding is generated via the construction of a theoretical system that maps the essentials of the phenomena under observation. To properly understand a given phenomena is to possess a conceptual schema that portrays with fidelity its major contours. The companionate function of prediction is highly consistent with this view of scientific understanding, as the availability of an accurate conceptual schema should enable one to make reliable predictions. Given an accurate map, one should be able to make sound predictions as to what route best leads to a given destination. As is often maintained, there is a *fundamental symmetry* between explanation and prediction. Although the term control occasionally carries with it unsavory connotations, it forms an obvious counterpart to the task of prediction. The primary goal of sound prediction is generally viewed as utilitarian; such prediction should typically (though not universally) enable individuals or societies to alter their circumstances in ways that will achieve desired ends. Thus, for example, a reliable theory of embryonic development might enable one to improve the life chances of the human fetus, to enhance poultry production in underdeveloped nations, or to decrease the rodent population in infested areas.

Yet one must carefully inquire into the conditions under which these traditional scientific aims may be realized. As Toulmin (1961) has pointed out, symmetry between understanding and prediction is hardly sacrosanct, and one may locate many instances in the sciences in which widely accepted theories make few predictions (namely, Darwinian theory), or in which reliable predictions are made without benefit of articulated theory (e.g., the early Chinese technology of gunpowder). When can we anticipate a fruitful linkage between theoretical description and point prediction? And might we consider severing the link between the two? At least one major condition necessary for a successful linkage would appear to be the availability of reliable or recurring phenomena. When the phenomena under consideration are either stable or recurring, one may hope to develop a theoretical description at t_1 upon which accurate predictions can be made about the state of nature at t_2. Thus, one's ability to predict depends importantly on the stability of the cause-effect relationship in question. Should either the stability or the ordered-change account of human development form an accurate template of human activity, successful prediction might be anticipated. The stability template assumes that life patterns are determined at an early period, and thus adult dispositions may at any time in history be predicted from accounts of early socialization. The ordered-change template generally assumes the existence of universal, ontogenetic trajectories in development, and is even more optimistic with respect to prediction. The course of development may not only be predicted in the present era, but barring major changes in human genetics, predictions may be made with respect to developmental trajectories in the distant future.

Yet, as our earlier analysis attempted to demonstrate, both of these positions seem questionable in light of the rapidly mounting support for plasticity in individual developmental trajectory. If development is importantly contingent on the peculiar confluence of historical circumstances as construed by the individual, and these perceived circumstances may be in a continuous state of unfolding, then we can neither anticipate a high degree of cross-time stability nor much in the way of universally recurring developmental sequences.

Theories attempting to map with accuracy those trajectories occurring during any particular era may have limited predictive value. This is not to say that *all* prediction is obviated. Just as people may undergo rapid and sometimes dramatic change in their perception of circumstance, so are they capable of maintaining a given perspective for long periods. And because these perspectives are usually shared within larger cultural groups, we may anticipate a certain amount of stability in developmental forms. For centuries, most children in Western culture have been far more exposed to interaction with females than with males. Although women's self-conception, along with their ideas concerning proper child care, has undergone considerable change over the centuries, it seems safe to say that the characteristic exposure of children to females during their first six years of life has remained relatively constant. Yet, as we also see, such regularity is precariously perched on the shoulders of shared conceptions of gender-related tasks within the culture, and such conceptions are subject to rapid alteration. Thus, existing regularity is essentially circumstantial and not endemic to human functioning.

We must, then, reexamine the traditional assumption that developmental psychologists may generate theoretical knowledge, the prime functions of which are prediction and control. Given a subject matter that seems to offer little in the way of an inherently recurring observation base, the hope of a primrose path to increasingly precise prediction is considerably reduced. Theories that enable reliable predictions to be made in one era may lose their capacity for prediction (and their relevance for control) in the next. This does not mean that the attempt to link theory and prediction should be altogether abandoned. The biologically oriented developmentalist may examine certain recurring similarities in periods of physiological maturation and decline. One may anticipate a higher degree of recurrence in those aspects of human functioning for which there do seem to be strong genetic inputs. And, to develop social policies within a given era, there is a strong need for theoretical description of human development during that period.

For certain purposes, it is useful to know what range of developmental sequences currently exist in the culture and with what relative frequency. It is useful to know, for example, what forms of preschool experience are related to later academic success, the degree to which both are related to subsequent feelings of personal well-being, and for what portions of the populace these relationships are valid. These relationships may wax and wane over time, but their theoretical description during a given era may lead to policy changes that could, at least temporarily, increase the number of people for whom feelings of personal well-being are attainable.

On the methodological side, the research on which such immediately applicable descriptive accounts are based would have to be far different in character than that currently prevailing. Small-scale observational or experimental studies that test the effects of single variables and reach publication long after execution are not likely to be of aid. As Bell and Hertz (1976, p. 7) have commented, "phenomena are changing faster than scientists have been able to produce useful conclusions about them . . . If developmental psychologists can offer only obsolete research findings to the public then why should the research be carried out?" Required are problem-oriented studies designed for rapid and efficient analysis of data and dissemination of the results within a specified time period. This form of research would function as a handmaiden to more general societal ends rather than posturing a contributor to fundamental or enduring knowledge.

B. THE ASSUMPTION OF EMPIRICAL EVALUATION

A second major assumption underlying the traditional empiricist orientation is that properly formed hypotheses are subject to empirical evaluation. Properly formed means that the major terms of the theory are unambiguously linked with the phenomena about which predictions are made (cf. Hempel, 1965). During the hegemony of logical positivism, the empirical validity of a given hypothesis was primarily linked to the frequency of its empirical confirmation. This line of thinking later became formalized in terms of the Bayesian concept of "antecedent probability." The greater the number of observed confirmations, the greater the antecedent probability that a given hypothesis is valid. Increments in the antecedent probability of a given hypothesis correspond to increments in "truth value." Although controversy continues, many feel this view has been supplanted by Popper's (1959) falsification theory. According to Popper, it is inappropriate to rest the validity of a hypothesis on the extent of its confirma- Any confirmation stands only as temporary support for a theory, as disconfirmations may always insubstantiate the theory. One er complete the process of confirmation. More important in establishing the validity of a theory, argued Popper, is the extent to which it resists attempts at falsification. Thus, the scientist is invited to generate observations that prove inconsistent with a theoretical contention. Only those theories open to falsification through empirical observation are deemed scientific in character.

The falsification argument has been attacked on a variety of philosophic grounds in recent years (cf. Lauden, 1977; Quine, 1953). However, neither the criterion of confirmation nor falsification can easily be sustained in light of present arguments. At the outset, if a theory is based on a given range of phenomena existing at t_1, and the phenomena are no longer existent at t_2, then the empirical evaluation of the theory at t_2 is rendered problematic. As Popper (1959, p. 45) has put it, "Only when certain events recur in accordance with rules or regularities, as is the case with repeatable experiments, can our observations be tested in principle by anyone . . . Only by such repetitions can we convince ourselves that we are not dealing with a mere isolated 'coincidence,' but with events, which on account of their regularity and reproducibility, are in principle inter-subjectively testable."

A second problem with the assumption of empirical evaluation is that, given a particular theoretical account, both confirmation and falsification may typically be secured by judicious selection of historical context. As is well recognized in the clinical domain, case histories furnish an inadequate basis for substantiating or disconfirming any theory of personality development or neurosis. Most case histories furnish an immense array of variegated events, and support (or disconfirmation) for one's theory may typically be found by selecting from the array just those exemplars that are required. Yet, as we now see, the developmental theorist faces much the same situation. If developmental trajectories are relative to historical context, as the previous analysis indicates, and each individual lives within a historical context that is, in certain respects, unique, then investigators are confronted with an immense range of observations potentially relevant to their theories. Investigators may thus select from this range as needs or interests dictate. In effect, both theoretical *confirmation and falsification importantly depend on the tactics of observational selection.* At the same time, once a given subculture is located within which support for a given theory may be found, confirmations can be generated *ad infinitum,* each of which misleadingly suggests that the theory is truly general.

A final shortcoming of the assumption of empirical evaluation in developmental research may be briefly outlined. As we have seen, there is a growing consensus in the discipline that people's behavior over time is damagingly unfixed. Developmental trajectories are potentie in number. Much the same argument would appear germane to he ceptual activity. That is, one may conceptualize the world in an infini ways, and which particular conceptual preferences exist may largely be a matter of historical contingency. Furthermore, one's employment of a given conceptual repertoire must typically be supported by the community of others with whom communication is necessary for personal well-being. Without a certain degree of correspondence in the way conceptual terms are used, communication is obviated. This condition of conceptual reliability raises fundamental questions concerning the capacity of the investigator to falsify a given theory of development. If any given observational pattern is subject to multiple conceptualizations over time, each of which is rendered valid through social support, then there is little way in which the investigator can confidently identify any given phenomenon. What counts as an observation of "prosocial" activity in one era, may be seen as "egotistical" or "conforming" in the next; what is taken as an indicator of "volition" in one historical period may later be seen as "habit" or "achievement motivation." In effect, one's contemporary array of examplars for a given theory are subject to continuous reinterpretation, any one of which may suggest that such theories were indeed "unfortunate." In the same way, an investigator can seldom be sure that today's observation of a given behavior pattern is conceptually the same or different from a pattern documented earlier in the life of a given individual. The same pattern of harsh and abrasive language may be viewed as "attention seeking" when adopted by a young person, but an indication of "social disengagement" when used by the elderly. Sexual questions posed by the adolescent may be classified as "healthy inquisitiveness"; for the middle-aged adult, the same activity may be termed "prurient." And, as investigators into lifespan continuity are painfully aware, it is exceedingly difficult to recognize consistency when measures of the same construct (namely, aggression, dominance, gregariousness, etc.) over the life span rely on different measures for different developmental periods. In effect, the conceptual meaning of a given behavior may importantly depend on the age of the individual in whom it is observed.

The primary result of such inherently ambiguous relations between concepts and observations is that one can never be certain when a given set of observations either confirms or falsifies a given theoretical claim about human development. In this respect, Meehl's (1978) summary views concerning the state of empirically validated theory in personality and social psychology seem no less applicable to developmental psychology:

> It may be that the nature of the subject matter in most of personology and social psychology is inherently incapable of permitting theories with sufficient conceptual power (especially mathematical development) to yield the kinds of strong refutations expected by Popperians, Bayesians, and unphilosophical scientists in developed fields like chemistry. This might mean that we could most profitably confine ourselves to low-order inductions, a (to me, depressing) conjecture that is somewhat corroborated by the fact that the two most powerful forms of clinical psychology are atheoretical psychometrics of prediction on the one hand and behavior modification on the other. Neither of these approaches has the kind of conceptual richness that attracts the theory-oriented mind, but I think we ought to acknowledge the possibility that there is never going to be a really impressive theory in personality or social psychology. I dislike to think that, but it might just be true. (p. 828)

Surely, for the developmental scholar, Meehl's conclusion is an unhappy one. Yet there is reason for resistance. Meehl may be correct with respect to the development of falsifiable theory. Yet there are immensely important roles to be fulfilled by general theories of development, even when such theories are neither testable nor lend themselves to purposes of prediction. It is to the role of theory in a universe of phenomenal fluctuation that we must now turn.

V. The Functional Utility of Life-Span Theory

When serious credence is given to arguments for the historical relativity of the developmental trajectory, along with the companionate view of the self-directed organism, traditional views of the nature and functions of scientific theory are critically challenged. These various arguments confront the traditional scholar with profound concerns: Should the primary theoretical focus be turned toward historically delimited description of high immediate utility but low transhistorical value? Of what value is highly abstract theory? Such theory seems to have little predictive utility in terms of the social problems facing the culture, nor is it open to convincing empirical evaluation. What reasons save those that are wholly self-serving can be offered for the scholarly elaboration of developmental theories such as those of Freud, Piaget, Werner, or the dialecticians, no one of which is sufficiently unambiguous that empirical assessment can be compelling? Should the developmental discipline shift its orientation sharply, then, toward historically centered description relevant to specific societal needs?

To answer these questions requires inquiry into the positive functions of general theories of development. If we abandon the traditional theoretical goals of prediction and control, what rationale remains to sustain the general theorist? One may argue that no rationale is required; theorists may continue their conjecture for the sheer intellectual joy of doing so. This argument cannot be refuted on any fundamental level. There is little reason to abandon the search for intellectual stimulation, whether in the form of the parlor game or the professional journal. However, for many, such self-centered pleasures lack nourishment; they simply do not furnish sufficient motivation for a life investment. Nor, on the wholly pragmatic level, can one anticipate the continued support of major institutions, both academic and governmental, should the sole concern of the developmental theorist be self-stimulation. Other rationales must be explored. In particular, we may consider three functions of developmental theory that are of cardinal significance over and above the problematic goals of prediction and control.

A. EXPLANATION AS A MEANS
TO COMMUNICATED INTELLIGIBILITY

Nothing within the present analysis militates against the central function of theory within traditional science, namely that of explaining the vagaries of experience. Given the press of an ever-changing sea of ambiguous events, the individual may frequently search for a means of determining "what there is" and "why." Theory offers a means of dissecting the flux; through theory the rough and tumble of passing experience is rendered orderly. Theory furnishes an essential inventory of what there is and ideally satisfies the individual's quest for why the units of the inventory are related as they are. In this way, theory furnishes a satisfying sense of understanding, along with terms enabling the individual to communicate this understanding to others. Thus, Freudian theory is highly useful in its capacity to demonstrate how seemingly diverse behavioral events across the life span are all expressions of a constant psychodynamic pattern. The chaotic and bizarre are thus transformed into a seemingly inexorable pattern; psychological sources are posited to make intelligible their existence and to suggest a cure. In the same way, other theorists rely on the concept of developmental stages to transform the immensely complex range of experiences into an orderly progression. In tying these stages to genetic sources or to social context, the theorist indicates "why" these stages occur as they do. And, in each case, the theorist furnishes terms of discourse, so that communication about experience is possible. The most broadly potent theories of the past century, including those of Darwin, Freud, Marx, and Keynes have all served in this capacity. Not one is falsifiable; not one contains a strong predictive capacity. Yet all have been universally important in furnishing intelligible understanding and associated language for communication.

Although these arguments are relatively elementary, there is a far more complex issue lingering in the wings. If such general theoretical structures are essentially untestable, then how is one to select among competing theories? Or, to rephrase the question, given a single compelling system of intelligibility, for what reason should one quest for a second? This question increases in impact in light of earlier arguments concerning contextual interpretation. As we saw, there is a fundamental ambiguity in linking abstract conceptual terms to empirical referents. Theories are difficult to test inasmuch as behavioral exemplars of any theoretical construct defie unambiguous specification over time. It appears that the conceptual terms of most abstract theoretical systems are sufficiently elastic with respect to the range of experiences to which they may be applied, that virtually all behavioral events might possibly be rendered intelligible from any coherent, abstract system (cf. Gergen, in press). The point seems well demonstrated in the case of psychoanalytic theory, a theory that has long proved satisfactory as a means of comprehending the immense range of experiences reported within the analytic process. In effect, the theoretical structure does not appear to have been vitally challenged bv any set of phenomena reported to analysts during the past five decades. The theoretical terms appear capable of convincing application within highly varying experiential contexts.

We find ourselves, then, faced with the dilemma of selecting among theories, none of which may be subject to empirical test, and each of which may be extended so as to explain virtually all human activity within certain periods of life. At this point, one might turn for help to the traditional but seldom used arsenal of comparative criteria for scientific theories. We might, for example, inquire into which formulation is the most parsimonious, the most logically coherent, the least ambiguous, or the most heuristically potent. However, when the dust is removed from these venerable criteria, we find little of sustenance. With increments in parsimony are frequently associated decrements in differentiation; because differentiation often increases the range of sensitization, parsimony comes with an attached cost. Reinforcement theories of development, for example, are highly parsimonious; however, in their failure to distinguish among various forms of reinforcement and the specific problems or promises attached to each, they lose their capacity for sensitization. Logical coherence is clearly an asset, but few available theories are obvious candidates for illogicality. Clear differences do exist among competing theories with respect to ambiguity, but again, clarity carries with it associated costs. The ambiguous theory, like the ambiguous poem, is often more evocative or suggestive. Further, with increments in ambiguity, theoretical terms are frequently rendered more flexible with respect to application; terms that are tied clearly to a given phenomenon cannot easily be generalized across contexts. Finally, the traditional criterion of heuristic potency loses its edge in light of the weaknesses of the falsification assumption. If empirical evidence cannot satisfactorily add to or subtract from the validity of abstract theoretical accounts, then theories spurring researchers into activity can scarcely be viewed as superior to those that do not. Thus, the innumerable attempts to test Piagetian theory cross-culturally may attest to the heuristic value of the theory. However, such research does little either to strengthen or weaken the evidential grounds of the theory, and one might reasonably view with dismay the abundant research activity stimulated by the theory. This is not to argue that the traditional criteria are irrelevant or dysfunctional; rather, each is problematic and together they do not take us far enough.

It appears, then, that traditional criteria offer little means for selecting one intelligibility system over another; nor is it obvious at this juncture why additional theoretical work is required of the discipline. Existing theory can, with skilled negotiation of conceptual meaning, account for virtually all life-span phenomena. A satisfactory answer to the question of "why multiple theories?" hinges on discussion of two additional functions of developmental theory.

B. THE GENERATIVE FUNCTION OF THEORY

There are two major senses in which one may gain theoretical understanding. As in the case of traditional empiricism, understanding is gained when one's conceptual system adequately maps the contours of an existing reality. One begins with the assumption of an existing reality, and it is this reality that furnishes the riddles to be solved by the discerning scientist. Theory is thus a means for representing the contours of nature and unlocking its secrets. For example, botonists may view themselves as confronting various forms of plant life and setting out to discover the conditions affecting growth and proliferation. This orientation toward theoretical understanding may be contrasted with a second in which such understanding entails the assignment of meaning to one's experience. One does not presume a given form of nature from this standpoint, but by assigning meaning to experience, creates interpretations that fashion the way in which nature is subsequently viewed. One does not "map an existing reality" from this standpoint but begins with constructions that dictate the synthesis of experience. Whereas the initial form of understanding is closely linked with positive–empiricist metatheory, the contrasting view finds its roots in the rationalist writings of Kant, Hegel, and others.

Thus far we have argued that understanding of the former variety has limited utility within the developmental sphere. There is no adequate way of assessing the degree of fit between a general theory and the presumed contours of nature. In effect, the empiricist program for science does not furnish adequate guidelines for the development of theory. In contrast, the rationalist form of understanding seems much favored by the emerging views of multiple developmental trajectories and the autonomous organism. If the individual is in continuous motion and may at any time move in novel ways, the contours of nature become obscure. When experience furnishes continuous flux, and repetition of experiential pattern is difficult to locate, a form of understanding that itself creates the contours of nature is favored. When experience is in constant flux, the very concept of "fact" loses its utility (Gergen, 1977). Under such conditions, the scientist may legitimately set out to render experience intelligible by creating its identity and its meaning.

In emphasizing the creation of reality through theory, the intention is not to revert to a skeptical solipsism. The question is not whether "there is something out there." We may safely join the broad ranks of those believing it more pragmatic to assume the existence of an external reality than not. However, when our experience of this presumed reality is suffused with ambiguity, when experience is multiplex and continuously changing, then any statement concerning "what there is" is rendered problematic. Any given statement serves to direct one's attention in such a way that one "experiences reality" in a way that is consistent with the theoretical statement. At the same time, the inherent richness of experience is diminished in doing so. Thus, for example, if one observes a large crowd of people, one encounters an immense array of everchanging stimuli. However, if one begins to search for the red pattern imbedded in the crowd, he or she soon begins to observe a dominant red form, and all other color variations recede into the background. When a second color is considered, and one's attentions are redirected, the color red recedes into oblivion, and the new color looms into view. In the same way, if a developmental theory directs attention to forms of mother–child "attachment" during a given period, one becomes sensitized to certain aspects of the child's activity, while others are ignored. Given the theory, one can see the obvious importance of attachment during this developmental period. Without the theoretical lens, attachment as an observational locus may recede into undifferentiated flux.

In addition to the "creation of entities," theoretical terms may also invest them with meaning, that is, convey the manner in which they are to be treated. To call a differentiated pattern of activity attachment suggests the manner in which one should respond, both conceptually and behaviorally. The term implies, in this case, a unit formation between individuals, a formation that would not be implied should an indicator of attachment, such as the tendency of the child to remain within close physical proximity to the mother, be described as "locating" activity or "power retention" (referring to the desire on the child's part to keep in view those objects over which it feels it possesses power). Similarly, the term attachment implies that one might look positively on such activity during the early developmental years but negatively as maturity is reached. Such evaluations are implied by the widespread cultural belief that mother and child should be attached during the formative years but that independence is necessary for maturity. In effect, the theoretical term not only creates the entity but establishes its theoretical and social significance.

From this perspective, the power of the theorist may be immense. The theorist who creates compelling theory is engaged in a form of ontological education. He or she teaches the culture "what there is" and "why." Furthermore, when sensitivities are thus educated, patterns of conduct within the culture may be altered as well. As one learns how to see, one also absorbs a logic for action. As we have seen, available theory frequently teaches one not only to perceive patterns of attachment, but to value such patterns in early stages of development and to view them skeptically in later periods. As a result of the theory, one may attempt to sustain the former patterns and discourage the latter. Prior to the theory, there is relatively undifferentiated flux and little demand for action; with the propounding of theory, there are discernible patterns and necessary actions.

Given the power of theory to shape both perception and action, we must raise the question of criteria. What forms of theory may be viewed as desirable? When should a theory be discarded? One major answer to such questions may be derived from distinguishing between theory that is consistent with, or reflective of common assumptions within the culture, and theory that is inconsistent with these assumptions. In the latter case, we may speak of generative theory (Gergen, 1978). *Generative theory* is that which *challenges the guiding assumptions of the culture, raises fundamental questions regarding contemporary life, fosters reconsideration of ex-*

isting contructions of reality, and by doing so, *furnishes new alternatives for action.* Let us consider more closely the two central components of generative theorizing along with arguments supporting such formulations.

C. THE GENERATION OF DOUBT

As we have seen, any given theoretical view simultaneously serves to sensitize and to create myopia; one sees more sharply, but remains blind to that which falls outside the realm of focus. Thus, it may be argued, any theory that commands widespread belief, that serves as the univocal view of reality within a given culture poses a threat to the culture. When experience has become truncated through what may be viewed as common sense assumptions concerning "what there is" and how it functions. there is only partial perception, reality carries but a single dimension. As one's actions are often consistent with one's views of the what and whys of experience, then the companion to partial perception is a delimited range of action. When a theory is used generatively, it will challenge the commonly shared construction of the world. It will generate doubt in such constructions, engendering flexibility and increasing the adaptive potential of an individual or a culture.

Freudian theory is perhaps the most generative developmental account yet devised. Initially the theory did much to unseat Victorian assumptions concerning the sexlessness of the early childhood period, and the antiseptic view of the relation between parent and child. More importantly, the theory called attention to the possibility of unseen and virtually impenetrable, unconscious connections between seemingly disparate events over the life span. Events that were phenotypically dissimilar and temporally dissociated could be related dynamically within the unconscious. In a broad sense, Freudian theory invited one to suspend belief in the phenomenal givens in contemporary life and to remain sensitive to unseen forces. One could scarcely ask a theory to provoke greater doubt in the common sense givens.

The rationale for multiple theories of life-span development should now be apparent. Because effective interchange among people demands a background of shared assumptions, the culture is continuously in the process of fabricating such assumptions concerning what exists, how it is related, and what therefore constitute reasonable actions. In effect, the culture is continuously in the process of molding common sense. As each new construction becomes absorbed into the assumptive bases of the culture, there is an associated constriction in perceptual capacity and a reduction in adaptive capability. Thus, at any point in time, there is a vital need for theory that challenges the shared assumptions of the times. The capacity for Freudian theory to generate doubt may now be largely exhausted. Much of the theory has entered the fund of common knowledge. As such knowledge is solidified, it is necessary to develop bold new theories of development that again thrust the culture into doubt.

D. THE FORMATION OF ALTERNATIVES

Closely allied with the generative function of creating doubt is that of furnishing alternative courses of action. Not only should generative theory give one reason to pause and reconsider current modes of activity, but ideally should point to other forms of actions and their potential results. One may here discriminate among generative conceptualizations that (*a*) succeed only in instigating doubt; (*b*) generate doubt and also *imply* alternative courses of action; and (*c*) those that fully articulate alternatives to current investments. It would be difficult to locate pure exemplars of these various categories. However, generatively orientated analyses do differ in the relative emphasis given to these various ends. A methodological critique, such as that mounted by Kurtines and Grief (1974) against Kohlberg's theory of moral development, does succeed is generating doubt about Kohlberg's analysis, but little is offered or implied by these investigators with respect to an alternative formulation. In contrast, Riegel's (1973) analysis of the cultural and economic underpinnings of current developmental theory, Sullivan's (1977) critique of Kohlberg's theory of moral development and the liberal social science ideology on which it is based, and Buck-Morss's (1975) assessment of the socioeconomic bias underlying Piagetian theory, all function both to generate doubt in the relevant theoretical scaffoldings and to imply alternatives. All might represent proper exercises of what Horkheimer (1972) has termed the ''critical attitude,'' and particularly so in their argument that an acceptance of contemporary theorizing can favor exploitative relations among persons. By implication, one is challenged to consider alternative theoretical forms that might favor the reconstruction of society along less exploitative lines.

Freedle's (1977) attempt to employ Thomian topological theory in building a developmental theory enabling both *p* and *not p* to be simultaneously true, along with his proposal for using nonclassical or deviant logics to understand certain forms of development, not only generates doubt in the currently existing theories of development, but succeeds in laying the scaffolding for important alternatives. However, Freedle's analysis falls short of the full generative demand inasmuch as it does not clearly elaborate alternative forms of action related to the orientation. Models are proposed, but their behavioral implications are left ambiguous.

Most desirable, from the present standpoint, are theoretical forms that enable one to perceive the shortcomings of existing positions and that liberate one from their behavioral implications. For example, if one were invested in the reconstruction of social institutions, what view of human development would most favor such reconstruction? If one seeks reforms in social policy vis-à-vis the aged population, could the aging process be reconceptualized in such a way that alternatives to the present policies might be favored? As argued elsewhere (Gergen & Basseches, in press), such formulations are particularly needed by practitioners and others whose major investments are in social change. Theorists who uncritically set out to describe contemporary patterns of development typically lend implicit support to the *status quo*. For those concerned with social change, compelling theoretical rationales are required to legitimize alternative forms of action at the conceptual or intellectual level.

E. THE VALUE–SUSTAINING FUNCTION OF THEORY

The preceding discussion furnishes ample prelude to a final significant role to be played by general theories of life-span development. To speak of the generative capacity of theories to create doubt and to foster new patterns of action clearly implies that any given theoretical commitment is problematic, and that the capacity to engage in both a pattern of activity and its negation is superior to either one of these options alone. This position cannot be justified either on strictly logical or empirical grounds. Traditionalists may also view this line of argument with dismay, for it suggests that one may be fully justified in attacking a theory, not because of its failure in accurate description or explanation, but merely because it is widely accepted. Essentially, it is being argued, one may justifiably dislodge a theory for valuational as opposed to nonvaluational purposes. In this case, the value behind the theory may be adaptive flexibility; however, other value investments may also serve as a basis for theoretical interpretation. Amplification of this point is required.

As we have seen, objective accuracy is not a criterion that can usefully be applied to general theories of development. If empirical verisimilitude can be abandoned as a major criterion for theoretical evaluation, and adaptive flexibility can be admitted as a value to be sought by theory, then should we not extend consideration to other potential values to be served by theory? One may argue that, should values become the common motivating force behind theory, the discipline would become a podium for ideological partisanship, and abnegate its venerable responsibility for rendering value-neutral accounts of reality. Should value investments be allowed to determine theoretical description and explanation, then the field could no longer lay claim to being a science; rather, it would become a form of secular religion.

Yet, as has become increasingly clear, it is naive to believe in the existence of theoretical accounts that do not favor certain forms of action over others, that do not add to the power, pleasure, fortune, or life chances of certain groups in society at the expense of others. As increasingly numerous accounts have shown, even the most pristine and innocuous theoretical accounts of human activity harbor numerous value implications. They do so in the selection of phenomena for study (thus lending such phenomena an importance not granted to potential competitors), the selection of terms enumerating these phenomena (theoretical terms indicate the value to be placed on various states and conditions), the selection of explanations (explanations place the locus of blame on varying persons or institutions), the image of the human functioning that they convey, and the choice of research methods (cf. Apfelbaum & Lubek, 1976; Buck-Morss, 1975; Gergen, 1977; Riegel, 1973; Sampson, 1978; Sullivan, 1977; Weber, 1949). We are not speaking here of the extent to which theorists' value investments have actually played an instrumental role in fashioning theory, nor of the extent to which personal values have guided the selection of method or data, all of which are matters to which philosophers of science have given considerable attention. Rather, the important point is that, in numerous ways, even the most disinterested theory conveys value implications. Theories insinuate themselves into culture in such a way as to alter the culture, to disrupt or to fortify certain cultural patterns, and such effects are of valuational importance to those who are so affected.

Given the inevitability of value-loaded theory, and the unsurmountable problems of establishing empirical validity, it would appear altogether appropriate to consider the value-sustaining potential of theory not as an inadvertent irritant, but as a primary function of theoretical endeavor. If theories do not adequately meet the traditional criteria of the positivist–empiricist paradigm, we may consider those ends toward which they are most efficacious. We need not consider theories less scientific for achieving these ends; rather, we must reconsider the concept of science as it is applied within the human sphere. In the present case, it would appear that theories properly function as implements for the sustaining of value positions. They may thus be judged according to their effectiveness in this capacity, and with respect to their agreement or disagreement with one's personal commitments. Theories that carry out the task poorly (for example, those seen as mere sentiments masquerading as theory, purely ideological or propagandistic), may be judged more harshly. And should a theory be found personally disagreeable, the way may be opened for critical reexamination and synthesis. Theories have long functioned to sustain values on an implicit level. Stability accounts favor patterns of behavior over the life span that are often inconsistent with those favored by ordered-change accounts (Gergen, 1977). Freudian theory may be viewed as traditionally moral in its implications (Rieff, 1961), whereas Kohlberg's theory of moral development may be viewed as sexist in implication (Sampson, 1978). One need not be dismayed that such theories sustain value investments. The major question is whether the theories are successful in enhancing the acceptability of the value commitments. Here the case is moot, as theorists have been less than willing to confront publicly the value bases of work that by traditional standards should be neutral. Future attention must be given to a means of linking theory and value in more effective ways.

VI. Summary

Conceptions of human functioning emerging within the life-span arena raise critical problems with respect to the function of theory and research from the traditional empiricist perspective. To extend the implications of current work is to cast considerable doubt on the capacity of theory to enhance prediction and control over time, and the capacity of science to furnish unequivocal corroboration or falsification of any given theory. These implications may be extended not only to psychological study more generally, but across the range of the social sciences as well. Although such views would appear pessimistic, they are so only to the extent that one remains steadfastly committed to a view of science once articulated but now largely abandoned within the philosophy of science. Life-span work thus lends itself to the development of an altered conception of scientific work, one that invites the theorist, on the one hand, to take seriously the valuational context in which his or her work is conducted and, on the other, to consider carefully his or her capacity for direct theoretical intervention into the course of human activity. Through the construction of systems of intelligibility, the theorist may essentially create the society of the future.

Acknowledgments

Support for the present analysis was furnished by the National Science Foundation (Grant No. 7809393). Additional gratitude is expressed to Nancy Datan. Mary Gergen, and Ellen Skinner for their careful appraisals of an earlier draft of the manuscript.

References

Apfelbaum, E., Lubek, I. Resolution vs. revolution? The theory of conflicts in question. In L. Strickland, F. Aboud, & K. Gergen (Eds.), *Social psychology in transition*. New York: Plenum, 1976.

Baltes, P. B., & Cornelius, S. W. The status of dialectics in developmental psychology: Theoretical orientation versus scientific method. In N. Datan & H. Reese (Eds.), *Life-span developmental psychology: Dialectical perspectives on experimental research*. New York: Academic Press, 1977, pp. 121–135.

Baltes, P., & Labouvie, G. Adult development of intellectual performance: Description, explanation, and modification. In C. Eisdorfer & M. P. Lawton (Eds.), *The psychology of adult development and aging*. Washington, D.C.: American Psychological Association, 1973.

Baltes, P. B., & Reinert, G. Cohort effects in cognitive development of children as revealed by cross-sectional sequences. *Developmental Psychology,* 1969, **1**, 169–177.

Baltes, P. B., & Schaie, K. W. On life-span developmental research paradigms, retrospects and prospects. In P. B. Baltes & K. W. Schaie (Eds.), *Life-span developmental psychology: Personality and socialization*. New York: Academic Press, 1973.

Bell, R. Q., & Hertz, T. W. Toward more comparability and generalizability of developmental research. *Child Development,* 1976, **47**, 6–13.

Bernstein, R. J. *The restructuring of social and political theory*. Philadelphia: University of Pennsylvania Press, 1978.

Birren, J. E. *Relations of development and aging*. Springfield, Ill.: Charles C Thomas, 1964.

Birren, J. E., & Woodruff, D. S. Human development over the life span through education. In P. B. Baltes & K. W. Schaie (Eds.), *Life-span developmental psychology: Personality and socialization*. New York: Academic Press, 1973.

Block, J. *Lives through time*. Berkeley, Calif.: Bancroft Books, 1971.

Borstelmann, L. J. Periodization in the history of American childhood. Paper presented at the Meeting of Cheiron. Washington, D.C., May 1976.

Botwinick, J. Learning in children and aged adults. In L. R. Goulet & P. B. Baltes (Eds.), *Life-span development psychology: Research and theory*. New York: Academic Press, 1970.

Brim, O. G., & Kagan, J. Constancy and change: A view of the issues. In O. G. Brim & J. Kagan (Eds.), *Constancy and change in human development*. Cambridge: Harvard University Press, 1980.

Buck-Morss, S. Socio-economic bias in Piaget's theory and its implications for the cultural controversy. *Human Development,* 1975, **18**, 35–49.

Buss, A. R. Generational analysis: Description, explanation & theory. *Journal of Social Issues,* 1974, **30**, 55–71.

Buss, A. R. *A dialectical psychology*. New York: Irvington, 1979.

Cronbach, L. J. Beyond the two disciplines of scientific psychology. *American Psychologist,* 1975, **30**, 116–127.

Datan, N. After the apple: Post-Newtonian metatheory for jaded psychologists. In N. Datan & H. Reese (Eds.), *Life-span developmental psychology: Dialectical perspectives on experimental research*. New York: Academic Press, 1977.

Demos, J., & Demos, V. Adolescence in historical perspective. *Journal of Marriage and the Family,* 1969, **31**, 632–638.

Dohrenwend, B. S., & Dohrenwend, B. P. (Eds.). *Stressful life events: Their nature and effects*. New York: Wiley, 1974.

Elder, G. H., Jr. *Children of the great depression*. Chicago: University of Chicago Press, 1974.

Elder, G. H., Jr. Social structure and personality: A life course perspective. In P. Baltes and O. Brim (Eds.), *Life-span development and behavior* (Vol. 2). New York: Academic Press, 1979.

Emmerick, W. Socialization and sex-role development. In P. Baltes & K. W. Schaie (Eds.), *Life-span developmental psychology: Personality and socialization.* New York: Academic Press, 1973.

Epstein, S. Traits are alive and well. In D. Magnusson & N. S. Endler (Eds.), *Personality at the cross-roads.* Hillsdale, N.J.: Erlbaum, 1977.

Freedle, R. Psychology, Thomian topologies, deviant logics, and human development. In N. Datan & H. Reese (Eds.), *Life-span developmental psychology: Dialectical perspectives on experimental research.* New York: Academic Press, 1977.

Gadlin, H. Child discipline and the pursuit of self: An historical interpretation. *Advances in child development and behavior* (Vol. 12). New York: Academic Press, 1978.

Gergen, K. J. Social psychology as history. *Journal of Personality and Social Psychology,* 1973, **26,** 309–320.

Gergen, K. J. Social psychology, science and history. *Personality and Social Psychology Bulletin,* 1976, **2,** 373–383.

Gergen, K. J. Social exchange theory in a world of transient fact. In E. Hamblin & J. Kunkel (Eds.), *Behavioral theory in sociology.* New Brunswick, N.J.: Transaction Books, 1977.

Gergen, K. J. Toward generative theory. *Journal of Personality and Social Psychology,* 1978, **36,** 1344–1360.

Gergen, K. J. Toward intellectual audacity in social psychology. In R. Gilmour & S. Duck (Eds.), *The development of social psychology.* New York: Academic Press, in press.

Gergen, K. J., & Basseches, M. The potentiation of psychological knowledge. In R. F. Kidd & M. Saks (Eds.), *Advances in applied social psychology.* New York: Academic Press, in press.

Gutmann, D. Parenthood: A key to the comparative study of the life cycle. In N. Datan & L. Ginsberg (Eds.), *Life-span developmental psychology: Normative life crisis.* New York: Academic Press, 1975.

Harré, R., & Secord, P. *The explanation of social behavior.* Totowa, N.J.: Littlefield Adams, 1973.

Hempel, C. *Aspects of scientific explanation and other essays in the philosophy of science.* New York: Free Press, 1965.

Hook, S. *Dialectical materialism and scientific method.* Manchester, England: Special supplement to the Bulletin of the Committee on Science and Freedom, 1957.

Hooper, F. Cognitive assessment across the life span: Methodological implications of the organismic approach. In J. Nesselroade & H. Reese (Eds.), *Life-span developmental psychology: Methodological issues.* New York: Academic Press, 1973.

Horkheimer, M. *Critical theory.* New York: Seabury Press, 1972.

Hultsch, D. F., & Hickey, T. External validity in the study of human development: Methodological and theoretical issues. *Human Development,* 1978, **21,** 76–91.

Huston-Stein, A., & Baltes, P. Theory and method in life-span developmental psychology: Implications for child development. In H. W. Reese & L. P. Lipsitt (Eds.), *Advances in child development and behavior.* New York: Academic Press, 1976.

Kagan, J., & Moss, H. A. *Birth to maturity.* New York: Wiley, 1962.

Kant, I. Critical examination of practical reason, 1788. In *Critique of practical reason and other works.* Trans. by T. K. Abbott. New York: Longmans, 1909.

Kurtines, W., & Grief, E. The development of moral thought: Review and evaluation of Kohlberg's approach. *Psychological Bulletin,* 1974, **81,** 453–470.

Kvale, S. Dialectics and research on remembering. In N. Datan & H. Reese (Eds.), *Life-span developmental psychology: Dialectical perspectives on experimental research.* New York: Academic Press, 1977.

Labouvie, E. W. The dialectical nature of measurement activities in the behavioral sciences. *Human Development,* 1975, **18,** 205–222.

Laudan, L. *Progress and its problems.* Berkeley: University of California Press, 1977.

Lieberman, M. Adaptive processes in late life. In N. Datan & L. Ginsberg (Eds.), *Life-span developmental psychology: Normative life crises.* New York: Academic Press, 1975.

Looft, W. Socialization and personality throughout the life span: An examination of contemporary psychological approaches. In P. B. Baltes & K. W. Schaie (Eds.), *Life-span developmental psychology: Personality and socialization.* New York: Academic Press, 1973.

Meacham, J. A. A transactional model of remembering. In N. Datan & R. Reese (Eds.), *Life-span developmental psychology: Dialectical perspectives on experimental research.* New York: Academic Press, 1977.

Meehl, P. E. Theoretical risks and tabular asterisks: Sir Karl, Sir Ronald, and the slow progress of soft psychology. *Journal of Consulting and Clinical Psychology,* 1978, **42,** 806–834.

Mischel, T. Psychological explanations and their vicissitudes. In W. J. Arnold (Ed.), *Nebraska symposium on motivation* (Vol. 23). Lincoln: University of Nebraska Press, 1975.

Mischel, W. *Personality and assessment.* New York: Wiley, 1968.

Montada, L., & Fillipp, S. H. Implications of life-span developmental psychology for childhood education. In H. Reese (Ed.), *Advances in child development and behavior.* New York: Academic Press, 1976.

Neisser, U. *Cognition and reality.* San Francisco: W. H. Freeman, 1976.

Nesselroade, J. R., & Baltes, P. B. Adolescent personality development and historical change: 1970–1972. *Monographs of the Society for Research in Child Development,* 1974, **39,**(1) Serial Number 154.

Nesselroade, J., & Reese, H. (Eds.), *Life-span developmental psychology: Methodological issues.* New York: Academic Press, 1973.

Neugarten, B. L. Adaptation and the life cycle. Paper presented at the meeting of the Foundations Fund for Research in Psychiatry, Puerto Rico, June 1968.

Neugarten, B. L., & Datan, N. Sociological perspectives on the life cycle. In P. B. Baltes & K. W. Schaie (Eds.), *Life-span developmental psychology: Personality and socialization.* New York: Academic Press, 1973.

Overton, W. F., & Reese, H. W. Models of development: Methodological implications. In J. R. Nesselroade & H. W. Reese (Eds.), *Life-span developmental psychology: Methodological issues.* New York: Academic Press, 1973.

Pearlin, L. Sex roles and depression. In N. Datan & L. Ginsberg (Eds.), *Life-span developmental psychology: Normative life crises.* New York: Academic Press, 1975.

Popper, K. R. *The logic of scientific discovery.* New York: Harper, 1968. (Originally published 1959).)

Quine, W. V. *From a logical point of view.* Cambridge, Mass.: Harvard University Press, 1953.

Reese, H. W. Discriminative learning and transfer: Dialectical perspectives. In N. Datan & H. Reese (Eds.), *Life-span developmental psychology: Dialectical perspectives on experimental research.* New York: Academic Press, 1977.

Reese, H. W., & Overton, W. F. Models of development and theories of development. In L. R. Goulet & P. B. Baltes (Eds.), *Life-span developmental psychology: Research and theory.* New York: Academic Press, 1970.

Rieff, P. *Freud: The mind of a moralist.* New York: Anchor, 1961.

Riegel, K. F. Time and change in the development of the individual and society. In H. Reese (Ed.), *Advances in child development and behavior.* New York: Academic Press, 1972.

Riegel, K. F. Dialectic operations: The final period of cognitive development. *Human Development,* 1973, **16**, 346-370.

Riegel, K. F. From traits and equilibrium toward developmental dialectics. In W. Arnold (Ed.), *Nebraska symposium on motivation.* Lincoln: University of Nebraska Press, 1975 (a).

Riegel, K. F. Toward a dialectical theory of development. *Human Development,* 1975, **18**, 50-64 (b).

Runyan, W. M. The life course as a theoretical orientation: Sequences of person-situation interaction. *Journal of Personality,* 1978, **46**, 569-593.

Sampson, E. E. Scientific paradigms and social values: Wanted—a scientific revolution. *Journal of Personality and Social Psychology,* 1978, **36**, 1332-1343.

Sarbin, T. R. Contextualism: A world view of modern psychology. In A. W. Landfield (Ed.), *1976 Nebraska Symposium on Motivation: Personal construct psychology* (Vol. 24). Lincoln: University of Nebraska Press, 1977.

Schlegel, A. Situational stress: A Hopi example. In N. Datan & L. Ginsberg (Eds.), *Life-span developmental psychology: Normative life crises.* New York: Academic Press, 1975.

Sullivan, E. V. A study of Kohlberg's structural theory of moral development: A critique of liberal social science ideology. *Human Development,* 1977, **20**, 352-376.

Toulmin, S. *Foresight and understanding.* New York: Harper & Row, 1961.

Tyler, L. E. *Individuality.* San Francisco: Jossey-Bass, 1978.

van den Berg, J. H. *The changing nature of man.* New York: Norton, 1961.

Weber, M. *The methodology of the social sciences.* Glencoe, Ill.: Free Press, 1949.

Weiss, J. R. Transcontextual validity in developmental research. *Child Development,* 1978, **49**, 1-12.

Whitehead, A. N. *Process and reality.* New York: Free Press, 1969 (originally published 1929).

Woodruff, D., & Birren, J. E. Age changes and cohort differences in personality. *Developmental Psychology,* 1972, **6**, 252-259.

Still Stable after All These Years:
Personality as a Key to Some Issues
in Adulthood and Old Age

Paul T. Costa, Jr. and Robert R. McCrae

GERONTOLOGY RESEARCH CENTER

NATIONAL INSTITUTE ON AGING

NATIONAL INSTITUTES OF HEALTH, BALTIMORE, MARYLAND

Abstract

A review of literature on personality and aging is presented in the context of a trait model of personality. It is argued that self-report trait methods offer an approach to the study of personality ideally suited to the requirements of longitudinal research. A formal trait model, incorporating the domains of Neuroticism, Extraversion, and Openness to Experience, is offered as an aid in both clarifying conceptual issues and organizing empirical findings. Clinical and projective studies of personality change in adulthood have provided evidence both for and against stability, but recent longitudinal studies using objective tests have shown little or no maturational change in personality. Rather than look for change, it is argued that developmental psychologists might better search for the mechanisms that promote stability. The primary relevance of personality to the study of adult development, however, is seen to be

LIFE-SPAN DEVELOPMENT
AND BEHAVIOR, VOL. 3

65

in its effects on the issues and problems with which the aging individual must cope. This is illustrated in applications to the male "midlife crisis," subjective well-being, and stressful life events. Future directions in the field of aging and personality include the refinement of trait measures, the synthesis of self-report with alternative methods, and investigation of the links between personality traits and the processes and mechanisms of coping.

I. A Trait Model of Personality and Aging

The present chapter grew out of an invitation from one of the editors to write a review of our own work and elaborate our views about the direction in which the field of personality and aging should go. We took him at his word; and the result is an interpretive review in which our own research is cited far more extensively than an impartial survey of the literature would justify. Furthermore, we have adopted a definite point of view and a tone that errs in the direction of "partisan zealotry" rather than of "benevolent eclecticism," in an attempt to "provide the reader with a vivid account . . ." (Maddi, 1976, p. 2), of our approach.

The belief that character or personality is set for life by the time the individual reaches adulthood has always been dominant. William James claimed that by the age of 30, character was "set like plaster." In the early days of personality psychology, the major modification of this position was the Freudian claim that the determination of personality was finished much *earlier* than 30—perhaps as early as 6 or 7 years. But increased interest in the psychology of aging has led a host of researchers to look for signs of development or change in personality in the later years of adulthood. Most often these studies, whether cross-sectional or longitudinal, have employed variables and measures derived from the individual difference or trait perspective. At the same time, the trait approach itself has been criticized and almost dismissed by interactionists, social learning theorists, and others who contend that traits and their measures are useless for understanding personalty and behavior.

We will argue that a new round of evidence establishing the claim for stability in trait dimensions during adulthood necessitates a revision of contemporary views on both personality theory and the field of aging and personality. Sophisticated trait models of personality *are* valid, but they do not show the kinds of changes in later life that it is currently fashionable to seek. Instead, they provide a stable, meaningful framework in which changes in health, social roles, cognitive functioning, or coping behavior can be examined and partially understood.

A. STATE OF THE FIELD

In her 1977 review, Neugarten claimed that the field of personality psychology was in disarray, crumbling under the attacks of social learning theorists (Mischel, 1968), humanistic psychologists (Maddi, 1976), and psychometrists (Fiske, 1974). The subfield of personality and aging appeared to be in even worse shape. The predominant theories of adult development (Erikson, 1950; Gutmann, 1964; Jung, 1933) were outgrowths of psychoanalytic approaches, which had been steadily sinking into disrepute for over a generation. The methodological critique of cross-sectional studies (which confound maturational changes with generational differences) offered by Schaie (1965) and Baltes (1968) had cast into doubt most of the accumulated evidence on age and personality, leaving only a handful of longitudinal findings on which to build, and these seemed to show no consistent pattern of age changes.

Neugarten's advice to personologists was that they should avoid ideological disputes and idle speculation, and concentrate on building a body of data and findings that could form the basis for a meaningful theory of aging and personality. This recommendation of empiricism is limited in usefulness, however. What facts, what data should we collect: attitudes? fantasies? nonverbal behavior? attributions? psychophysiological responses? Without the implicit or explicit guidance of theory, observations are not likely to be meaningful. Methodological problems cannot be avoided simply by proclaiming theoretical neutrality: Theories and facts must go hand in hand, and a crisis affecting one necessarily affects the other.

As the 1980s commence, it is possible to view this pessimistic outlook as the darkness before the dawn. The field of personality itself has seen a renewal of confidence, and the results of longitudinal studies of aging have played a central role in this rebirth (Block, 1977). In addition, longitudinal studies have provided a tentative answer to the question of whether there are age-related changes in personality, and pointed toward other significant topics of research. Somewhat surprisingly, the "breakthrough" that we feel has restored confidence to personality psychology was not the proposal of a new conceptual model or paradigm but a return to one of the oldest models: trait theory.

Neugarten complained that broad concepts, often clinically inspired, were unoperationalizable, and narrow concepts trivialized much research. Trait psychology has always offered the hope of a meaningful solution to this dilemma. By most definitions, traits are generalized tendencies toward thoughts, feelings, and behaviors, and thus escape the constricting narrowness of many strictly behavioral approaches. At the same time, traits have historically been tied to measures (usually self-report scales) that operationalize them. If a researcher can demonstrate the validity and utility of a trait measure, he or she has simultaneously shown the generality and operationalizability of the associated concept. Trait measures, when properly developed and employed, can provide the basic data that Neugarten rightly demanded as a foundation for theories of personality and aging.

But the bluntly empirical nature of trait measures has contributed in the past to their low esteem in the field, as conceptual and theoretical elegance is not required. Moreover, although anyone can invent a concept and create a scale, "The authors of many of the instruments . . . were either unaware of the importance of construct validity or . . . could not be bothered to undertake the complex and arduous task of establishing the construct validity of the devices" (Kelly, 1975, p. viii). Indeed, such scales have multiplied past any reasonable number; as a result, the literature consists of a great body of findings that do not cumulate into any meaningful pattern of results. The studies in a recent and thorough review of longitudinal research over the full life span (Moss & Susman, 1980) demonstrate the bewildering variety of concepts and measures used in the field and the enormous difficulty of attempting to integrate results. Neugarten pointed out that life-span developmental psychologists have been more concerned with telling us *how* to study the life span than telling us *what* to study. The same criticism can be leveled at methodologically oriented trait psychologists.

The *premise* of this chapter is that there is a solution to this problem, and that, using this solution, many of the important issues of aging and personality can be approached in a far more constructive manner than has typified the field. Once again, we believe the solution has been available for many years. What is clearly needed is a trait *model* or system; and factor analysts like Cattell (1950, 1973), Guilford (Guilford, Zimmerman, & Guilford, 1976) and Eysenck (1960, 1967) have offered candidates for several decades. Personality researchers in general, and gerontologists in particular, have failed to recognize the power of these models to organize and synthesize results. A review of the literature that disregards the empirical and conceptual structure of traits and measures is likely to yield only a litany of confusion. The review offered here is organized by topic and presented in the context of a model we find useful. This means, of course, that the review will be unabashedly interpretive. In addition to the standard list of personality and aging literature reviews (e.g., Chown, 1968; Neugarten, 1963, 1973, 1977; Riegel, 1959; Schaie & Marquette, 1972; Schein, 1968), more neutral reviews have been offered by Moss and Susman (1980), Gynther (in press), and Siegler (in press).

B. THE NEO TRAIT MODEL OF PERSONALITY

Too often, psychology, and personality theory in particular, have suffered from the tendency of each new theorist to cast away old theories and start from scratch (the factions in psychoanalytic circles having set an unfortunate precedent in this regard). We all know that science depends upon an accumulation of knowledge; somehow we must find a way to salvage the best from past systems while still allowing for change and growth.

Empirically based trait models offer a good starting place. Despite the theoretical and technical differences among Eysenck (1960), Cattell (1973), and Guilford (Guilford, Zimmerman, & Guilford, 1976), which tempt many to dismiss them all, all three have *empirically* converged at either the first or second order of analysis on two basic dimensions of temperament. These are *N,* Eysenck's "Neuroticism," Cattell's "Anxiety" and Guilford's (low) "Emotional Health," and *E,* Eysenck's "Extraversion," Cattell's second order "Exvia," and Guilford's "Social Activity." Whereas the "true" number of dimensions of human personality is a metaphysical rather than a scientific question, a long history of fact finding shows that *at least* the two dimensions of Extraversion and Neuroticism must be reckoned with in any personality model. To these two, our research suggests the addition of a third broad domain, which we call *O,* Openness to Experience. Hence the acronym, "NEO."

Our research reported here was conducted primarily on participants in the normative aging study (Bell, Rose, & Damon, 1972). This sample was composed of over 2000 male volunteers, mostly veterans, who were screened at entry for physical health and geographic stability. All but the lowest socioeconomic levels were well-represented; and, in comparison to the general population, higher educational levels were found, particularly in the oldest men. Participants ranged in age from the twenties to the nineties.

Because the primary focus of the Normative Aging Study was originally physical health and aging, a regular cycle of psychological measurement was not planned, and time-sequential designs were not employed. Instead, a one-time battery was administered to about 1100 subjects between 1965 and 1967 that included the 16PF (combined A and B forms, 1962 edition), the Strong Vocational Interest Bank (SVIB), the Allport–Vernon–Lindzey (1951) Scale of Values (AVL), and the General Aptitude Test Battery (GATB). Factor analyses (Costa, Fozard, & McCrae, 1977; Costa, Fozard, McCrae, & Bossé, 1976) of SVIB and GATB scales were used to reduce the number of variables to more manageable proportions.

Between 1975 and 1977, a number of new personality measures were mailed to subjects, including the Crowne–Marlowe Social Desirability Scale (Crowne & Marlowe, 1964), the EASI-III Temperament Survey (Buss & Plomin, 1975), the Eysenck Personality Inventory (EPI; Eysenck & Eysenck, 1964), the Experience Inventory (Coan, 1972), and scales to measure psychological well-being (Bradburn, 1969), life events (Holmes & Rahe, 1967), positive affect, and the midlife crisis. Data from all these measures will be mentioned in later sections of this chapter.

We first encountered the structure we have come to call the NEO model

TABLE I

Factor Loading in Three Age Groups[a]

	Factor I: Neuroticism			Factor II: Extraversion			Factor III: Openness		
	1[b]	2[c]	3[d]	1	2	3	1	2	3
EIP neuroticism	76	79	79						
EASI-III									
General emotionality	81	83	84						
Fear	67	59	73	−52					
Anger	73	66	72						
Impulse inhibition	56	72	73						
EPI extraversions				70	63	76			
EASI-III									
Sociability				72	72	71			
Tempo				57	69	56			
Vigor				66	74	66			
Sensation seeking	39			50	31	50		43	
Positive emotions[e]				62	47	66		45	
EI Openness									
Phantasy	35	32		−40			68	61	66
Esthetics							62	62	63
Feelings	51	49	49					40	38
Actions						59	66	58	43
Ideas							75	55	73
Values							59	35	60

[a] Varimax rotation of three principal components, decimal points omitted; all loadings above .30 shown.

[b] $N = 206$ men aged 36–51.

[c] $N = 132$ men aged 52–57.

[d] $N = 197$ men aged 58–85.

[e] Scale added to EASI-III (Costa & McCrae, 1978).

in a cluster analysis of the scales of the 16PF (Costa & McCrae, 1976). In addition to Neuroticism and Extraversion clusters, we found a group of scales consisting of I (Tenderminded), M (Imaginative), and Q1 (Liberal Thinking), which were interpreted as constituting a domain of Openness to Experience. We were later able to show that scales in the Experience Inventory (EI), yielding independent measures of openness to phantasy, esthetics, feelings, actions, ideas, and values, joined these 16PF scales in forming a third factor (alongside Neuroticism and Extraversion) when a joint factor analysis was conducted (Costa & McCrae, 1978). When we substitute Eysenck's E and N scales and temperament scales taken from Buss and Plomin's (1975) EASI-III Temperament Survey for the 16PF scales, the same factor structure emerges. Table I demonstrates this by offering three replications on different age cohorts. Only one scale—Openness to Feelings—is consistently misplaced, and even it has modest loadings

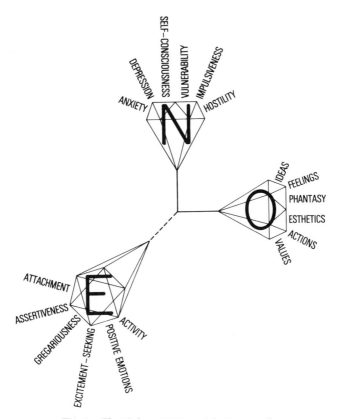

Fig. 1. The 18-facet NEO model of personality.

on the expected factor in two cases. To the extent that deviations from the predicted structure are present, a need to improve upon the particular measures used is indicated. But more importantly, the same general pattern is found in the 16PF itself, the 16PF with the EI, and the EI with the EPI and EASI-III scales. Every theoretical construct must be operationalizable, but too often constructs and even entire theories are built upon a single instrument or procedure. The NEO model, shown in Fig. 1, has the virtue of being operationalizable through a variety of measures. Parallels to some or all of these factors can also be seen in the ratings of interpersonal behavior (Bales, 1970) and in peer ratings (Norman, 1963), suggesting that the results cannot be discarded as "method variance" or brushed away as an artifact of self-report methodology.

We will postpone a more detailed description of the model and its measures to a later section; our purpose for introducing the model here is to illustrate how the psychology of aging can be illuminated by a conceptual model of personality. Empirically, the three domains of Neuroticism,

Extraversion, and Openness have demonstrated their utility by their ability to predict and explain a number of important attitudes, behaviors, and feelings. Traits are admittedly weak in making specific behavioral predictions, but they excel in the breadth of phenomena to which they are relevant. A quick summary of the empirical correlates of measures from these domains can also serve as a way of fleshing out the trait descriptions.

Individuals high in Neuroticism, although not necessarily clinically neurotic, do show the following characteristics: they complain more about their health, on both physical and psychiatric sections of the Cornell Medical Index (though we have no evidence that they are actually physically sicker; McCrae, Bartone, & Costa, 1976); they are more likely to smoke than less neurotic men, and less likely to quit (McCrae, Costa, & Bossé, 1978); they are heavier smokers, and report more reasons for smoking. Similarly, they drink more alcohol, and are more likely to have drinking problems (Nuttall & Costa, 1975). They have other problems, too: As we will see, they report more difficulties in sexual adjustment and financial troubles. They appear to be somewhat more likely to be separated or divorced. On measures of intellectual functioning, they perform a little worse, perhaps because they are less well able to cope with the stress of the testing situation (Costa *et al.*, 1976). Not surprisingly, Neuroticism is also related to unhappiness, dissatisfaction with life, and low subjective well-being (Costa & McCrae, 1980).

Although Neuroticism is thus a pervasive part of the individual's personality, it would not be expected to influence all aspects of life. And in fact, the values and occupational interests of our men were consistently unrelated to levels of Neuroticism.

Extraversion, on the other hand, shows up most clearly in these areas. We found correlations as high as .60 between extraversion and dimensions of occupational interest obtained from a factor analysis of the SVIB (Costa *et al.*, 1977). The occupations to which extraverts are attracted are not surprising: They prefer to be social workers or business administrators, advertising men or lawyers. Introverts, by contrast, prefer such occupations as architect, physicist, or carpenter; jobs in which accomplishing a task is more central than dealing with people. Though they drink no more than introverts, when extraverts do drink, it is more likely to be in company or with members of the opposite sex. Extraverts seem to value power and humanitarian goals somewhat more than introverts do (Costa & McCrae, 1977). And, as we will show in detail a little later, extraverts are happier, with more positive affect and general well-being.

Occupational choices are also influenced by the third dimension, Openness to Experience (Costa & McCrae, 1977, 1978). Open men are more likely to prefer the occupations of psychologist, psychiatrist, or minister, and less likely to prefer the jobs of banker, veterinarian, and mortician. They have higher scores on AVL measures of theoretical and aesthetic values, and lower scores on religious and economic values. They perform somewhat better on measures of both verbal and performance intelligence. Openness also shows an influence on many of the major life events that have proved so important in conceptions of both stress and the life span: Open men are more likely to quit a job, or be demoted, or begin an entirely new line of work; they are more often involved in lawsuits. Some of these outcomes are desirable, some are undesirable. Correspondingly, we find that Open men are higher on both positive and negative affect scales: That is to say, their lives are more eventful, and they experience both the good and the bad more forcefully.

We have cited our own work exclusively here; these lists of correlates could be meaningfully multiplied many times by consulting the work of Eysenck or Cattell. But it was our experience with this model that convinced us that a trait approach was not only useful, but essential, as an element of personality theory. The conceptual advantages of adopting this model have been equally impressive to us. We have learned to differentiate seriousness from depression; impulsiveness from excitement, or sensation-seeking; and the need for variety from the need for activity. We are learning how to integrate concepts from social psychology (Rokeach, 1960), psychoanalytic ego psychology (Kris, 1952), humanistic psychotherapy (Rogers, 1961), and gerontology (Chown, 1961) into a single domain of traits. And, as a result of these conceptual mappings, we feel better able to make sense of the "booming, buzzing confusion" of the literature on aging and personality. We can group apparently dissimilar studies (using scales with a variety of labels for the same underlying construct) and look for replicability of results; we can occasionally explain apparent contradictions. The NEO model provides a conceptual framework in which to evaluate conceptual similarities and differences from a variety of theoretical sources and for a variety of practical applications.

Our enthusiasm for a trait model of personality is probably not shared by most gerontologists. Traits are enduring dispositions, whereas maturational change in personality has often seemed to be the El Dorado of life-span developmental psychologists. Sociologists who have examined the behavior of aging men and women have noted the "persistence of life style" (Maddox, 1968) and coined the phrase "continuity principle" (Havighurst, McDonald, Maeulen, & Mazel, 1979) to describe it. Schaie and Gribbin (1975) have commented that "for the period of adulthood, a stability model seems plausible for many variables . . . notably . . . many personality variables" (p. 67). And yet the quest for age-related changes in personality goes on. We are not likely to win much attention or sympathy for enduring traits until we have confronted the issue of whether or not personality changes with age.

II. Stability of Personality

A. CLINICAL EVIDENCE OF STABILITY AND CHANGE

Clinical assessments of personality, in which the investigator obtains information through direct personal interaction with the subject, carries a particular kind of force as a form of scientific evidence. Although interview-based assessments and ratings do not typically have the objectivity or reliability of standardized procedures, they do benefit from flexibility in content and from the ability of the interviewer to utilize nonverbal cues, such as posture, tone-of-voice, or gestures, in forming an impression of the person as a whole. Similarly, projective and open-ended measures are often considered media in which the whole person can be seen more readily than in standardized inventories. This holistic quality makes the observations and opinions of those who have spent time with aging men and women a good starting point for a review of stability and change. The opinions are mixed.

On the one hand, theories of adult development have invariably sprung up in this context. Jung's clinical practice, Buhler's (1935) analysis of personal biographies, Levinson's (1978) intensive interviews, and Gutmann's (1964) projective tests have formed the basis for models of personality change with age. Age differences and even longitudinal changes (Ames, 1965) in Rorschach responses have been observed. Certainly many of us have the clear impression that there must be significant changes in personality, when such clear changes in expressiveness are seen (Bromley, 1978).

On the other hand, there is also a body of clinical evidence arguing for stability in personality. When, as part of a study on the midlife crisis (Costa & McCrae, 1978), we asked a sample of normal adult men to describe in their own words if and how they had changed in the past 10 years, we were disappointed to find that the great majority perceived no changes worth mentioning. Moss and Susman (1980) remind us that the recidivism rates in the treatment of psychopathology are painful evidence of the stability of abnormal characteristics in the face of massive efforts to change the individual.

Interviews concerned with identifying the coping styles of older people have noted that these are typically continuations of styles used throughout adulthood (Reichard, Livson, & Peterson, 1962). Adjustment types

(Neugarten, Crotty, & Tobin, 1964) do not appear to be found dispropor-
tionately in any one age group. Similarly, Lowenthal and Chiraboga (1972)
reported that distress in the "empty nest" period of life is consistent with
lifelong patterns of maladjustment.

A number of researchers have looked for age differences or changes in
projective measures. Verbal productivity in response to TAT or Rorschach
cards is generally reduced in older populations (Kahana, 1978), but many
have argued that this reflects declines in perceptual or cognitive functioning
rather than personality change (Caldwell, 1954; Chown, 1968; Overall &
Gorham, 1972). Thus, when Eisdorfer (1963) compared the responses of
community-dwelling aged in a high IQ group with norms from younger
subjects, he found no differences. A variety of cross-sectional projective
studies showing no age differences might be cited (see Kahana, 1978), but
such studies tended to use variables scored idiosyncratically, and so did not
lend themselves to the kind of comparison and summarization that would
be necessary to properly evaluate them.

Longitudinal studies are less common. Using TAT measures of needs for
Power, Affiliation, Aggression, and Achievement, Skolnick (1966) reported significant 20-year stability coefficients ranging from .21 to .34.
Britton and Britton (1972), in a sample aged 65 to 85 at the beginning of the
study, used TAT cards to measure "adequacy in initiating action, . . . self-
confidence, intellectual functioning, happiness, social status, and interpersonal acceptance" (p. 47). A total score showed correlations ranging from
.21 to .52 for 17 men, and from .27 to .53 for 29 women, over periods of 3,
6, and 9 years. Despite the heterogeneity of the content in these ratings and
the small sample size, half of these correlations were statistically significant. Considering the short-term reliability of these kinds of tests, correlations of this magnitude must be construed as evidence of stability.

Q-sort methodology allowed Block (1971) to quantify and compare information gathered through a number of different (and not directly comparable) procedures on a sample of 171 men and women. Q-sort ratings on
senior high school students correlated significantly with ratings based on
interviews conducted when the subjects were in their middle thirties. The
average correlations across all individuals was .56 for men and .54 for
women. Although some subjects were distinctly more stable than others,
the clear trend was toward stability in the relative prominence of personality characteristics within the individual.

Finally, Mussen, Eichorn, Honzik, Bieber, and Meredith (in press)
reported the stability of cognitive and personality ratings in a sample of 53
women rated at age 30, and then independently at age 70. Ratings were
made on single, 7-point scales. Of 16 personality characteristics, 10 showed
significant retest correlations, notably Cheerfulness ($r = .28$), Excitability

(r = .24), and Talkativeness (r = .52). Different interviewers, who talked for a few hours with subjects, tended to get similar impressions of personality traits, despite the fact that 4 decades had elapsed between interviews.

We have presented at some length the clinical evidence for stability, whereas only mentioning the theories that argue for change or development. In part, this reflects our evaluation of the literature; in part, the difficulties of summarizing evidence for the alternate position. Those who claim stability tend to agree; those who find differences show little unanimity. Jung tells us old people should express the complement of their youthful personality. Erikson looks for ego integrity versus despair. Gutmann seeks a change in ego processes from active toward magical mastery. Neugarten claims increased "interiority," and Rorschach (1942) finds the inner lives of the elderly to be constricted. Some or all of these claims may be true, but the failure of most of these theorists to provide reliable and valid measures and investigative procedures to support their claims casts considerable doubt. Perhaps the claims of stability and change from these nontrait approaches can be reconciled by an investigator who has had far more experience in the field than we:

> The direction of personality change, then, from middle to old age seems to be one of increased inner orientation; increased separation from the environment; a certain centripetal movement which leads to increased consistency and decreased complexity and in which the synthesizing and executive qualities, in maintaining their centrality, maintain also the continuity of the personality. (Neugarten, 1964, pp. 198–199)

B. CORRELATIONAL EVIDENCE OF STABILITY

"Continuity of personality" can mean any of several things. The simplest measure is given by the retest correlation coefficient. In the short run, these coefficients are correctly interpreted as evidence of the reliability of the measure, as it can usually be assumed that the measured characteristic will not change during the short interval. When taken over a period of years, however, high correlations are evidence of stability in the characteristic or trait itself. Only long-term longitudinal data on substantial samples can be used to assess stability in this way.

Fortunately, the last few years have seen the ripening of several major longitudinal studies, the results of which have converged on the conclusion of long-term stability in adulthood. Siegler, George, and Okun (1979) found the 2-year stability of Form C of the 16PF scales (average r = .50) to equal or excel the 2-week retest values in a sample of 331 men and women aged 45 to 70 at first measurement. Using the MMPI, Leon, Gillum, Gillum, and Gouze (in press) reported 30-year stability in a sample of 71 normal men with a mean age at retest of 77. Despite the limited variation on most MMPI scales in a normal population, all coefficients were significant, with a median retest correlation of .39. The highest correlation was on the nonpathological scale Social Introversion, where a coefficient of .74 was seen.

Using 16PF measures in a sample of adult males (aged 25 to 82 initially), we reported 10-year stability correlations ranging from .58 to .69 for Anxiety or Neuroticism and from .70 to .84 for Extraversion in three age groups. Individual scales measuring traits in the domain of openness ranged from .44 for Imaginativeness to .63 for Tendermindedness (Costa & McCrae, 1977, 1978). Two other constructs relevant to Openness, Rigidity and Dogmatism, have shown similar levels of retest stability in German samples of adults 55 and older (Angleitner, 1976; Riegel, Riegel, & Meyer, 1967). Data from the Baltimore longitudinal study of aging (Costa, Mc-Crae, & Arenberg, 1980) gives additional evidence of stability using the Guilford–Zimmerman Temperament Survey (GZTS) scales over 6- and 12-year intervals for males ranging in age from 17–85. The average 12-year retest coefficient for all 10 scales in a sample of over 200 men was .73—somewhat higher than the 1-year retest reliability cited in the GZTS manual (Guilford *et al.,* 1976).

C. CHANGES IN MEAN LEVELS

Many researchers think of stability in terms of mean levels. After all, there is substantial correlation between measures of intelligence in early childhood and in adulthood, yet there is also a powerful developmental increment in intellectual ability over this period. Conceivably, age might have a similar effect on personality, uniformly raising or lowering the level of a trait, while maintaining the relative ordering of individuals. It is possible, if hazardous, to infer such developmental changes from cross-sectional differences in the level of traits, and a host of researchers have done so. Neugarten (1977), like many others, finds the results confusing and contradictory, although a consistent difference in introversion seems to be found.

Far more useful are longitudinal studies, especially when they include an age range that can simultaneously provide evidence of cross-sectional differences. Although some complications arise, we would normally expect a true aging effect to show up both as mean level changes over time and as cohort differences.

Three studies have concurred in finding no maturational effects in the Neuroticism domain. Using four measurement points 2 years apart on their sample of 331 men and women over age 45, Siegler, George, and Okun

(1979) found no main effects for time or for cohort on Form C 16PF scales C (Stable), L (Suspicious), O (Guilt-prone), Q3 (Controlled), or Q4 (Tense). We also (Costa & McCrae, 1978) found neither age differences nor change on these scales in a sample of 140 men aged 25 to 82 retested after 10 years. Douglas and Arenberg (1978), who supplemented longitudinal and cross-sectional analyses with cross-sequential and time-sequential designs, found no effects attributable to maturation on any of the scales in the GZTS "Emotional Health" factor: Emotional Stability, Objectivity, Friendliness, and Personal Relations. The size of their sample (915 men) and the reliability of the measures make this finding of "no difference" particularly powerful evidence of stability.

In the Extraversion domain, results are similar but not quite so unanimous. Siegler *et al.* (1979) again found no main effects for age or time on Scales A (Outgoing), E (Assertive), F (Happy-go-lucky), H (Adventurous), or Q2 (Independent). We found no effects for A, E, F, or H, and only a longitudinal effect for Q2—suggesting perhaps secular change and a time-of-measurement effect. Douglas and Arenberg (1978) found no differences in GZTS Sociability, and cross-sectional differences only on Ascendance; but they did find both cross-sectional and longitudinal declines in General Activity, the third component of the "Social Activity" factor. Although this appears to support the argument for a maturational decline in level of activity, it should be noted that the change was quite small—only .125 standard deviation over a 6-year period. Similarly, Leon *et al.* (in press) reported a significant increase in Social Introversion, amounting, however, to only .3 standard deviation over a period of 30 years. In view of these findings, the often repeated claim that introversion increases in later life (e.g., Chown, 1968) should be reevaluated. What changes do occur (i.e., are statistically significant) in healthy men and women are so small as to be of little practical significance or consequence.

Adequate measures of the full domain of Openness have not been available for use in longitudinal studies. If we consider the 16PF scales I (Tenderminded), M (Imaginative) and Q1 (Liberal thinking) as representative of this domain, we can note that Siegler *et al.* (1979) found no main effects, and that we found cross-sectional differences only in a sample of 404 men retested after 11 years. Angleitner (1976), using the Riegel and Riegel (1960) scales, reported longitudinal increases in personal rigidity, and decreases in general rigidity and dogmatism in a German sample of 93 men and women measured at four time points. He cautions, however, that the time effects account for only 1–2% of the variance: "Statistically confirmed though it may be, this effect seems inconsequential in terms of total variance" (p. 78).

Three of the scales in the Douglas and Arenberg (1978) study do not fit easily into our three-domain model: Restraint and Thoughtfulness, which form a third factor in the GZTS; and Masculinity. Of these, the first two show no maturational change in level, whereas Masculinity shows a decline of about .125 standard deviation (or half an item on a 30-item scale) over a 6-year period. Stability of personality is not limited to traits within our model.

D.   STRUCTURAL INVARIANCE

One final issue of stability can be raised. The possibility remains that variables that do not themselves increase or decrease in level may yet take on new relations to other variables (Baltes & Nesselroade, 1973). This structural approach, pursued by Craik (1964), Bendig (1960), and Coan (1966), was historically the beginning of our involvement with trait theory. We were interested in seeing whether or not the relation between traits changed with age: Perhaps there would be a differentiation into more complex dimensions, or perhaps the nature of the personality dimensions would change, not quantitatively, in level, but qualitatively, in their structure and relationships. We selected cluster analysis as the most appropriate technique for looking at personality structure and did cluster analyses of 16PF scales within three age groups.

Initial results showed similar structures in Extraversion and Neuroticism, but some variation in Openness. When better measures of Openness were obtained from the Experience Inventory (EI), the structure of all three domains showed itself to be age invariant. Perhaps the clearest evidence of that is provided by Table I, where clearly similar results can be seen in three age cohorts. Parallel analyses on the GZTS (McCrae, Costa, & Arenberg, in press) also show age-invariant factor structures in three age groups.

E.   COMMENTS AND CONCLUSIONS

Studies reviewed in these last sections have all used self-report methods. Response set, defensiveness, and more-or-less deliberate falsification all pose threats to the validity of self-report measures. Nevertheless, the practice of combining many items into scales can give personality questionnaires a reliability that ratings or other types of measurement often do not possess; and ultimately the intimate knowledge that one possesses of oneself cannot be matched by the most skilled clinician.

But does this very knowledge artificially contribute to the stability of self-report scores over long periods of time? Epstein (personal communication, May, 1979) has argued that old people may retain and report an image of the personality that they had at younger ages, and thus appear more stable than they actually are. Yet, when Woodruff and Birren (1972) compared personality test scores gathered in 1944 with retests 25 years later, and with retrospection accounts of how subjects believed they had answered in 1944, they found a rather different state of affairs. There was no evidence of change in the retest, but there were significant differences between the actual 1944 scores and the retrospective accounts of them. This suggests that, at least on a conscious level, individuals do not minimize change; they exaggerate it. Subjectively people may change; objectively they do not seem to.

How does all this talk of stability square with Neugarten's (1977) statement that we all "know" personality changes with age—though we cannot demonstrate it scientifically? Admittedly, many things do change with age. Physical, perceptual, and cognitive abilities generally decline. Sexual vigor and interest decrease. Social roles alter drastically, and events like retirement and widowhood produce major changes in the behavior of individuals. Responses to projective test stimuli decrease with age. Bromley (1978) has argued that changes in mobility and expressive capacity lead to radical changes in the "stimulus value" of old people and thus to change in *our perception* of their personality. And it can be admitted that there are unmistakable age changes in the specific behaviors that express enduring traits: "Activity" in older persons is likely to be gardening rather than football. But all these changes do not amount to change in personality, for personality is not the totality of behavior, but rather "a stable set of characteristics and tendencies that determine those commonalities and differences in the psychological behavior . . . that may not be easily understood as the sole result of the social and biological pressures of the moment" (Maddi, 1976, p. 9).

The conclusion that personality is stable requires several qualifications, however:

1. We do not know how early in development personality "stabilizes." A representative national sample of 1628 tenth grade males was retested after eight years. Substantial increases were seen in self-esteem and in drug use, whereas aggressive behavior declined. In terms of relative ordering of scores, however, the authors concluded that: "the dominant picture that emerges from this research is not change but stability. Again and again, with respect to attitudes, aspirations, self-concepts, and behaviors, we found that differences correlated with different experiences in the late teens and early twenties generally pre-dated the actual experiences" (Bachman, O'Malley, & Johnston, 1978, p. 221).

2. We have little evidence on the cross-cultural generalizability of our conclusions. But Grombach (1976), reviewing personality research from the

Bonn study, one of the few longitudinal studies conducted outside this country, showed stability in most measures, which tended to confirm cross-sectional findings that "activity, mood, ego control, and self-confidence are to be explained less by age than by 'syndromes' of personality variables . . . and by 'destiny' (education, profession, social status . . .)" (p. 52).

3. We are woefully weak in large-scale longitudinal studies on women. However, the results of the Bonn and Duke studies provide tentative evidence that women will show comparable stability to men.

There are still a number of ways in which personality change may be found. Within our model, there is relatively little longitudinal evidence on the stability of Openness. Other personality variables, such as locus-of-control or persistence, which do not fit into any of our domains, may show change. Unconscious, intrapsychic variables inaccessible to self-report methods may change. Change may be a characteristic of discernible subgroups (Block, 1971) or may be mediated by the occurrence of major life events or by intelligence (Bergmann, 1978).

But at some point we should begin to reconsider the advisability of continuing our quest for developmental changes in personality. Rather than be disheartened by this, the student of personality interested in continuity or change should, we believe, reformulate goals. Instead of looking for the mechanisms by which personality changes with age, we should look for the means by which stability is maintained. Are traits genetically determined, and therefore as stable as genetic influences? Do individuals choose or create environments that sustain the behavior that characterizes them? Are we locked into our nature by the network of social expectations around us? Do early childhood influences continue to operate beyond the reach of corrective experiences? And within any one of these perspectives—genetic, behavioral, social-role, or psychoanalytic—by what mechanisms are we enabled to assimilate the changing experiences of a lifetime to our own nature? How do we cope, or adapt, or defend so as to preserve our essential characteristics unchanged in the face of all the vicissitudes of adulthood and old age? *These* are questions for the student of personality and aging.

III. The Influence of Personality on Aging Processes: Three Examples

The conclusion that age has little impact on the major dimensions of personality might seem at first to signal the end of the field of aging and personality, or at least call for a new theoretical approach to personality in which change, or the possibility of change, is present. But only a narrow understanding of the field of aging could support this view. Objectively measured personality still has a crucial role in the study of aging, because it has pervasive influences on many or even most of the issues and problems with which the aging person has to cope. In fact, we believe that an understanding of the aging process is subject to serious distortion if it does not take into account the role of stable individual differences.

Since this is an important point, let us restate it, somewhat differently. Neugarten, in a famous dictum, has defined adult development as "the changing basis within the individual for adaptation to life." What we propose is to turn this dictum on its head, and to define the major contribution of personality to the study of aging as "the stable basis within the individual for adaptation to a changing life."

As a general principle, we would suggest that any psychological research on aging routinely examine the effects of Neuroticism, Extraversion and Openness, much as sex and socioeconomic status are now examined. In support of this strategy, we can offer our experience in three areas of particular interest to gerontologists: The male midlife crisis, subjective well-being, and stressful life events. In all three cases, consideration of personality has shed light on the issues, suggesting radical reinterpretation, or resolving old paradoxes, or opening a new perspective. We have not, of course, "reduced" these issues to trait psychology, but we feel we have shown the contribution of our trait model to an understanding of each.

A. THE MALE "MIDLIFE CRISIS"

The idea of stages of adult development, long proposed and cherished by many in the field, has seen a remarkable revival in recent years. Books by Levinson (Levinson *et al.,* 1978) and Gould (1978) have stated formally the theories Sheehy (1976) popularized so well. The midlife crisis in particular has attained the status of a folk concept, freely invoked by novelists, commentators, and neighborhood gossips. Clearly, the popular acceptance of the idea has outstripped its scientific foundation (Brim, 1976).

Working with an honors student (Cooper, 1977), we attempted to answer empirically one of the points of controversy surrounding the crisis: When does it occur? Levinson claimed that the crisis came between 40 and 45; Gould, more tentatively, had suggested 37 to 43. A content analysis of writings on the midlife crisis led to the development of an inventory (the MLC scale) of characteristics and concerns that should typify men in this period. To be faithful to the original clinical context in which the crisis had been "discovered," we made some clinical judgments on the basis of responses to some open-ended questions. Very few of our men showed clear signs of a "crisis," but the few that did scored significantly higher on

TABLE II

Mean *t*-Scores for Midlife Characteristic Scales by Four Age Breakdowns

Characteristic	35–45 / 46–55		37–43 / 44–55		35–54 / 55+		40–45 / 50–55	
Inner turmoil	49.9	50.0	47.7	50.2	50.0	49.6	50.4	50.2
	(46)	(103)	(25)	(121)	(138)	(76)	(38)	(62)
Inner orientation	50.4	50.7	51.2	50.6	50.5	49.2	50.8	51.2
	(44)	(106)	(23)	(124)	(139)	(74)	(36)	(63)
Change in time	47.8	50.0	48.1	49.7	49.2	51.8	47.9	51.2
perspective	(47)	(103)	(26)	(121)	(140)	(74)	(39)	(60)
Sense of failing power	46.8	50.1	45.9	49.7	49.2	52.2*	47.1	51.0
	(47)	(101)	(26)	(119)	(137)	(76)	(39)	(59)
Rise in repressed parts	49.2	50.7	49.2	50.4	50.3	49.4	49.0	51.3
of self	(46)	(104)	(25)	(122)	(139)	(74)	(38)	(61)
Marital dissatisfaction	51.6	49.8	50.4	50.4	50.5	48.8	52.2	47.7
	(46)	(104)	(26)	(121)	(139)	(78)	(38)	(61)
Job dissatisfaction	50.2	51.5	49.7	51.6	50.8	48.1	50.7	53.1
	(46)	(99)	(25)	(117)	(135)	(65)	(38)	(57)
Life viewed as tedious,	49.8	50.8	48.4	50.9	50.6	49.0	50.0	51.3
boring	(47)	(107)	(26)	(125)	(143)	(73)	(39)	(63)
Disharmony with	51.0	50.2	50.2	50.5	50.6	48.9	51.0	49.9
children	(40)	(96)	(23)	(111)	(126)	(62)	(35)	(56)
Sense of separation	48.8	49.8	46.7	50.0	49.5	52.7	49.3	48.4
from parents	(41)	(64)	(24)	(78)	(99)	(28)	(33)	(33)
Total midlife scale	50.7	49.1	51.3	49.4	49.9	50.9	51.3	47.0
	(24)	(42)	(13)	(52)	(61)	(19)	(21)	(20)

* *p* < .05.

7 of the 10 sections of the scale we had constructed, giving some support to its claim of validity.

When we examined the scores of 233 men aged 35 to 79 on our MLC scale in several alternative age groupings, we found, somewhat to our surprise, *no age differences at all.* Table II shows the results of the first study (Cooper, 1977). Only one *t*-test reached the .05 level of significance, and it was in the wrong direction! This finding was too important to leave unreplicated. We empirically selected the best items from the original scales and administered them to an entirely new sample of 315 men, ranging in age from 33 to 79 (Costa & McCrae, 1978). Once again, no differences were found between age groups. The midlife crisis, whatever it was, did not appear to be confined to the midlife.

The MLC scale did show some highly significant relations—but to Neuroticism, not to developmental stage. We found a correlation of .51 between scores on the MLC and the Eysenck N scale—almost high enough to justify the use of the MLC as a measure of Neuroticism. But what about the direction of causality? Were men going through the crisis temporarily

neurotic, as Levinson had suggested? Or was the crisis simply one more in-
cident in a life-long history of maladjustment? Fortunately, we had
measures of Neuroticism taken 10 years earlier. Although the correlations
were smaller (from .19 to .36), the findings, replicated on scales, C, L, O,
Q3 and Q4 of the 16PF, are unequivocal: The crisis-prone men had been
more or less neurotic for at least 10 years, and probably for all their adult
lives.

These findings do not necessarily mean that there is no midlife crisis, nor
that the apparent crisis is only a disguised form of Neuroticism. They do,
however, cast grave doubt on the claim that everyone goes through a crisis,
or that there is any particular portion of the adult age span in which crises
are concentrated. Instead, they suggest that neuroticism in adult men *is
likely to take the form of* more job dissatisfaction, marital troubles, concern over failing health, and so on. Block reports that better adjusted adolescents have more stable Q-sorts than the worse adjusted. We suspect that
these more neurotic individuals do not become well adjusted; rather, they
change from adolescent forms of Neuroticism—immaturity, delinquency,
acting out—to more "adult" forms, like the midlife crisis. This "symptom
substitution" is a form of change related to age and yet consistent with the
stability of the underlying disposition of Neuroticism.

The moral is simple: Before making claims for new developments in personality, researchers should first demonstrate discriminant validity, to be
sure they are not dealing with the established dimensions of Neuroticism,
Extraversion, or Openness.

B. SUBJECTIVE WELL-BEING

A second issue that has received much attention in the field of gerontology is morale, life satisfaction, or happiness among the elderly. The
disengagement theory of aging led to a body of research on the factors
related to successful aging, usually measured as psychological or subjective
well-being. A number of researchers in the field of aging and adult development (George, 1978; Liebermann, 1978) have concluded that personality is
more crucial to life satisfaction and adaptation than such objective circumstances as age, income, race, or sex. Indeed, in Larson's (1978) review
of the gerontological literature, only self-reported health consistently has
correlations as high as .40 with measures of subjective well-being, and, as
we know, self-reported health is powerfully influenced by Neuroticism.

We have demonstrated (Costa & McCrae, 1980), in a large sample of
adult males that happiness (measured in a variety of ways) is related to both
Extraversion and Neuroticism. Not surprisingly, adjusted and extraverted
men are happier than neurotic and introverted men. Correlations for Ex-

traversion measures ranged from .13 to .29; for Neuroticism measures, from − .19 to − .50. All correlations were in the predicted direction; 15 of 16 were statistically significant.

But more interesting than these results was the discovery that one of the recurring puzzles of the literature on subjective well-being was understandable by reference to our model. Bradburn (1969), a leader in the field of survey research on well-being, devised a scale with two sets of questions: positive affect and negative affect. He found that, although both of these were related to overall estimates of happiness, they were unrelated to each other, and tended to have different external correlates. Similarly, Andrews and Withey (1976) asked subjects to rate the "good" parts of their life and the "bad" parts separately. They found no correlation between these ratings, although both predicted global happiness.

We think we have been able to show the reason for this curious independence of "good" and "bad," positive and negative affect. Positive affect, or satisfaction with life, is in considerable measure an expression of Extraversion. Negative affect, or dissatisfaction, reflects the contribution of Neuroticism. Since Extraversion and Neuroticism are independent, satisfaction and dissatisfaction must also be. So enduring are the effects of these two personality dimensions that we were even able to predict well-being scores from personality data collected 10 years previously.

But what has all this to do with gerontology? If well-being or morale is to be used as a criterion of adjustment to aging or a measure of the quality of life, or as a dependent variable in studies on the effects of housing, social programs, or other interventions on behalf of the elderly, it must be understood in its own right. The fact that enduring personality dispositions appear to influence happiness far more than objective circumstances should give pause to those who wish to use morale as a measure of the quality of life, as adjusted extroverts will tend to find satisfaction in almost any life situation, whereas the neurotic will never be pleased. The fact that both activity and positive affect are expressions of Extraversion should caution against any *causal* interpretation of correlations between activity and life satisfaction: Old introverts may even resent the intrusions of well-meaning social directors attempting to increase their activity levels. The fact that both self-reported health and negative affect are correlates of Neuroticism should temper the conclusion that health is a major determinant of happiness, and programs designed to improve the health of the elderly should probably not use psychological well-being as an outcome measure. And the fact that measures of subjective well-being are influenced not only by Neuroticism but also by Extraversion argues against their use as measures of mental health. There is nothing pathological about introversion, yet older introverts are classified as less mentally healthy by measures that include "zest" as a component of adjustment. The idea that life-long introverts should become socially active to be adjusted to old age seems absurd. Yet this is one implication of the prevailing use of moral measures. An informed use depends upon an understanding of subjective well-being in the context of Neuroticism and Extraversion.

C. STRESSFUL LIFE EVENTS

Major life events—marriage, divorce, illness, retirement, death of loved ones—have been the focus of much research, primarily for two reasons. First, such events have been construed as stressors, and hypothesized to be precursors of physical illness (Rahe, 1972). Second, a number of gerontologists have noted that it is the predictable succession of these events that constitutes the basic plotline of adult development (Lowenthal, Thurnher, & Chiriboga, 1975). However else they may be seen, some of these events are also behaviors, and important behaviors at that.

Sensitive to the charge that personality does not predict behavior, we decided to examine the scores of individuals who had or had not experienced certain life events, concentrating our attention on events that were relatively common in our sample and that were more objective. We used a modification of the Holmes–Rahe (1967) schedule of life events, and looked at personality before and after a 10-year period in which the events occurred, although unfortunately we did not have the same measures at both times. The results were intriguing: Virtually all the events over which subjects could be expected to have any control were related to, and sometimes predicted by, personality, in meaningful ways. Thus Neuroticism measures were higher in subjects with sexual and financial problems, and among those who were divorced in the interval; occupational promotions went to the more intelligent. But most interesting to us were the findings on the new dimension of Openness to Experience.

Table III shows that subjects who moved, were separated, were divorced, were demoted, quit or began new lines of work, or who were involved in lawsuits were higher in total Openness, and usually on at least two of its facets. These events are among the most important in aging theories that stress roles and role transitions. Are voluntary role changes characteristic of open people? Do these voluntary changes cause as much stress, or are open people better able to handle the stress of new role demands? Or is the direction of causality reversed: Do life events promote Openness, and if so, how long do the effects last?

It must be emphasized that these results are extremely tentative at this point. Events were relatively rare, so that few subjects fit into the yes categories. The magnitude of differences is quite small—not surprisingly,

TABLE III

Mean Openness Differences in Life Event Groups [a]

	N	Total	Esthetics	Feelings	Actions	Ideas	Values
Moved to a new place of residence:							
Yes:	314	7.20*	NS	NS	NS	NS	NS
No:	493	4.55					
Was separated:							
Yes:	65	11.05**	3.51*	2.69*	NS	NS	0.12***
No:	742	5.08	2.24	1.57			−1.66
Was divorced:							
Yes:	48	10.43*	NS	NS	NS	NS	0.00*
No:	759	5.27					−1.62
Got a job demotion:							
Yes:	42	10.21*	4.02*	NS	NS	NS	NS
No:	765	5.32	2.25				
Quit a job:							
Yes:	57	11.70***	NS	NS	NS	0.79*	0.65***
No:	750	5.11				−0.54	−1.68
Began a new line of work:							
Yes:	223	8.85***	NS	NS	7.83*	0.24**	−0.68***
No:	584	4.33			7.13	−0.71	−0.84
Involved in a lawsuit:							
Yes:	58	11.91***	3.51*	3.00**	8.51*	NS	−.022*
No:	749	5.09	2.25	1.56	7.23		−1.62

[a] No significant differences in Phantasy.
* $p = .05$.
** $p = .01$.
*** $p = .001$.

when one considers the number of factors beyond the individual's control that determine events. Finally, we have not yet had an opportunity to replicate the findings. But even these results are strong enough to remind us that human beings are not passive reactors who, in the language of life stress research "incur life events." People take an active part in creating their lives, and an understanding of personality is necessary to an understanding of life.

IV. New Directions for Research

It seems curious to list trait research as a new direction for the field of personality and aging. But so unpopular has it become, and yet so crucial is it to the field that we must treat it here. The data already presented show several of the applications of the model; more detail on the conceptualization of traits seems to be in order now.

A. THE RENAISSANCE OF TRAITS

The great theoretical debates in personality have traditionally pitted psychodynamic against behavioral perspectives, with the "third force" of humanistic psychology sometimes also a contributor. Trait psychologies have been largely ignored as a theoretical camp, although measures generated by the individual differences approach have been used by almost everyone. The first crisis in trait psychology occurred in the 1950s and 1960s, when response sets, particularly social desirability, were recognized as a possible contaminant of trait measures. "Paper-and-pencil" became a term of opprobrium, despite the many advantages of objective inventories over projective tests and clinical ratings. In the late 1960s, Mischel (1968) wrote an enormously influential critique in which he claimed that personality traits themselves must be called into question. Within a few years, it was the accepted opinion of most psychologists that traits were dead, as discredited as phlogiston or the ether.

But traits were not dead, as Epstein (1977) and many others (Hogan, DeSoto, & Solano, 1977; Livson, 1973) began to argue. Block (1977), who had earlier (1965) defended self-report measures against the response-set hysteria, prepared a forceful rebuttal to Mischel. He showed that a more careful reading of the literature could find evidence of both stability and predictive validity for some traits, and insisted that the trait approach must be judged by its *best* exemplars, not its worst; Block thus anticipated the need for a good trait model.

The renaissance of trait theory that can be observed today was made possible by a reformation of trait research. Both method and theory learned from the criticism of the past two decades. Measures can be controlled for social desirability, without adopting the nihilistic attitude that self-reports are *nothing but* response sets. Table IV, for example, gives the correlations of two scales—the Crowne–Marlow Social Desirability Scale and the Eysenck Lie Scale—with measures that we have discussed earlier in this chapter. As might be expected, scales measuring Neuroticism and Openness to Experience are correlated with both social desirability scales. But the *magnitude* of the correlation is quite modest, usually below .30. These correlations are much too small to account for relations observed using these instruments, as the statistical technique of partial correlation can easily show. It is also noteworthy that the two social desirability scales show a much higher correlation with each other ($r = .57$) than either shows with our personality scales, thus contributing to the case for con-

TABLE IV

**Correlations of Neuroticism, Extraversion, and Openness Measures
with Scales of Social Desirability**

	Crowne–Marlowe social desirability[a]	EPI lie scale[b]
EPI neuroticism	−.31***	−.22***
EASI-III:		
General emotionality	−.33***	−.21***
Fear	−.29***	−.16***
Anger	−.33***	−.20***
Impulse inhibition	−.32***	−.24***
EPI extraversion	−.02	−.10**
EASI-III:		
Sociability	.19***	.05
Tempo	.03	.08*
Vigor	.12***	.10**
Sensation seeking	−.11***	−.13***
Positive emotions[c]	.01	−.02
Total openness (EI)	−.21***	−.24***
Phantasy	−.25***	−.23***
Esthetics	−.03	−.02
Feelings	−.25***	−.19***
Actions	.05	−.06
Ideas	−.06*	−.12**
Values	−.21***	−.25***

* $p = .05$.
** $p = .01$.
*** $p = .001$.
[a] $N = 559$ with EPI, 903 with EASI-III, 823 with EI.
[b] $N = 582$ with EPI, 566 with EASI-III, 562 with EI.
[c] Scale added to EASI-III (Costa & McCrae, 1978).

vergent and divergent validity. Finally, note that scales in the important domain of Extraversion are virtually unrelated to Social Desirability scales. These kinds of data demonstrate the improvement in contemporary scales over such dated instruments as the Bernreuter or Humm–Wadsworth inventories. Douglas Jackson's (1974, 1978) work on the Personality Research Form and the Jackson Personality Inventory is an additional demonstration of sophisticated test development. Incidentally, his conclusion that laymen can write good items if the nature of the trait is clearly spelled out (Jackson, 1975) is consistent with our experience. One need only compare the simple, clear, straightforward items of, say, Buss and Plomin's EASI-III Temperament Survey (1975), with the questions of Cattell's 16 Personality Factors Questionnaire (16PF) to see the change in self-report strategy. Yet the simple five-item Sociability Scale of the EASI-III correlates about as highly (.58) with the Eysenck Personality Inventory (EPI) E scale as does the five-scale Extraversion cluster of the 16PF.

In addition to these essentially technical improvements, there have been theoretical and conceptual advances. The best trait theorists of the past, most notably Gordon Allport, have always had a sophisticated view of trait psychology. The ease with which paper-and-pencil measures can be administered has led, however, to a quantity of thoughtless research and "theorizing." Mischel and other behaviorist critics have done us a service in pointing out the resulting confusion and mistakes. The arguments over these issues are sometimes involved, and have been given at length elsewhere (cf. Magnusson and Endler, 1977), but it may be useful if we make explicit our guiding assumptions:

1. Traits are generalized dispositions to thoughts, feelings, and behavior and endure over substantial periods of time.

2. Traits do relatively little to determine single, specific behaviors (which are chiefly governed by other influences that may be broadly construed as situational), though they do show an appreciable influence over behaviors summed or averaged over long periods of time and situations (cf. Epstein, 1977; McGowan & Gormly, 1976).

3. Traits are *inherently* interactive. Thus, trait anxiety is the tendency to experience fear or apprehension *when threatened;* sociability involves the predisposition to be friendly *when other people are present;* and so on. We would argue that recent work on person–situation interactionism is mostly relabeling; and despite new methods of analysis (Endler & Hunt, 1966) this approach does not introduce a new and distinct conceptual model.

4. Traits are neither static nor merely reactive. They include dynamic, motivating tendencies to seek out situations that allow the expression of certain behaviors. The individual who is open to ideas reads books, attends lectures, discusses new ideas, ponders them at length, and otherwise actively pursues them.

5. As generalized dispositions that are manifested in a variety of concrete behaviors, the enduring quality of traits is wholly consistent with the observable changes in behavior that occur with age. The anxious person, who is afraid of rejection in high school and of economic recession in adulthood, will probably be afraid of illness and death in old age. Kagan (1971) has labeled these changes "heterotypic continuity."

6. Traits need not be inherited or biologically based. Allport (1937, 1961), Murray (1938) and more concretely Eysenck (1967) all have postulated a physiological basis for traits, usually without a direct evidential basis. We take the position that the *origin* of traits is a question that can safely be left open for the present. Most probably a number of causes

contribute to the formation and maintenance of traits, and a premature attempt to adopt a theoretical stance on this issue is unwise.

7. Traits do form a useful level of scientific analysis. Mischel's (1977, p. 335) latest charge that they demand, rather than provide, explanation sounds like old-fashioned reductionism. Researchers who want to explain the mechanisms underlying traits are free to do so, but those who wish to use traits as "primitive terms" in an epistemological sense are likewise free to do so.

8. Finally, and perhaps most importantly, we have come to realize that trait theory, like all theories, has a range and focus of convenience (Kelly, 1955). We would be among the first to state that traits are of little utility in predicting the responses of particular individuals at particular times. Role demands, cognitive structures, or histories of reinforcements may be more promising explanatory principles here. But trait measures are useful in examining specific behaviors in large groups of people—in predicting election results, perhaps, or screening for mental illness. And traits are useful in describing and predicting psychologically important global characteristics of individuals. Because they are sensitive to the generalities in behavior, trait approaches are particularly useful in giving a holistic picture of the person, as so many personality psychologists demand. It is this summarizing and abstracting feature of trait language that makes it useful to laymen when they describe others.

It is also this feature, among others, that makes a trait approach ideal as a method for the study of personality and aging. The radical interactionist, who believes that personality can be studied only by observing behavior in different situations, would probably never attempt to address such global issues as how (if at all) personality changes with age. If different reactions were observed in young and old, would this be evidence of changing situations or changing personality? Would there be any reason to do longitudinal research, other than to confirm cross-sectional observations? Would the data collected 10 years ago be of any use at all to a behaviorist or interactionist who does not recognize the stability of personality?

Trait psychology, by contrast, is clearly complementary to the aims of longitudinal research. Variables thought to endure over time are observed over time. Data collected at earlier times are directly relevant to present research; where stability has been demonstrated, earlier measurements can even be used as a "proxy" for contemporaneous measurement. The impact of naturally occurring life events that intervene between one measurement and another can be analyzed in quasi-experimental designs. The existence of stable traits allows the accumulation over time of a multitude of measures with which no subject could, in good conscience, be burdened at

a single time. Multiple measures extend the predictive and construct validity, the "nomological net" of particular constructs, and, even more basi-
cally, permit replication of findings. We know of no better or more feasible
way to observe "the facts" about aging and personality than by studying
the intercorrelations of such a body of measures.

B. AN ELABORATON OF THE NEO MODEL

The NEO model is a particular version of a trait approach that accords
attention to three groups of traits. As we have not developed a position on
the origin or function of these trait domains, and as we do not have formal
definitions of them, we will not dignify our ideas with the title of "theory."
We have found, however, that these are powerful constructs; giving us
both a sense of understanding and an ability to form reasonable expectation about what data will show. One way to communicate these constructs
is by showing their external correlates; another is by identifying their
elements. A description of our most recent operationalization of the model
may serve this purpose.

Given the importance of personality in understanding aging, the accurate
conceptualization and measurement of traits becomes one of the priority
tasks of gerontologists. On the one hand, we believe that existing measures
of at least two dimensions, Neuroticism and Extraversion, are serviceable,
and can and should be used by researchers. On the other hand, we also feel
that there is considerable room for improvement and have therefore embarked on the process of creating and validating a new personality inventory. In particular, we are devoting considerable attention to the specification of more focused *facets* of each of the three domains. The global
estimates of E and N provided by Eysenck's EPI do not allow much precision in showing which *forms* of either trait domain are most characteristic
of a person. Eysenck himself (1963) has considered breaking the E scale
into "sociability" and "impulsivity" components. An inventory providing
measures of half a dozen forms or facets of Extraversion or Neuroticism
would allow both a more fine-grained analysis and the opportunity to
replicate basic relations on different scales in the same instrument. In principle, we sympathize with Cattell's attempts to articulate the traits that collectively define a domain, but in practice, our own (unpublished) item factor analysis and those of others (Eysenck, White, & Soueif, 1969; Howarth
& Browne, 1971; Karson & O'Dell, 1974) show that the 16PF is not an acceptable measure of specific facets. Whereas Cattell's second-order factors
of Anxiety or Neuroticism and Extraversion are valid measures of those
constructs, the same cannot be said of his first-order scales, which show little evidence of discriminant validity, and generally unacceptable levels of
reliability.

In designing our own instrument, we have attempted to specify the major components of each domain. This is a problem of "content validity," and there is no perfect logical or theoretical way to insure that we have succeeded. At the least, we hope the facets will represent a good sample of the traits in each domain; each scale should also measure a trait of interest in its own right.

We now distinguish six facets of Neuroticism: Anxiety, Hostility, Depression, Self-consciousness, Impulsiveness, and Vulnerability. Anxiety and Hostility contain elaborations of the negative emotions of fear and anger. Under the label of *Anxiety,* we include the tendency to experience fear, panic, worry, apprehension; also a higher characteristic level of tension and nervousness. The trait-anxious person is high-strung, easily startled, and fearful. *Hostility* is a comparably generalized conceptualization of the affect of anger. Individuals high in this trait tend to be irritable, quick to take offense, and hot-tempered. Interpersonally, they tend toward suspicion, aggression, and perhaps paranoia.

Another pair of affects that theoretically complement each other are guilt and shame, affects that are used to direct the behavior of the individual in socially acceptable ways. The facet of *Depression* includes not only a dispirited, melancholic disposition, but also the tendency to experience excessive guilt, and thus corresponds to Cattell's "Guilt-proneness." Chronic low self-esteem, a classic symptom of depression, is also included here. *Self-consciousness* is conceived as the general trait that comprises shame, along with excessive shyness, feelings of social inferiority, and a particular sensitivity to ridicule or teasing. Those high in self-consciousness are often embarrassed.

In addition to the affective manifestations of Neuroticism, there are also two behavioral facets. *Impulsiveness* in our model must be distinguished from the extraverted "impulsivity" of Eysenck. Impulsiveness here is the tendency to give in to temptations, to feel overwhelmed by desires and drives; it is essentially reactive. Eysenck's "impulsive" person might eat a whole cake on a dare; our impulsive person would eat it all because he was unable to stop. Impulsiveness can be viewed as a failure in the ability to deal with internal conflicts and the pressures of desires. *Vulnerability,* by contrast, refers to the inability to cope with external pressures and difficulties. Conceived as a component of Neuroticism, Vulnerability corresponds to a characterological inadequacy in facing or dealing with problems or stress. Regression, panic, dependency, and breakdown are among the manifestations of Vulnerability, and this facet probably comes closest to Neuroticism as "the predisposition to neurosis."

In the domain of Extraversion we also identify six facets. We have broken sociability into two components: Attachment and Gregariousness.

Attachment refers to a warm, friendly style of personal relations and contrasts with the formal, detached manner of introverts. *Gregariousness* implies only a desire to be surrounded by people, and seems to reflect a need for greater quantities of social interaction and stimulation. A third interpersonal facet of Extraversion is *Assertiveness,* a trait found in the GZTS (as Ascendance) and in the 16PF. Interpersonal dominance is also a part of Assertiveness. The opposite pole of each of these three facets is most accurately characterized as a preference to avoid forceful social interaction. Thus, introverts are distant rather than hostile, self-sufficient rather than shy, independent rather than submissive.

We also distinguish three temperamental facets of Extraversion. *Activity* is a compound of Buss and Plomin's Tempo and Vigor, and resembles Guilford's General Activity. Incidentally, it appears to be highly related to Type-A behavior syndrome as measured by the Jenkins Activity Schedule (Glass, 1977). *Excitement-seeking* is similar to stimulus- , sensation- , or thrill-seeking, and probably best corresponds to what Eysenck calls the "impulsivity" component of Extraversion. Excitement-seeking is a proactive disposition that may contribute to risk-taking; we do not regard it as pathological. Finally, we incorporated into our administration of the EASI–III a scale measuring *Positive Emotions,* the propensity to experience such affects as joy, happiness, laughter, and excitement. Positive Emotions is our most distinctive contribution to the conceptualization of Extraversion, for whereas Cattell has a scale "Happy-go-lucky versus Sober" and Eysenck notes the jocularity of extroverts, no one appears to have conceptualized the distinction between positive and negative emotional states as relevant to the definition of Extraversion. The factor analyses presented in Table I demonstrate that Positive Emotions forms a part of the Extraversion domain.

We have already published a description of the six facets of Openness to Experience (Costa & McCrae, 1978). The Experience Inventory, which measures Openness to *Phantasy, Esthetics, Feelings, Actions, Ideas,* and *Values* formed the nucleus around which our new scales were built. We have added new items, particularly to the Feelings facet, to improve the scales, but the basic structure is unchanged.

We do not wish to give the impression that the NEO model exhausts the "personality sphere." Personality includes more than just traits, although traits play an indispensable role in personality description and theory; and the NEO model does not even claim to cover all important traits. Masculinity–femininity, for example, seems to be separate; and several pieces of evidence have led us to consider the need for a new domain of self-control. The NEO model is provisional, but it seems to cover enough important traits to form a useful starting point for future research on personality and aging.

C. ALTERNATIVE METHODS OF RESEARCH

This review has been admittedly partisan. We use a particular approach and methodology, and we feel that we have demonstrated the utility of that approach. But we cannot deny the legitimacy of other ways of studying personality and aging, or the need to look at phenomena that escape the notice of trait methods. Bromley (1978) has advocated the use of the case study method, which attends to idiographic material to which standardized instruments are necessarily insensitive. Projective techniques offer a time-honored method that may be useful in eliciting material the individual is unwilling or unable to accurately report. Interviews have a flexibility that questionnaires lack, and, for some purposes, the best instrument for measuring a phenomenon is the intuition of a skilled clinician. Those who see personality as a process rather than as a structure will be obliged to observe individual cases repeatedly, perhaps through the course of a significant transition like retirement.

We would only suggest that these methods be supplemented by self-report measures of the most important dimensions of personality. Short measures taking only a few minutes to administer and seconds to score can provide a context in which other results can be seen and interpreted; at the least they can provide hints to alternative hypotheses about the meaning of results. The speculation that "interiority" is comparable to introversion could be quickly tested; the clinician's impression of a midlife crisis could be evaluated in the context of the characteristic neuroticism of the subject.

Such comparisons, regularly made, might well establish the discriminant validity of nontrait, or non-self-report methods—might show the unique contributions they make to an understanding of aging. But where other methods are used exclusively, the skeptic is likely to wonder whether the same results might not have been obtained more quickly and easily from self-report methods.

D. AGING, STRESS, AND COPING

Few problems are of more practical importance or more theoretical interest than stress and coping. For the aging adult, whose occupational and family choices have already been made, coping with the expected and unexpected stresses of life constitutes the major challenge of life. Theoretically, the varieties of coping styles and the adequacy of coping efforts form the core of individual difference models of personality. We think work in personality can contribute substantially to research in this field, and were pleased to find a similar opinion expressed by Lieberman (1978, p. 125): "Our results would also suggest that a strict personality position emphasizing intrinsic processes over the life span, a position that certainly has not been a popular one in the personality field during the past ten years, still merits consideration. To explain adaptation, such a model may prove to be more fruitful than models using social characteristics as their primary explanatory framework."

Adaptation, adjustment, or coping have been central issues in gerontological research, and an array of different perspectives and problems has appeared. Because established roles represent a major part of one's adaptation to life, new roles, such as career shifts, widowhood, or retirement, have been conceived as "normative life crises" (Datan & Ginsberg, 1975). Key questions here involve the issue of "on-time" versus "off-time" transitions (Neugarten, 1977) and whether different coping strategies are effective for different age groups. Another class of major stressors is provided by eruptive life crises like illness, divorce, and unemployment. An extensive but controversial (Brown, 1974) line of research has implicated such disruptive events in the development of illness. More closely controlled research, investigating individual differences in reactions to stress and examining psychological and social consequences as well as medical consequences, is clearly needed.

Personality is sometimes defined as the organization of mechanisms for adaptation or coping, and the three domains of personality in our model each have important implications for the process of coping. Neuroticism is the most obviously relevant, since it appears to be an index of the vulnerability of the individual to stress of all kinds. An earlier section showed the impact of Neuroticism on well-being scores, which are sometimes used to operationalize levels of coping or adaptation (Siegler, Cleveland, & Ramm, in preparation).

Whereas Neuroticism seems to measure the general adequacy of coping resources, Openness appears instead to define a dimension of alternative adaptive strategies: One maximizing the input of new information to find the best possible solution; the other minimizing new information to reduce disturbance of the existing order. A comparison of the relative advantages of being open or closed in different age groups would be of particular interest, as closedness and rigidity are stereotypically associated with old age.

Extraversion, too, is relevant to coping outcomes and styles. As we have seen, extraverts of any age are more likely to *appear* adjusted when measured on happiness or life-satisfaction. More importantly, extraverts may be better able to find and utilize social supports when these become crucial in old age. However, as Carp (1977) points out, the ideal support systems may differ for different kinds of people, and social planners may wish to recommend alternative interventions for introverts and extraverts.

At a more molecular level, a number of researchers (Haan, 1977; Lazarus & Cohen, 1976; Pearlin & Schooler, 1978) have begun to identify and evaluate specific coping mechanisms that are commonly used. In conjunction with trait information, these approaches offer the best hope of pinpointing which techniques are best for particular individuals in particular situations. We agree with Neugarten (1977, p. 644) that "it is personality which is the pivotal factor in adaptation to aging" and we feel that traits provide the stable structure of personality within which the aging individual copes, adapts, defends, compensates, or adjusts. The synthesis of coping mechanisms with trait models is a major task of the future.

Acknowledgment

Research in this chapter was supported in part by the Medical Research Service of the Veterans Administration (Normative Aging Study).

References

Allport, G. W. *Personality: A psychological interpretation.* New York: Holt, 1937.

Allport, G. W. *Pattern and growth in personality.* New York: Holt, Rinehart & Winston, 1961.

Allport, G. W., Vernon, P. E., & Lindzey, G. *Study of Values: Manual of directions.* Boston: Houghton-Mifflin, 1951.

Ames, L. B. Changes in the experience balance scores on the Rorschach at different ages in the life span. *Journal of Genetic Psychology,* 1965, **106**, 279–286.

Andrews, F. M., & Withey, S. B. *Social indicators of well-being: Americans' perceptions of life quality.* New York: Plenum, 1976.

Angleitner, A. Changes in personality observed in questionnaire data from the Riegel Questionnaire on Rigidity, Dogmatism, and Attitude toward Life. In H. Thomae (Ed.), *Patterns of aging: Findings from the Bonn Longitudinal Study of Aging.* Basel: Karger, 1976.

Bachman, J. G., O'Malley, P. M., & Johnston, J. *Adolescence to adulthood: Change and stability in the lives of young men.* Ann Arbor, Mich.: Institute for Social Research, 1978.

Bales, R. F. *Personality and interpersonal behavior.* New York: Holt, Rinehart & Winston, 1970.

Baltes, P. B. Longitudinal and cross-sectional sequences in the study of age and generation effects. *Human Development,* 1968, **11**, 145–171.

Baltes, P. B. & Nesselroade, J. R. The developmental analysis of individual differences on multiple measures. In J. R. Nesselroade & H. W. Reese (Eds.), *Life-span developmental psychology: Methodological issues.* New York: Academic Press, 1973.

Bell, B., Rose, C. L., & Damon, A. The Normative Aging Study: An interdisciplinary and longitudinal study of health and aging. *Aging and Human Development,* 1972, **3,** 5–17.

Bendig, A. W. Age differences in the interscale factor structure of the Guilford-Zimmerman Temperament Survey. *Journal of Consulting Psychology,* 1960, **24,** 134–138.

Bergmann, K. Neurosis and personality disorder in old age. In A. D. Isaacs & F. Post (Eds.), *Studies in geriatric psychiatry.* New York: Wiley, 1978.

Block, J. *The challenge of response sets.* New York: Appleton-Century-Crofts, 1965.

Block, J. *Lives through time.* Berkeley, Calif.: Bancroft Books, 1971.

Block, J. Advancing the psychology of personality: Paradigmatic shift or improving the quality of research. In D. Magnusson & N. S. Endler (Eds.), *Personality at the crossroads: Current issues in interactional psychology.* Hillsdale, N.J.: Erlbaum, 1977.

Bradburn, N. M. *The structure of psychological well-being.* Chicago: Aldine, 1969.

Brim, O. G. Jr. Theories of the male mid-life crisis. *Counseling Psychologist,* 1976, **6,** 2–9.

Britton, J. H., & Britton, J. O. *Personality changes in aging: A longitudinal study of community residence.* New York: Springer, 1972.

Bromley, D. B. Approaches to the study of personality changes in adult life and old age. In A. D. Isaacs & F. Post (Eds.), *Studies in geriatric psychiatry.* New York: Wiley, 1978.

Brown, G. W. Meaning, measurement, and stress of life events. In B. S. Dohrenwend & B. P. Dohrenwend (Eds.), *Stressful life events: Their nature and effects.* New York: Wiley, 1974.

Buhler, C. The curve of life as studied in biographies. *Journal of Applied Psychology,* 1935, **19,** 405–409.

Buss, A. H., & Plomin, R. *A temperament theory of personality development.* New York: Wiley, 1975.

Caldwell, B. McD. The use of the Rorschach in personality research with the aged. *Journal of Gerontology,* 1954, **9,** 316–323.

Carp, F. M. Morale: What questions are we asking of whom: In C. N. Nydegger (Ed.), *Measuring morale: A guide to effective assessment.* Washington, D.C.: Gerontological Society, 1977.

Cattell, R. B., *Personality: A systematic theoretical and factual study.* New York: McGraw-Hill, 1950.

Cattell, R. B. *Personality and mood by questionnaire.* San Francisco: Jossey-Bass, 1973.

Chown, S. M. Age and the rigidities. *Journal of Gerontology,* 1961, **16,** 353–362.

Chown, S. M. Personality and aging. In K. W. Schaie (Ed.), *Theory and methods of research on aging.* Morgantown, W. V.: West Virginia University, 1968.

Coan, R. W. Child personality and developmental psychology. In R. B. Cattell (Ed.), *Handbook of multivariate experimental psychology.* Chicago: Rand McNally, 1966.

Coan, R. W. Measurable components of openness to experience. *Journal of Consulting and Clinical Psychology,* 1972, **39,** 346.

Cooper, M. W. An empirical investigation of the male midlife period: A descriptive, cohort study. Unpublished undergraduate honors thesis, University of Massachusetts at Boston, 1977.

Costa, P. T., Jr., Fozard, J. L., & McCrae, R. R. Personological interpretation of factors from the Strong Vocational Interest Blank scales. *Journal of Vocational Behavior,* 1977, **10,** 231–243.

Costa, P. T., Jr., Fozard, J. L., McCrae, R. R., & Bossé, R. Relations of age and personality to cognitive ability factors. *Journal of Gerontology,* 1976, **31,** 663–669.

Costa, P. T., Jr., & McCrae, R. R. Age differences in personality structure: A cluster analytic approach. *Journal of Gerontology,* 1976, **31,** 564–570.

Costa, P. T., Jr., & McCrae, R. R. Age differences in personality structure revisited: Studies in validity, stability, and change. *Aging and Human Development,* 1977, **8,** 261–275.

Costa, P. T., Jr., & McCrae, R. R. Objective personality assessment. In M. Storandt, I. C. Siegler, & M. F. Elias (Eds.), *The clinical psychology of aging.* New York: Plenum, 1978.

Costa, P. T., Jr., & McCrae, R. R. The influence of extraversion and neuroticism on subjective well-being: Happy and unhappy people. *Journal of Personality and Social Psychology,* 1980, *38,* 668–678.

Costa, P. T., Jr., McCrae, R. R., & Arenberg, D. Enduring dispositions in adult males. *Journal of Personality and Social Psychology,* 1980, *38,* 793–800.

Craik, F. I. M. An observed age difference in response to a personality inventory. *British Journal of Psychology,* 1964, **55,** 453–462.

Crowne D. & Marlowe, D. *The approval motive.* New York: Wiley, 1964.

Datan, N., & Ginsberg, L. *Normative life crises.* New York: Academic Press, 1975.

Douglas, K., & Arenberg, D. Age changes, cohort differences, and cultural change on the Guilford-Zimmerman Temperament Survey. *Journal of Gerontology,* 1978, **33,** 737–747.

Endler, N. S., & Hunt, J. McV. Sources of behavioral variance as measured by the S-R Inventory of Anxiousness. *Psychological Bulletin,* 1966, **65,** 336–346.

Eisdorfer, C. Rorschach performance and intellectual functioning in the aged. *Journal of Gerontology,* 1963, **18,** 358–363.

Epstein, S. Traits are alive and well. In D. Magnusson & N. S. Endler (Eds.), *Personality at the crossroads: Current issues in interactional psychology.* Hillsdale, N.J.: Erlbaum, 1979.

Erikson, E. *Childhood and society.* New York: Norton, 1950.

Eysenck, H. J. *The structure of human personality.* London: Methuen, 1960.

Eysenck, H. J. Smoking, personality, and psychosomatic disorders. *Journal of Psychosomatic Research,* 1963, **7,** 197–130.

Eysenck, H. J. *The biological basis of personality.* Springfield, Ill.: Charles C Thomas, 1967.

Eysenck, H. J., & Eysenck, S. B. G. *Manual of the Eysenck Personality Inventory.* London: University Press, 1964.

Eysenck, H. J., White, P. O., & Souief, M. I. Factors in the Cattell Personality Inventory. In Eysenck, S. J. & Eysenck, S. B. G. (Eds.), *Personality structure and measurement.* San Diego, Calif.: Knapp, 1969.

Fiske, D. W. The limits for the conventional science of personality. *Journal of Personality,* 1974, **42,** 1–11.

George, L. K. The impact of personality and social status factors upon levels of activity and psychological well-being. *Journal of Gerontology,* 1978, **33,** 840–847.

Glass, D. C. *Behavior patterns, stress, and coronary disease.* Hillsdale, N.J.: Erlbaum, 1977.

Gould, R. L. *Transformations.* New York: Simon & Schuster, 1978.

Grombach, H. H. Consistency and change of personality variables in late life. In H. Thomae, (Ed.), *Patterns of aging: Findings from the Bonn Longitudinal Study of Aging.* Basel: Karger, 1976.

Guilford, J. S., Zimmerman, W. S., & Guilford, J. P. *The Guilford-Zimmerman Temperament Survey handbook: Twenty-five years of research and application.* San Diego: Knapp, 1976.

Gutmann, D. L. An exploration of ego configurations in middle and later life. In B. L. Neugarten (Ed.), *Personality in middle and later life.* New York: Atherton, 1964.

Gynther, M. D. Aging and personality. In J. N. Butcher (Ed.), *New directions in MMPI research.* Minneapolis, Minn.: University of Minnesota Press. In press.

Haan, N. *Coping and defending.* New York: Academic Press, 1977.

Havighurst, R. J., McDonald, W. J., Maeulen, L., & Mazel, J. Male social scientists: Lives after sixty. *The Gerontologist,* 1979, **19,** 55–60.

Hogan, R., DeSoto, C. B., & Solano, C. Traits, tests, and personality research. *American Psychologist,* 1977, **32,** 255-264.

Holmes, T. H., & Rahe, R. H. The social readjustment rating scale. *Journal of Psychosomatic Research,* 1967, **11,** 213-218.

Howarth, E., & Browne, J. A. An item factor-analysis of the 16 PF *Personality,* 1971, **2,** 117-139.

Jackson, D. N. *Personality Research Form manual* (Rev. ed.). Port Huron, Mich.: Research Psychologists Press, 1974.

Jackson, D. N. The relative validity of scales prepared by naive item writers and those based on empirical methods of personality scale construction. *Educational and Psychological Measurement,* 1975, **35,** 361-370.

Jackson, D. N. Interpreter's guide to the Jackson Personality Inventory. In P. McReynolds (Ed.), *Advances in psychological assessment* (Vol. 4). San Francisco: Jossey-Bass, 1978.

Jung, C. G. *Psychological types.* New York: Harcourt, Brace, & World, 1933.

Kagan, J. *Change and continuity in infancy.* New York: Wiley, 1971.

Kahana, B. The use of projective techniques in personality assessment of the aged. In I. C. Siegler, M. Storandt, & M. F. Elias (Eds.), *The clinical psychology of aging.* New York: Plenum, 1978.

Karson, S., & O'Dell, J. W. Is the 16 PF factorially valid? *Journal of Personality Assessment,* 1974, **38,** 104-114.

Kelly, E. L. Forward. In K. T. Chun, S. Cobb, & J. R. P. French, Jr. (Eds.), *Measures for psychological assessment: A guide to 3,000 original sources and their applications.* Ann Arbor, Mich.: Institute for Social Research, 1975.

Kelly, G. A. *The psychology of personal constructs* (Vols. 1, 2). New York: Norton, 1955.

Kris, E. *Psychoanalytic explorations in art.* New York: International Universities, 1952.

Larson, R. Thirty years of research on the subjective well-being of older Americans. *Journal of Gerontology,* 1978, **33,** 109-125.

Lazarus, R. S., & Cohen, J. B. Theory and method in the study of stress and coping in aging individuals. Paper presented at the Fifth W. H. O. Conference on Society, Stress, and Disease: Aging and Old Age, Stockholm, Sweden, June 14-19, 1976.

Leon, G. R., Gillum, B., Gillum, R., & Gouze, M. Personality stability and change over a 30-year period—middle age to old age. *Journal of Consulting and Clinical Psychology,* in press.

Levinson, D. J., Darrow, C. N., Klein, E. B., Levinson, M. H., & McKee, B. *The seasons of a man's life.* New York: Knopf, 1978.

Lieberman, M. A. Social and psychological determinants of adaptation. *Aging and Human Development,* 1978-1979, **9,** 115-126.

Livson, N. Developmental dimensions of personality: A life-span formulation. In P. B. Baltes & K. W. Schaie (Eds.), *Life-span developmental psychology: Personality and socialization.* New York: Academic Press, 1973.

Lowenthal, M. F., & Chiriboga, D. Transition to the empty nest. *Archives of General Psychiatry,* 1972, **26,** 8-14.

Lowenthal, M. F., Thurnher, M., & Chiriboga, D. *Four stages of life.* San Francisco: Jossey-Bass, 1975.

Maddi, S. R. *Personality theories: A comparative analysis* (3rd ed.). Homewood, Ill.: Dorsey Press, 1976.

Maddox, G. L. Persistence of life style among the elderly: A longitudinal study of patterns of social activity in relation to life satisfaction. In B. L. Neugarten (Ed.), *Middle age and aging: A reader in social psychology.* Chicago: University of Chicago Press, 1968.

Magnusson, D. & Endler, N. S. (Eds.). *Personality at the crossroads: Current issues in interactional psychology.* Hillsdale, N.J.: Erlbaum, 1977.

McCrae, R. R., Bartone, P. T., & Costa, P. T., Jr. Age, anxiety, and self-reported health. *Aging and Human Development,* 1976, **7,** 49–58.

McCrae, R. R., Costa, P. T., Jr., & Bossé, R. Anxiety, extraversion, and smoking. *British Journal of Social and Clinical Psychology,* 1978, **17,** 269–273.

McCrae, R. R., Costa, P. T., Jr., & Arenberg, D. Age invariance in the factor structure of the Guilford-Zimmerman Temperament Survey scales. *Journal of Gerontology,* in press.

McGowan, J., & Gormly, J. Validation of personality traits: A multicriteria approach. *Journal of Personality and Social Psychology,* 1976, **34,** 791–795.

Mischel, W. *Personality and assessment.* New York: Wiley, 1968.

Mischel, W. The interaction of person and situation. In D. Magnusson & N. S. Endler, *Personality at the crossroads: Current issues in interactional psychology.* Hillsdale, N.J.: Erlbaum, 1977.

Moss, H. A., & Susman, E. J. Constancy and change in personality development. In O. G. Brim, Jr. & J. Kagan (Eds.), *Constancy and change in human development.* Cambridge, Mass.: Harvard University Press, 1980.

Murray, H. A. *Explorations in personality.* New York: Oxford, 1938.

Mussen, P., Eichorn, D. H., Honzik, M. P., Bieber, S. L., & Meredith, W. M. Continuity and change in women's characteristics over four decades. *Journal of Gerontology,* in press.

Neugarten, B. L. Personality changes during the adult years. In R. G. Kuhlen (Ed.), *Psychological backgrounds of adult education.* Chicago: Center for the Study of Liberal Education for Adults, 1963.

Neugarten, B. L. Summary and implications. In B. L. Neugarten (Ed.), *Personality in middle and late life.* New York: Atherton Press, 1964.

Neugarten, B. L. Personality change in late life: A developmental perspective. In C. Eisdorfer & M. P. Lawton (Eds.), *The psychology of adult development and aging.* Washington, D.C.: American Psychological Association, 1973.

Neugarten, B. L. Personality and aging. In J. E. Birren & K. W. Schaie (Eds.), *Handbook of the psychology of aging.* New York: Van Nostrand Reinhold, 1977.

Neugarten, B. L., Crotty, W. J., & Tobin, S. Personality types in an aged population. In B. L. Neugarten (Ed.), *Personality in middle and later life.* New York: Atherton Press, 1964.

Norman, W. T. Toward an adequate taxonomy of personality attributes: Replicated factor structure in peer nomination personality ratings. *Journal of Abnormal and Social Psychology,* 1963, **66,** 574–583.

Nuttall, R. L., & Costa, P. T., Jr. Drinking patterns as affected by age and by personality type. Paper presented at the 28th Annual Scientific Meeting of the Gerontological Society, October 2, 1975, Louisville, Ky.

Overall, J. E., & Gorham, D. R. Organicity versus old age in objective and projective test performance. *Journal of Consulting and Clinical Psychology,* 1972, **39,** 98–105.

Pearlin, L. I., & Schooler, C. The structure of coping. *The Journal of Health and Social Behavior,* 1978, **19,** 2–21.

Rahe, R. H. Subjects' recent life changes and their near future illness reports: A review. *Annals of Clinical Research,* 1972, **4,** 393–397.

Reichard, S., Livson, F., & Peterson, P. G. *Aging and personality.* New York: Wiley, 1962.

Riegel, K. F. Personality theory and aging. In J. E. Birren (Ed.), *Handbook of aging and the individual.* Chicago: University of Chicago Press, 1959.

Riegel, K. F., & Riegel, R. M. A study on changes of attitudes and interests during later years of life. *Vita Humana,* 1960, **3,** 177–206.

Riegel, K. F., Riegel, R. M., & Meyer, G. Socio-psychological factors of aging: A cohort-sequential analysis. *Human Development,* 1967, **10**, 27–56.

Rogers, C. R. *On becoming a person: A therapists's view of psychotherapy.* Boston: Houghton-Mifflin, 1961.

Rokeach, M. *The open and closed mind.* New York: Basic Books, 1960.

Rorschach, H. *Psychodiagnostics.* New York: Grune & Stratton, 1942.

Schaie, K. W. A general model for the study of developmental problems. *Psychological Bulletin,* 1965, **64**, 92–107.

Schaie, K. W., & Gribbin, K. Adult development and aging. In A. R. Rosenzweig & L. W. Porter (Eds.), *Annual Review of Psychology* (Vol. 26). Palo Alto, Calif.: Annual Reviews, 1975.

Schaie, K. W., & Marquette, B. Personality in maturity and old age. In R. M. Dreger, (Ed.), *Multivariate personality in honor of Raymond B. Cattell.* Baton Rouge, La.: Claitor's Publishing, 1972.

Sheehy, G. *Passages: Predictable crises of adult life.* New York: Dutton, 1976.

Schein, V. E. Personality dimensions and needs. In M. W. Riley & A. Foner (Eds.), *Aging and society* (Vol. 1). *An Inventory of research findings.* New York: Russell Sage Foundation, 1968.

Siegler, I. C. The psychology of adult development and aging. In E. W. Busse & D. G. Blazer (Eds.), *Handbook of geriatric psychiatry.* New York: Van Nostrand Reinhold, in press.

Siegler, I. C., Cleveland, W. P., & Ramm, D. Stress and adaptation in later life: Strategies, resources, and events. In preparation.

Siegler, I. C., George, L. K., & Okun, M. A. A cross-sequential analysis of adult personality. *Developmental Psychology,* 1979, **15**, 350–351.

Skolnick, A. Stability and interrelationships of thematic test imagery over twenty years. *Child Development,* 1966, **37**, 389–396.

Woodruff, D. S. & Birren, J. E. Age changes and cohort differences in personality. *Developmental Psychology,* 1972, **6**, 252–259.

The Development of Wisdom across the Life Span: A Reexamination of an Ancient Topic

Vivian P. Clayton

TEACHERS COLLEGE
COLUMBIA UNIVERSITY

and

James E. Birren

ANDRUS GERONTOLOGY CENTER
UNIVERSITY OF SOUTHERN CALIFORNIA

Abstract

The concept of wisdom is explored for its potential in describing and explaining unique and progressive aspects of performance in adulthood not yet captured heretofore in well-researched domains. The concept itself has had an extensive history and played a major role in the maintenance of societies and in the development of the individual. A summary of its position in ancient Western and Eastern traditions is presented. This historical perspective is followed by an empirical analysis of the structure of human qualities guiding the behavior of individuals perceived as being wise in contemporary society. An examination is made of the relationship between wisdom and specific developmental theories that have considered progressive aspects of change in adulthood, and the most basic questions facing researchers interested in relating wisdom to the life cycle are raised.

I. Introduction

Research in the field of life-span developmental psychology has tended to neglect those qualities that might be unique to and representative of development in late adulthood. Emphasis has been placed instead on cognitive and personality variables that emerge in childhood. Such variables may or may not have relevance to the last half of the life cycle (Labouvie-Vief & Chandler, 1978). Furthermore, much of this research has tended to parallel the orientation of our culture by focusing on the irreversible, decremental aspects of performance in later life. Within the last decade, however, there has been growing interest in exploring the potentially unique and progressive aspects of performance in adulthood and old age (Baltes & Labouvie, 1973; Baltes & Willis, 1977; Labouvie-Vief, 1976, 1977; Riegel, 1975; Schaie, 1977–1978). Particularly in the area of cognitive development, recent findings have challenged the decremental view of adult development by presenting evidence for the plasticity of intelligence as well as demonstrating the large influence that contextual variables may have when compared with the role of biological factors in adult intellectual performance (Baltes & Willis, 1979a; Labouvie-Vief, Hoyer, Baltes, & Baltes, 1974; Schaie, 1979; Schaie & Gribbin, 1975).

Wisdom is probably the one aspect of human life-span development most written about in the traditional literature of the world. It has always had an association of a positive nature with the later years of life (Birren & Renner, 1977). Those older individuals who possessed wisdom often held positions of social consequence and were given respect in their communities (Adler, 1955). There is a growing awareness and impetus to create meaningful roles for the postretirement segment of our population (Birren & Woodruff, 1973). Wisdom might prove to be one important criterion variable to be considered for qualifying individuals for such positions. Introducing the concept of wisdom could also provide the field of life-span developmental psychology with an attribute that represents a progressive aspects of growth in the later years of life.

The major purpose of this chapter, therefore, is to reintroduce an ancient concept with strong historical validity to a field that will allow for exploration of its psychological validity as well. We hope examining the concept of wisdom will open up new perspectives for the study and understanding of adult development and possibly provide a model descriptive of successful adaptation during the later years of life.

II. A Historical Perspective on Wisdom

It will be apparent in the following historical review that mankind has, for ages, used the term "wisdom" to refer to a positive quality inherent in the mature person. The behavioral display of wisdom was considered to be desirable and methods of encouraging its expression were described in ancient texts. Wisdom appeared to blend the qualities of cognition, emotion, and intuition. Widely varying cultural traditions acknowledged that it could be acquired with time, though not necessarily a product of chronological age alone.

Though the exact origins of the term "wisdom" remain obscure, wisdom appears to be more frequently and extensively the subject of discussion in the ancient books of East and West of 2000 years ago than in modern texts (Conze, 1958). The ancients seemed to have not only a greater yearning for wisdom, but also a greater interest in understanding what wisdom was and how it could be gained. Wisdom is the focus of such books in the Eastern tradition as the Hindu *Vedas* (Yogananda, 1946) and the Buddhist *Dhammapada* (Thomas, 1950). In the Western disciplines, discussion of wisdom is found in the literature of the Old and New Testaments (Paterson, 1972; Rad, 1972) as well as in prominent Sophic texts of the ancient Greek culture (Lobsang, 1965). Despite mutual reverence for wisdom, Eastern and Western traditions held different viewpoints on how wisdom could be achieved. Though a comprehensive presentation remains beyond the scope of this chapter, the major features of the Western and Eastern traditions will be highlighted.

A. WESTERN TRADITION

The Biblical approach to wisdom is represented in what is known as the wisdom literature (e.g., Book of Solomon, Job, Proverbs, Ecclesiastes, Epistle of James, Apocrypha; McFayden, 1921, Noth & Thomas, 1955; Perdue, 1977; Rad, 1972). This body of literature presents three fairly distinct paths that were available for pursuing wisdom. Two of these paths emphasized the power of the intellect.

The first of these paths was formal and available only to the privileged class (Oesterley, 1927). The young sons of noblemen or wealthy merchants were treated to an education that prepared them to be statesmen, diplomats, and administrators in high government posts. The educational system made efforts to teach its students an empirical rather than subjective approach in conducting the business of state. The ideas emphasized were logic, rigor, and probity. The training condemned a man who was rash or garrulous in his speech. It rewarded those who applied a sharp and disciplined mind to every facet of a situation before committing themselves to an opinion or a policy. Explicit permission and encouragement were given to challenge political and religious authority for, reflecting the training's emphasis on objectivity, the world and its problems were to be treated as they were and not as they ought to be (Noth & Thomas, 1955).

The second path was also pedagogical and logical in emphasis, though it was less formal than the first (Paterson, 1972). This approach to wisdom involved listening and learning from one's parents. It was almost mandatory in these ancient times to listen, obey, and honor the instruction of one's parents. This less formal manner of teaching prescribed modes of personal conduct as well as informed the young of the whims of human nature. Examples of this method of acquiring wisdom can be found in the Book of Proverbs in the Old Testament. This Book is a compendium of instruction and advice given to Jewish youths by professional sages in the postexilic period (Perdue, 1977). It is not surprising that many proverbs begin with the words, "My son . . . ."

Both these methods relied heavily on man's cognitive capacity to learn; both utilized teaching as a helpful tool; wisdom, in both paths, represented a type of knowledge to be acquired. The third path available for pursuing wisdom involved minimal efforts at learning and maximum adherence to faith (Rad, 1972). Wisdom, in other words, came to man not through his own efforts but as a divine gift. The Lord was the ultimate judge and fear of Him would lead man to wisdom. The purpose of this particular path to wisdom was not only to make man cognizant of God, but also to regulate human conduct (Garnett, 1940). Aquinas (1951), in describing this particular path states, "Since the regulation of human conduct by the divine law belongs to wisdom . . . in order to make a beginning, man must, first of all, fear God and submit himself to Him" (p. 101).

All three Biblical paths specified acquisition of a certain type of knowledge. The knowledge itself, however, was somewhat different depending on which path the seeker pursued. Those sons of noblemen who pursued formal education were given insights into the ways of conducting matters of business and state; those who pursued the informal process of receiving instruction from parents were given codes to guide their personal conduct; those who adhered to God's word as the means for acquiring wisdom were taught to believe in Mosaic law.

Possibly as a consequence of this diversity, the meaning of wisdom, as it can be inferred from these ancient texts, was far from uniform. Knowledge, the desire and ability to learn, and understanding, were the qualities most frequently associated with wisdom. Solomon was noted additionally for his cunning, moral discernment (I Kings 3:9; 12) and grasp of justice (I Kings 3:28). Wisdom was equated with prudence (Proverbs 8:12), and with strength as well (Proverbs 8:24).

Not only were there multiple meanings attributed to wisdom in the Bible, but this quality was also associated with both young and old people (McFayden, 1921). Cultural conditions might have been responsible for the superimposition of the life-span orientation on the acquisition and application of wisdom. As long as there was pressure to honor and revere the elders, an inevitable struggle between the young and old over the authority of the father or elders seemed to exist. This authority was oftentimes misused by the older individuals. Questioning the wisdom of the elders by a younger person is expressed concisely in the following passage from the Book of Job:

> Elihu had waited to speak to Job because they were older than he. And When Elihu saw that there was no answer in the mouth of these three men, he became angry. And Elihu . . . answered: I am young in years,/ and you are aged;/ Therefore I was timid and afraid/ to declare may opinion to you./ I said, "Let days speak, and many years teach wisdom."/ But it is the spirit in man; the breadth of the Almighty that/ makes him understand. It is not the old that are wise,/ nor the aged who understand what is right./ Therefore I say, "Listen to me. Let me also declare my opinion. (Job 32:5-10)

The epic of Susanna, in the Apocrypha, also captures the theme of the young not only questioning the sagacity of the old, but triumphing over them through the application of impartial judgment. According to the Talmud, a body of recorded oral history, it was acknowledged that one could be old without being wise (Sol. 4:8-9, 16). Conversely, the ancient rabbis held that one could have the basis of wisdom through the pursuit of knowledge without being old. As two of the prescribed methods for acquiring wisdom involved teaching, it is not surprising that when doubt was expressed about an elder's wisdom, it was in the area of his intellectual prowess. Rabbi Elisha B. Avyah was quoted as saying, "What does learning when old resemble? It is like writing on blotted out paper" (Bokser, 1951, p. 59).

Despite battles between young and old as to who could possess and apply wisdom, the dimension of time was often credited as a way of providing a person with wisdom, particularly in its relationship to experience. "An educated man knows many things/ and one with much experience/ will speak with understanding./ He that is inexperienced knows few things. . ." (Ben Sira 34:9-10).

B. GREEK TRADITION

Literature of ancient Greece reflects less concern with the age at which wisdom could be acquired; rather it constantly raises the question of whether man could even possess wisdom. This question was related to the fact that the Greeks made a distinction between philosophical wisdom and practical wisdom.

Aristotle equated philosophical wisdom with the highest branch of speculative science, metaphysics, whose purpose it was to investigate first principles and causes. Philosophical wisdom connoted the highest form of knowledge, representing an understanding of the ultimate nature of things. It was believed that only God could possess such knowledge. In the *Apology,* for example, Socrates told his accusers that his cross-examination of the pretenders to wisdom was a duty imposed upon him by the oracle who declared that there was no man wiser than himself. To understand the oracle's meaning, he tried to seek out wisdom in other men, but he said at his trial, "I found that the men most in repute were all but the most foolish. My hearers always imagine that I myself possess the wisdom which I find wanting in others, but the truth is, O Men of Athens, that only God is wise, and by his answer, he intends to show that the wisdom of men is worth little or nothing; he is only using my name by way of illustration, as if he said, 'He, O men, is the wisest'" (Adler, 1955, p. 1103).

If philosophical wisdom was concerned with the ultimate nature of things, practical wisdom was concerned with the ultimate good for man. To illustrate the distinction between this double aspect of wisdom, Aristotle used the example of the early Greek sages. "We say Anaxagoras, Thales, and men like them have philosophical but not practical wisdom when we see them ignorant of what is to their own advantage . . . they know things that are remarkable, admirable, difficult, and divine, but useless; viz., because it is not human goods they seek" (Adler, 1955, p. 1104).

Although Aristotle might have believed the possession of philosophical wisdom to be beyond human powers, he nevertheless felt that man should attempt to "seek the knowledge that is suited to him" (Adler, 1955, p. 1105). The individual could attempt to reach this most divine virtue by being inquisitive and curious. Curiosity was manifested in those who questioned, probed, investigated, and made efforts to seek out answers to the mysteries of life. Those who never raised questions about the purpose of life, who never tried to analyze or understand the nature of existence, were those who could not bridge the gap between practical and philosophical wisdom.

To the Greeks then, wisdom connoted the highest form of knowledge; it represented an understanding of the ultimate nature of things as well as an understanding of the ultimate good for man. The Greeks connected moral and character implications with being wise (Garnett, 1940). An individual was not thought of as being wise unless he acted wisely; to act wisely was a reflection of good, moral behavior (Nogar, 1966). Achieving wisdom, therefore, did not represent the mere accumulation of facts, but also represented a knowledge of good and evil.

C. EASTERN TRADITION

Like the Western tradition, the Eastern tradition treated wisdom as a particular type of knowledge that was concerned with understanding the meaning of life, of God, and of the relationship between man and the universe. The Western approach, however, stressed the importance of the intellect and reason for pursuing wisdom. The Eastern tradition, represented by Zen Buddhism, Taoism, Sufism, and Hinduism, shared the conviction that too much intellectual, rational analysis would seriously hinder enlightenment, the term used to describe the attainment of wisdom (Cragg, 1976; Humphreys, 1961; Lin, 1948; You, 1972). In these Eastern disciplines, the wise individual was the one who had developed direct, experiential knowledge of the meaning of life rather than the one who did not have the experience but who did much reasoning about it.

According to Tart (1975), an enlightened man was able to "see things as they actually are" (p. 15). To be able to see things as they actually are required, first and foremost, an understanding of one's own nature that was not distorted and an acceptance of the vicissitudes of life that brought suffering, as well as joy. Whereas the intellect was considered the faculty responsible for perceiving, discriminating, and conceptualizing about reality, it was not considered the faculty that allowed man to grasp the actual nature of reality itself. This was due to the very nature of the intellect which, in performing the above functions, created a separation between the individual and the perceived object. Words, the tools of conceptualization, were not considered to be able to take the place of experience. The wise individual, therefore, evidenced his wisdom not by telling others what the ultimate nature of reality was, but by teaching people how to experience it for themselves. The human abilities that gave man the opportunity to experience directly were intuition and compassion. These qualities, acting as sensing devices, provided man with qualitatively different ways of evaluating information that were equally as important as the intellect. Eliminating intuition and compassion in man would make certain kinds of knowledge inaccessible, thereby blocking his path to enlightenment (Cragg, 1976).

In the Eastern approach, the path to enlightenment was aided by two things: meditation and having a teacher (Pelletier & Garfield, 1976). The purpose of meditation was to train the individual how to quiet and free the conscious mind of all thoughts and preconceptions—a necessary precursor to clear perception, to being able to see things directly. An analogy that might help explain one of the functions of meditation is provided by this Zen parable, *A Cup of Tea:*

> Nan-in, a Japanese master during the Meiji era (1868–1912) received a university pro-
> fessor who came to inquire about Zen. Nan-in served tea. He poured his visitor's cup
> full, and then kept pouring. The professor watched the overflow until he no longer could
> restrain himself. "It is overfull. No more will go in!" "Like this cup," Nan-in said,
> "You are full of your own opinions and speculations. How can I show you Zen unless
> you first empty your cup?" (Reps, 1961, p. 5)

After the mind is emptied of thought through meditation, focus and concentration are thought to develop, allowing the individual to "become one with the object meditated on, whether that object is an external, physical object or a spiritual object or concept" (Tart, 1975, p. 20).

A teacher was also considered a necessary component on the path to enlightenment. The teacher was a person who had obtained enlightenment himself. The relationship between student and teacher was based upon a commitment to see things as they actually are. This commitment was translated into directly experiencing human nature and the nature of reality. This was accomplished through the use of *koans,* which were problems given by the teacher to his disciples. The answers to koans were not amenable to solution through the use of the intellect; as their purpose and solution were tied to mirroring the paradoxes within man's own nature, only contemplation and intuition could help a student understand them. Examples of these paradoxical propositions are: "Let me hear the sound of one hand clapping; walk while riding on a donkey" (Suzuki, 1960, p. 49).

The teacher also gave the student another type of opportunity to experience human nature by conveying the only thing the teacher could convey directly (i.e., his own existence). This is reflected in an old Hassidic saying, "When I go to my tsaddick I don't study torah, I watch him tie his shoe laces." Again in this approach, words are by-passed.

When enlightenment was achieved, the Eastern tradition spoke of transformations in behaviors and the reorganization of values (Owens, 1975). The enlightened individual would be more compassionate and would orient his life around helping others; he would evidence tranquility, and the desire to acquire fame and power would cease along with the fears of old age, sickness, death, or poverty. The attitude toward the past would be one of gratitude, toward the present, of service, and toward the future, of responsibility (Pelletier & Garfield, 1976).

There was a relationship between chronological age and reaching enlightenment in the Eastern disciplines. This relationship, however, was more determined by the time needed to experience things directly than by any specific qualities of age itself (You, 1972). Enlightenment, therefore, did not come merely with getting older; only those who practiced meditation and were committed to seeking and understanding the ultimate nature of things were likely candidates for achieving wisdom.

Zen Buddhism has always been distinctly opposed to written doctrine that dictates how to live or ways to think (Owens, 1975). Within the Hindu tradition, however, those who committed themselves to seeking enlightenment were urged to divide their time on earth into four general periods. The first part of the life cycle, known as Brahmacarya, was a period to be devoted to training the mind and body for spiritual practice in later life. A teacher was considered necessary during this training to act as a guide and advisor. The second part of the life cycle, known as Jarhastya, was to be devoted to work and family. When one became a grandfather, the next period, known as Vansprastya, was said to begin. It was during this period that one was to leave home to prepare the spirit. It was to be a time of retreat, where social bonds were loosened. The last period of one's life, known as Samayasa, was to be a time of renunciation, during which the individual would be awaiting enlightenment and freedom from all earthly bonds and desires (Yogananda, 1946).

In summary, both in ancient Eastern and Western traditions, discussions were held about the qualities of wisdom, how it might be acquired, and what its general relationship was to the life cycle. Although the present review is not comprehensive, nor based on a systematic analysis, it appears that ancient sources contained statements about wisdom and that these statements reflected a belief that wisdom was a desirable attribute of human behavior that varied from person to person according to his pursuit of its development. Overall, it seems that all traditions described wisdom as being a type of knowledge involving a quest to understand the meaning and purpose of life; all traditions perceived that this type of knowledge was reflected in behavior; all saw that a period of tutelage was necessary to acquire wisdom. There was agreement that time was a necessary component for acquisition of wisdom. Both life experience and the direct experiencing of life were considered important elements. The Eastern and Western traditions did not agree on what human abilities were needed or essential for obtaining wisdom or what type of educational procedures would be most effective to instill the individual with this particular type of knowledge.

III.   Toward an Empirical Definition of Wisdom

The previous historical review strongly suggests that, for some time, mankind has held the conviction that there is a superior, complex, and desirable form of knowledge called wisdom that reflects an underlying understanding and experience of the ultimate nature of reality and man's relationship to this reality. Eastern and Western traditions differed in the emphasis placed on which human qualities were harnessed to achieve this type of knowledge. Nevertheless, the intellect, the emotional, and intuitive capacities were all mentioned as faculties that might help man achieve this ultimate form of knowledge over time.

A contemporary definition of wisdom, taken from the Oxford Unabridged Dictionary (1933) reads as follows, "The capacity of judging rightly in matters relating to life and conduct; soundness of judgment in the choice of means and ends." Particular types of judgments, therefore, are one way wisdom might be manifested in behavior. It would be of interest to know what the contemporary perception is of the corresponding, underlying human abilities, and whether these perceptions are uniform or change as individuals increase in age.[1]

A.   MEANING OF WISDOM: AN EMPIRICAL STUDY

To address these issues, an empirical investigation was undertaken for the explicit purpose of examining the underlying structure of wisdom as it is perceived by individuals across the life span. The methods of analysis reflected the complexity of this goal; detailed information on procedure can be obtained from Clayton (1976).

As the historical perspective highlighted the multidimensional nature of wisdom, a multidimensional scaling algorithm, TORSCA8 (Torgerson, 1958) was used. Multidimensional scaling (MDS) analyses have already been demonstrated as effective tools in developmental research (Arabie, Kosslyn, & Nelson, 1975; Howard & Howard, 1977; Kosslyn, Pick, & Farello, 1974) and are recommended when attempting to define those psychological variables whose underlying dimensions are not known in advance (Guilford, 1954). The MDS algorithm was preceded with an individual difference analysis, Points of View (Tucker & Messick, 1963), which allowed for differences between subjects in their perceptions of wisdom to emerge.

---

[1] An interesting and forceful historical piece on the concept and role of wisdom in old age is an article by G. Stanley Hall published in 1921 in the *Atlantic Monthly*. This article was written anonymously but was later acknowledged by Hall in his 1922 book on senescence (note by editors).

Participants consisted of 83 individuals representing three age–cohort levels drawn from the university community: 16 male and 15 young female adults (N = 31; mean age = 21.3 years), 11 male and 12 female middle-aged persons (N = 23; mean age = 49.2 years), and 15 male and 14 female older persons (N = 29; mean age = 70.1 years). The young adults were students in an introductory course in gerontology; the middle-aged individuals were faculty and staff members of the Andrus Gerontology Center of Los Angeles; the older participants were all volunteers in the same center. All subjects had completed a minimum of 2 years of college. This sample clearly consisted of well-educated individuals.

The stimuli used for this investigation were generated by young, middle-aged, and older people in an earlier pilot study (Clayton, 1975b) as descriptors of wise individuals. These descriptors were: *experienced, intuitive, introspective, pragmatic, understanding, gentle, empathetic, intelligent, peaceful, knowledgeable, sense of humor,* and *observant.* Three more stimuli were included for the investigation summarized here. As all of the descriptors had been generated in relation to a wise individual, the adjective *wise* was added to this list of descriptors. It was designed to serve as the centroid in the MDS representations. To examine how individuals across the life span perceived the relationship between wisdom and age, as well as the relationship between wisdom and themselves, the adjective *aged* and the pronoun *myself* were also included. A total of 15 words, therefore, were used in the MDS task.

The task consisted of having subjects judge the similarity of the members of each of the 105 pairs of the stimuli (i.e., all possible nonredundant combinations of the 15 descriptors). Judgments were recorded on a scale from 1 to 5, with 1 representing the highest degree of similarity, and 5 representing the least degree of similarity between a pair of stimuli.

To examine whether or not there were differences across subjects in their perception of similarity among the 105 stimulus pairs, judgments were first analyzed using the Points of View individual differences procedure (Tucker & Messick, 1963). The results of this analysis revealed significant individual differences in the judgment of the pairs between cohorts. No sex differences were found. As a consequence, a separate vector for each cohort, representing mean similarity judgments across the 105 pairs, was submitted to the MDS algorithm, TORSCA8 (Torgerson, 1958). Preliminary solutions were obtained in spaces of one to six dimensions for each age group. Kruskal's (1964) stress index was used to determine the extent to which the distances in space deviated from the ordinal distance input data. For each cohort, these stress values were plotted to determine the optimal dimensionality (Shepard, Romney, & Nerlove, 1972). For all cohorts, the elbow in the stress values appeared to be over the third dimension. The fifth and

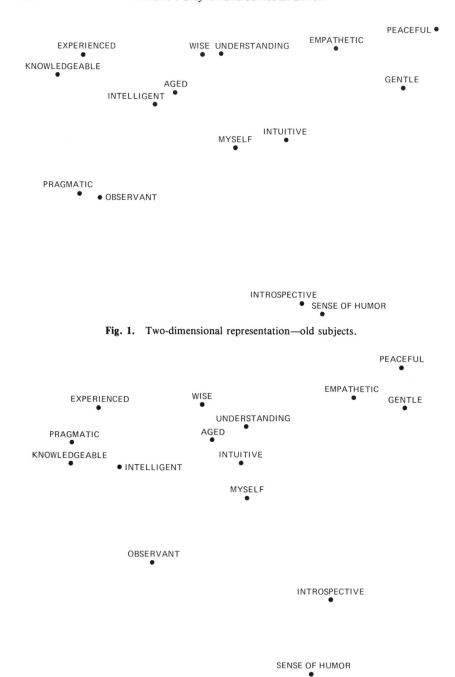

Fig. 1.   Two-dimensional representation—old subjects.

Fig. 2.   Two-dimensional representation—middle-aged subjects.

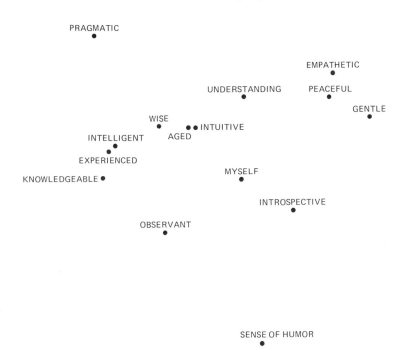

Fig. 3. Two-dimensional representation—young subjects.

sixth dimensions in all solutions yielded relatively small improvements in stress. They were not included, therefore, in subsequent analyses.

To facilitate comparisons across cohorts as well as aid the interpretation of the structures, the solutions were rotated to congruence using Case II of Cliff's (1966) orthogonal rotation program. After the axes across structures were aligned, spatial representations were created. The first two axes for each age group are presented in Figs. 1, 2, and 3. The dimension loadings for the three axes across age groups are represented in Table I. As all the stimuli were initially generated to describe a wise individual, the stimulus *wise* was used as the centroid in all interpretations. Structural differences as well as similarities were observed across cohorts. The structural similarities will be reported first, followed by a description of the structural differences.

B. STRUCTURAL SIMILARITIES ACROSS COHORTS

An examination of the spatial arrangement of stimuli in Figs. 1, 2, and 3 shows all representations to be cluster structures, with interpretable nonorthogonal components occurring within the clusters. One of these clusters reflected an affective component of wisdom. It extends from *wise* to

TABLE I
Dimension Loadings across Age Groups

Age	Stimuli	Dimensions		
		1	2	3
Young	Aged	−.06	.05	.41
	Empathetic	.36	.22	−.14
	Experienced	−.32	−.01	.14
	Gentle	.47	.09	.08
	Intelligent	−.31	.00	−.22
	Introspective	.25	−.16	.14
	Intuitive	−.06	.05	−.36
	Knowledgeable	−.33	−.08	−.01
	Myself	.10	−.07	−.13
	Observant	−.15	−.25	−.22
	Peaceful	.34	.15	.27
	Pragmatic	−.35	.33	.04
	Sense of humor	.14	−.58	.03
	Understanding	.08	.15	−.05
	Wise	−.15	.06	.01
Middle-aged	Aged	−.04	.10	.61
	Empathetic	.36	.22	−.21
	Experienced	−.39	.19	.25
	Gentle	.53	.19	.13
	Intelligent	−.33	.02	−.30
	Introspective	.29	−.37	.16
	Intuitive	.02	.03	−.49
	Knowledgeable	−.47	.03	−.10
	Myself	.04	−.07	.00
	Observant	−.24	−.26	−.22
	Peaceful	.51	.31	.17
	Pragmatic	−.47	.09	−.17
	Sense of humor	.24	−.64	−.05
	Understanding	.05	.13	−.11
	Wise	−.08	.20	.00
Old	Aged	−.14	.10	.76
	Empathetic	.32	.23	−.25
	Experienced	−.43	.21	.29
	Gentle	.54	.11	.25
	Intelligent	−.22	.07	−.42
	Introspective	.24	−.52	.28
	Intuitive	.18	.03	−.54
	Knowledgeable	−.52	.14	−.08
	Myself	.04	−.06	.07
	Observant	−.38	−.24	−.23
	Peaceful	.63	.31	.04
	Pragmatic	−.43	−.23	.10
	Sense of humor	.31	−.53	−.12
	Understanding	−.03	.22	−.06
	Wise	−.11	−.22	.09

peaceful in the middle-aged and older subjects' structures and from *wise* to *peaceful–empathetic* in the younger participants' structure. In addition to these stimuli, *understanding* and *gentle* were also located near this cluster of stimuli across structures. The other cluster seemed to represent a reflective component of wisdom. It extended from *wise* to *introspective* in all three groups. In addition to these stimuli, *intuitive* and *myself* were consistently located near this component.

When the pattern of dimension loadings for the third axis was examined in Table I, another general similarity was found. In all cohorts, the three stimuli having the highest negative loadings were *intuitive, intelligent* and *observant*. In the middle-aged and older groups' structures, the two stimuli having the highest positive loadings were *aged* and *experienced*. The highest positive loading for the young subjects was also *aged,* followed, however, by *peaceful* and then by *experienced* and *introspective*. Only a tentative interpretation, based on prevailing stereotypes, could be made for this particular pattern of dimension loadings. As *intuitive, intelligent,* and *observant* are not attributes conventionally associated with chronological age, whereas *aged* and *experienced* usually are, this last axis might be suggestive of a perceived developmental, age-related component of wisdom.

C. STRUCTURAL DIFFERENCES BETWEEN COHORTS

The most important difference found across representations was that the underlying structure of wisdom seemed to become more differentiated with an increase in the participant's age. Examination of the stimuli that fell neither in the reflective nor affective components lends support to this interpretation. In the older participants' structure, there are two distinct clusters on which the remaining stimuli are located. One cluster extends from *wise* to *knowledgeable,* with *experienced* falling fairly close to this cluster. Whereas these qualities are clearly time-dependent, they are not necessarily age-related. This cluster, therefore, seems to be representing a time-related component of wisdom. The other cluster extends from *wise* to *pragmatic–observant,* with *aged* and *intelligent* falling nearby. This cluster appeared to be representing a fairly specific cognitive component of wisdom. An examination of the middle-aged participants' representation of wisdom shows these two clusters beginning to separate; for the young, they are still undifferentiated, forming a more general cognitive component.

Other age differences were observed in relation to the relative positions of several stimuli. In the older subjects' structure, all the stimuli fell near or close to one of the four components identified in their solution, suggesting a less ambiguous perception of the attributes of a wise individual. In the middle-aged participants' structure, *observant* did not fall near any of the identified clusters. In the younger subjects' representation of wisdom, however, both *observant* and *sense of humor* became part of another cluster that extended from *pragmatic* to *sense of humor*. This cluster might be representing a serious–light dimension of wisdom. More stimuli would need to fall between these two extreme points, however, before such an interpretation could be fully acceptable.

Age differences were also observed in the position of the stimulus *aged* across representations of wisdom. In the young and middle-aged participants' representations, *aged* fell much closer to the reflective component of wisdom, whereas in the older participants' representation *aged* appeared to be associated with the cognitive component.

D. AGE DIFFERENCES IN POSITION OF STIMULI RELATIVE TO THE ATTRIBUTE "WISE"

To examine the degree of perceived similarity between *wise* and the other 14 stimuli across age groups, the interpoint distances between *wise* and the remaining stimuli were analyzed in a one-way multivariate analysis of variance. The main effect for age was significant, F $(28,134) = 2.04$, $p < .01$, indicating differences across groups in the position of the 14 stimuli relative to *wise*. Univariate analyses were therefore examined for each of the 14 stimuli with age as the independent variable. No significant differences were found for the stimulus *myself.* The older participants did not judge themselves as possessing more or less of this attribute than did the middle-aged or younger subjects. Significant differences were found for the stimulus *aged,* F $(2,80) = 3.22$, $p < .05$; *experienced,* F $(2,80) = 5.25$, $p < .01$; *understanding,* F $(2,80) = 4.32$, $p < .01$; and *empathetic,* F $(2,80) = 3.17$, $p < .05$. Scheffé post hoc tests indicated that both young and middle-aged participants placed *aged* and *experienced* closer to *wise* than did the older participants ($p < .05$). These results indicate that *aged* and *experienced* were less associated with *wise* by participants in their later years, whereas *understanding* and *empathetic,* qualities of an affective nature, were judged as being more similar to *wise* as participants increased in age.

E. DISCUSSION

The major purpose of this investigation was to examine the structure of the concept of wisdom as it is perceived by individuals across the life span. The results from this scaling study confirmed the multidimensional nature of wisdom suggested by historical and anecdotal documentation. Wisdom was perceived by these educated individuals as an attribute representing the *integration* of general cognitive, affective, and reflective qualities. It is interesting to note that all age groups were consistent in the identification of the reflective component, characterized by the qualities of introspection and intuition, and the affective component, characterized by the qualities of understanding, empathy, peacefulness, and gentleness. These two components were considered essential in the pursuit of enlightenment in the Eastern disciplines. Consistency across groups was also found in the identification of a component of wisdom possibly perceived as age-related, or developmental. These similarities in structure across age groups are important. They satisfy one of the prerequisites for validating a new hypothetical construct, namely, that of consistency in meaning across age-related reference systems (Cronbach & Meehl, 1955).

Differences between cohorts occurred in the perceived organization of the specific qualities that clustered within the general cognitive component, the dimension of wisdom most valued in ancient Western disciplines. Two cognitive components were present in the older subjects' structure of wisdom that merged in the middle-aged and younger subjects' representations of wisdom. One of these components seemed to identify time-dependent qualities (e.g., knowledge and experience) that are not necessarily age-related. The other components focused on the specific cognitive qualities of intellect, pragmatism, and observation. Future research investigations might consider exploring the relationship between this perceived differentiation across age–cohort groups in the underlying cognitive component and the actual ontogenetic and cohort-related changes in cognitive structures that are well documented in life-span developmental literature (Baltes & Willis, 1977, 1979a).

In light of the long-held belief that age brings wisdom, an unexpected age difference was found in the analysis of interpoint distances between *wise* and the 14 other stimuli. The older participants placed the stimulus *aged* significantly farther from *wise* than either the young or middle-aged participants. It appeared, then, that the older individuals were least accepting of the more positive, age-related stereotype. This supports Rokeach's (1973) finding of the effect of age on terminal value-system stability. It is also consistent with findings that older people, in fact, believe more strongly in the negative stereotypes about old age than do younger persons (McTavish, 1971; Neugarten, Moore, & Lowe, 1965). The results, furthermore, indicated the absence of a perceived relationship between the participant's own aging process and wisdom. The older participants did not judge themselves as personally possessing more or less wisdom than did the middle-aged and young participants. Unlike the two younger groups, however, the older participants perceived the affective qualities of understanding and empathy as being much more similar to wisdom than chronologial age or experience.

The specific structural differences in the conception of wisdom raise a number of intriguing questions for future research. If the Oxford English Dictionary's behavioral definition of wisdom proves empirically accurate, would the judgment or decision rendered by an older individual reflect greater empathy than that of his younger counterpart? During what portion of the life cycle does the individual perceive that chronological age alone is not highly related to wisdom? How does this perception develop? The cross-sectional nature of this first empirical attempt to elucidate the underlying structure of wisdom precludes answers to this inquiries. Longitudinal or sequential investigations and use of age–cohort representative or comparable samples will help clarify which of these structural differences in the concept of wisdom are the product of ontogentic factors and which are the result of sociocultural influences.

IV.　Wisdom and Development

The previous sections have described wisdom as a type of knowledge and as a perceived multidimensional attribute of the individual. The intent of the present section is to focus on the relationship between this concept and the process of development. Models that have generated or commented on progressive aspects of change in adulthood will be examined for their potential contributions in promoting research on wisdom. The most basic questions facing investigators interested in relating wisdom to the life cycle will then be raised.

Models of development have or imply different perspectives on the nature of man, on his relationship to the universe, and perhaps most critical, on the definition and direction of change in the life cycle (Baltes, Reese, & Lipsitt, 1980; Lerner & Ryff, 1978, Overton & Reese, 1973; Reese & Overton, 1970). As the nature and direction of changes in wisdom across the life-span are unknown, an exclusive preference for a particular model or theory from which to examine and design empirical investigations would be extremely short-sighted. At this stage of theory building and creating testable hypotheses, the nature of wisdom itself should have a bearing on the nature of the theory that will evolve and the methods of investigation to be adopted.

There are several existing developmental models that have either postulated or have the structural framework to examine progressive, adult-centered growth. These theories will be acknowledged and the major strengths and weaknesses inherent in trying to apply them to the concept of wisdom will be highlighted. This examination will not be systematic, but rather will focus on what contribution extant models and theories might make in promoting research and understanding of the development of wisdom.

A. MODELS OF DEVELOPMENT

1. Erikson

Erikson's (1968) theory of development is the only theory considered that specifically embeds wisdom in a life-cycle framework. Wisdom is considered a virtue that emerges in the last stage of life, representing the successful mastery of specific developmental tasks and resolution of stage-specific crises (Erikson, 1959). The major strength of Erikson's approach to wisdom lies in his recognition of the importance of social change and its relation to the developing individual. It has been observed (Clayton, 1975a) that the prevailing sociocultural conditions in contemporary society offer very few channels for the expression and maintenance of wisdom. The implication of Erikson's model is that, unless wisdom has validity as a social concept, its recognition and development in the individual is difficult, if not impossible.

Another asset of Erikson's model for the study of wisdom lies in the epigenetic principle that is responsible for directing the individual through the major developmental stages. Whereas Erikson represents wisdom as a virtue emerging in the very last years of life, the epigenetic principle states that each virtue is present in earlier stages although in forms reflective of the different levels of life complexity and experience (Erikson, 1964). Erikson's model, therefore, does not entirely exclude the possibility that wisdom is a quality, the development and expression of which represents an ongoing process as well as an end product in the life cycle.

Erikson's model, however, also has some disadvantages for the process of validating wisdom as a psychological construct. His model is methodologically weak, and attempts to operationalize the relevant adulthood stages have not proved very successful (Gruen, 1964; Lowenthal, 1977). His approach, furthermore, is content-bound to the area of social–emotional development, having little to offer in the way of insights as to how the intellectual or reflective components of wisdom are utilized in the psychosocial evolution of the individual.

2. Kohlberg

Erikson's eighth stage of development serves as the launching pad for Kohlberg's (1973a, 1973b) postulation of a seventh stage following the postconventional period of moral development. In Erikson's last stage, the developmental task is to resolve what has been the meaning of the individual's life. Such questions as "Why live?" and "How face death?" are the focus of inquiry at this stage and are triggered when the individual realizes his own life is soon to end. To Kohlberg (1973b), these questions signify the individual's progression to a seventh stage in moral development. Acknowledging that these questions are more ontological than moral, he states that they cannot arise on a psychologically serious level until a man has attained moral principles and lived a life in terms of these principles for a considerable length of time. The postconventional stage, furthermore, only offers an imperfect integration or resolution of the problem of life's meaning.

Kohlberg does not think the questions that require attention in this seventh stage are resolvable on purely logical or rational grounds as moral questions are. He suggests, instead, that they are resolved by a shift in perspective that occurs within the individual. The shift in perspective is analogous to a reversal in a figure–ground relationship. The individual shifts from seeing himself as the center of the universe to identifying with the universe and seeing himself from this perspective. What results is that the individual senses the unity of the universe in which he is but one element. The acquisition of this nondualistic, nonegoistic orientation signals resolution to these ontological questions. Due to the nonlogical nature of the emergence and resolution of these ontological inquiries, Kohlberg hypothesized that this seventh stage does not fit the notion of a stage in the structural sense.

Kohlberg's perspective has made several contributions for understanding the development of wisdom. Even if he has only descriptively captured the perspective the wise individual might hold, he has offered the field a valuable suggestion that attainment of such a perspective is not based on logical structures or resolvable through rational reasoning. Kohlberg might also be offering a particularly useful observation (i.e., that wisdom is evoked as much by the nature of the questions raised as by the type of answers given). By suggesting the potential incompatibility of exploring wisdom within a structural framework, he has raised the issues of which methodological tools will prove most useful in operationalizing wisdom and determining its developmental relationship to the individual. Another potential contribution Kohlberg could be making for the empirical study of wisdom is the conceptualization of its relationship to moral development. Historically, many of the questions that evoked wisdom were those that involved problems of human conduct (Garnett, 1940). An understanding and integration of moral principles, therefore, might be a necessary precursor to rendering wise and appropriate judgments.

There are also shortcomings inherent in Kohlberg's perspective. He does not adequately specify the mechanisms that explain how an individual progresses from the postconventional stage to stage seven. His view might be limited in suggesting that questions concerning the meaning of life are solved or only contemplated at the end of one's life. He might be making a significant observation (i.e., that questions evoking the use of wisdom are triggered when one is confronted with the finitude of one's own life). This can occur, however, as a consequence of other experiences distributed throughout the life span. Car accidents, death of parents, serious illness, or loss of any kind might trigger these ontological inquiries. In addition, Kohlberg is not very clear in specifying the nature of the nonlogical mechanisms that are the basis of the seventh stage and that resolve these ontological inquiries. He does suggest that contemplation is involved (Kohlberg, 1973b), highlighting the need to better understand the role played by the reflective component of wisdom in the development of the individual.

3. Piagetian Views

Several investigators have also addressed the issue of adult-specific progressive cognitive change within a Piagetian framework (Arlin, 1975; Gruber, 1973; Riegel, 1973b). Representative of the organismic model, Piaget conceives of development as proceeding toward an end state (Piaget, 1970a). This end state is cognitive maturity, reflected in attainment of the formal operational stage. With formal operations, the individual can engage in abstract thought, explore hypotheses on a mental level, solve complex verbal problems, and employ proportionality and combinatorial systems in problem solving (Inhelder & Piaget, 1958). Attainment of the formal operational stage signals to Piaget (1970b) that the individual can effectively adapt to a great variety of problems and assimilate a number of novel situations. When an individual reaches this stage in adolescence, he can acquire new knowledge, but the underlying logical structures undergo no further modification. The cognitive structures, therefore, have reached a high degree of equilibrium.

One serious limitation to Piaget's approach in describing and explaining adult-specific stages is its emphasis on organismic, maturational mechanisms that direct development to the exclusion of a consideration of the role that historical factors might play in cognitive evolution (Baltes & Willis, 1979b, Riegel, 1975a). By emphasizing normative, universal patterns of development, the structural nature of Piaget's theory does not provide a framework for understanding potential interindividual variability in the development of wisdom. Indeed, increasing empirical evidence suggests that, as early as adolescence, differential contextual influences do affect the performance of formal operations (Clayton & Overton, 1976; Denney, 1974; Papalia & Del Vento Bielby, 1974; Piaget, 1972).

Arlin (1975) and Gruber (1973), furthermore, have proposed that there are unique adult-centered tasks that the logical operations of the formal period alone are not structurally able to solve. These adult-centered tasks focus on problem-finding (e.g., creative thought, the envisioning of new questions, and the discovery of new heuristics). Arlin (1975) obtained preliminary data suggesting a sequential, hierarchical relationship between problem-solving and problem-finding. She did not specify, however, what operational properties are inherent to the problem-finding stage that make it qualitatively different from formal operations, nor has she specified the antecedent determinants responsible for advancing the individual from one stage to the next.

4. Cognitive Dialectics

Riegel (1973b) and Chandler (1975) have also identified an adult-centered task, that of being presented with multiple coexisting and logically equiprobable alternatives. The individual must choose a course of action that openly contradicts other choices available. According to Piaget (1970b), a high level of equilibrium is obtained by the formal operational period, and contradictions cannot be entertained because of the logical nature of thought processes. This had led Riegel (1973c; also see Labouvie-Vief & Chandler, 1978) to state that the structures of the formal operational stage fail to represent adequately the dialectical nature of thought and emotions of mature individuals. Riegel (1973b), in fact, has proposed a modification of Piaget's model of cognitive progression in which the basic dialectical nature of thought is incorporated into each developmental stage. At all intellectual levels, therefore, the individual is able to comprehend the interdependence of form and content, cause and effect. Attainment of formal operations, therefore, is not a sufficient precursor to attaining a dialectical understanding of the nature of man and his relationship to the environment.

The dialectical approach to development shares many features with the Eastern disciplines' perception of the basic nature of the universe, the accurate perception of which entitled a man to be called wise (Tart, 1975). A core tenet of both perspectives is the acknowledgment that change is a fundamental property of all phenomena at both an individual and social level. The focus is on processes, activities, or transformations rather than on products or end states (Riegel, 1973c). In this respect, both dialectical and Eastern disciplines support Arlin's (1975) findings of a shift from a problem-solving to a problem-finding orientation in some adults. In Eastern disciplines, the very purpose of the koan was to highlight to the disciple the nonlogical, contradictory, impermanent nature of the universe. The nature of koans was such that the intellect alone could never produce a full understanding of them. The following brief dialogue between Kopp (1976) and a Zen master, talking over the possibility of suicide, captures some of these dialectical notions: "Dying is no solution," the sage affirmed. "And living?", I asked. "Nor living either," he conceded, "but who tells you there is a solution?" (p. 197).

Our models of aging could conceivably be altered if, in fact, achievement of a dialectical perspective characterized the type of knowledge held by an individual who has been developing wisdom. We would begin to view the older person who has wisdom as a seeker who is still exploring life, rather than as an individual who has found and can provide the answers to pressing ontological questions. A wise person would simply not know the answer to, "What is the meaning of life?" any more than an innocent child. A wise person, however, would know that he did not know and this knowledge would be evidence of his wisdom.

B. SUGGESTIONS FOR RESEARCH

The review of the models holding potential for exploring wisdom within a life-span framework have uncovered several important issues for future research. Behavioral criteria that might be used to identify and measure the performance of wise individuals will be drawn from the historical documentation and the reported empirical investigation; three perspectives (evolutionary, cross-cultural, and developmental) that hold potential for structuring future research endeavors will then be outlined. In our view, these perspectives, with roots in modern scientific, humanistic, and life-span inquiry, hold much promise for translating thoughts about wisdom beyond the symbolic presentations of myth, common sense, religion, philosophy, and literature into specific research questions amenable to empirical analysis. It is important to stress that the issues raised within each perspective are intended to highlight this conceptual framework and, by no means, to represent a comprehensive overview of all the issues that will need to be addressed.

1. Behavioral Criteria

A major task for researchers interested in operationalizing the construct of wisdom will be to identify behavioral criteria that will successfully isolate relatively wise from unwise individuals. This is a task posing considerable difficulty, as the criteria may change along with the individual's position in the life cycle. Acknowledging this real limitation, the historical review provides a number of descriptive suggestions.

The historical review established wisdom as a type of knowledge concerned with the nature of man and how he relates to the environment, both in its personal and universal aspects. Possession of this type of knowledge was believed to be manifested in an individual's actions, judgments, values, and personality characteristics. According to the ancient Greeks, a wise individual's actions were considered moral and ethical; his judgments, usually offered in situations of an interpersonal nature, reflected the nonlogical, paradoxical nature of reality.

Solomon's wisdom, for example, was illustrated in the judgment he gave the two women who claimed the same child. Examining his solution, it is interesting to note that it lacked rationality (i.e., to cut the child in half), but reflected a clear understanding of human nature. Indeed, the biological mother's instinctual cry upon hearing Solomon's judgment really determined who the mother was. Another striking feature of Solomon's solution is that it represented a basic contradiction, supporting Riegel's (1975) dialectical position. In the face of a request to preserve life, the solution suggests curtailment of life.

A wise person's values, according to the ancient Eastern tradition, reflect a reduced attachment to material wealth, fame, and power, and stronger attachment to less externally defined criteria of "success in life," namely, personal freedom, health, and happiness (Kapleau, 1965). Thus, the personality of a wise individual has been described in ancient Eastern sources as being childlike without being childish (You, 1972); the individual is highly flexible, sensitive, and able to be entirely in the moment. Suzuki (1960) captured some of these qualities in a description of his master. "When he meets Buddha, he talks in the fashion of a Buddha; when he meets a patriarch, he talks in the fashion of a patriarch; when he meets a hungry ghost, he talks in the fashion of a hungry ghost" (p. 34). The empirical investigation, furthermore, has suggested that receptivity to wisdom-related knowledge could depend upon an individual having, in combination, affective, reflective, as well as intellectual capabilities.

2. Evolutionary Perspective

The literature on wisdom is frequently associated with the postreproductive years. Therefore, it may be useful in future work to explore a possible relation of wisdom to species survival, both in historical and contemporary contexts (Wilson, 1978). In preliterate societies, for example, the precise recollection and recitation of a tribe's history could have considerable import in helping the culture survive through difficult times. What is wisdom's contribution to survival and adaption to the advantages and disadvantages of old age in our technological society? If wisdom is highly correlated with time and represents a knowledge related to understanding the meaning of life, a longer life might imply a more thorough comprehension of this type of knowledge. Examination of the relative amounts of wisdom in short-lived versus long-lived families could shed some light on this issue.

Another evolution-related perspective stems from the fact that, historically, wisdom was considered a viable social and political concept as well as a personological, individual quality (Rad, 1972). Ancient Athens, for example, was considered the seat of wisdom (Adler, 1955). It appears that in our contemporary world, however, wisdom has less social significance or status. Bertrand Russell (1969) noted this when he commented, "that although our age far surpasses all previous ages in knowledge, there has been no correlative increase in wisdom" (p. 123). What factors have contributed to the decreased social saliency of wisdom over the ages? Related to evolution is also wisdom's potential relationship to neurobiological development. Smith (1978), in his article on selfhood, notes that questions of an ontological nature (e.g., whence we came into the world, why we are here, and what happens when we die) are an inherent side effect of the development of language and symbolization. Neurobiological research on the development of consciousness in man (Ornstein, 1972), therefore, might also provide fruitful avenues along which to proceed for operationalizing wisdom as a life-span developmental construct.

3. Cross-Cultural Perspective

Wisdom has the benefit of cross-cultural validity as well as historical relevance. Future research investigations will need to examine the concept of wisdom in other cultures to identify what aspects of wisdom (e.g., type of knowledge, methods of transmission, manner of development) are universal and transcend the standards and values of a particular society. Wisdom may play a more important role in other cultures, and we may compare consequences for mental and social roles for the elderly in the light of such an emphasis.

4. Developmental Perspective

A developmental perspective focuses on exploring how the individual achieves wisdom in the course of a lifetime.

In line with some current analytic models of life-span development, one goal would be the identification of the specific age-graded, history-graded, and nonnormative (Baltes *et al.,* 1980) life-event determinants that are necessary for the emergence and maintenance of wisdom. It could be that it is the joint knowledge and experience of each of the three influence systems listed (age-graded, etc.) that is a necessary, though not sufficient, condition for the emergence of wisdom.

Another proposition for future investigations is that the development of wisdom is not hindered by normative, maturational changes that lead to decline (e.g., the loss of physical strength, slowing in psychomotor speed) but utilizes those skills that undergo improvement in performance over time such as indices of information, verbal knowledge, and introspection (Gutmann, 1977; Horn & Cattell, 1966, 1967; Schaie & Gribbin, 1975). Contextual factors that are time- but not age-dependent need particular consideration. Although wisdom has always been associated with advancing age, the empirical analysis of wisdom presented earlier indicated that not all old people are necessarily perceived as being wise. Type, number, timing, and ways of processing life experience might prove to be significant factors related to the achievement of wisdom. Contextual variables examined should include not only events, but people-related interactions as well.

The developmental functions for the concept of intelligence have been elucidated over a broad range of the adult years, largely because of longitudinal assessment and utilization of sequential strategies. It will be a challenge to measure the particular life-course developmental functions for the intuitive and affective components. It will be of interest to see if the functions differ across cohorts from epoch to epoch as in the specific case of intellectual development. The historical review suggested that wisdom, by the nature of the type of knowledge it represents, is timeless, as opposed to time-bound. Translating this into the life-span developmental orientation, empirical research will need to determine if wisdom-related knowledge evidences a greater degree of interindividual universality than intellectual knowledge. If it does, it suggests that methods of transmitting wisdom-related knowledge may be less formal (e.g., through father–son linkages) than the methods we employ to transmit intellectual knowledge (e.g., attendance at school).

Awareness of measurement issues in the life-span orientation might help shape a methodological framework appropriate for the study of wisdom. The issues of structural and quantitative change, measurement equivalence, and the competence–performance distinction might prove to be useful in long range research investigations. As a multivariate life-span quality, representing the integration of perceived cognitive, affective, and reflective abilities, the structural organization of wisdom might not remain invariant over time; ability levels might not remain the same. Sensitivity to the possibility of structural as well as quantitative changes over time would be important. The issue of measurement equivalence is central to the task of developing assessment techniques for measuring behaviors, actions, judgments, and personality characteristics of wise people. Different sets of predictive validity criteria might be needed, depending on the level of wisdom the individual possesses. Finally, ability-intrinsic versus ability-extrinsic factors, known to developmental psychologists as the issue of competence versus performance, might also prove central to empirical research. Wisdom, in its early life manifestations, for example, might be more of a state, specifically evoked and initiated by a situation. In later phases of the life cycle, after the individual has experienced and absorbed basic patterns and cycles, it might become more of an internalized trait, inherent to the individual and somewhat freed from action.

Description of the major wisdom-related developmental functions across the life cycle and explanation of the antecedent mechanisms responsible for its development should occupy research investigations for many years to come. The life-span orientation also holds much promise for use of intervention strategies designed for the purpose of helping people realize and optimize their wisdom. Intervention research in late adulthood and old age presents a generally consistent pattern of positive outcomes (Baltes *et al.*, 1980; Labouvie-Vief, 1976) supporting evidence of intraindividual plasticity. In this context, there is much to be gained from closely examining the ancient Eastern and Western traditions' approaches to wisdom, particularly with respect to the concept's link with the learning process. Future research investigations will need to explore the validity of various pedagogical methods for transmitting wisdom-related knowledge. The effects of role modeling, and creation of situations that give the student the opportunity to experience this type of knowledge directly must be created and compared to the more traditional ways of transmitting knowledge represented in our present educational systems. If receptivity to wisdom-related knowledge proves to be dependent upon cognitive, affective, and intuitive evaluations, the Western educational systems might become increasingly susceptive to dealing not only with intellectual but also intuitive and affective abilities.

V. Summary and Conclusions

Research in the field of life-span developmental psychology has tended to neglect those qualities that might be unique to, and representative of, development in late adulthood. The concept of wisdom has always enjoyed a positive association with the later years of life; in the past, it has also had social significance as a model for adults and as a guiding principle for ancient societies. With an increasing proportion of our population reaching the later years of life, there appears to be more momentum to create meaningful roles for the postretirement segment of our population. Wisdom might prove to be one important criterion variable for qualifying individuals for such roles. It might also be an emergent and advantageous quality of development in later life and descriptive of successful adaptation to the later years. The purpose of this chapter, therefore, has been to launch an exploration of wisdom and consider its relevance to life-span development.

The concept itself has an extensive history and has played a major role in the maintenance of societies and in the development of the individual. A summary of its position in ancient Eastern and Western traditions is presented. Both traditions considered wisdom to be a type of knowledge involving an understanding of ontological issues and both believed that a period of tutelage and the passage of time were necessary components in the acquisition of this type of knowledge. The Western tradition stressed the importance of the intellect and reason, whereas ancient Eastern traditions shared the conviction that too much intellectual analysis would impede its acquisition. The Eastern disciplines stressed the importance of contemplation and compassion. Eastern and Western traditions did not agree, therefore, on the differential importance of the human abilities essential for obtaining wisdom or the kind of educational procedures best suited for its development.

To assess what human abilities were perceived to underlie the behaviors of wise individuals, a multidimensional scaling analysis of the concept was undertaken. The results from this empirical investigation indicated that young, middle-aged, and older individuals all perceived wisdom as a multidimensional attribute involving the *integration* of general cognitive, affective, and reflective components. Age differences in the perceived structural organization of wisdom were also found. Older individuals identified a time component of wisdom. Unlike the two younger groups, they also perceived the affective qualities of understanding and empathy as being more similar to wisdom than to chronological age or to experience. This latter finding was further supported by the absence of a perceived relationship between the participant's own aging process and wisdom. The older individuals, in other words, did not judge themselves as possessing more or less wisdom than did the middle-aged or younger individuals, though the two younger groups attributed wisdom to the older persons.

The next section of this chapter examined the relationship between wisdom and specific developmental theories that have considered progressive aspects of change in adulthood. Some aspects of Erikson, Kohlberg, and Piaget's approaches to development judged to be particularly promising for the study of wisdom were highlighted. In addition, it was noted that the recent concern with dialectics has several features in common with the ancient conceptualization of the type of knowledge held by wise individuals. Identification of the postformal operational stage of problem finding was also seen as holding promise for understanding the orientation adopted by wise individuals in adult-centered tasks. Embedding wisdom in a developmental framework encompassing the entire life span might also affect our models of aging. The older person who has wisdom would be perceived as a seeker who is still exploring life, rather than as an individual who has found and can provide the answers to pressing ontological questions.

A major task for researchers interested in operationalizing the construct of wisdom will be to identify relevant behavioral criteria that will isolate relatively wise from unwise individuals. The historical review and empirical investigation suggest that wisdom is manifested in an individual's actions, judgments, values, and personality characteristics. A wise individual has affective, reflective, as well as intellectual skills for evaluating information and knowledge. Three perspectives; evolutionary, cross-cultural, and developmental, are proposed for structuring future research investigations. The evolutionary perspective focuses on how wisdom is related to species survival; the cross-cultural perspective captures research designed to identify the universal and culture-specific features of wisdom; the developmental perspective focuses on how the individual achieves wisdom in the course of a lifetime.

In this chapter, wisdom has been described as a type of knowledge, as a multidimensional attribute, as a guiding principle of ancient societies, as well as an untapped potential of the individual. If having wisdom is an advantage during adulthood, and old age, a broader appreciation of its cultivation within the individual, and rewards for the social contributions made by those who possess it, is warranted. Presently, our technological society encourages productivity rather than reflection and values problem-solving abilities rather than perceiving the assets of a broad questioning approach. The benefits, therefore, of turning our research efforts towards adult-centered tasks and the psychological processes of mature adults may spread the realization that knowledge explosions of mastery of specific developmental tasks are not enough. In themselves, they do not lead to the well-being of the individual nor do they necessarily help in the acquisition of wisdom.

Acknowledgments

The research reported in this chapter was supported, in part, by a predoctoral dissertation research grant from the Administration on Aging, Department of Health, Education and Welfare. A number of colleagues read a draft version of this chapter, and provided insightful comments. For this effort we wish to thank K. W. Schaie, G. Vaillant, J. Whiting, S. Brent, and J. Amodeo.

References

Adler, M. *The great ideas: A syntopicon of great books of the western world.* Chicago: Encyclopedia Britannica, 1955.

Aquinas, T. *The wisdom of Thomas Aquinas.* New York: Peter Pauper Press, 1951.

Arabie, P., Kosslyn, S. M., & Nelson, K. E. A multidimensional scaling study of visual memory of 5-year-olds and adults. *Journal of Experimental Child Psychology,* 1975, **19,** 327–345.

Arlin, P. K. Cognitive development in adulthood: A fifth stage? *Developmental Psychology,* 1975, **11,** 602–606.

Baltes, P. B. Life-span developmental psychology: Some converging observations on history and theory. In P. B. Baltes & O. G. Brim (Eds.), *Life-span development and behavior* (Vol. 2). New York: Academic Press, 1979.

Baltes, P. B., Reese, H. W., & Lipsitt, L. P. Life-span developmental psychology, *Annual Review of Psychology,* 1980, **31,** 65–110.

Baltes, P. B., & Labouvie, G. V. Adult development of intellectual performance: Description, explanation, and modification. In C. Eisdorfer & M. P. Lawton (Eds.), *The psychology of adult development and aging.* Washington, D.C.: American Psychological Association, 1973.

Baltes, P. B., & Willis, S. L. Toward psychological theories of aging and development. In J. E. Birren & K. W. Schaie (Eds.), *Handbook of the psychology of aging.* New York: Van Nostrand Reinhold, 1977.

Baltes, P. B., & Willis, S. L. The critical importance of appropriate methodology in the study of aging: The sample case of psychometric intelligence. In F. Hoffmeister (Ed.), *The evaluation of old-age-related changes and disorders of brain functions.* Heidelberg: Springer, 1979. (a)

Baltes, P. B., & Willis, S. L. Life-span developmental psychology, cognitive functioning and social policy. In M. W. Riley (Ed.), *Aging from birth to death.* Boulder, Colo.: Westview Press, 1979. (b)

Birren, J. E., & Renner, V. J. Research on the psychology of aging: Principles and experimentation. In J. E. Birren & K. W. Schaie (Eds.), *Handbook of the psychology of aging.* New York: Van Nostrand Reinhold, 1977.

Birren, J. E., & Woodruff, D. S. Human development over the life span through education. In P. B. Baltes & K. W. Schaie (Eds.), *Life-span developmental psychology: Personality and socialization.* New York: Academic Press, 1973.

Bokser, B. Z. *The wisdom of the Talmud: A thousand years of thought.* New York: Philosophical Library, 1951.

Chandler, M. J. Relativism and the problem of epistemological loneliness. *Human Development,* 1975, **18,** 171–180.

Clayton, V. Erikson's theory of human development as it applies to the aged: Wisdom as contradictive cognition. *Human Development,* 1975, **18,** 119–128. (a)

Clayton, V. The meaning of wisdom to young and old in contemporary society. Paper presented at the meeting of the Gerontological Society, Louisville, October, 1975. (b)

Clayton, V. A multidimensional scaling analysis of the concept of wisdom. Unpublished doctoral dissertation, University of Southern California, 1976.

Clayton, V., & Overton, W. Concrete and formal thought processes in young adulthood and old age. *International Journal of Aging and Human Development,* 1976, **7,** 237–245.

Cliff, N. Orthogonal rotation of congruence. *Psychometrika,* 1966, **31,** 33–42.

Conze, E. *Buddhist wisdom books.* New York: Harper & Row, 1958.

Cragg, K. *The wisdom of the Sufis.* New York: New Directions, 1976.

Cronbach, L., & Meehl, P. Construct validity in psychological tests. *Psychological Bulletin,* 1955, **52**, 281-302.

Denney, N. Classification abilities in the elderly. *Journal of Gerontology,* 1974, **29**, 309-314.

Erikson, E. *Identity and the life cycle.* New York: International University Press, 1959.

Erikson, E. *Insight and responsibility.* New York: Norton, 1964.

Erikson, E. *Identity, youth and crisis.* New York: Norton, 1968.

Garnett, C. B. *Wisdom in conduct: An introduction to ethics.* New York: Harcourt Brace, 1940.

Gruber, H. E. Courage and cognitive growth in children and scientists. In M. Schwebel & J. Raph (Eds.), *Piaget in the classroom.* New York: Basic Books, 1973.

Gruen, W. Adult personality: An empirical study of Erikson's theory of ego development. In B. Neugarten (Ed.), *Personality in middle and late life.* New York: Atherton, 1964.

Guilford, J. P. *Psychometric methods.* New York: McGraw-Hill, 1954.

Gutmann, D. The cross-cultural perspective: Notes toward a comparative psychology of aging. In J. E. Birren & K. W. Schaie (Eds.), *The handbook of the psychology of aging.* New York: Van Nostrand Reinhold Company, 1977.

Hall, G. S. (anonymous). Old age. *Atlantic Monthly,* January 1921.

Horn, J. L., & Cattell, R. S. Refinement and test of the theory of fluid and crystallized intelligence. *Journal of Educational Psychology,* 1966, **57**, 253-170.

Horn, J. L., & Cattell, R. S. Age differences in fluid and crystallized intelligence. *Psychologica,* 1967, **26**, 107-129.

Howard, D. V., & Howard, J. H. A multidimensional scaling analysis of the development of animal names. *Developmental Psychology,* 1977, **13**, 108-113.

Humphreys, C. *The wisdom of Buddhism.* New York: Random House, 1961.

Inhelder, B., & Piaget, J. *Growth of logical thinking from childhood to adolescence.* New York: Basic Books, 1958.

Kapleau, P. (Ed.). *The three pillars of Zen.* Boston: Beacon Press, 1965.

Kohlberg, L. Continuities in childhood and adult moral development revisited. In P. B. Baltes & K. W. Schaie (Eds.), *Life-span developmental psychology: Personality and socialization.* New York: Academic Press, 1973. (a)

Kohlberg, L. Stages and aging in moral development: Some speculations. *Gerontologist,* 1973, **13**, 497-502. (b)

Kopp, S. *If you meet the Buddha on the road, kill him.* New York: Bantam Books, 1976.

Kosslyn, S. M., Pick, H. L., Jr., & Fariello, G. R. Cognitive maps in children and men. *Child Development,* 1974, **45**, 707-716.

Kruskal, J. Multidimensional scaling by optimizing goodness-of-fit to a nonmetric hypothesis. *Psychometrika,* 1964, **29**, 1-28.

Labouvie-Vief, G. Toward optimizing cognitive competence in later life. *Educational Gerontology: An International Quarterly,* 1976, **1**, 75-92.

Labouvie-Vief, G. Adult cognitive development: In search of alternative interpretations. *Merrill-Palmer Quarterly,* 1977, **23**, 227-263.

Labouvie-Vief, G., & Chandler, M. Cognitive development and life-span developmental theory: Idealistic versus contextual perspectives. In P. B. Baltes (Ed.), *Life-span development and behavior.* New York: Academic Press, 1978.

Lavouvie-Vief, G., Hoyer, W., Baltes, M. M., and Baltes, P. B. Operant analysis of intellectual behavior in old age. *Human Development,* 1974, **17**, 259-272.

Lerner, R. & Ryff, C. Inplementation of the life-span view of human development: The sample case of attachment. In P. B. Baltes (Eds.), *Life-span development and behavior* (Vol. 1). New York: Academic Press, 1978.

Lin, Y. *The wisdom of China.* London: M. Joseph, 1948.

Lobsang, R. *The wisdom of the ancients.* London: Transworld Press, 1965.

Lowenthal, M. F. Toward a sociopsychological theory of change in adulthood and old age. In J. E. Birren & K. W. Schaie (Eds.), *The handbook of the psychology of aging*. New York: Van Nostrand Reinhold, 1977.

McFayden, J. E. *The wisdom books*. London: J. Clarke, 1921.

McTavish, D. G. Perceptions of old people: A review of research methodologies and findings. *The Gerontologist Third Report*, 1971–72, 90–101.

Neugarten, B. L., Moore, J. O., & Lowe, J. C. Age norms, age constraints, and adult socialization. *American Journal of Sociology*, 1965, **70**, 710–717.

Nogar, R. *The wisdom of evolution*. New York: New American Library, 1966.

Noth, M., & Thomas, D. W. *Wisdom in Israel and the ancient near east*. Leiden: E. J. Brill, 1955.

Oesterley, W. *The wisdom of Egypt and the Old Testament in the light of the newly discovered teaching of Amen-em-ope*. New York: Macmillan, 1927.

Ornstein, R. *The psychology of consciousness*. San Francisco: W. H. Freeman, 1972.

Overton, W., & Reese, H. W. Models of development: Methodological implications. In J. R. Nesselroade & H. W. Reese (Eds.), *Life-span developmental psychology: Methodological implications*. New York: Academic Press, 1973.

Owens, C. Zen Buddhism. In C. Tart (Ed.), *Transpersonal psychologies*. New York: Harper & Row, 1975.

Oxford English Dictionary. Oxford: Oxford University Press, 1933.

Papalia, D. E., & Del Vanto Bielby, D. Cognitive functioning in middle and old adults: A review of research based on Piaget's theory. *Human Development*, 1974, **17**, 424–443.

Paterson, J. *The wisdom of Israel*. New York: Abingdon Press, 1972.

Pelletier, K., & Garfield, C. *Consciousness East and West*. New York: Harper & Row, 1976.

Perdue, L. *Wisdom and cult: A critical analysis of the views of cult in wisdom literatures of Israel and the ancient near east*. Missoula: Scholars Press, 1977.

Piaget, J. *Genetic epistemology*. New York: Columbia University Press, 1970. (a)

Piaget, J. *Structuralism*. New York: Basic Books, 1970. (b)

Piaget, J. Intellectual evolution from adolescence to adulthood. *Human Development*, 1972, **15**, 1–12.

Rad, G. *Wisdom in Israel*. New York: Abingdon Press, 1972.

Reese, H. W., & Overton, W. Models of development and theories of development. In L. R. Goulet & P. B. Baltes (Eds.), *Life-span developmental psychology: Research and theory*. New York: Academic Press, 1970.

Reps, P. *Zen flesh, zen bones*. New York: Doubleday, 1961.

Riegel, K. F. Developmental psychology and society: Some historical and ethical considerations. In J. R. Nesselroade & H. W. Reese (Eds.), *Life-span developmental psychology: Methodological issues*. New York: Academic Press, 1973. (a)

Riegel, K. F. Dialectic operations: The final period of cognitive development. *Human Development*, 1973, **16**, 346–370. (b)

Riegel, K. F. An epitaph for a paradigm. *Human Development*, 1973, **16**, 1–7. (c)

Riegel, K. F. From traits and equilibrium towards developmental dialectics. In W. Arnold (Ed.), *Nebraska symposium on motivation*. Lincoln: University of Nebraska Press, 1975. (a)

Rokeach, M. *On the nature of human values*. New York: Free Press, 1973.

Russell, B. *The autobiography of Bertrand Russell 1944–1969* (Vol. 3). New York: Simon and Schuster, 1969.

Schaie, K. W. Toward a stage theory of adult cognitive development. *Journal of Aging and Human Development*, **8**(2) 1977–1978, 129–138.

Schaie, K. W. The primary mental abilities in adulthood: An explanation in the development of psychometric intelligence. In P. B. Baltes & O. G. Brim, Jr. (Eds.), *Life-span development and behavior* (Vol. 2). New York: Academic Press, 1979.

Schaie, K. W., & Gribbin, K. Adult development and aging. *Annual Review of Psychology,* 1975, **26**, 65-96.

Shepard, R. N., Romney, K., & Nerlove, S. *Multidimensional scaling: Theory and applications in the behavioral sciences.* New York: Seminar Press, 1972.

Smith, B. On Selfhood. *American Psychologist,* 1978, **33**, 1053-63.

Suzuki, D. T. Lectures on Zen Buddhism. In E. Fromm, D. T. Suzuki, E. R. DeMartino, *Zen Buddhism and psychoanalysis.* New York: Harper & Row, 1960.

Tart, C. (Ed.). *Transpersonal psychologies,* New York: Harper & Row, 1975.

Thomas, E. J. *Tripitaka, the quest of enlightenment: A selection of the Buddhist scriptures.* London: Murray, 1950.

Torgerson, W. S. *Theory and methods of scaling.* New York: Wiley, 1958.

Tucker, L. R., & Messick, S. An individual difference model for multidimensional scalings. *Psychometrika,* 1963, **28**, 333-367.

Wilson, E. O. *On human nature.* Cambridge: Harvard University Press, 1978.

Yogananda, P. *The autobiography of a yogi.* Los Angeles: Self Realization Fellowship, 1946.

You, Y. H. *Wisdom of the far east.* Washington, D.C.: Far Eastern Research and Publications Center, 1972.

Aging and Parenthood in the Middle Years

Alice S. Rossi

UNIVERSITY OF MASSACHUSETTS

AMHERST, MASSACHUSETTS

Abstract

This chapter reviews the two primary theoretical models of adult development in the middle years—the normative-crisis model, and the timing-of-events model. Applying a life-course perspective, the samples of middle-aged subjects in recent research are shown to have special cohort characteristics in common; and applying a biosocial perspective, research on the middle years is found to neglect physiological variables. Research findings are reported from an exploratory study of middle-aged mothers of early adolescent children, in which life-course and biosocial perspectives guided the design. Several dimensions of age are analyzed in relation to chronological age of the mothers: subjective age identification, desired age, ideal age, and minimum death age. Actual maternal age is then analyzed for its relation to aging and cohort membership, both of which are shown to be relevant to an understanding of the mother-child relationship during early adolescence.

I. Introduction

The central question posed in the exploratory research reported in this chapter was a deceptively simple one: does the age of a mother make a difference to the family world experienced by early adolescents, and if so, how and why does maternal age matter? The question was posed from four perspectives on human development: (*a*) life-span developmental psychology; (*b*) the sociology of the life course; (*c*) biosocial science; and (*d*) family sociology. In isolating phases of the life span—early adolescence and middle age—developmental psychology was relevant to the question. In focusing on contemporary parents of early adolescents, the historical sensitivity to cohort differences made a sociological perspective on the life course relevant. In dealing with phases of the life span in which individuals undergo significant physiological as well as social psychological changes, a biosocial science perspective was relevant. And in specifically focusing on the relationship between parent and child rather than on individual development in early adolescence or middle age, family sociology entered the problem formulation.

The exploratory nature of the research must be stressed from the outset. The findings are offered only in an illustrative way. Precisely because we wished to blend the perspectives of several disciplines, and to explore the utility of new empirical definitions for some key concepts, the project, on a shoestring budget was limited to a small local sample of 68 families. As elaborated in what follows, this also determined both subjects and method: written questionnaires in a mail survey to mothers of early adolescent children. Hence the intent of both the study and this chapter is as much problem formulation as research reporting.

In this introductory section, we shall position our central research question against the backdrop of the four disciplinary perspectives noted. In doing so, we shall make assertions more fully amplified in the sections that follow.

A. PARENTING IN THE MIDDLE YEARS

Parents of early adolescents are, for the most part, adults in their middle years. There are of course exceptions: A birth to a teenage girl can lead to an under-30-year-old mother of a 14-year-old child. The drop in age of menarche, relaxed sexual standards, and resistance to effective contraception by teenagers has in fact produced a recent upturn in the number of such teenage pregnancies and births. But taking a more typical restriction of births to the age range from 20 to 35, within which most births now take place, still means the mother of one 14-year-old might be 34, whereas the mother of another 14-year-old might be 50. In our sample, the age range of mothers of at least one early adolescent child between 12 and 16 years of age was 33 to 56 years of age, a span of 5 years for the adolescent children and 23 years for their mothers. Hence the literature on the middle years in developmental psychology was relevant for what it might illuminate about adult development in the middle years in general, and of parenting in specific. We found, however, serious limitations to this literature in formulating our research: It deals largely with men, with job and career progression more than family role development; it varies in how middle age is defined, and typically contains little more than a few ritual comments on the relevance of physiological aging factors to the changes observed in midlife.

While there has been heightened attention to the middle years in recent developmental research, it is often as an unintended consequence of research focused on quite other periods of the life line. Some research on old age has used middle-aged subjects simply to provide a comparative criterion, without any specific theory concerning adult development in the middle years. So too, as adolescence was extended through longer formal schooling, and policy issues focused on facilitating occupational choice in advanced technical and scientific specialties in the post-Sputnik era, research attention extended from late adolescence to early adulthood. Kenniston (1970) coined the label of "Youth" to capture this new phase between adolescence and full adulthood, but again the extension forward into adulthood from adolescence, like appending middle age to research on old age, was not guided by theoretical interests in development in early adulthood. In the same way, as the social sciences were sensitized to the cohort and historical dimensions of age and away from maturational change assumptions when faced with age differences, longitudinal studies were given priority, with the result that studies begun in earlier decades were reactivated and their subjects newly approached at a time when they were in their early to middle years. A number of projects are now under-way, if not yet in print, that are follow-up studies from samples begun with adolescents of high school or college age, who are now in their thirties and forties. Their focus has been either on career progression or the timing of job and family events.

The recent spurt of newly published studies on the middle years deals largely with particular birth cohorts, subjects first studied in childhood in the decade of the 1920s or early 1930s. Prominent examples of this are George Vaillant's *Adaptation to Life* (1977), reporting the results of a 30-year follow-up of Harvard sophomores into their late forties and fifties, and Glen Elder's work (Elder, 1974; Elder & Rockwell, 1976) on the Oakland Growth and Berkeley Guidance study samples, also adults in their late forties and fifties by 1970. These longitudinal studies have been joined by cross-sectional investigations of the middle years (e.g., in Daniel Levin-son's *The Seasons of a Man's Life* (1978), Marjorie Lowenthal's *Four Stages of Life* (Lowenthal, Thurnher, & Chiriboga, 1975), of which one is middle age, and Lillian Rubin's *Women of a Certain Age* (1979). More popularized analyses of the middle years are represented by Gail Sheehy's bestseller, *Passages* (1977), and Roger Gould's *Transformations* (1978).

From the perspective of our concern for aging and parenthood in the middle years, and how parental age affects the family world experienced by early adolescents, there is little help from such life-span research on the middle years. This is either because the focus is typically on individual growth and change along the life line, with no attention to the age of children in relation to the ages of their parents, or because parenting per se was not the focus of the research.

B. FAMILY STAGES OR FAMILY CYCLES

Whereas psychologists paid little attention to parenting in the middle years, sociologists have tended to study little else but parenting in midlife. Yet ironically, family stage typologies have been defined, not in terms of parental age, but in terms of the age of the youngest child. A typical exam-ple is Hill's (1964) nine-stage model of the family cycle, with such stage labels as "Establishment" (newly married, childless); "New Parents" (married, a child under 3), or "Postparental" (married, no children at home). Such typologies have little utility for our purposes because each stage embraces a wide span of years among parents: a postparental phase may include people in their sixties as well as those in their forties, depending on the timing, number, and spacing of births. Recent inquiry also suggests problems in the age-referent of postparental definitions. Borland (1978) has shown that the postparental phase is not typical of married people in their forties, a decade we would surely include in any phase definition of middle age, but in their fifties. From Institute of Survey Research (ISR) quality of life survey data, she shows that until men and women pass their 55th birthday, the modal household in the United States was a married couple with at least one child under 18 still living at home. With a very broad definition of middle age from 35 to 64 years of age, this would mean only one in four couples are postparental (Borland, 1978). It therefore seems inappropriate to define middle age as the span of years between the departure of the youngest child and an adult's retirement, for it would exclude entirely too many middle-aged adults who are still actively involved in rearing and supporting adolescent children.

One might also question whether and when any parent becomes postparental. The label itself suggests the termination of a role, when what may transpire is better described as a transition to a new phase of parenting. The lengthened period of time for advanced schooling means economic responsibility for children until they reach their early twenties, and the high unemployment rate among young people under 25 often means economic responsibility for children over 18 who are neither working nor attending school. In 1976, 18% of 16–19-year-olds were unemployed, and 12% of 20–24-year-olds, with higher rates for males than females in these age groups (U.S. Department of Labor, 1977). It is curious that although the extension of schooling has been discussed from the point of view of a new stage of life among contemporary young people, the implication for parenting (i.e., that parenting too has a new phase), has been neither noted nor researched.

For our research purposes, it seemed clear that there was sufficient variation in the timing of births and family size to expect a wide range in the chronological ages of parents of early adolescent children, and hence the opportunity to explore whether or not parental age, specified in terms of physiological change, family role development, or cohort membership, illuminated both important but neglected aspects of adult development in the middle years and the emotional and social climate in the families of young adolescents.

C. PARENTAL AGING AND ADOLESCENT STRESS

The family sociologist's interest in social relations, if blended with a concern for peak periods of physiological change along the life line, might contribute to a better understanding of both sides of the parent–child relationship. We know, from previous work, that early adolescence involves a great deal of physical growth and change, erratic levels of endocrine secretion, and major transitions in the social ecology of the child—change in schools, shifts from family to peers, early experimentation with heterosexual relations, and so on (Hamburg, 1974). It was the special blend of biological and social–psychological change in early adolescence that sparked our interest in this phase of child development in the first place.

But this was equally true of the parents of young adolescents, particularly older parents in their forties who are experiencing their own endocrine irregularity and change, and a whole range of new manifestations of aging in their bodies—skin, hair, teeth, vision, body shape, muscle tone, daily rhythm, sleep needs, among others. The key insight in formulating the research was the hypothesis that the "winding down" parent may be as hard for adolescents to live with as the "winding up" adolescent is difficult for the parents to live with. Yet strained family relationships involving adolescents tend to be interpreted in terms of either the child's biopsychological changes, intergenerational clashes in values, pathological qualities in the parental marriage or in relations to the adolescent. Similarly, when sociologists note that the low point of morale and satisfaction among parents tends to be when their children are adolescents, and the postparental phase by comparison shows an improvement in morale and satisfaction (Deutscher, 1964, 1969; Feldman & Feldman, 1975; Spanier, Lewis, & Cole, 1975; Troll, 1971), the interpretation again focuses on the adolescent, either the volatile quality of the child at this age in testing the limits of parental tolerance, or the economic squeeze on the parents supporting their children through the most expensive phase of child rearing (Oppenheimer, 1974, 1976, 1977). But the parents' own developmental stress may be a contributor in both instances, feeding into the adolescents' stress, or complicating parental ability to cope with a growing-up child while they deal with their own aging, mortality issues, or shifts in time perspective. Hence research on the physiological components of aging, and the psychological meaning of age to the parents of adolescent children could illuminate not only an important dimension of adult development in the middle years, but adolescent development and family development as well.

D. LIFE–COURSE PERSPECTIVE

An exciting development of the past decade in the social sciences has been the fertile interaction between the fields of historical demography, social history, and family studies in sociology. Elder (1978a) has given a good review of this history, made an important contribution to its development (Elder, 1978b), and demonstrated the importance of blending historical sensitivity with family analysis in his *Children of the Great Depression* (1974). A life-course perspective focuses on the pathways through the age-differentiated life span in the major role domains of life, and involves the search for social patterns in the timing, duration, spacing, and order of events along the life line (Elder, 1978b).

The life-course perspective has several intellectual roots: One is the use of a demographic concept of cohort (Ryder, 1965) particularly as this has affected the new specialty of age stratification in sociology (Riley, 1972, 1976), and a process view of family development (e.g., Rodgers, 1973). Elder's (1974) analysis of the long-lasting effects of the differential impact of the depression on California families is a good example of the use of historically based structural factors to illuminate adult behavior and values of a particular cohort, illustrating Ryder's (1965) point that "a cohort is distinctly marked by the career stage it occupies when prosperity or depression, peace or war, impinge on it" (p. 846). It was the blending of the demographic concept of cohort with sociological ideas of family development that stimulated the collaborative work by family historians, demographers, and sociologists in the analysis of 1880 census data, now brought together in a remarkable collection of essays in Tamara Hareven's (1978) *Transitions: The Family and the Life Course in Historical Perspective.*

Cohort analysis and a life-course perspective are having a growing impact on sociology, nowhere more apparent than in family studies, which increasingly show sensitivity to the historical context within which subjects grow up and live out their adult lives. Young people's access to jobs, timing of marriage, size of family, and employment of women is more likely now than in the past to be examined in terms of the size of one cohort compared to others; cohort size in turn reflects, on an aggregate level, the impact of historical events on individual life decisions, and carries far-reaching consequences as differentially sized cohorts ripple through the age-stratification system (Riley, 1972, 1976; Ryder, 1978).

Life-course research has benefited by the existence of data sets on relatively narrow birth cohorts (e.g., the Berkeley Guidance Study, in which all the subjects were born in 1928 or 1929, or the Oakland Growth

Study of slightly older subjects, born in 1920 and 1921). This narrow age range permitted a careful tracing of the impact of historical events upon highly specific cohorts as they moved through the life line. Life-course researchers have added social and economic variables to early family influences in our schemes accounting for adult behavior, tracing whether and how these early external social factors affected subsequent adult choices and life styles. Thus Bennett and Elder (1979) have shown how maternal employment during the depression, as mothers adapted to the harsh press of the times on family economy, continued to influence the work histories of their daughters, and even the daughters' wishes for their own daughters' life plans several decades later.

But life-course sociologists have contributed little to theories about adult development. It is our reading that recent sociological efforts to disentangle maturational from cohort and period effects do not have any theoretical concern for phases of adult development; indeed, they typically have more interest in the effects of historical time or cohort size and composition, than in the process of aging. In political sociology, for example, the substantive interest is apt to be on political attitudes, party affiliation, and work alienation. Through the use of national surveys that included measures on these political or work variables in surveys administered at several points in time, sociologists can disentangle maturational from cohort effects (e.g., Bengston & Cutler, 1976), following an analysis model similar to that of life-span psychologists (e.g., Nesselroade & Baltes, 1974), though with adult rather than adolescent subjects. But the sociologists engaged in such analysis are more apt to be testing a theory of political behavior or of historical change in political processes than a theory of aging or adult development; hence their delight with the robustness of cohort or historical effects which they have the theories to interpret.

The life-span developmental psychologist faces a rather different dilemma from the life-course sociologist: Because there is no general theory of adult development, and because adulthood lasts such a long time, it is difficult to select a meaningful cohort of adults for study of age-related maturational processes, much less to attempt to differentiate such processes from the cohort and period effects that qualify or constrain maturational interpretations of age-difference findings. Perhaps this is why so much of the recent literature with a life-span perspective is illustrative of efforts at conceptual refinement or programmatic calls for new research, rather than of empirical demonstrations of the analytic utility of the perspective on adulthood.

In approaching a research project on contemporary middle-aged parents of early adolescents, there are limits to the applicability of the life-course perspective. One can be sensitive to the demographic characteristics of the rather broadly defined birth cohorts represented by the parents and the children they have produced. Knowing the parents' ages permits a sketch of the historical events taking place at selected points along their life lines. Knowing that these middle-aged parents produced the baby boom, and that most of their families are relatively large by today's fertility standards, we can explicitly explore the impact of family size upon the parents' report of the difficulty of adolescent child rearing in the inflationary 1970s. These are important qualifiers if they guard against the tendency to interpret findings as reflections of maturational phase or parental role rather than as the cohort-specific characteristic of large family size in an inflationary period of social and economic history.

We have drawn upon both the life-span and the life-course perspective in formulating the research on aging and parenting in the middle years. Toward that end, it is useful to examine recent research on the middle years by life-span psychologists, and to assess that work through the filter of life-course and biosocial perspectives. It is to this review and assessment that the next section of the chapter is addressed. We shall then cull, from that review, several issues for exploration with the data from the pilot study of middle-aged mothers of adolescents, and conclude with some suggestions for future research on the middle years.

II.   Life-Span Theories of Development in the Middle Years

Two perspectives can be identified in recent work on adult development in a life-span framework: a normative-crisis model, on the one hand, and a timing-of-events model, on the other. They are not specific to development in the middle years, but apply in a more general way to the long stretch of adulthood. But they are either explicitly or implicitly present in most of the research on middle age. We shall first sketch the major foci of each life-span model and then review them from a life course and biosocial perspective.

A.   NORMATIVE–CRISIS MODEL

The Erikson (1959) theory of life-cycle development has been followed, if not always acknowledged, by those who adhere to a crisis model of adult development. This theory assumes an inherent ground plan to all human development: Erikson argued that, as in embryological development, each developmental task has its "time of special ascendancy," and that if a task appropriate to a given phase of life is not resolved, it impairs development in all subsequent phases of life. Thus the resolution of an "identity" task in adolescence is a precondition to the successful resolution of an "intimacy" task in early adulthood. "Integrity" in old age is premised on successful resolution of the "generativity" issue of middle adulthood. This model grew out of work on child development, and is similarly premised on the notion of a patterned sequence of stages, each with appropriate physical, emotional, and cognitive tasks to be accomplished. Though far less precise when applied to adult phases of the life line, it has generally been assumed that Erikson's sixth stage, centering on the task of developing the capacity for intimacy, spans the years of early adulthood from 20 to 40, whereas the seventh stage, focusing on generativity issues, spans the years from 40 to 65 (Havighurst, 1973).

Erikson never, to my knowledge, spoke of a "midlife crisis," but those who do have built upon his theories and incorporated the idea of crisis as a normal part of adult development. In Vaillant's (1977) study as in Levinson's (1978), the implicit assumption is that the middle years involve a necessary period of crisis and self reevaluation that, once resolved, ushers in a new phase of life with significant changes in the older self. While Vaillant rejects the high drama of more popularized writings on the midlife crisis (Sheehy, 1977), his case examples and summary project exactly this view of the middle years as a watershed during which both outer-life structure and inner concept of self undergo profound change. As he puts it: "men leave the compulsive, unreflective busywork of their occupational apprenticeships and once more become explorers of the world within" (Vaillant, 1977, p. 220). This is very similar to the process charted in Levinson's study of men in their forties, though with a difference in timing: Where Levinson claims this shift never occurs before 38 or later than 43, Vaillant suggests much greater variation, "at age forty, give or take as much as a decade."

With variation as great as from 20 years in Vaillant's study (30–50) to only 5 years in Levinson's study (38–43), it remains an open question what exactly is changing in these men's lives and why. Since Levinson did not study any men over 45, he may simply not have been able to examine the full range of critical change in midlife. Clearly he has not examined men undergoing the more specifically physiological changes of the late forties and early fifties. What does show in both studies is the fact that the dominant role domain in the lives of men from early adulthood into their forties is the overwhelming priority of work commitment and career progression. In the Levinson study, for example, as we watch the men move from their twenties to their mid forties, at each step it is work that defines their central priority: The selection and testing of self against choice through the occupational formation process in their twenties, settling down into an occupational niche in their thirties, the confrontation of earlier dreams with the reality of attainment in their forties. In both studies, the shift in midlife is from this high centrality of work to greater investment in family and private life, which means, in turn, that significant emotional accessibility of men to their children takes place only when the children reach adolescence, and to their wives only in the second decade of marriage. Indeed, although 80% of Levinson's subjects were married by the age of 28, he claims "most men in their twenties were not ready to make an enduring commitment to wife and family and they were not capable of a highly loving, sexually free, and emotionally intimate relationship" (Levinson, 1978, p. 107).

Levinson makes much of the role of career mentors in the work histories of the male subjects, but it may be that it was their wives who played the role of "intimacy mentors" to the men during their twenties and thirties. If so, this makes the developmental task in early adulthood in the Levinson men consistent with Erikson's life-cycle theory, but inconsistent in the case of women in early adulthood. It implies that women, typically younger than their husbands, have already resolved the intimacy issue by their twenties, whereas men are still engaged in the task.

It is not an unfair conclusion to suggest that neither the concept of crisis nor the specification of cause has been established in studies of midlife transitions in the normative crisis model of adult development. Brim's (1976) caution is worth noting here. In pointing out that the field of adult development is similar to child development 50 years ago in its exploration of age-linked developmental sequences, he says: "like child development then, it (adult development) is in real danger from pop culture renderings of life stages, from the public seizing on the ideal of age-linked stages of development, such as the 'male midlife crisis', just as it seizes on astrology and tea-leaf reading" (p. 7).

B. TIMING-OF-EVENTS MODEL

The key idea in the timing-of-events model is that adult development is not paced by crises, but by a sense of the "average expectable life cycle" as Butler and Lewis (1977) put it. Stress along the life line is not inherent in developmental transitions as in the normative-crisis model, but a manifestation of asynchrony in the timing of life events. It is the unanticipated event, not the anticipated, that is likely to represent the traumatic event. Thus not to marry by 35 or to become a widow at 35 may trigger anxiety because the individual's cultural expectation of appropriate timing has been violated.

Neugarten (1964, 1968, 1973, 1979) has been a leading proponent of this view, and suggests that a psychology of the life cycle is not a psychology of crisis behavior as much as it is a psychology of timing. Thus she has suggested, that in midlife, people do not undergo crises but a normal gradual change in their time perspective, in which "life is restructured in terms of time-left-to-live rather than time-since-birth" (Neugarten, 1968, p. 97), a shift that is accompanied by heightened introspection, stock-taking and interiority. She suggests, further, that chronological age is no longer the positive marker that it was early in life, that middle-aged men and women "look to their positions within different life contexts—body, career, family—rather than to chronological age for their primary cues in clocking themselves" (Neugarten, 1968, p. 94).

Part of the reason for the gradual nature of this shift in time perspective, Neugarten suggests, stems from the fact that phasing in the different contexts of life are not always synchronous: A man may be "on time" in phase of work, but "off time" as a father of a preschool son born in a late or second marriage. This suggests an ironic qualification of the general theory: Asynchrony *across* the major domains of life reduces stress, whereas asynchrony *within* a domain increases it, an echo of the subjective perception of organic equilibrium that is a consequence of finely articulated but differentiated body clocks. Asynchrony in *one* body system—pulse, respiration, kidney secretion beyond the normal range—is stressful and an index of possible disease; but asynchrony *across* body systems is a necessary condition for health and subjective equilibrium (Luce, 1970). It is also an open question whether stress and a crisis of transition may not occur when a *number* of expected events coalesce in a very short time period, as suggested by research on life events and stress (Dohrenwend & Dohrenwend, 1974).

The assumption in the timing-of-events model is that there is no overarching life-span ground plan of adult development. The phasing, the shifts in self-definition are largely structured by age norms rooted in culture and society, not in biology. Chronological age is not a meaningful marker because the major life events in the middle part of life occur at very different ages to different people. It might appear that, precisely because of the great variance of social and psychological attributes in relation to chronological age, there is an excellent opportunity for research to establish the relative contribution of the timing and sequencing of both social and biological events and processes, but to date, there have been no studies directed to such questions.

The timing-of-events theory has in fact born more fruit in the life-course perspective and in historical demography than in developmental psychology or in family sociology. Modell, Furstenberg, and Strong (1978), Elder and Rockwell (1976), and Uhlenberg (1978) have all done interesting cohort analyses to study shifts in the timing and sequencing of life events over the past century. They showed that there was far more variation in the timing and sequencing of such events as school entry and exit, marriage, departure from parental household, death or incapacity of spouse, in the nineteenth century than the mid-twentieth century.

On the other hand, the life-span theory of timing-of-events may have emerged in a period of social history—the 1950s and early 1960s—more stable and with a more expectable life cycle than either before or since. Many indicators in the late 1970s suggest a new period of increased variance in both the timing and sequencing of life events. Age norms are more fluid; more people marry, divorce, and remarry; increasing numbers of children spend time first in two-parent, then one-parent, then two-parent households. Neugarten, who had been a proponent of the view that it is asynchrony that triggers stress, has recently described the current period from the point of view of a more "fluid life cycle, one marked by an increasing number of role transitions, the disappearance of traditional timetables, and the lack of synchrony among age-related roles" (Neugarten & Brown-Rezanka, 1978, p. 4). If this is so, and the general theory of stress related to asynchrony holds, one would predict elevated stress at decision points along the life line for many adults during the current period of age-norm flux and departure from expected timetables.

One is left with many unanswered questions concerning midlife development with either of the two life-span perspectives. Despite its origins in, and congeniality with, an ontogenetic framework, the normative-crisis perspective has cut its link to biology as surely as the timing-of-events perspective has. The very loose and broad definition of age range that characterizes the Eriksonian stages of adult development has clearly not facilitated any research attention to age-related physiological changes and their psychological impact. The insistence of the timing-of-events psychologists that chronological age does not matter because of the great variation in the social timing of life events, has similarly worked against the emergence of research designed to test the contribution of aging indicators to psychological state or social relationships. In the following section, we turn to a more focused discussion of the major limitations of life-span models as they are illuminated by an application of a life-course and a biosocial perspective.

III. Limitations of Current Models of Adult Development

A. COHORT PARTICULARITY

We have noted earlier that almost all the research on middle-aged adults in the past decade, whether from cross-sectional or longitudinal studies, concerns people born between the early 1920s and the early 1930s. The

Berkeley Guidance Study involves the 1928–1929 cohort; the Oakland Growth Study, the 1920–1921 cohort. Vaillant's (1977) Harvard study was based on 95 men from the classes of 1942–1944; with 22 as the average age at college graduation, the sample is then largely from the birth cohort of 1920–1922. Though Rubin (1979) does not tell us exactly what year she interviewed her sample of 160 middle-aged women, assuming it was 1977 and the women ranged from 35 to 54 at that time, they were born between 1923 and 1942; with a median age of 47, the median birth cohort is thus placed at 1930. Levinson's (1978) men, interviewed in 1968 when they were in their late thirties and early forties, are also from the 1923 to 1933 cohort. Even the women studied in an alumnae survey of her class in the late 1950s on which Friedan (1963) developed the profile of unease and ennui of women with a "problem without a name" are women born in the decade of the 1920s.

Most of what we know in American social science research about middle age has therefore come from people who were either born during or spent their early childhood in families that experienced the depression. The older men of the 1922–1932 birth cohort were subject to the draft in World War II, the younger, during the Korean War in the 1950s. Furthermore, their adulthood after military service, the forming of their families, and the progression of their careers took place in an era with special economic characteristics. As a very small demographic cohort, reflecting the lowered birth rate that began in the late 1920s and persisted through the depression years of the 1930s, post World War II adults benefited from the combination of membership in a small cohort and an expanding economy, particularly in the growing professional and technical fields. This means there was both opportunity and pressure for high productivity and easy career advancement as their lives and work histories unfolded in the 1950s and the 1960s. Unlike their fathers' experience of loss of jobs and talent underutilization, today's middle-aged men may have aspired well beyond their earliest expectations and they may have been overutilized by job demands in an era of easy promotions. The profile of the midlife men in Levinson and Vaillant's studies may strike a future developmental researcher as burned out at a premature age, rather than reflecting a normal developmental process all men go through so early in life.

The women in this cohort of middle-aged adults show a reciprocal profile to that of the men. They represent the cohort that pioneered the modern equivalent of the nineteenth century frontier, in the settlement of suburbia in the post World War II period. At the same time, they were attracted to domesticity that far exceeded in affluent possibilities what their mothers experienced in the lean years of the 1930s, but were more isolated from kin and friends by distance and the pressure on time and energy that flowed from their most striking characteristic—the large size of their families. Ryder (1978) has suggested that the combination of suburban homes with greater indoor and outdoor space to absorb children and rising incomes from an expanding economy encouraged a relaxation of contraceptive usage and easy acceptance of third and fourth pregnancies during the 1950s and early 1960s.

But in the 1950s, few parents realized that a birth spacing pattern of 2 years in a society increasingly requiring 4 years of postsecondary schooling to enter skilled occupations would produce unprecedented financial pressure on them as parents when the children reached late adolescence. Numerous middle-aged parents in recent years have coped with the financial expense of supporting two adolescents through postsecondary schooling simultaneously. Demographers have studied what they call the "life-cycle squeeze" in this cohort during their middle years, which they trace to the gap between life-style aspirations, the rising cost of rearing children in adolescence, and family income. Oppenheimer (1976) has pointed out, for example, that in 1969, child care costs for men between 35 and 44 were 97% higher than for men just ten years younger, whereas their earnings were only 15% higher than the younger men's. Families responded to this squeeze in much the way they did in the past. Whereas, in the nineteenth century, a primary family adaptive strategy involved taking in boarders (Hareven, 1978), in the 1950s and 1960s, the adaptive strategy has been the sharp increase in paid employment of married women. In either case, it is typically a family decision, an adaptive strategy that bridges the gap between living standard aspirations and real income (Oppenheimer, 1977).

Quite apart, then, from any maturational age-related stress and change in the middle years, the present cohort of middle-aged adults has been subject to a good deal of economic and social stress from large families, overextended budgets, the need to depart from expected life styles as women joined the labor force and men felt the pressure to overinvest in jobs to make ends meet. At the same time, if there is truth in the idea that it is the unanticipated event that produces stress, one would predict higher levels of stress in women than in men, since their roles have been reactive to unanticipated economic pressure as children entered adolescence, rather than as players in a scenario they planned in advance and hence expected. With larger homes and larger families, residence in suburbia that typically involves travel of some distance to places of employment, and more continuous employment histories than they anticipated as younger women, the stage has been set for middle-aged women to experience stress and work overload that fully matches that of the men in their cohort.

One last characteristic of the cohort of contemporary middle-aged adults is relevant here. In studies by Levinson (1978) and Vaillant (1977), one is struck by the close articulation between men's psychological development and chronological age. The highly specified timetable Levinson proposes as a general developmental characteristic of men's lives may be a reflection of the bureaucratic organization of work in an industrial economy. The tight sequence of male schooling and career progression may simply reflect the phasing of modern business and professional life that facilitates an orderly expectable timetable for men through life. Chronological age under such economic circumstances becomes a reasonable proxy for routinized career progression. Indeed Neugarten (1968) reported, from her studies of middle-aged men in the early 1960s, that they "perceive a close relationship between life line and career line" (p. 96). No invarient developmental pattern has been confirmed by such studies, however, for the close correspondence between age and career stage may flow from the opportunities and pressures unique to American society at a particular stage of development at a particular point in history.

B. NEGLECT OF PHYSIOLOGICAL FACTORS

Whereas the life-course perspective is extremely useful in grounding recent studies of the middle years in the particularity of social place and historical time, it is of little use in assessing studies where strictly maturational variables are concerned.

Life-course researchers to date have concentrated their efforts on broad structural variables of an economic or demographic variety, typically through the use of aggregate census data by means of ingenious linkages between records of births, marriages, deaths, property ownership, migration. With either type of data, they can only "infer" the social and economic pressures on individuals and families concerning major life decisions. Life-span psychologists, by contrast, have had direct contact with living subjects and, at least in the early phases of the major longitudinal studies, included variables dealing with physical growth and development along with psychological variables. Physical and mental health was in fact a motivating concern in the initiation of the Harvard Grant Study, in an effort to break from traditional clinical concentration on pathology; emotional well-being and adaptation continued as a major focus of Vaillant's follow up study of the Harvard sophomores in middle age.

By and large, however, neither the normative-crisis nor the timing-of-events approaches of the life-span psychologists have made much room in their theoretical thinking for physiological variables. There is a shadowy reference to the curve of expansion during the first half of the life span and its contraction in the later years, but in close-up studies of individuals moving through the middle years, there is no effort to measure physical aging and to relate this empirically to measures of personality, social role, cognitive style, ability, and so on. This neglect is all the more striking in light of the intellectual origins of the Erikson life-cycle theory in biology and medicine. In addition, his association in Vienna as a young researcher with Charlotte Bühler meant early intellectual exposure to her efforts to conceptualize the life cycle in terms that embraced biological as well as psychological and social variables (Bühler, 1933; Frenkel, 1936; Frenkel-Brunswick, 1968). In American social science during the 1930s and 1940s, biological processes received attention in theories and research on child development, but, with the approach of World War II, adults were increasingly viewed as bodyless. Partly in reaction to the misuse of biology among earlier social scientists, and to the political manifestation of eugenicist and genocidal ideas during the fascist era in Europe, American social science in the 1940–1960 period showed an enchantment with the concepts of culture and social structure, and the methods of science and statistics. In the 20 years since 1960, historical comparisons have competed with cultural comparisons as the cutting edge of the social science disciplines. Today, there is a danger that life-course sociologists and historians may tempt life-span psychologists even further away from biological variables than their crisis and timing-of-events models have already done.

However fascinating cultural and historical variation is, a central goal of all efforts to view the life span from birth to death in an overarching developmental framework remains the search for relatively invariant processes that hold to a large degree in all cultures and in all periods of time. With a now vastly enriched and still increasing storehouse of knowledge of other times and other cultures, it should be far easier than a quarter-century ago to test for variance and consistency of age and gender-related phenomena. Of even greater importance, however, is getting on with the job of formulating research that includes physiological variables and explores how they relate to, are explained by, or overridden by psychological and social processes in adult development. To do this means to abandon broad definitions of middle age as a 20–25-year phase of the life span, and to narrow research attention to specific age ranges within which known biological changes take place that might illuminate or be illuminated by psychological and social changes. A sequential longitudinal design, for example, could span the menopause, and chart maturational, cohort and individual differences using direct measures of physiological, psychological, and social variables.

Gender differences in the middle years are prime candidates for such biosocial research. The growth, peaking, and waning of gender differentiation in psychological attributes and social roles is matched by physiological sexual dimorphism along the same life curve. Whereas the emergence of gender differentiation by early adulthood can be and has been explained on the ground of cumulative socialization into traditional gender roles, the same learning theory model underlying this explanation would predict no loss of gender differentiation past the age of 45, for by then there has been a quarter-century of reinforcement experience. Yet a good deal of evidence suggests a shift away from sharp sex-related differentiation in the second half of life. Since major changes occur in endocrine functioning during both the decade of increasing sexual dimorphism—puberty and adolescence—and of decreasing sexual dimorphism— the middle years from 45 to 55—it is at least a plausible hypothesis that physiology is implicated in the observed psychosocial changes. The fact that Bühler and her associates spoke of this pattern, based on biographic data from both living subjects in the 1920s and written evidence from diaries and biographies of deceased subjects who lived in the nineteenth century, further strengthens the possibility that this pattern holds across historical time and therefore transcends any cohort or cultural particularity of middle-aged subjects in the 1960s and 1970s.

There is a remarkable consistency to the observations by developmental psychologists on the direction of change in women compared to men in the decade from 45 to 55 years of age. Many of these studies note a shift from an active, agentic orientation of young males to a more passive orientation in later years (Cumming & Henry, 1961; Gurin, Veroff & Feld, 1960; Kuhlen, 1964; Peck & Berkowitz, 1964; Rosen & Bibring, 1968). Responses to TAT stories in the Kansas City samples of middle-aged and older adults (40–49, 50–59, 64–71) suggested a decline already visible in the two middle-aged groups in ego involvement and ego energy (Gutmann, 1964; Neugarten & Gutmann, 1968). Gutmann (1975) found sex role reversals with age in three totally dissimilar societies, on the basis of which he proposed that a shift takes place from dominance toward nurturance with increasing age of men, and the reverse pattern, from nurturance to dominance, in women. A similar gender role reversal has been noted by social anthropologists in ethnographic accounts of other societies (e.g., Murphy & Murphy, 1974). A comparison of the characteristics of middle-aged men and women with an older preretirement group in Lowenthal's (1975) study also suggests an increase in assertive independence with age among the women and an apparently emotionally satisfying reverse trend between the two older age groups of men. Shifts in sexual interest and speed of arousability show declines as men age but a retention or an increase in agentic sexual interest among women as they age (Rubin, 1979). Neugarten and Gutmann (1968) concluded, from an analysis of age, sex, and social class differences in Midwest samples, that as women age they become "more tolerant of their own aggressive, egocentric impulses," whereas as men age, they become more tolerant of their "nurturant and affiliative impulses" (p. 71).

That these age–sex trends show up so consistently suggests that chronological age is tapping some underlying changes in biological functioning, and hence it is difficult to agree with the same psychologists who claim chronological age is no longer a meaningful marker on the life span. Much of the evidence in support of the latter assertion is based on several investigations of women in the menopausal years. This research suggests that, contrary to assumptions in the social sciences and medicine, menopause is rarely a crisis to women; there is more dread in the anticipation than difficulty in the experience; and far from being upset at the loss of an important biological function, most women feel relief to have it behind them (Neugarten & Kraines, 1965; Neugarten, Wood, Kraines, & Loomis, 1968). The sharpest difference found by age of women on a 35-item menopause attitude measure was on a factor called "postmenopausal recovery." Inspection of sample items on this factor suggests that far more than menopause per se is involved in the age contrasts: Women in the criterion group of 45–55 years and the older comparison group of women 56–65 are most dissimilar from the two younger comparison groups (21–30 and 31–44 years of age): The older woman is more self-confident, calmer, freer to do things for herself. The sharpness of the age contrast can be illustrated with one item: The percentage agreeing to the item "After the change of life, a woman feels freer to do things for herself," is 74 and 65% among the two age groups *over* 45, only 16 and 24% in the two age groups *under* 45 years of age (Neugarten *et al.,* 1968). The trend with age is consistent with the shift from affiliation and dependency to more agentic, autonomous orientations among the older women.

There are two reasons for caution in interpreting the results from such research on the menopause. If postmenopausal women report more confidence, freedom, autonomy, there is no reason to assume that this has anything to do with sheer cessation of menses. As Neugarten notes, many of the women in the 45–55-year-old age group were happy to have done "not only with menstruation and its attendant annoyances, but also with the mothering of small children" (Neugarten *et al.,* 1968, p. 200). Release from child-care responsibilities and economic pressure, having the house to themselves and their husbands, and increased time and energy for nonfamily activities, are implicated. But this does not mean that endocrine changes as a part of the physiological changes in the decade from 45–55 did not contribute to the psychosocial changes. To fasten on menopause per se may be very misleading, for it may be other aspects of aging that involve at least a temporary period of adjustment difficult for women, which when accomplished lead to a release of new energies and a revised conception of self in the fifties. Whether a woman is menstruating or not is private knowledge; grey hair, wrinkles, drowsiness, age spots, thickening of the waistline, bifocal glasses, are the indicators of aging that matter in social interaction. Endocrine changes contribute to these signs of aging and, until they have been measured directly and related to psychological variables, it is premature to conclude that physiology is insignificant, that chronological age does not matter, or that it is the timing of events and a shift in time perspective that are critical viewpoints on middle age.

It should be noted that the ability to directly assay hormonal secretion level with any reliability has a very short history, and research that links hormonal levels to social behavior with human subjects is only beginning to appear in the literature (Doering, 1980; Kling, 1975; Leshner, 1978; Mason, 1975). It is not clear as yet which specific androgen is related to aggressive behavior, for example, and current efforts are under way to determine from blood assays whether it is serum androstenedione, serum testosterone, testosterone-binding globulin or free testosterone concentration or some combination that is related to fight–flight responses. One recent study found that testosterone and free testosterone concentration tended to rise after the age of 60 in human females, whereas estrogen and androstenedione decline (Purifoy, Koopmans, & Tatum, 1979). Current debate also involves the question of whether it is the balance between estrogens and androgens that matters rather than secretion level of one or the other taken separately. More generally, one could hypothesize that underlying the shift to more assertive behavior on the part of human females from midlife on is a change in the androgen–estrogen ratio, with androgen becoming more biologically active and influential as the estrogens drop. Just the reverse endocrine pattern may hold for human males, with estrogens having more effect on behavior as androgens drop. But specific research to link inter- and intragender variation in hormonal level to change in human psychological or social behavior is only now under way.

IV. Research Design Criteria

Several criteria follow from this assessment of life-span research on adult development from a life-course and biosocial perspective, which determined the design of the study of aging and parenthood in the middle years.

A. CRITERIA FROM A BIOSOCIAL PERSPECTIVE

Three criteria pertinent to the research design followed from a concern for the biological dimension of development. One was to concentrate on early adolescents, following the definition of early adolescence from previous work as the 5-year span from 12 through 16 years of age (Hamburg, 1974; Kagan & Coles, 1972), to maximize the presence of dramatic biological and social psychological changes in the child. The second was to try to obtain considerable variance in the age of the parents of such adolescents, to have women at different stages of the aging process in the middle years. The third criterion was to develop a variety of approaches to the variables of age and aging. On the latter, to explore not menopausal status but the rapidity and the degree of aging the women have experienced in recent years of a kind that is highly visible to others and likely to have psychological significance to the woman.

On the age variable itself, an effort was made to provide a more phenomenological understanding of the meaning of age through two empirical approaches. One is a set of open-ended questions on what the women saw as the best and worst things about being the age they are now, and what had been the best and worst thing that happened to them in the past year. A second approach to age was to permit a statistical analysis of the subjective aspects of age, by asking women to give a specific age in response to questions such as how old they feel or how old they would like to be. To provide some linkage to age norms, we asked their judgment of what the best age is for a woman or a man to be.

B. CRITERIA FROM A LIFE-COURSE PERSPECTIVE

Three criteria were suggested by the life-course perspective in designing the research. One was the timing and variation of major events in the lives of the middle-aged women; age at marriage and at first birth, current ages of the children, and total family size. Since such ages in the fielding year (1978) could be readily translated into historical time, the same information contributed to the second criterion, a largely descriptive one of placing the research subjects in cohort or historical time, to increase interpretive sensitivity in the quantitative analysis and as a base for predicting whether and how the findings from this particular cohort of middle-aged parents might differ looking ahead to parents who will be in the middle years in the 1980s.

The third criterion suggested by a life-course perspective was to obtain information that cuts across the major domains of life. Aging and parenting do not exist in a vacuum but may be influenced by, or exert an influence on, the quality of personal experience in marriage, the division of responsibility in household maintenance, relations to people outside the family at work or through community involvement. The following sections will concentrate on the results under the first two of these life-course criteria.

V. Fielding and Sample Characteristics

In the best of all possible worlds, a research design to explore aging and parent–child relations in the middle years would include as subjects both parents and adolescent children, and data would consist of direct rater observation of aging status, medical measures on endocrine levels and health status, and interview and written materials to cover psychological and social variables. The reality, however, necessitated an exploratory project, as the work was done on a small biomedical research grant that provided less than $1000 for expenses beyond the salary of one research assistant. Hence, the first decision of the research venture was to concentrate on a small sample of local families, with data obtained from a self-administered questionnaire mailed to the mothers. Although there are no data from adolescents themselves or from their fathers, we assume that any developmental differences among the mothers meant that the family worlds within which early adolescents were living differed in social and psychological atmospheres. Daily exposure presumably has subtle effects upon everybody who shares the intimate space of a common household, and hence maternal age differences increase the probability that some part of the variation among adolescents may be linked to the aging, cohort membership, or life circumstances of their mothers.

A. FIELDING

The sample was drawn from street directories in two small towns in western Massachusetts. Only intact families were selected, in which the wife's listed age was between the early thirties and the middle fifties. This age range was selected to maximize variance in maternal age yet locate families containing children in early adolescence. Letters of invitation were sent with return postcards giving information on family composition and willingness to fill out a survey. Telephone follow-up calls were made to those not returning postcards. Of the original sample drawn from the directories, explicit refusals were made by 20% of the women, with another 20% excluding themselves or being excluded by the researcher on the grounds of not having children, not having an early adolescent child as yet, or only having grown children in their twenties. A few women eager to participate in the study were retained in the sample although they had no children in the 12–16 age range.

B. SAMPLE CHARACTERISTICS

The 68 women in the study were a diverse group in terms of educational attainment and socioeconomic status. A third had no more than a high school education, whereas 20% have had some graduate work or hold an advanced degree beyond the bachelor's. The educational attainment of their husbands was even more polarized than the women's; 40% of the husbands have not gone beyond high school, whereas 34% have degrees beyond the bachelor's. Similarly, the income range (total household income in 1978) was from $8000 to $56,000; 34% of the families had incomes of less than $15,000, 25% over $30,000. Two-thirds of the women were employed at the time of the study, slightly higher than national labor force participation rates of women in intact families with children aged 6–13 (59.3%) and 14–17 (58.5%) (U.S. Department of Labor, 1979, Table 6). Slightly less than 20% were attending some kind of educational institution. Half of the employed women rated their jobs negatively in terms of salary or promotion opportunity, but 75% found their jobs above average (on a 7-point rating scale) in interest and task variety, and two-thirds reported overall satisfaction with their jobs. The women were about equally divided between Protestants (47%) and Catholics (43%); only two women were Jewish, and five reported either no or other religious affiliations. Ethnicity was not inquired into but the predominant national origin among Catholics in this part of the state is Polish.

Chronological age is a major variable in the analysis to follow, and hence it is important to report in detail the age distribution of the women subjects. Current age will be used both as a dichotomized variable in sketching the major differences between younger and older mothers, and as a continuous variable in regression analyses to test the independence of age as an index of aging from social, family stage, or cohort dimensions of age. Figure 1 shows the actual case distribution of the subjects by current age and birth cohort, and the mean age of the women when current age was dichotomized.

There is a difference of 8 years in the mean age of the women in the two groups (39.5 for younger mothers, 47.5 for older mothers). Note, too, that all but six women are between the ages of 36 and 50: Younger mothers are for the most part in their late thirties and the early forties (36 to 43), whereas the older mothers are in their late forties (45–51). Hence the younger mothers are all in their premenopausal years, the older mothers

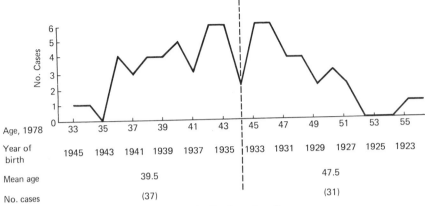

Fig. 1. Age distribution of mothers.

largely in their menopausal years, and only 2 of the 31 older mothers are postmenopausal. Although the younger mothers are still in their fertile years, all but two of the women in the sample responded "definitely not" (and they said "probably not") when asked if they planned any additional children in the future. In historical terms, the older mothers were born in the late 1920s through the early years of the depression (1927–1933); the younger mothers were born in the depths of the depression but before the onset of World War II (1935–1942).

In a period of rapid change in marriage and family formation, it is also important to investigate cohort differences that might be tapped by chronological age. Because educational attainment has increased with successive cohorts in recent decades, and the fertility rate rose sharply between 1946 and 1957, and then declined steadily from 1959 to the present time, one might expect the older mothers to show larger families and lower educational attainment levels than the younger mothers.

Table I shows that there were no significant differences between the two age groups in this sample on status characteristics of either the wife or the husband. If anything, the older mothers showed a slightly higher proportion with education beyond a college degree than did the younger mothers. This was not the case for the husbands' educational attainment, suggesting some of the older mothers may have returned for additional schooling during the past decade as their children began to enter their teens. Their residence close to a public university would also facilitate securing further education after a period of withdrawal. The only status factor worth special note suggests a career progression associated with chronological age: For both employed wives and husbands, there was a higher proportion

TABLE I

Status Characteristics of Spouses and Family by Age of Mother

Status characteristic	Total	Younger mothers	Older mothers[a]
Wife's education			
High school graduate or less	44.8	41.7	46.4
Some college or BA	22.4	30.5	14.9
Some graduate work or advanced degree	32.8	27.8	38.7
100% =	(67)	(36)	(31)
Husband's education			
High school graduate or less	39.7	40.5	38.9
Some college or BA	23.5	24.3	22.6
Some graduate work or advanced degree	36.8	35.2	38.5
100% =	(68)	(37)	(31)
Wife's current occupation			
Professional	48.6	50.0	47.1
Managerial–administrative	10.8	—	23.5
Sales–clerical	27.0	25.0	29.4
Blue collar	13.6	25.0	—
100% =	(37)	(20)	(17)
Husband's occupation			
Professional	38.2	38.9	41.4
Managerial–administrative	27.9	22.2	37.9
Sales–clerical	20.6	33.3	7.0
Blue collar	13.2	5.6	13.7
100% =	(68)	(36)	(31)
Total family income			
Under $15,000	21.2	27.3	17.2
$15,000–$25,000	30.3	30.3	34.4
Over $25,000	48.5	42.4	48.3
100% =	(66)	(33)	(29)

[a] None of the age differences reach statistical significance on a chi-square test.

in managerial and administrative positions in the older than in the younger age groups; because this was matched by a decrease with age in the proportion in sales and clerical positions but not in representation in professional occupations, it may be that the older women and their husbands had advanced from lower-level sales and clerical jobs to more responsible managerial positions in the same occupational context. Several marginal comments in the questionnaires were consistent with this interpretation: All were older women who noted recent promotions to supervisory positions in a firm or public agency they or their husbands had worked in for some years.

C. MARRIAGE AND FAMILY FORMATION

There was considerable variation in the age at which the women married their current husbands and in their age at the birth of their first child. On average the women were 24.1 years of age at the time of their present marriage, whereas their husbands were on average 27.9 years of age. This is higher than national norms due to the higher educational attainment of the subjects and the later age at which remarriages take place. Approximately one in four of the marriages involved a previously married spouse. Table II summarizes several demographic and social characteristics of first marriages compared to remarriages among the younger and older mothers. As seen in the table, the mean age of wives in first marriages was about the same for younger (20.6) and older (20.3) women, whereas the husbands of the older women were slightly older (26.1) than the husbands of the younger women (23.9), perhaps reflecting the marriage postponement of older men who served in the military. Both wives and husbands who had been married previously were approximately a decade older at the time of their current marriage, than those in a first marriage for both. Thus among older mothers, marriages involving at least one previously married partner involved wives who were on average 31 and their husbands 36 when they married, compared to 20 for wives and 26 for husbands in first marriages. A comparable pattern was shown for the younger women.

There was also some suggestion that the remarriages were based on a more mature knowledge of the partner, for Table II shows that a larger proportion of the women knew their husbands for 2 years or more in cases of remarriage than they did in the case of first marriages.

Family size did not significantly differentiate younger from older mothers. In fact, the younger mothers have slightly larger families (3.51) than older mothers (3.42 children on average). Family size was strongly affected by marital history: Those with a prior marriage had larger families than the couples in first marriages. There was an even sharper difference in family size if "both remarried" cases are separated from those of only one spouse having been married previously: A mean family size of 4.73 for the "both remarried" cases, to only 2.57 for the "one spouse remarried" group, a highly significant difference (χ^2, $p < .006$). This is due to the fact that when both partners were previously married, they both tended to bring children into the second marriage and then had at least one additional child; where only one partner had been married before, he or she tended to be childless at the point of the second marriage.

The variance in age at which the present marriage was formed is shown graphically in Fig. 2, a range for the women of 15–42, but when "outlyer" cases were omitted, there was an effective range, within which 80% of the

TABLE II

**Marital and Family Characteristics of First Marriages
versus Remarriages[a] by Age of Mother**

Characteristic	Younger mothers		Older mothers	
	First marriage	Remarriage	First marriage	Remarriage
Percent first marriage	71.4% (35)		74.2% (31)	
$\overline{X}$ Age of wife at present marriage	20.6	29.3	20.3	30.8
$\overline{X}$ Age of husband at present marriage	23.9	36.6	26.1	35.8
$\overline{X}$ Family size	3.36	3.70[b]	3.17	4.13[b]
Percent knew husband 2 years or more before marriage	28.0%	40.0%	26.0%	52.1%
Percent married less than one year at birth of 1st child	38.1%	33.0%	27.2%	38.0%

[a] Present marriage is first marriage for wife only, husband only, or neither. Sixty-one percent of remarriage cases involve prior marriage of both husband and wife.

[b] Family size varies considerably when remarriage is divided into "one spouse remarried" versus "both remarried": Mean family size is 2.57 where one spouse only was married before, 4.73 where both spouses were married before.

marriages were contracted, of 19–30. For the husbands, the full range was 17–51, but the counterpart effective range was 20–36. The more skewed distribution of age of husbands than of wives reflected the much greater age difference in remarriages: a full 53% of the cases in which both spouses were married before involved a husband 10 or more years older than his

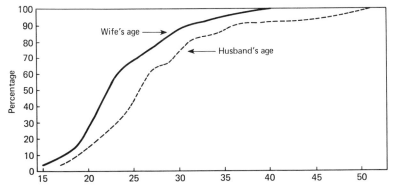

Fig. 2. Cumulative percentage distribution of age at current marriage for wives and husbands.

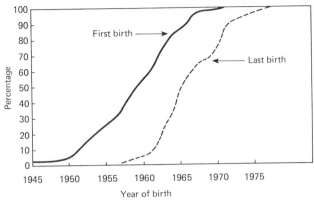

Fig. 3.   Cumulative percentage distribution of first and last births by year of birth.

wife, compared to 14% where only one partner was married before, and 4% for intact first marriages.

The childbearing years of the women were as variable as those of marriage formation. The women ranged in age at first birth from 16 to 39. First births took place between 1945 and 1970; last births took place between 1957 and 1976. Figure 3 shows the cumulative curves of childbearing for first and last births against this historical time frame, and Fig. 4 shows the high degree of overlap in the years of childbearing for the younger and older mothers.

It is clear from the charted timing of births that the older and younger mothers were bearing children during years in which the national birth rate underwent dramatic change. The two age groups in fact overlap in giving birth to both first and last children during the years 1957 to 1965 (see Fig. 4). That the older mothers showed on average the same family size as the

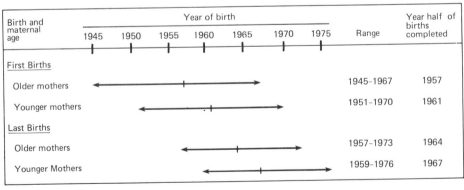

Fig. 4.   Historical timing of first and last births by age of mother.

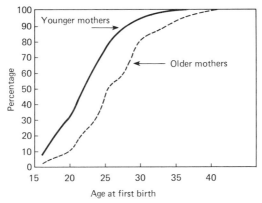

Fig. 5. Cumulative percentage distribution of age at first birth by age of mother.

younger mothers was a consequence of two factors: the chronological age at which they began childbearing and the historical time period during which first births occurred. The older women actually showed an older age at first birth (mean of 25.8) than the younger mothers (22.3): They were part of the cohort whose marriage formation was influenced by wartime and postwar adjustment, hence they married and bore a first child at a slightly older age than the young women whose families were begun during an era of early marriage and births. Figure 5 shows this age–timing contrast between the two groups of women.

However, the era in which the first births took place were high birth-rate years, so that the older women, although beginning the childbearing phase of their lives at an older age, had their children in an era of high birth rates. The effect of this factor can be seen if the years of first births are divided at 1959 when the national rate began to decline: The final family size of women whose first birth took place before 1959 was 4.13, while the family size of women whose first birth took place after 1959 was only 2.97. Because all but two of the women claimed that they planned to have no additional children, the smaller family size for those who had children in the more recent period probably does not reflect uncompleted family formation.

Table III brings together several threads in the data presented in Tables I and II, in terms of which we can follow the adult development of the mothers and the development of the oldest and youngest child in the families they formed, against the historical context of the 1940–1978 period. This is done separately for the younger and older mothers so that we can place their development and that of their children in the framework of recent social history. Older mothers were in their twenties in the 1950s and in their thirties during the 1960s; their children were in elementary school in the 1960s and have moved through high school and post-

TABLE III

**Median Age of Younger and Older Mothers,
First and Last Born Children, in Historic Context**

Age of mother and children	1940	1950	1960	1970	1978
Older mothers					
Age of mother	9	19	29	39	47
Age of oldest child			3	13	21
Age of youngest child				6	14
Younger mothers					
Age of mother	1	11	21	31	39
Age of oldest child				9	17
Age of youngest child				3	11

secondary schooling in the 1970s. Some of the oldest children have already married and begun families of their own within the past few years, and the youngest child is only now moving into adolescence.

By contrast, younger mothers were at much earlier phases of family formation in the 1960s, when they were in their twenties, while their children were, for the most part, too young to be affected by the political climate of the late 1960s and early 1970s. Hence it may be the older children of the older mothers who were most affected by the social and political events of recent years, whereas it may have been the mothers themselves in the younger cohort who were affected. Indirect support for this possibility is found in responses to the question, "Does any member of your family have any of the following problems?" (Responses were given separately for weight, drug, alcohol, emotional, and "other" problems and coded in terms of which member of the family was involved.) The woman herself was involved more often in the total problems cited by younger mothers than by older mothers (19 of 46 problems among younger mothers—42%— to 6 of 39 problems among older mothers—15%). By contrast, a child was involved more often in the problems cited by older mothers (64%) than by younger mothers (37%). There were only three families with a drug or alcohol problem that involved the mother herself, all three among the younger mothers. The four families of older mothers that had a drug or alcohol problem involved a father and/or a child, not the mother.

Looking ahead, we can calculate the age the women subjects will be when they have completed their child-rearing responsibilities, by relating their current ages to the age of their youngest child. Taking 21 as the age when most parents will be free of the financial burden of child rearing, and when most children will have completed their schooling and left the parental household, Fig. 6 shows a mean age for mothers of 52 at the termina-

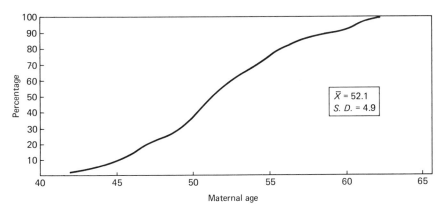

Fig. 6. Cumulative percentage distribution of maternal age when child rearing is completed (defined as age of mother when youngest child turns 21).

tion of child-rearing responsibility, with a range from 42 to 63. Being on the average 5 years older than their wives, most husbands in the study families will carry financial responsibilities for their children until late in their fifties. There is a similarity here with national data. As noted before, Borland (1978) has shown that until men and women pass their fifty-fifth birthday, the modal household in 1971 was a married couple with at least one child under 18 still at home. For the current cohort of middle-aged adults, having had large families means a small portion of the middle years will be spent in child-free households. For a number of the families in the study, the departure of the youngest child will only occur within a few years of their father's retirement.

From this introduction to the sample and to the younger compared to the older mothers, it can be seen that whereas the total sample bore the clear mark of the historical period during which they moved into adulthood, married, and formed their families, the two age groups of the mothers did not show any marked status differentiation apart from predictable occupational progression and an associated income rise with age.

VI. Dimensions of Age

Turning 5 is a source of pride and an occasion of celebration for most youngsters and their families. Turning 50 may be a more bittersweet occasion for condolence along with congratulation. The meaning of age and of time has been explored most intensively among the elderly (Kalish, 1976; Kalish & Reynolds, 1976; Kastenbaum, 1966; Kastenbaum & Aisenberg,

1972; Reynolds & Kalish, 1974). Those who have explored subjective age identification and age norms have reported a consistent tendency for widespread subjective age identification outside chronological age-group membership. Cutler (1975), for example, examined the subjective age iden- tification of three broad age categories of 18–35, 36–59, and 60 or older and found approximately the same level of identification among both the youngest and the oldest group: roughly 38% of the 18–35-year-olds iden- tified themselves as "young" and 38% of the 60 and older adults identified themselves as "old." There is clearly a lot of identification forward along the life span among the young, and a lot of identification backward to younger ages among the old (Bengston & Cutler, 1976; Cutler, 1974, 1975).

We were fortunate to obtain access to some unpublished data on dis- crepancy between actual age and subjective age from a large sample of adolescents and their parents (Kandel, 1979). The item asked for the specific age respondents "think of themselves" as being, which permitted the construction of discrepancy scores (both older and younger than actual age) for adolescents and their parents of specific actual ages. Figure 7 charts the pattern shown in the responses of adolescent girls and their mothers. There is a clear tendency for the middle-aged mothers to show an increasingly larger proportion with a "younger" age identification, and lit- tle identification with older ages, in the age range from the early thirties to the late fifties. Adolescent girls, by contrast, have a strong tendency to think of themselves as older than they are that declines as they approach their twenties. Data on fathers show very much the same tendency as the mothers, whereas adolescent boys retain a high level of thinking of themselves as older between 16 and 19 (data not shown), in contrast to the sharp drop among the girls shown in Fig. 7.

There were no data from adults in their twenties in Kandel's (1979) sam- ple, but the contrast between adolescents under 20 and adults over 30 shown in the figure suggests the twenties and early thirties may be the phase of life with the closest relation between mental self-image and actual self. Adolescents may hold an image of the young adult they hope to become, whereas middle-aged and older adults hold a self-image of the younger adult they have been. If this is so, one should find an equivalence between actual age and subjective age identification among young adults, but to date we have not located any study that confirms this.

It is interesting to consider our study families in light of the pattern shown in Fig. 7. Assuming the trends shown among the adolescent girls and their mothers are for the most part maturational, the picture evoked here is of daughters absorbed by images of an older self and mothers by images of a younger self. The missing link, young adults in their twenties, could be the older siblings (or oldest children) who have left the parental home and

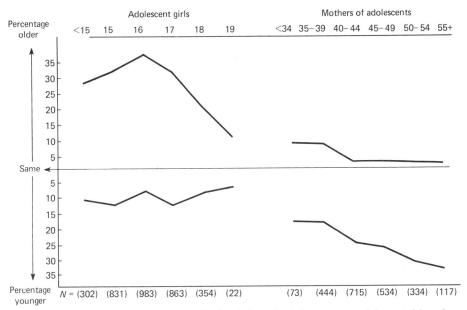

Fig. 7. Discrepancy between perceived and chronological age among adolescent girls and their mothers: Percentage who think of themselves as younger or older than they are. (Unpublished data from 1972 New York State sample, provided by Denise Kandel, Department of Psychiatry, Columbia University [Kandel, 1979].)

are at that stage of life toward which the younger adolescent yearns and which many mothers hold a private image of themselves still being.

This is of course a slight exaggeration, for the trend shown in Fig. 7 deals only with departure from acceptance of age; the majority of both adolescents and adults think of themselves as the age they actually are. Kandel's (1979) data have not been analyzed for the determinants of departure from age acceptance, which will be a major focus in the analysis of the meaning of age to the women in our study.

We begin with an overview of these dimensions, followed by a comparison of how younger mothers differ from older mothers in their subjective views on age. This will be followed by a more intimate profile of the meaning of current age based on responses to open-ended questions dealing with the best and worst aspects of their present age. We then explore some of the determinants of subjective age (the age women feel most of the time) and desired age (the age they would like to be). In that context, we will introduce the physiological measure of aging symptoms and explore its robustness as a correlate of chronological age and independence from other age-related factors such as stage of family life and the press of family worries and pleasures.

A. THE MANY MEANINGS OF AGE

Figure 8 shows three of the six ways we explored the meaning of age to the women subjects (along with their chronological age to provide a comparative anchor): *subjective age,* as measured by the question "Most of the time I feel as though I were about age . . ."; *desired age,* as indexed by the item "If I could be any age I wanted right now, I would like to be . . ."; and *minimum death age,* as measured by the item "I would like to live to at least the age of. . . ." It is quickly apparent from an inspection of the cumulative curves in Fig. 8 that most women not only feel younger than they are in actuality, but want to be younger still. There is also greater variance on subjective and desired age than in actual age. Although 23 years separated the youngest from the oldest subject, there was a range of 69 years in subjective age (from a 36-year-old woman who said she felt 16 to a 45-year-old woman who claimed she felt 85) and a range of 35 years in desired age (from 16 to 51).

There is no support in these data for the view that women do not want to be younger than they are. On average, they would like to be 10 years younger than they are (33 was the average desired age, 43 was their average actual age). In fact, not a single woman wanted to be older than she was: Women who gave a desired age of 50 or 51 were actually those ages, so the range on this variable is from a desire to be very young to acceptance of actual age.

On average, the women expressed a desire to live to be at least 75, short by only a few years from female longevity norms in the late 1970s, but there is a surprisingly wide range to the minimum death age—from 55 to 85. At first we thought the choices under 65 were probably given by younger women, on the assumption that women under 40 might consider any age over 55 to be somewhat unreal (like being over 30 from the perspective of a 16 year old). As it turned out, however, this was not the case. The short life projections came from women in their late forties and early fifties. One such woman, with the youngest death age (55) was herself 51, so she was projecting a mere four more years of life. Further inspection of her case showed that her youngest child was now 14, which meant she wanted to live until that child was 18. This was the pattern for five of the six cases of women with short life preferences. The single exception was a 52-year-old woman who said she hoped to live to at least the age of 60, with the marginal notation "if I am lucky." Elsewhere in the questionnaire she volunteered the information that she had been recently diagnosed as having breast cancer. (Her two children will be 15 and 25 when she is 60.) But five of the six women who gave short life preferences (under 65) would have children just turning 18 when they reached the minimum death age, sug-

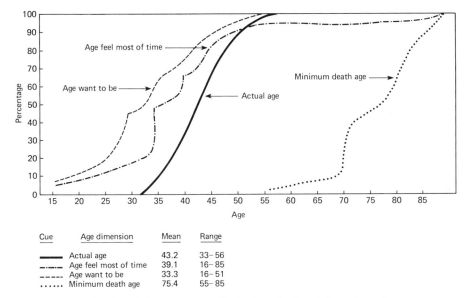

Fig. 8. Cumulative percentage distribution of selected dimensions of age.

gesting that they consider 18 a subjective marker to when their own responsibilities for actively rearing children come to an end. Financial help that continues to flow from parent to child after 18, for school expenses, establishing a household, or easing bouts of youthful unemployment, may not be experienced as active child rearing the way daily care and supervision of children and high school adolescents are. Such financial help can come as readily (and from a larger earnings base) from fathers as from mothers, so in an indirect way these data are consistent with Kalish and Reynolds' (1976) finding that incapacity and death is more threatening to men than to women on the grounds of inability to care for dependents (also see Diggory & Rothman, 1961). Although we did not ask how long the women expected to live, in light of the distribution of minimum death age and the presence of a rather large minority who gave an age under 65, it is doubtful that our data are consistent with the suggestion of Reynolds and Kalish (1974) that people want to live to an older age than they expect to live.

Table IV shows the correlations among the six subjective measures of age and actual age, and permits a first approximation to interpreting the response distributions shown separately in Fig. 8. The high correlation (.774) between actual age and the age people at a first meeting think the women are suggests a realistic component to the women's sense of themselves in the eyes of others. By contrast, the far more modest positive

TABLE IV

Pearson Correlation Coefficients between Age Variables[a]

Age variable	Actual age	People think	Age feel	Age want to be	Best age for woman	Best age for man	Minimum death age
Actual age	—	.774***	.208*	.041	-.100	.073	.000
People think		—	.189	.086	-.094	.061	-.104
Feel most of time			—	-.145	-.187	-.294*	-.408**
Want to be				—	.733***	.473**	.225*
Best age for woman					—	.677***	.168
Best age for man						—	.139
Minimum death age							—

[a] Statistical significance shown in this and all subsequent tables will be indicated by asterisk notations as follows:

*** = .000–.001
** = .002–.009
* = .01–.05
+ = Borderline significance, .06–.10

relationship between actual age and subjective age (.208) suggests the presence of experiences and attributes that are not age-specific, but play a role in stimulating the feeling of being older or younger than they are. Desired age, as suggested by the distance between its curve and actual age in Fig. 8, has no relationship to chronological age (correlation of .041), again suggesting the presence of either individual attributes and life experiences or the influence of age norms.

Age norms are implicated by the evidence of a highly significant correlation (.733) between desired age and the "best age" for a woman to be. Those who give very young ideal ages tend themselves to want to be much younger than they are; those who give older ideal ages are more accepting of their current age. Age norms themselves are subject to change, and the further finding that the women's actual age and ideal age is negatively related ($-.100$) suggests some loosening of the tendency to hold youth more desirable than maturity. The negative correlation here suggests a cohort factor in this direction, for it means younger mothers are showing a slight tendency to give older ideal ages than the older mothers do.

Two correlations in Table IV, viewed together, suggest an important thread in the meaning of age as an escape route from current stress or personal despair: Subjective age shows a strong negative relationship to minimum death age ($-.408$), whereas desired age is significantly positive in relationship to minimum death age (.225). That is, it is women who feel young who project long futures for themselves, whereas those who feel older than they are, show short life preferences. Those who accept their current age wish to live long lives; those who want to be much younger than they are give themselves very short futures. To the extent women have internalized a youthful ideal for women, the prospect of aging and death may be dire and conflictual, a prospect resolved by cutting back on expected and desired longevity so that old age does not have to be experienced. Early death expectations are then an escape from the necessity of dealing with age when cultural ideals are anchored in youth. There are no other data in the study to pursue the normative component to these responses any further, but we shall explore in what follows which aspects of the current life situations of the women contribute to their unease with their present age and corresponding escape to a youthful past or shortened future.

Table V summarizes, in the form of means and range, the pattern shown by younger mothers and older mothers to the meaning of age items. The most significant finding shown here is the much greater discrepancy between actual age and desired or ideal ages for older than for younger mothers. Older mothers are on average 8 years the seniors of the younger mothers, but their ideal and the age they want to be is slightly younger than the averages for the younger mothers. Consequently, desired age on

Alice S. Rossi

TABLE V

Meanings of Age Profile of Younger and Older Mothers:
Mean and Range (in brackets)

Age variable	Younger mothers		Older mothers	
Actual age	39.5		47.5	
		(33–43)		(44–56)
Age people think you are	34.6		40.8	
		(25–45)		(34–50)
Age feel most of time	37.5		40.9	
		(17–70)		(16–85)
Age want to be	33.6		32.9	
		(17–43)		(16–51)
Best age for a woman to be	33.0		31.0	
		(21–40)		(20–44)
Best age for a man to be	34.9		33.7	
		(24–45)		(25–42)
Minimum death age	75.6		75.2	
		(60–85)		(55–85)

average falls short of actual age by 6 years for the younger mothers but by 15 years for the older mothers.

If this age difference is a cohort phenomenon, desired age may shift closer to actual age as norms change toward more positive feelings about the second half of life. An increasingly aged population and improved health in the older years may take time to reach the individual consciousness of people in midlife, for their image of the elderly may be stored in memories of their grandparents and older kin of earlier cohorts of the elderly. If the age difference is a maturational phenomenon, we can expect younger women to follow the lead of older women in the next decade of their lives by looking backward to youth more than they do now. With cross-sectional data, we cannot directly confirm a cohort interpretation. But, to the extent we can show either an aging or a family phase correlate to subjective and desired age, we strengthen the maturational interpretation and hence indirectly lower the probability of cohort relevance to the interpretation. We turn to this issue later in this section.

B. THE "BEST" AND THE "WORST":
A QUALITATIVE LENS ON AGE AND AGING

Open-ended questions on the best and worst aspects of their current age and of the past year provide a narrower lens through which to view the tone and the most salient aspects of the lives of the younger and older mothers in the study. Three general patterns were striking in the comments of our subjects. One was the high salience of family roles, as indicated by the frequency with which their responses were in terms of events in the lives of family members rather than in self-referent terms. For example, when asked what the worst thing was about her present age, one woman said "the fights between my teenagers and their father," another that "the children are not yet grown up enough to be independent." Two-thirds of the responses to what were the best and the worst things that happened in the past year were in terms of family members. Although the question about being your present age was expected to elicit personal references to aging, family members were again found to be a frequent reference. Thus family members were the focus of 40% of the responses to the best thing about being their present age. By contrast, it was only on the question concerning the worst thing about current age that family members largely disappeared and the self and aging emerged strongly: Only 14% of the references here were to family, the remainder to aging issues. The family emerged as the locus of pleasure and the self as the locus of worry.

A second general tendency was for younger mothers to mention family members more frequently than older women on the worst thing probes, and less frequently on the best thing, a tendency that held in responses to both the age and past-year questions. The third general pattern was for children to be referred to more often than spouses by the older mothers (a child to husband ratio of 3:1) compared to younger mothers (a ratio of 2:1).

It was when the women focused specifically on themselves that a decided difference in tone between the younger and older mothers was sensed. The younger women seemed aware of beginning signs of aging (less agility, not snapping back as quickly from late hours, difficulty keeping weight down), whereas the older women responded on a deeper level, often with a note of despair. Table VI juxtaposes some of the responses in terms of self of the younger and older women to the question about their current age. No younger woman said there was nothing good about her present age as did a 51-year-old mother, nor did any younger mother speak in terms of fear and depression concerning the future, or the closing down of options for change in the years ahead.

The same upbeat versus downbeat contrast by the age of the women is shown in their comments about the past year. On the best thing that happened to them, younger women reported things that were clearly markers in their own accomplishments: earning degrees after returning to school; changing an occupation from gym teaching to computer science; getting a new job teaching handicapped children; reelection to a school committee. By contrast, the older mothers were more likely to mention pleasurable experiences rather than accomplishments (a treasure found at a tag sale, a trip

TABLE VI

"Best" and "Worst" Things about Current Age, by Age of Mother (Self-referent responses only)

Younger mothers	Older mothers
Best thing	**Best thing**
. . . I'm learning to accept some of my faults, sort out exactly what is important to me.	. . . There's nothing good about being my age.
. . . I just like what I am these days.	. . . I don't care so much what other people think of me.
. . . I'm quieter, more tolerant and patient with everybody these days.	. . . I just do what I want, never mind what others think.
. . . I'm not yet too old to remember what it's like to be young and not too young to be insensitive to the old.	. . . Just having more time for myself to do what I want.
. . . Just a good feeling that these are the best years of my life and nice to realize it.	. . . It's nice to have time to yourself but find I am too old to do a lot of things I'd like to do.
	. . . I'm not yet 60! and satisfied with years past.
Worst thing	**Worst thing**
. . . Weight is getting hard to take off.	. . . I get depressed. I'm more nervous. The future is more frightening.
. . . I don't like wearing stronger glasses; bifocals ahead.	. . . I feel my time for being young is over but I have not developed a good perspective about being old.
. . . I can't stay up til the wee hours without feeling it.	. . . A terrible sense of time passing much too quickly.
. . . I can begin to understand that midlife brings declining physical ability.	. . . I often feel terribly afraid of illness and death.
. . . I can't play the same game of tennis anymore.	. . . Lack of zip; I mind terribly the loss of energy.
. . . Most of the people in my age range are dull and dead-ended.	. . . I'd rather be young and independent.
. . . I am a bit concerned whether it's too late to reach my professional goals.	. . . Hard to get going physically. Mentally I can be on the job before my body leaves the bed, but body resists.
	. . . Terrible sense of waste of previous years.
	. . . Lingering fears that hold me back from being all I want.

to New York), with a flatter tone ("nothing special, just more time to do less.") The same contrast in tone and scale of event was caught in their responses to the worst thing that happened: Younger women mentioned things like "swamping our boat off the Connecticut shore," "not being completely happy with my co-workers," "feeling disappointed in a friend." By contrast, the worst things cited by older women were more deeply embedded in physical and emotional trauma: "finding out I had a malignant breast tumor," "a long spell last spring when I was deeply depressed," "very serious doubts about my future."

This is not to say it is only their own physical pathology that older women reported. They also cited worrisome events involving their kin and their husbands more than the younger women did. It was only the older mothers who reported such events as a suicide attempt by an elderly mother with a history of depression, a move into a nursing home by a father, a husband's mother coming to live with the family. The older mothers were entering a period in life as the "sandwich" generation, when obligations to and worry about the aging of their parents competed with the needs of their own children and husbands, and pressures from work both in the home and on the job. There was a difference as well, in the kinds of things involved when the husband was referred to: Older women cited illness, unemployment, a breakdown in communication with their husbands, whereas younger women more typically struck a positive note, "continuing a great marriage," "taking a long vacation with my husband alone." In light of the average age difference between husbands and wives, most husbands of the older women were in their fifties, when unemployment often hits those with less secure jobs in the private sector (20% of the sample reported their husbands were unemployed for a month or more during the preceding year). Health issues were also more serious and can be not only life-threatening but livelihood-threatening as well, particularly for self-employed craftsmen and business men whose work is premised on physical strength and health. The longitudinal study of health through the life span sponsored by the National Institute of Aging shows some deterioration of health for both sexes between the third and fourth decade of life and continued deterioration into the fifth decade for men but less so for women (U.S. Department of HEW, 1979). Hypertension in a man's fifth decade and reproductive system disturbance and illness in a woman's late forties is a combination more probable for the older mothers than for the younger mothers.

Travel, vacations, and sexuality were all referred to by both older and younger mothers, but again with a difference in emphasis and tone. The older women stressed the stimulation of travel itself, whereas the younger women spoke of getting away with their husbands. Older women only made two references to sex, both with a note of relief that they "couldn't get pregnant." There were no references to sex being better as a physical and emotional experience. Younger women who made reference to sexuality cited conflict surrounding sexual affairs: "Going through a stormy period when I found he had an affair going," and "I had a small affair which my husband found out about, then swatted at me with that knowledge anytime he could." Though conflict was clearly present, there was also more zest, engagement, and pure pleasure running as a thread through the younger women's comments that is less prevalent in the comments of the older women.

The ambivalence, flat tone, and aura of depression that characterized so many comments from the older women, may be an indication of the years of transition they are passing through. Unfortunately we have few women well into their fifties, when one might predict, based on the general sex reversal noted earlier, the older women will have changed to a more hopeful and envigorated conception of themselves and their own lives. We shall see at least some evidence in a later section, that they are now taking very great pleasure in a new way from their relations with their children. To some degree they are showing the pressures of the complex responsibilities they are carrying, for children, homes, jobs, with periodic unemployment and occasional illness, all in addition to their own private responses to growing older.

It is striking how strongly their relationship to their husbands correlates with numerous aspects of their lives. On items designed for a Life Satisfaction score, satisfaction with their marriage was significantly related to satisfaction with their homes (.354), neighborhood (.299), social life (.591), whereas the only item that correlated to satisfaction with their relations to their children was time for themselves (.366). Men's earning ability, job location, and social availability determined the community they lived in, often the neighborhood, and what they did socially. As their financial pressures ease, households contract in size, and accommodation is made to aging, the older women may develop renewed zest and pleasure in their lives in the decade ahead.

C. SUBJECTIVE AGE IDENTIFICATION

To explore the correlates and determinants of subjective age identification, a score was constructed based on chronological age and the age the women felt "most of the time." Subjective age was subtracted from actual age, so that a " + " on the score indicated women felt younger than they were, and a " − " indicated the women felt older than they were. Table VII ranks the characteristics associated with feeling older or younger than ac-

TABLE VII

Correlates of Subjective Age Identification[a]

Index[b]	Pearson correlation coefficient
Family role competence (wife)	+.332**
Educational attainment	+.304**
Work drive (employed women)	+.263*
Social activities	+.237*
Children's domestic help	+.223*
Aging symptoms	+.087
Total pleasures	+.059
Family interaction	+.054
Marital interaction	+.024
Family problems	−.073
Medication	−.132
Family size	−.138
Marital disagreement	−.204*
Continuous employment history	−.213*
Worries re husband	−.223*
Worries re children	−.242*
Total worries	−.247*
Daily exhaustion	−.266*
Worries re self	−.273*

[a] Positive coefficients mean feeling younger, negative coefficients feeling older than chronological age.

[b] Operational definitions of indices are given in Table XVII at the end of the chapter.

tual age. (Operational definitions of the indices shown in the table are given at the end of the chapter in Table XVII.) Feeling younger is associated with higher educational attainment, competence in family roles, high work drive, having help from children in domestic management, and social activities away from home, many of which were engaged in by the woman alone (e.g., club meetings, church, cultural events).

Feeling older than one's actual years was related to marital disagreement, continuous employment over the family cycle, worries about spouse, children, self, and large-sized families. Whereas symptoms of aging were not correlated with feeling older, health issues were implicated by the correlation with taking medication, daily exhaustion, and worry about health and one's future, which are items on the Self-Worry score.

Many of the variables associated with the subjective age score were themselves intercorrelated. For example, educational attainment and family role competence were positively correlated (.339), as were marital disagreement and worries (.358). A regression analysis permitted the isolation of independent effects of these strong correlates of subjective age identification. As seen in Table VIII, all four variables contributed indepen-

TABLE VIII

Regression on Subjective Age Identification Score[a]

Predictor variable	Beta coefficient
Family role competence	+.252*
Educational attainment	+.196*
Marital disagreement	−.183*
Total worries	−.163*
Aging symptoms	−.133*
Total pleasures	+.075
R^2 = .267*	
N = (62)	

[a] Subjective age subtracted from actual age, so a positive Beta coefficient means feeling younger than actual age, a negative beta coefficient means feeling older than actual age. Predictor variables operationally defined in Table XVII at the end of the chapter.

dently to the subjective age identification score: Feeling younger was associated with both educational attainment and family role competence, whereas marital disagreement and high worry scores were associated with feeling older. Total worries contributed a significant negative coefficient but total pleasures, although associated with feeling younger, did not reach significance. Note that, whereas the Aging Symptoms score did not correlate significantly with subjective age identification, it contributed a significant independent effect to feeling older in the regression equation.

From this analysis, subjective age identification seemed to be rooted in three dimensions of the women's lives: (*a*) the social and emotional climate of their immediate environment, as seen in the effect of the marriage, involvement in social and work roles away from home, the sheer size of the family, and help with home maintenance; (*b*) in the competence and drive of the women, as shown by the contribution of work commitment, educational attainment, and family role competence; and (*c*) in the aging process itself. Disturbance in family relations, aging rapidly in recent years, and heavy responsibilities tipped the age identification to older ages, whereas competence, achievement, and high energy tipped the identification to younger ages.

At a more general level, these data tell us something about the women's implicit assumptions about the life span itself. Why should having a college degree be associated with feeling young and a high school degree with feeling old? Why is being competent in family roles not an index of maturity and acceptance of one's present age instead of with feeling young? There was an implicit linkage of culturally valued attributes with a youthful age identification and culturally devalued attributes with an older age identification. Thus it is achievement, competence, delegation of work to others and autonomy that were linked with youth and feeling young, whereas stress, worry, waning energies, and exhaustion were linked with age and feeling older. A structural characteristic of being in the "middle," whether this refers to a position in a stratification system, a lineage, or a position on a life line, may encourage looking up and down a hierarchy in social space, backward and forward in the time frame represented by the life span. The clustering of variables associated with youthful and older age identification strongly suggests the transitional perspective of a midpoint in life, an age that perhaps does not yet provide a corrective to the cultural calculus of youth with all things bright, strong, and good, and of age with all things dark, weak, and stressful.

D. AGING SYMPTOMS

It is appropriate at this juncture to look more closely at the actual process of aging as measured in our data, because it will be of central importance as we shift attention to desired age of the women. As noted previously, we did not include direct measures of menopausal status or menopausal symptoms, but preferred to tap a wider range of aging symptoms with a high probability of occurrence in the years of life represented in the sample. The emphasis was largely on those things easily reported and easily perceived by others who interact with the women, and we assume these may have far more relevance to her sense of self, her intimate relationships, and perspectives on her past and future, than whether or not her ovarian follicles ripen and permit conception. Table IX provides the marginals on the nine items that comprised the Aging Symptoms Index.

Sensory functions such as vision and hearing, and the condition of our teeth may be assumed to change in one direction: They either remain what they were as we age, or they get worse. It is rare for eyes, ears, or teeth to improve except as we compensate by wearing glasses, hearing aides, or having teeth reconstructed. Consistent with this reasoning, Table IX shows fewer than 5% of the women reporting any improvement in eyesight, condition of teeth, or hearing. By contrast, weight, body shape, hair, and health are all things we can by voluntary acts significantly change and improve: Voluntary diet and exercise control, medical and cosmetic correction are the means. So we found not only a number of women reporting that these conditions were now worse than they were 5 years ago, but 20% or more reporting that they were better than they were.

Rating oneself on these nine factors undoubtedly carries with it more than a dispassionate assessment of self. There were, no doubt, other aspects

TABLE IX

Aging Symptom Marginals

Aging symptom	Rating[a]		
	Worse now	No change	Better now
Eyesight	48.5	47.1	4.4
Shape of body	43.2	33.8	22.1
Teeth	38.2	58.4	2.9
Energy level	38.2	41.2	20.6
Weight	35.3	41.2	23.5
Sex life	27.8	42.6	29.4
Health	25.0	50.0	25.0
Hearing	16.2	82.8	1.0
Hair condition	11.8	69.1	19.1

[a] Question read: "How would you rate yourself today compared to 5 years ago, on each of the following: better 5 years ago, no change, better now."

of their lives than body changes involved for many of the women who rated themselves. Hence it is particularly important to establish how closely the index relates to chronological age, and which of the elements in the index are more closely related to age than others. Table X shows the distribution of the Aging Symptoms Index with as fine an actual age classification as the small sample permitted, but it is clear that there was a decided elevation of aging symptoms in the oldest of the three age groups of women represented here: Women in the oldest group, largely in their late forties, showed a significant concentration at the high end of the index and a corresponding low proportion at the low end of the index. Closer inspection showed that more younger women reported a gain of weight and a loss of body shape than did older women, suggesting that some aging processes occurred before others, in this instance, weight gain during the early thirties when many of the women had their last few children. By contrast, the one item that seemed most likely to carry social and psychological components in addition to aging per se—sex life—was the most strongly related to age of all the variables in the index: 45% of the older women versus only 11% of the younger women reported a deterioration in their sex lives as compared to 5 years ago. This sharp contrast probably reflected change in sexual desire of husbands in their fifties along with change in the women's interest and pleasure in sex.

One further step established the linkage of the aging symptoms score to chronological age and its independence from family stage: A regression of actual age, family size, and age of youngest child showed that only chronological age was significantly related to aging symptoms (beta coefficient of

TABLE X

Aging Symptoms and Age of Mother

	Age of mother		
Aging symptoms score	33–40	41–45	46–56
Low (2 or less)	60.1	52.4	23.8
Moderate (3–4)	27.3	28.6	33.4
High (5–9)	12.6	19.0	42.8[a]
100% =	(21)	(23)	(21)

[a] Statistically significant from two younger age groups at .05 level.

.312, $p < .003$), whereas family size and youngest child's age were not significant (beta coefficients in the .04 range; R^2, $p < .05$, was .147).

Hence, we concluded that the Aging Symptoms score may be used as it was intended, as a measure of physiologically based change in the aging process. A good example of how the variable works to illuminate the lives of the middle-aged women can be seen in Table XI, in which the dependent variable is Daily Exhaustion Level. This index is based on three ratings on how frequently the women feel exhausted at the end of the day—physically, mentally, emotionally. In Table XI we have regressed the Aging Symptoms Index together with chronological age, and two family variables one might predict would affect Daily Exhaustion Level: The sheer number of people the women deal with each day, as measured by family size, and the age of the youngest child as an index of the extent of maternal supervision required in child rearing. It is evident in the results that aging changes and not chronological age per se contributed to daily exhaustion: Aging symptoms were the strongest predictor of daily exhaustion, with chronological age contributing nothing in addition. Age of the youngest child did not contribute anything over and above the other variables in the equation,

TABLE XI

Regression on Daily Exhaustion Score

Predictor variable	Beta coefficient
Aging symptoms	+.348**
Family size	+.281*
Actual age	−.006
Age of youngest child	−.053
$R^2 = .187*$	
$N = (59)$	

whereas family size was second only to aging symptoms in elevating daily exhaustion.

E. DESIRED AGE

It will be recalled (Figure 8) that the age variable most strongly tipped to youth was Desired Age, the age women reported they would like to be if they "could be any age they wanted." Half the women, in fact, wanted to be under 30 years of age. Not a single woman wanted to be older than she was, so that the range on this variable had an upper limit of actual age, meaning the women accepted the age they were as the most desirable one for them to be, down to a very youthful desired age in late adolescence. Figure 9 demonstrates the marked contrast between the younger and older mothers in the gap between desired and actual age (represented as the space between the dotted·curves for the younger mothers, and between the solid line curves for the older mothers). The question pursued in this section is how to interpret the strong emphasis on youth in the desired age responses, and why the older women showed an even greater youth preference than the younger women.

There are three major interpretations we might entertain for the emphasis on youth in the Desired Age responses. The first is a *cultural accent on youth:* If a society stresses strength and action, aging is apt to be devalued and death to be feared. Hence women may simply be showing an internalized cultural norm in so strongly preferring to be young. With the aging of the population, a secular trend away from this heavy focus on

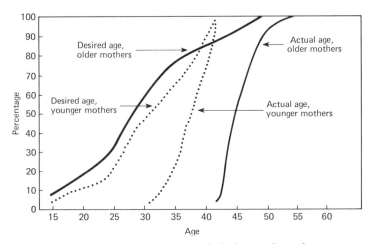

Fig. 9. Cumulative percentage distribution of desired age and actual age among younger (...) and older (——) mothers.

youth would explain the difference between the younger and older mothers as cohort differences: With each younger group entering their middle years, one would predict smaller proportions with youthful age desires. This is consistent with the difference seen in Fig. 9 between the younger and older mothers. The fact that Desired Age was significantly correlated with Ideal Age further supported this cultural and cohort interpretation.

A second interpretation would focus on *maternal identification with children*. The women subjects are currently very intensely involved with child rearing, have relatively large families and major commitments to their roles as mothers. The parent–child relationship is a two-way relationship in terms of influence: Hence the mothers' desire to be young may simply index their acceptance of or openness to the values espoused by their children. Older mothers may have seen many of their oldest children struggle with value issues of a personal and political variety during the past decade, whereas few younger mothers have yet had a child in late adolescence. Hence older mothers, through identification with their children and influence by them, may show youthful age preferences. If this is so, then one might expect mothers with strong preferences to be young to find it easier to relate to their own adolescent children than women who accept their current age as the most desirable age to be.

A third interpretation would view the youthful age desires as an *escape response to current stress*. This stress might have three major sources: Unhappiness in primary roles in the family (disturbed relations with spouse and children, for example); anxiety engendered by maturational factors such as the signs of aging they are currently experiencing; and the particular crunch of the current historic period that is exerting special and unprecedented pressures on middle-aged parents. We have already seen evidence to support the second of these interpretations concerning stress, for the older mothers showed an elevated level of aging symptoms, and we can explore the contribution of this variable to desired age. The first stress interpretation is also one we can pursue empirically since we have measures on the marital and parent–child relationships. The third stress interpretation must remain relatively untapped empirically, though economic pressure may be inferred where family size is great. This builds on demographic work on the life-cycle squeeze middle-aged parents are currently experiencing, which was discussed earlier.

With a small sample, there are limitations to the number of variables one can enter into a regression equation; hence we show three different sets of predictor variables in Table XII, to test the alternate interpretations just outlined. Equation (1) includes variables relevant to the immediate primary relations as a source of stress prompting an orientation to youth rather than acceptance of age: scores on the frequency of marital disagreement;

TABLE XII

Regressions on Desired Age

Regression equation	Predictor variable	Beta coefficient	R^2
(1)	Educational attainment	+.321**	
	Aging symptoms	−.277*	
	Total pleasures	+.183*	
	Marital disagreement	−.162	
	Total worries	−.033	.209*
(2)	Family size	−.380**	
	Aging symptoms	−.278*	
	Educational attainment	+.140	
	Age of youngest child	+.114	
	Actual age	−.029	.270**
(3)	Family size	−.461***	
	Age at first birth	−.391**	
	Aging symptoms	−.251*	
	Educational attainment	+.227*	
	Actual age	−.091	.345**

level of pleasure taken from relations with husband and children; its counterpart, a level of worries about relations with spouse and children; and the aging symptoms score, to test whether or not the maturational indicator of stress contributed to youthful age desires independent of the family-rooted worries. Educational attainment is included on the notion that competence and knowledge may work against acceptance of cultural emphasis on youthful appearance and for an acceptance of the maturity associated with being older.

The regression results in Eq. (1) (Table XII) clearly support the stress interpretation on both family and maturational grounds: Physiological aging is more significant in its contribution to youthful age desires than the worries score; marital disagreement, though not statistically significant, is in the predicted direction of escape from current stress. Gratification and pleasure in current family relations are related to age acceptance, as shown by the significant positive beta (.183). Knowledge and competence, as tapped by educational attainment, emerged as the strongest predictor of age acceptance in Eq. (1).

It is possible, however, that educational attainment is a key predictor not simply because of its association with competence and knowledge, but as a proxy for a strong correlate, family size (better educated women have smaller families), which may be important here because it taps degree of economic pressure on families rearing adolescents. Hence in Eq. (2) we retain educational attainment and aging symptoms, and add family size. We also add actual age so that the aging symptoms can be tested for their independence of chronological age. The last predictor is age of youngest child in the family, which can serve the purpose of controlling for the impact of family stage, as rearing young children may be more stressful than older children and lead to the escape response of youthful age desires on the part of the mother.

The results are again consistent with the stress interpretation: Family size replaced educational attainment as the most powerful predictor of youthful age preference, whereas aging symptoms survived with independent effects over and above chronological age. Family stage also contributed in the sense that having older children was related to greater current age acceptance, but this was not statistically significant. The total amount of variance explained has also increased in Eq. (2) over Eq. (1).

Equation (3) takes the final step in this exploration of the stress interpretation of desired age. Here the predictor variables are similar to Eq. (2) except for the substitution of maternal age at first birth instead of age of youngest child, on the reasoning that women who have very late first births have had a longer pre-child-rearing early adulthood and may in retrospect feel some nostalgia for that stage of life from the vantage point of midlife heavy responsibilities for rearing young children. The results again clearly supported the interpretation that emphasizes stress on the grounds of family responsibilities and ambivalence toward growing old, which together triggered an escape toward youthful age desires.

It is, of course, not possible to say exactly what it is about past youth that the women wanted. Some women may yearn to return to the actual lives they lived during their early adult years. For others, and we suspect this applies particularly to those now carrying heavy family responsibilities or who are in marriages that are not very gratifying, the youthful orientation may represent a fantasy of going back in time to undo or make other choices about marriage and family size than they, in fact, made in those years.

The implication is strong from this analysis that the women who wished to be young did so out of stress in their current personal lives or reaction to aging, and not that they were showing an identification with youthful values, as the cultural interpretation held. When life is going well, the women seem to be saying, they have no desire to be younger than they are. But for many middle-aged women, life does not go well.

A more direct test of the second interpretation (i.e., that the mothers identify with their children's values), is to inquire whether women who wish to be much younger reported less difficulty in rearing adolescents than women who accepted their age. The analysis shows that quite the opposite holds: the younger the women wanted to be, the more difficult they reported rearing both early adolescents ($-.335$) and late adolescents ($-.278$) to be. (The latter correlation is based only on those mothers who presently have a child in late adolescence.) Hence we reject the interpretation that youthful age preferences stem from maternal identification with children.

An important line of inquiry for future research is the impact of the parents' subjective age and desired age upon their actual relations with adolescent children, how the children themselves experienced a family in which the parents were yearning backward to their own youth, and how the aging parent provided a different emotional climate than a younger parent for children at the same stage of adolescence. If youthful age desires of the parents were from identification with the values of youth, one might predict amicable relations between the two generations, or at least tolerance on the part of the parents for the values and behavior of their children that differed from their own at a comparable stage of life. But when the youthful age desires stem from bitter disappointment with the parents' own lives and difficulty in adjusting to aging, the impact on the children may be very different. It might suggest to children that growing up and adult status is worrisome and disappointing. If the parents yearn for youth as an escape from stress in their current lives, they may be rivalrous with their children as the latter approach full adult sexual status, applying pressure on their children to make choices they would have made rather than what is most appropriate to the child's own qualities and preferences. Still other parents with difficulty accepting their age may reject a mature style of relating to the child and seek to be pals to their young when the children would prefer models of maturity and stature.

VII.   Dimensions of Parenting

In this section, we will first examine the differences between younger and older mothers in the role domains in which they derived more pleasure than worry, sketch the trends shown in child rearing difficulty by age of the child and the characteristics of the mother, and examine how maternal age and aging impacted upon the relationship with one particular early adolescent in the study families.

A.   PLEASURE-WORRY BALANCE

Family roles involve a good deal of emotional investment and a great amount of time, and are very apt to involve both positive and negative affect. One can find enormous pleasure in children, a home, and a spouse, and still experience frequent and intense irritation and worry. Bradburn (1969) has in fact shown that a top rating of personal happiness hinges on a balance of both positive and negative experiences, not the absence of the latter. Marital happiness studies suggest that sheer duration has an effect in reducing gratification (Feldman & Feldman, 1975; Rollins & Feldman, 1970; Spanier *et al.*, 1975). What a happiness curve might look like for parenthood happiness is not known, though family stage analyses suggest a decline when children are adolescents and an upturn again with the birth of grandchildren. Thus satisfaction or happiness varies both through time and across role domains in life.

To operationalize the balance notion, we obtained separate ratings for both pleasure and worry on such family dimensions as the woman's relations with children, her husband's relations with the children, the marital relation, husband's and children's health, children's behavior, and the woman's own health and view of her own future. Total scores were developed for pleasures and for worries, and subscores on each for spouse, children, and self. When the Total Pleasure and Total Worry scores were regressed on a general life Satisfaction index, significant coefficients were found for both (Pleasures, .442; Worries, − .237), with a highly significant R^2 of .296.

The subscores provide a useful overview to a striking contrast between the younger and older mothers. From the qualitative material, the stress interpretation of aging symptoms, and the determinants of subjective age, one would predict that older women would show a pleasure–worry balance more tipped to the worry side than younger women on the Self subscore, but how the age groups would differ in the balance between pleasure and worry where children and spouse are concerned was less apparent from previous analyses. Table XIII provides the overall profile for such an assessment. There was very little difference in either the mean Pleasure or Worry score among younger mothers across the three spheres of self, spouse, and children. The older mothers showed a very different profile; the mean pleasure score on children was very high, and the worry score on Self was also high. Viewed together, it is clear, that in balance, the older mothers showed more gratification in children than in marriage or the self. (On one of the three items in the Self–Worry score, only 13% of the older women reported they did not worry at all about their own future, compared to 46% of the younger women.)

When all the references to children were culled from the open-ended questions and examined for differences between the younger and older mothers, it was clear that having an older child settled in adult family and work roles provided a great deal of gratification to the older women. Perhaps the fact that their oldest children were adolescents in the late 1960s

TABLE XIII

**Balance of Pleasures and Worries Concerning Children,
Husband, and Self, by Age of Mother (Mean Score)[a]**

Score subject	Type	Younger mothers		Older mothers	
Children	Pleasures score	80.0		85.4	
	Worries score	35.1		32.1	
	Net balance		+ 44.9		+ 53.3
Husband	Pleasures score	78.2		67.1	
	Worries score	29.1		44.0	
	Net balance		+ 49.1		+ 23.1
Self	Pleasures score	78.8		69.4	
	Worries score	29.5		51.8	
	Net balance		+ 49.3		+ 17.0

[a] Children and self scores are four-item scores (4–12 score range), and husband score a three-item score (3–9 score range.) All scores converted to 0–100 scale to facilitate cross-score comparison. A "+" net balance indicates extent to which mean Pleasures Score exceeds mean Worries Score.

and early 1970s gave a special edge of pleasure to their being settled in jobs and families. The women made such comments as: "I am delighted with the girls my sons have married and happy to welcome each grandchild"; "after a bad start, my son is straightened out and happily married"; "it's great being a grandmother and having all the older children about settled down." Robert LeVine's (1978) comment about the Gusii apply to western Massachusetts as well: "The reproductive career . . . is not limited to the individual's own procreation, but includes that of his or her offspring" (p. 292).

What was less expected was the spillover effect this experience had upon the older mothers' relationship with their remaining children at home. Several women drew the comparison directly: "I am enjoying the teenage years of my younger children in a way I never did with the older ones"; "I did not really enjoy my older children when they were young. I was a very concerned and unsure mother"; "I feel I can really enjoy the younger ones now and do; we have great fun together"; "It's so much easier to take an adolescent's moods when you've been through it before." The impression is strong that with one child successfully settled, the women feel more confident about their ability to cope with the passage of their younger children through adolescence.

Younger mothers are at a rather different stage of individual and family development. Their comments about their children show concern for issues of accomplishment and of problem behavior: "Sue got admitted to the boarding school she wanted"; "The twins made all-state orchestra this year"; "A son who dropped out of high school returned to school this year." Car accidents, a child put on probation because of delinquent behavior, and another child left behind a full grade at school were among other comments the younger mothers made. Household conversation and emotional atmosphere will affect and be affected by *all* the children in a family, both those at home and those away from home. From the perspective of the young adolescents in the families, those with older siblings are sure to catch the pleasure of their mothers as a new kind of family event is celebrated: a wedding, a home purchase, the birth of a grandchild. If the older mother contributes some edge of disquiet from her personal response to aging, and the parents give off signals of marital friction and bickering, the remaining early adolescents are exposed to a complex and very different family context than their older siblings experienced. Whereas the older mother may be more competent and self-assured in dealing with the last young adolescent in the family, she may communicate some of her own personal stress and lack of assurance about the future. In contrast, the younger mother may be less confident of her parenting skills in dealing with a young adolescent but share with and communicate to the adolescent child a confident and hopeful view of the future.

Both the qualitative comments of the mothers, and our speculation as to their meaning and probable impact on the child in the family, compound the age of the mother with birth order of the child. Even the pleasure and worry scores do not differentiate what dimension of age affects the quality of relations with children as we were able to infer from earlier analyses of aging in relation to subjective and desired age. To the extent possible, the remaining sections attempt to disentangle the specific dimensions of age as they bear upon the relationships between the mothers and their early adolescent children.

B. DIFFICULTY OF CHILD REARING BY AGE OF CHILD

Because all the mothers have seen at least one child through some part of early adolescence, and many have seen children through late adolescence, they bring an experienced eye to an assessment of the difficulty of rearing children at various ages. The women show a clear distinction in their ratings of child rearing difficulty between children through the age of eleven, and children between early and late adolescence. The general trend is from relatively easy child rearing for youngsters under 2 to increasing difficulty in late adolescence. Figure 10 also shows a comparable trend in the mothers' assessment of the child's difficulty in growing up (broken lines), with a slight tendency for greater difficulty for the parent in the early years, and for the child in the adolescent years.

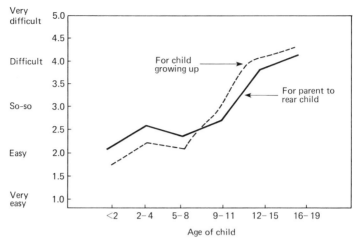

Fig. 10.   Mean ratings on developmental and child rearing difficulty by age of child.

Rather different maternal characteristics relate to child rearing difficulty with very young children than to older children. We regressed several characteristics of the mothers on reported child rearing difficulty for five specific ages of children, an analysis shown in Table XIV, in which three quite distinct patterns emerged. The educational attainment of the mothers showed a reversal with the age of the child: Better-educated mothers rated child rearing to be more difficult than less well-educated women in the early years of child development (particularly the troublesome testing period between 2 and 4 years of age), whereas by adolescence, the trend reversed and better-educated women rated dealing with late adolescents to be much easier than did less well-educated women. We suspect there are two factors involved here: Education matters far less in relations between parents and the very young child, since child rearing at this stage involves teaching basic language and motor skills at which parents of all levels of sophistication may be quite competent. But educated parents may seek to order life's affairs in a predictable manner that early child rearing is bound to upset, so they may find early child rearing upsetting to their daily routines and life styles. Once children reach adolescence, an educated parent may have more in common with the high school or college age child than less well-educated parents have. A second factor may have to do with the expense of rearing children, which goes up with the age of the child. Consequently, better-educated parents of adolescent children, with higher status jobs and higher income, may find it easier on both financial grounds and shared interests to deal with adolescent children than less well-educated parents.

Family size shows a rather different pattern. In the judgment of the

TABLE XIV

**Regression on Child Rearing Difficulty by Age of Child
(Beta Coefficients)**[a]

Predictor variable	Age of child				
	Under 2	2–4	9–11	12–15	16–19[b]
Family size	−.016	−.153	−.176	.337*	.527**
Age at first birth	.233	.212	−.030	.266*	.240
Educational attainment	.335*	.383*	−.117	−.109	−.364*
Current maternal age	.053	.108	.142	−.047	−.098
R^2	.157*	.168*	.057	.149*	.183*

[a] Positive beta coefficients indicate difficult child rearing, negative betas, easy child rearing; for example, better-educated women find rearing children under 2 more difficult (.335) and rearing adolescents less difficult (−.364) than less well-educated women.

[b] Excluding mothers who have not yet had a child in late adolescence.

women in the study, rearing very young children is easier if one had a lot of experience (i.e., a number of children), but as the children grow into adolescence, the pattern reverses, reaching the most significant beta coefficient in the table by late adolescence (.527), when the larger the family, the more difficult child rearing is reported to be. Again, it is likely that the range of problems presented by the very young child is much narrower, less individuated from one child to the next, than those of more fully developed near-adult adolescent children. The larger the family, the greater the possibility that problems in their lives will affect the atmosphere of the family. Having had one baby may give good preparation for dealing competently with a second or fourth, but having had one adolescent does not necessarily prepare the parent to deal effectively with the third adolescent in the family. In addition, a large family at later stages of family development will involve acute financial pressure on the parents, so "difficulty" involves the earning capacity of the parent, not simply interpersonal skills, understanding of child development, and special characteristics of the child at that stage.

Age at first birth shows yet a third pattern: Except for the latency period of 9 to 11, the older the mother was at the birth of a first child, the more difficult she reported it was to rear children. Our findings are similar to those of Daniels and Weingarten (in preparation) that women who had their first birth in their late twenties or early thirties found adjustment to early parenting much more difficult than those who timed births in the early twenties: Life had jelled for the older first-time parent and the timing itself reflected an orderly decision to complete schooling and become established in careers before taking on family responsibilities. For such women, the near impossibility of keeping firm control of a day's events with an infant or toddler in the family may take a heavier toll, making the child rearing experience far more difficult than for a younger woman with less set ways, less focused goals, greater flexibility and capacity to bend with the press of unexpected daily events. Our findings suggest that late timing of first parenting continues to have an effect at later stages of child rearing as well: The older a woman at first birth, the more difficult child rearing is reported to be, not only with toddlers, but with adolescents.

We assume the global ratings of child-rearing difficulty made by the women are at least in part rooted in their own experience rearing children at various ages, but the ratings undoubtedly also reflect aspects of the mothers' experiences that have little to do with specific relationships with specific children. Thus the finding that late first birth is associated with child-rearing difficulty may carry some stress rooted in being off time as mothers of young children when most women their own age have older children. In the next section, we avoid these potentially contaminating factors by concentrating on how maternal age and aging affect the relationship with one specific early adolescent child in the family, about whom a number of special questions were asked.

C. MATERNAL AGE, AGING, AND RELATIONSHIP TO EARLY ADOLESCENT CHILD

Families vary to such an extent in the number, spacing, and sex of children, that it is difficult in a sample of any size to control for all the appropriate structural characteristics of family composition when one focuses on a particular dyad involving one child and one parent. The best we can do in narrowing attention to the relationship between early adolescents and their mothers is to resort to a dummy variable for sex of child and birth-order position. In the regressions used in this section, these controls are identified as daughter = 1, son = 0, and last born (youngest child) = 1, oldest, middle, and only child = 0.

The first analysis step was to pinpoint the relative contribution of maternal age and aging symptoms to either the perceived difficulty of rearing early adolescent children or the specific reported emotional closeness to a given early adolescent child in the family. Table XV shows that maternal age was slightly implicated in child rearing difficulty whereas aging symptoms of the mother were not; but in emotional closeness to the early adolescent child, the pattern reversed: Here it was aging symptoms in the mother that reduced the closeness to the child. As aging symptoms are related to youthful desired age on the part of the mother and stress in the marital relationship, this may also involve a tendency to more daydreaming, a shift to interiority in the woman, less accessibility to her children; with the result

TABLE XV

**Regression on Difficulty of Childbearing and Emotional Closeness
to Early Adolescent (Beta Coefficients)**

Predictor variable	Child rearing difficulty	Emotional closeness
Maternal current age	.146	− .122
Aging symptoms	.003	− .224*
Early adolescent:		
Daughter[a]	− .022	.169
Last born[a]	− .161	.065
R^2	.113	.131

[a] Dummy variables: daughter = 1, son = 0; last born = 1, first born, middle and only = 0.

that there is less emotional closeness to the early adolescent. This is clearly a speculation, but it is consistent with a further finding that older mothers both encourage less sociability in their early adolescents, and report these children to be less sociable. In a regression including family size and maternal age, with dummy variables on sex and birth order of the adolescent, the only significant predictor of the rated sociability of the child was maternal age (a beta coefficient of − .304*): The older the mother, the less sociable she rated her child to be.

A rather different set of factors come into play in stimulating tension with early adolescents. Our data suggested a decided cohort dimension that not only illuminated the slightly more distant quality of the emotional tone of mother–child relationships among the older mothers, but a source of the difficulty reported in child rearing. We asked the mothers in the study how often their early adolescents were critical of them on five issues: for the clothes they wore, being old-fashioned, their outlook on life, being too strict, and talking about when they were their children's age. A *Mother Criticism* score was devised from these items. We also asked whether the early adolescent had engaged in a series of behaviors that could be labeled "limit testing": smoking cigarettes, drinking wine or beer, smoking marijuana, drinking whiskey or other hard liquor, kissing and/or petting, and hitchhiking. The score based on these six items is labeled *Limit Testing*. We asked the mothers, for each of these behaviors, what their response would be or was to such behavior: Would they accept it as part of growing up, disapprove but say nothing; or disapprove and talk to the child or scold him or her. The score based on these items was labeled *Maternal Disapproval of Limit Testing*.

The mothers' current age showed quite strong correlations with these measures: .203 with Mother Criticism, − .569 with Limit Testing, and + .271 with Maternal Disapproval of Limit Testing. The older the mother, the less apt the early adolescent was reported to engage in limit testing, the more critical the child was of the mother, and the more mothers disapproved of limit testing on the behaviors involved in the score. Regressing both Age and Aging Symptoms together with Mother Criticism and Maternal Disapproval of Limit Testing showed the most significant predictor of emotional closeness to the child was Mother Criticism: the more critical the child was of the mother, the more distant the relationship to the child reported by the mother (a beta coefficient of − .339*). Because only a small proportion of the early adolescents had actually engaged in the limit testing behavior, the Maternal Disapproval score was the more useful variable in the next step of the analysis. Table XVI shows maternal age to be a very strong predictor of disapproval of the child's limit testing: The older the mother, the more she disapproved of such experimentation on the part of the child, independent of a control variable like church attendance that one might expect to relate to such moralistic standards, or to educational attainment of the mother, which one might expect to be related to a loosening of such standards. Neither variable showed any significant contribution to maternal disapproval independent of maternal age.

Phase of family development was even more predictive of maternal disapproval than the age of the mother: The older the youngest child in the family, the less the mother disapproved of limit testing by an early adolescent. This suggested that women relax their restrictions on adolescent experimentation over time, as well as apply less rigid standards to younger children once they have seen that older children survive such adolescent experimentation as they mature. The process of change along the course of family development makes it all the more striking that maternal age survives as a significant predictor as well. We may be tapping a significant cohort difference here: The older mothers may have themselves engaged in less limit testing in their youth than the younger mothers. In addition, the younger mothers were themselves in their twenties in the 1960s and may have engaged in experimentation with drugs and sex, thus adding to the original cohort difference, adult change in response to the relaxed mood of the historical period in which they were young adults. It will be remembered too, that it was only the younger mothers who had a drug or alcohol problem or who reported extramarital affairs. Consistent with this interpretation, maternal age was negatively correlated with the encouragement of the quality of "unconventionality" (− .301) by the mother or the extent to which she rated her early adolescent as being "unconventional" (− .261).

Thus, whereas aging seems to be associated with maternal withdrawal and youthful fantasies, and consequently less emotional closeness to and more difficulty in rearing adolescent children, this second set of factors

TABLE XVI

**Regression on Maternal Disapproval of Limit Testing
Behavior by Early Adolescent**

Regression equation	Predictor variable	Beta coefficient
(1)	Maternal current age	.344*
	Age, youngest child	−.476**
	Frequency, church attendance	.118
	$R^2 =$	.235*
(2)	Maternal current age	.375*
	Age, youngest child	−.506**
	Family size	.021
	Educational attainment	.008
	$R^2 =$	.224*

rooted in cohort and historical period characteristics also has an effect upon the parent–adolescent relationship. More than younger mothers, older mothers were criticized by their adolescent children, held more rigid standards for behavior, and disapproved of the child's limit testing. Although we cannot discount the possibility of psychological rigidity and denial as part of the older mother's reaction to her own "winding down" as the child "winds up," we suggest there are cohort and historical effects showing through the age variable as well. Thus, culture, history, and biology all contribute to our understanding of adult development in the middle years and its impact on the emotional climate within which the young grow to maturity.

VIII. Conclusions

We shall briefly summarize the major findings from the exploratory research reported in this chapter, sketch what the next research steps could appropriately be in following up the leads of this analysis, and discuss the question of whether the next generation of middle-aged parents will have similar or different characteristics from those found in research on contemporary middle-aged adults.

The chapter has explored several dimensions of maternal age, weighing the areas in which chronological age serves as an indicator of physiological change and aging in the middle years, as the carrier of cohort characteristics, or a marker to family and child development phases. We have found that marital discord, aging itself, worries about self, spouse, and children all contributed to feeling older than chronological age and wanting to be younger. There was strong evidence that the contemporary cohort of middle-aged adults did not accept their age but yearned to be young or to have a chance at different options taken in youth than those they had in fact chosen. The implication of the findings is that middle-aged mothers who look longingly in the direction of youth or darkly ahead to a premature death, do so not out of an internalized cultural norm glorifying youth so much as out of circumstances of interpersonal, role, and aging stress.

We have shown some evidence that subjective and desired age have an effect independent of chronological age upon the relationship to children in the family: Women who want to be younger than they are report greater difficulty rearing adolescent children than women who accept their age, and women who have recently experienced an elevation of aging symptoms report less emotional closeness to their early adolescent children. There were suggestions of cohort differences between younger and older mothers that reflected the differential impact of the past decade on women in their twenties compared to those in their thirties, and on the older children in the study families who moved through adolescence during those years. We have also suggested that today's middle-aged parents have carried a particularly heavy, and perhaps cohort-specific burden of responsibilities as a consequence of the large and closely spaced families they have produced, during an historic period marked by rising educational expectations and runaway inflation.

The focus on the physiological process of aging suggests some common issues that confront every generation of middle-aged adults. Each generation will confront the menopause, the signs of aging in their bodies, their own mortality, increased concern for the health and survival of their spouses, the conflicts produced by tugs of obligation and love to both their aging parents and adolescent children, and will bring different experiences to bear as they rear a last child from those involved in rearing a first child. Whereas the next generation of middle-aged parents will be spared part of the midlife squeeze because of the smaller size of their families, the impact of their own aging is apt to occur during the years they are rearing adolescents as a consequence of the later age at which marriage and families are being formed in the 1970s. The women in the next cohort of middle-aged parents may differ from their mothers in having an expectation of relatively continuous employment through the family cycle, and hence experience fewer jolts from unexpected turns of events that differed from their youthful expectations of adulthood.

It is always tempting to write research summaries with a more "conclusive" tone than they merit, and this is clearly a special danger in summarizing an exploratory piece of research on a small sample. There is a clear need for future research to devise better and more varied measures of aging, subjective age identification, and stress indicators. The study needs to be replicated on a larger sample with data from fathers as well as from mothers, and directly from adolescent children rather than reported by the parents. And we need to take seriously the importance of direct measurement of endocrine levels, health status, external and valid indicators of the degree of aging perceived by others in the environment of our subjects, and to relate such measures to interview data on social characteristics, the quality of family relationships, and the subjective self-image of middle-aged adults.

Finally, we need to be alert to social, economic, and political indicators of historical change so that we are aware in advance of fielding a study, the probable parameters within which our observations will hold, and what variables will tap the degree of exposure to and involvement of our subjects with the changes taking place in the larger society. Unless we do this and do it well, we shall continue to indulge in post hoc interpretations of the probable impact rather than the measured impact of social change or historical events on the people we study. It may be, for example, that the close linkage between chronological age and career progression that has marked the past few generations of American men, is undergoing gradual but significant change. There are already signs that, as women adapt the male career pattern, more men are shifting to women's past styles of relating to the job world. Evidence of this is seen in men's later age at job entry, earlier retirement, elevated discontent with the lockstep job ladders of factory work, greater involvement in schooling throughout the adult years (one-third of all college students are now over 25 years of age); more career switching in midlife, now facilitated by married women's continuous employment, more flexible time scheduling, increased part time employment (15% of all jobs in the United States are now part time); and an improved job market for unmarried employees as a consequence of the lesser mobility of married workers with dual careers to coordinate.

Business and management observers have also suggested that the structure of work in American society is undergoing a shift from the lockstep pattern of schooling and job scheduling of mature industrialism, to a postindustrial pattern of greater flexibility, more interspersing of school and work, a more subtle adaptation between family and work patterns (Hirschhorn, 1977, 1979). Hirschhorn (1979) and Berkeley (1971) have also suggested that a new organizational form is emerging in the advanced sectors of the economy, based on temporary, task-centered teams rather than bureaucratized job ladders, which will mean far less solidity to expected job promotion, location, even job skills, for future workers in the labor force. This will call for either dispelling the assumption that young people can chart a life plan in advance, or being prepared to experience basic changes at points when settling down to stable job and family lives is expected.

As researchers concerned with adult development, we need to be alert to these indicators of the direction of change in the larger society. If we also build change indicators into our research designs, we will be adding the measures we need to assure that our research findings illuminate the similarities and differences between our contemporary middle-aged subjects and their successors in middle-aged cohorts of the future.

TABLE XVII

Indices and Operational Definition

Index	Operational definition
Aging symptoms	9-item score on things "better 5 years ago" than now: health, eyesight, hearing, energy level, body shape, sex life, hair condition, weight, teeth.
Children's domestic help	5-item score on frequency of children's help with household chores: meal preparation, clean up, clothes care, shop for food, clean house.
Daily exhaustion	3-item score on frequency of daily mental, physical, and emotional exhaustion.
Employment history	Level of employment (none, part time, full time) at 5 family stages in terms of age of youngest child.
Family interaction	5-item score on frequency with which total family (parents and children) do things together: eat breakfast, eat dinner, discuss local news, visit friends, talk intimately an hour or more.
Family problems	5-item score on presence of problems of any family member: weight, emotional, drug, alcohol, other.
Family role competence	Ratings from "far below" to "far above" average on three roles as spouse, parent, home manager. Separate scores for wife and husband.
Life satisfaction	6-item score on satisfaction–dissatisfaction ratings: house, neighborhood, social life, relation to spouse, relation to children, time for self.
Limit testing	6-item score on early adolescent re: smoking cigarettes; drinking wine or beer; smoking marijuana; drinking whiskey or other hard liquor; kissing and/or petting; hitchhiking.
Marital disagreement	6-item score on frequency of disagreement with husband on: money, politics, chores, relations to relatives, how to handle children, sex relations.
Marital interaction	5-item score on frequency of doing things alone with husband: eat breakfast, eat dinner, discuss local news, visit friends, talk intimately for an hour or more.

(Cont.)

TABLE XVII (CONT.)

Index	Operational definition
Maternal disapproval of limit testing	6-item score on mother's acceptance or disapproval of limit-testing behavior of early adolescent. Same items as Limit Testing score.
Medication	9-item score on frequency of taking medication in past month for: pain, upset stomach, chronic illness, headache, sleep, nerves, stay awake, improve mood, increase energy.
Mother criticism	5-item score on frequency of criticism of mother by early adolescent child: being old fashioned; being too strict; clothes mother wears; outlook on life; talking about when they were child's age.
Social activities	6-item score on frequency of attendance: church, club–organization meetings, sports events, eating out, sports participation, cultural events.
Subjective age identification	Actual Age minus Age Feel most of the time.
Total worries, total pleasures	Ratings on extent of Worry and of Pleasure, total scores and subscores re spouse, children, self: husband's health, relation to children, relation to wife, children's health, children's behavior, relation to father, relation to mother; respondent's health, thinking about own future, relation to children and husband.
Work drive	4-item score on ratings on probability of staying on current job if income not needed, job terrible but no other available, child needed attention, husband wanted wife to stay home.

Acknowledgments

Part of the support for data gathering and analysis of the study reported here came from a Biomedical Sciences Support Grant at the University of Massachusetts, for which the author is grateful. Special thanks are also due to graduate students in family sociology and human life-cycle seminars who contributed ideas during the instrument-design phase of the research: to Janet Gans for help during the fielding; to Beth Shapiro for coding; and to Lucy Fischer, Beth Shapiro, and Aida Rodriquez for computer work. Very special thanks are here acknowledged to readers of an earlier draft of the manuscript: James Wright, Bernice Neugarten, Pamela Daniels, Kathy Weingarten, Orville G. Brim, Frank Furstenberg, and Glen H. Elder, Jr.

References

Bengtson, V. L., & Cutler, N. E. Generations and intergenerational relations: Perspectives on age groups and social change. In R. H. Binstock & E. Shanas (Eds.), *Handbook of aging and the social sciences.* New York: Van Nostrand Reinhold, 1976.

Bennett, S. K., & Elder, G. H., Jr. Women's work in the family economy: A study of depression hardship in women's lives. *Journal of Family History,* 1979, **4**(2), 153–176.

Berkeley, G. E. *The administrative revolution: Notes on the passing of the organization man.* Englewood Cliffs, N.J.: Prentice-Hall, 1971.

Borland, D. C. Alternatives in the definition of middle age: Postparental life stage or chronological age, an assessment. Paper presented to 73rd annual meeting, American Sociological Association, September 1978.

Bradburn, N. *The structure of psychological well-being*. Chicago: Aldine, 1969.

Brim, O. G. Theories of the male mid-life crisis. *Counseling Psychologist,* 1976, **6,** 2–9.

Bühler, C. *Der menschliche lebenslauf als psychologisches problem*. Leipzig: S. Hirzel, 1933.

Butler, R. N., & Lewis, M. I. *Aging and mental health*. St. Louis: Mosby, 1977.

Cumming, E., & Henry, W. H. *Growing old: the process of disengagement*. New York: Basic Books, 1961.

Cutler, N. E. The effects of subjective age identification among old and young: A nation-wide study of political, economic, and social attitudes. Unpublished paper presented at the twenty-seventh Annual Meeting of the Gerontological Society, Portland, Oregon, 1974.

Cutler, N. E. Toward a political generations conception of political socialization. In D. C. Schwartz & S. K. Schwartz (Eds.), *New directions in political socialization research*. New York: Free Press, 1975.

Daniels, P., & Weingarten, K. *Sooner or later*. New York: Norton, (in preparation).

Deutscher, I. The quality of postparental life: Definitions of the situation. *Journal of Marriage and the Family, 1964,* **26,** 52–59.

Deutscher, I. From parental to postparental life: Exploring shifting expectations. *Sociological Symposium,* 1969, **3,** 47–60.

Diggory, J. C., & Rothman, D. Z. Values destroyed by death. *Journal of Abnormal and Social Psychology,* 1961, **30,** 11–17.

Doering, C. H. The endocrine system. In O. G. Brim, Jr. & J. Kagan (Eds.), *Constancy and change in human development*. Cambridge: Harvard University Press, 1980.

Dohrenwend, B. S., & Dohrenwend, B. P. (Eds.) *Stressful life events*. New York: Wiley, 1974.

Elder, G. H., Jr. *The children of the Great Depression*. Chicago: University of Chicago Press, 1974.

Elder, G. H., Jr. Approaches to social change and the family. *The American Journal of Sociology, Supplement,* 1978, **84,** S1–S33. (a)

Elder, G. H., Jr. Family history and the life course. In T. K. Hareven (Ed.), *Transitions: The family and the life course in historical perspective*. New York: Academic Press, 1978. (b)

Elder, G. H., Jr., & Rockwell, R. C. Marital timing in women's life patterns. *Journal of Family History,* 1976, **1,** 34–53.

Erikson, E. Identity and the life cycle: Selected papers. *Psychological Issues,* 1959, (whole no. 1).

Feldman, H., & Feldman, M. The family life cycle: Some suggestions for recycling. *Journal of Marriage and the Family,* 1975, **37,** 277–284.

Frenkel, E. Studies in biographical psychology. *Character and Personality,* 1936, **5,** 1–34.

Frenkel-Brunswik, E. Adjustments and reorientation in the course of the life span. In B. Neugarten (Ed.), *Middle age and aging*. Chicago: University of Chicago Press, 1968.

Friedan, B. *The feminine mystique*. New York: Norton, 1963.

Gould, R. L. *Transformations: Growth and change in adult life*. New York: Simon & Schuster, 1978.

Gurin, G., Veroff, J., & Feld, S. *Americans view their mental health*. Monograph Series, No. 4. New York: Basic Books, 1960.

Gutmann, D. An exploration of ego configurations in middle and later life. In B. L. Neugarten (Ed.), *Personality in middle and late life*. New York: Atherton Press, 1964.

Gutmann, D. Parenthood: A key to the comparative study of the life cycle. In N. Datan & L. H. Ginsberg (Eds.), *Life span developmental psychology: Normative life crises*. New York: Academic Press, 1975.

Hamburg, B. A. Coping in early adolescence: The special challenges of the junior high school period. In S. Arieti (Ed.), *American handbook of psychiatry*. New York: Basic Books, 1974.

Hareven, T. K. (Ed.), *Transitions: The family and the life course in historical perspective*. New York: Academic Press, 1978.

Havighurst, R. J. History of developmental psychology: Socialization and personality development through the life span. In P. B. Baltes & K. W. Schaie (Eds.), *Life-span developmental psychology*. New York: Academic Press, 1973.

Hill, R. Methodological issues in family development research. *Family Process*, 1964, **3**, 186–206.

Hirschhorn, L. Social policy and the life cycle: A developmental perspective. *Social Service Review*, 1977, **51**, 434–450.

Hirschhorn, L. Post-industrial life: A U.S. perspective. *Futures*, August 1979, 287–298.

Kagan, J., & Coles, R. (Eds.). *From twelve to sixteen: early adolescence*. New York: Norton, 1972.

Kalish, R. A. Death and dying in a social context. In R. H. Binstock & E. Shanas (Eds.), *Handbook of aging and the social sciences*. New York: Van Nostrand Reinhold, 1976.

Kalish, R. A., & Reynolds, D. K. *Death and ethnicity: A psychological study*. Los Angeles: University of California Press, 1976.

Kastenbaum, R. On the meaning of time in later life. *Journal of Genetic Psychology*, 1966, **109**, 9–25.

Kastenbaum, R., & Aisenberg, R. *The psychology of death*. New York: Springer, 1972.

Keniston, K. Youth as a stage of life. *The American Scholar*, 1970, **39**, 631–654.

Kling, A. Testosterone and aggressive behavior in man and nonhuman primates. In B. E. Eleftheriou and R. L. Sprott (Eds.), *Hormonal correlates of behavior*. New York: Plenum Press, 1975.

Kuhlen, R. G. Developmental changes in motivation during the adult years. In J. E. Birren (Ed.), *Relations of development and aging*. Springfield, Ill.: Charles C Thomas, 1964.

Leshner, A. I. *An introduction of behavioral endocrinology*. New York: Oxford University Press, 1978.

LeVine, R. A. Comparative notes on the life course. In T. K. Hareven (Ed.), *Transitions: The family and the life course in historical perspective*. New York: Academic Press, 1978.

Levinson, D. J. *The seasons of a man's life*. New York: Knopf, 1978.

Lowenthal, M. F., Thurnher, M., & Chiriboga, D. *Four Stages of life*. San Francisco: Jossey-Bass, 1975.

Luce, G. G. *Biological rhythms in psychiatry and medicine*. Public Health Service Publication No. 2088. Washington, D.C.: United States Government Printing Office, 1970.

Mason, J. W. Emotion as reflected in patterns of endocrine integration. In L. Levi (Ed.), *Emotions: Their parameters and measurement*. New York: Raven Press, 1975.

Modell, J., Furstenberg, F. F., Jr., & Strong, D. The timing of marriage in the transition to adulthood: Continuity and change, 1860–1975. *American Journal of Sociology, Supplement*, 1978, **84**, S120–S150.

Murphy, Y., & Murphy, R. F. *Women of the forest*. New York: Columbia University Press, 1974.

Nesselroade, J. R., & Baltes, P. B. Adolescent personality development and historical change: 1970–1972. *Monographs of the Society for Research in Child Development*, 1974, **39**, (whole no. 1).

Neugarten, B. L. (Ed.). *Personality in middle and late life*. New York: Atherton, 1964.

Neugarten, B. L. The awareness of middle age. In B. L. Neugarten (Ed.), *Middle age and aging*. Chicago: University of Chicago Press, 1968.

Neugarten, B. L. Personality changes in adult life: A developmental perspective. In C. Eisdorfer & P. Lawton (Eds.), *The psychology of adult development and aging*. Washington, D.C.: American Psychological Association, 1973.

Neugarten, B. L. Time, age and the life cycle. *American Journal of Psychiatry*, 1979, **136**, 887–894.

Neugarten, B. L., & Brown-Rezanka, L. Midlife women in the 1980s. Testimony before the Select Committee on Aging, United States House of Representatives, September, 1978 (Mimeo).

Neugarten, B. L., & Gutmann, D. Age–sex roles and personality in middle age: A thematic apperception study. In B. L. Neugarten (Ed.), *Middle age and aging*. Chicago: University of Chicago Press, 1968.

Neugarten, B. L., & Kraines, R. Menopausal symptoms of women in various ages, *Psychosomatic Medicine*, 1965, **27**, 266–273.

Neugarten, B. L., Wood, V., Kraines, R. J., & Loomis, B. Women's attitudes toward the menopause. In B. L. Neugarten (Ed.), *Middle age and aging*. Chicago: University of Chicago Press, 1968.

Oppenheimer, V. K. The life cycle squeeze: The interaction of men's occupational and family life cycles. *Demography*, 1974, **11**(2), 227–245.

Oppenheimer, V. K. The Easterlin hypothesis: Another aspect of the echo to consider. *Population and Development Review*, 1976, **2**, 433–457.

Oppenheimer, V. K. The sociology of women's economic role in the family. *American Sociological Review*, 1977, **42**, 387–406.

Peck, R., & Berkowitz, H. Personality and adjustment in middle age. In B. L. Neugarten (Ed.), *Personality in middle and late life*. New York: Atherton, 1964.

Purifoy, F. E., Koopmans, L. H., & Tatum, R. W. Steroid hormones and aging: Free testosterone and androstenedione in normal females aged 20–87 years, 1979 (unpublished manuscript).

Reynolds, D. K., & Kalish, R. A. Anticipation of futurity as a function of ethnicity and age. *Journal of Gerontology*, 1974, **29**, 224–231.

Riley, M. W. Age strata in the society. In M. W. Riley, M. Johnson, & A. Foner (Eds.), *Aging and society: A sociology of age stratification*. New York: Russell Sage Foundation, 1972.

Riley, M. W. Age strata in social systems. In R. H. Binstock & E. Shanas (Eds.), *Handbook of aging and the social sciences*. New York: Van Nostrand Reinhold, 1976.

Rodgers, R. H. *Family interaction and transaction: The developmental approach*. Englewood Cliffs, N.J.: Prentice-Hall, 1973.

Rollins, B. C., & Feldman, H. Marital satisfaction over the family life cycle. *Journal of Marriage and the Family*, 1970, **32**, 20–28.

Rosen, J. L., & Bibring, G. L. Psychological reactions of hospitalized male patients to a heart attack: Age and social class differences. In B. L. Neugarten (Ed.), *Middle age and aging*. Chicago: University of Chicago Press, 1968.

Rubin, L. B. *Women of a certain age: The midlife search for self*. New York: Harper & Row, 1979.

Ryder, N. B. The cohort as a concept in the study of social change. *American Sociological Review*, 1965, **30**, 843–865.

Ryder, N. B. A model of fertility by planning status. *Perspectives*, 1978, **19**(6), 369.

Sheehy, G. *Passages: Predictable crises of adult life*. New York: E. P. Dutton, 1977.

Spanier, G. B., Lewis, R. A., & Cole, C. L. Marital adjustment over the family life cycle: The issue of curvilinearity. *Journal of Marriage and the Family*, 1975, **37**, 263–275.

Troll, L. E. The family in later life: A decade review. *Journal of Marriage and the Family*, 1971, **33**, 263–282.

Uhlenberg, P. Changing configurations of the life course. In T. K. Hareven (Ed.), *Transitions: The family and the life course in historical perspective.* New York: Academic Press, 1978.

U.S. Department of Labor, Bureau of Labor Statistics. *Who are the unemployed? A chartbook.* Bureau of Labor Statistics Bulletin 1965, 1977.

U.S. Department of Labor, Office of Information, *News,* October 31, 1979.

Vaillant, G. *Adaptation to life.* Boston: Little Brown, 1977.

Female Sexuality through the Life Span

Judith Long Laws

SYRACUSE UNIVERSITY
SYRACUSE, NEW YORK

Abstract

Shortcomings of a sparse research literature on sexuality in older persons are discussed. The framework for a life-span approach to human sexuality is presented, based upon a developmental model for sexual identity. Published research is reviewed in terms of information on the vicissitudes of three major forms of sexual expression. Effects of physical aging,

LIFE-SPAN DEVELOPMENT
AND BEHAVIOR, VOL. 3

marital status, opportunity, and individual differences in sexual motivation are assessed. Cross-sectional and life-history research strategies are evaluated. Suggested foci for future research include the development of a measure of sexual motivation, the relationship among forms of sexual expression at a point in time and over time, and the emergence of themes of sexual alienation or sexual agency over the life span.

Sexuality—here defined as *the individual's capacity for pleasure from intimate physical contact*—is a vital human attribute that is manifest in every stage of the life cycle. Gerontologists who have written on this topic are mindful of the vitality of sexuality in older persons. Thus Goldfarb (1965) places sexual expression in the context of self-actualization, referring to elders as "capable providers of pleasure to self and others" (p. vii). Rubin (1965) links sexual expression to the need for physical touch, surely a lifelong concern. Stein and Etzkowitz (1978) hold that the developmental tasks of work, sexuality, reproduction, and intimacy span the adult years. Existing research offers ample evidence for the persistence of sexual interest and sexual expression in the later decades of life. Indeed, one wag has suggested sex as the answer to Butler's question, *Why Survive?*

I. Researching the Sexuality of Older Persons

A search of the professional literature indicates that the sexuality of older persons has been neglected by gerontologists and sex researchers. By any standard, older individuals were underrepresented in Kinsey, Pomeroy, & Martin (1948, 1953). Kinsey *et al.* included in the studies only 56 women over the age of 60. Several of the scarce contributions of elderly women in particular (Christenson & Gagnon, 1965; Christenson & Johnson, 1973) are subsamples drawn from the Kinsey files. Masters and Johnson (1968) had only 54 respondents falling between 60 and 78; most of these were under 70. In the Duke studies, respondents were 60 or above at the start of the research in 1955 (Verwoerdt, Pfeiffer, & Wang 1969). Kinsey *et al.*'s (1953) discussion of older males is limited to a few pages; and that of older females is even more limited. All of the research to date suffers from an additional flaw: The respondents are too young. The proportion of the elderly population that is over 75 is increasing, and we have virtually no information on which to base projections. It is anticipated that, by the year 2000, 45% of the elderly (over 65) population will be 75 or older. Moreover, the sex ratio, which favors women at 65 (69 men for every 100 women), becomes more extreme at later ages: It is currently 77 : 100 among persons 65–74 and 48 : 100 at 85 and older. Extant sex research unfortunately reflects neither the age nor the sex structure of the elderly population.

Because the aged population is plentiful, and its sexuality is neither a rare nor exotic phenomenon, the lack of research becomes, in itself, something requiring explanation. Some of the factors that appear to affect the quantity or quality of research in this area include: (*a*) Resistance to sexual topics; (*b*) failure to disaggregate; (*c*) lack of historical perspective; (*d*) anomalies in conceptualizing sexuality; and (*e*) sex bias.

A. DIFFICULTIES OF SEX RESEARCH WITH ELDERLY POPULATIONS

Although most professionals in gerontology express prosex attitudes, Yeaworth and Friedeman (1975) note that there is wider acceptance of the idea of infantile sexuality than of sexuality in older people. Pfeiffer (1969) reports that relatives of the elderly are discomfited by their participation in sex research. This discomfort may not be limited to lay people. More than one gerontologist has suggested that the paucity of research on older persons' sexuality can be attributed to gerontologists' unexamined resistance to the idea of probing into their parents' sexual secrets.

In addition, attitude surveys indicate a perceived disjunction between sex and the elderly: Both young and old hold stereotyped views of the elderly as sexless and uninterested in sex (Golde & Kogan, 1959; Kogan & Shelton, 1962).

Perhaps for some of these reasons, persons outside the sex-research community are prone to overestimate the difficulties of securing responses to questions on sexual topics. Others exaggerate the nonrepresentativeness that may be introduced by volunteer bias. This question has rarely been investigated empirically. However, Udry and Morris (1967), Wilson (1975), and Kaats and Davis (1970) have achieved encouraging results in checking the validity of their research on college and national samples.

These two biases—imagining that sex research is "touchier" than it is, and stereotyping of older people—are dangerous to the degree that they elude the researcher's awareness. The guarded quality of parent–child communication about sexuality can potentially carry over into the researcher's adult years. A type of cognitive incest taboo may be internalized by most children in our society: that is, an avoidance of thinking of their parents in sexual terms. This results directly from the parental teaching that Schaefer (1973) calls "the Big Lie": that children are asexual (and, conversely, that parents are too). If, as young people, we learn to shield our sexual behavior from parental knowledge, that posture may well persist throughout the life span. Conversely, we as children shield ourselves from knowledge of our parents' sexuality. Unfortunately, this scruple seems to generalize to all adults (i.e., persons older than ourselves). This not only retards research on the sexuality of older persons, but, when such research is carried out, different cohorts are grouped together, resulting in the neglect of their differing histories.

B. THE PROBLEM OF FAILURE TO DISAGGREGATE

We have already seen that most studies of sexual behavior and attitudes underrepresent older people. Perhaps for this reason, researchers have not disaggregated older respondents in their analyses. In failing to do so, they have overlooked the demonstrated effects of educational attainment and birth cohort that may be particularly important for women. Among women who would now be considered elderly, Kinsey *et al.* (1953, pp. 299, 339) found dramatic differences in accumulated incidence of premarital coitus. Historic studies summarized in the following sections contradict many of the myths concerning older women's sexual motivations, capacities, and histories. It seems likely that readers and researchers alike know very little about women who attained adulthood before the "Feminine Mystique." Moreover, they tend to view these inappropriately aggregated women from the perspective of the "liberated" 1960s and 1970s. Such distortions suggest a crucial role for historical studies affording information on cohorts of women who may be completely neglected in research that utilizes cross-sectional strategies.

C. LACK OF HISTORICAL PERSPECTIVE

The clearest argument for the value and distinctiveness of historical perspective on women's sexuality can be found in the following three studies. They differ from current "establishment" sex research in (*a*) the spectrum of sexual behaviors with which they are concerned; (*b*) the dimensions of significance with which respondents invested their sexuality; and (*c*) the birth cohorts represented.

One of the earliest known empirical studies of women's sexual experience was conducted by Clelia Duel Mosher (Jacob, 1979), herself a character of some historical interest.[1] The respondents in her study, women born

---

[1] Clelia Duel Mosher, born in 1863 into a family of (male) physicians, put herself through college and devoted herself to researching and debunking myths about women's incapacities. At 32, she entered the new Johns Hopkins School of Medicine. After graduation, she continued her research as a professor at Stanford. She volunteered and served in World War I. The data reported here remained unpublished at her death in 1940 (K. A. Jacobs, Clelia Duel Mosher, *Johns Hopins Magazine,* 1979, **30**(3), 9–16).

around the period of the Civil War, seemed to refute stereotypes about Victorian women and their sexuality. The 47 histories in Mosher's survey span 30 years, beginning in 1892; 17 were completed before 1900, 14 between 1913 and 1917, and 5 in 1920. Most respondents were college graduates and married to college graduates. Of those responding to a question about work before marriage ($N = 38$), 30 had been employed.

Questions on the survey included the level and source of premarital sex information, frequency and preferred frequency of intercourse, sleeping arrangements, frequency of orgasm, purposes of intercourse, contraception, and sexual initiation. Respondents' comments included reflections about their conjugal relations and husbands' part in their sexual satisfaction. Of the 41 women answering a question on sexual desire, 35 reported that they desired intercourse independent of their husbands' interest. Most women were orgasmic, although the wording of the question did not permit the author to assess frequency of orgasm. Failures to achieve orgasm (under conditions of sexual arousal) were reported as "nerve racking," whereas achieving orgasm increased at least one respondent's regard for her husband (Jacob, 1979, p. 14).

Opinions about the purposes of intercourse revealed much of the ethos of marital sexuality, at least in this privileged stratum. Those who thought reproduction was the sole purpose were in the minority; 24 marked "pleasure" as one purpose; 13 thought intercourse was "a necessity" for both sexes, and 9 for men only; 15 thought it was a necessity for neither. Some respondents, asserting the value of intercourse as an expression of love's passion, opined that regulating coital frequency by desired family size was inappropriate. This sample endorsed both marital coitus and contraception; at least 30 of the respondents used some form of birth control.

A pioneering study in the survey research tradition was one by Davis (1929) that explored in detail the sexual experience of an early generation of college women. The particular emphasis was on lesbian attachments, but a detailed sexual history was taken with parallel attention to heterosexual and homosexual involvements. This study gave thoughtful attention to issues of sexual identity and ethics as well as to sexual expression.

In Davis' 1929 study (as in Mosher's a generation earlier), there appears to be a moral reservation about intercourse. This does not take the form of the guilt of premarital sex familiar in the 1950s and 1960s, but rather the older idea of sensual indulgence as being of lower moral worth than abstinence. None of the (Freudian) theoretical sequelae of guilt were apparent in respondents expressing these sentiments: Neither sexual interest nor orgasmic competence was inhibited. Nevertheless, a number of women stated abstinence as an ideal which was hard to live up to.

Another research report casts light on the question of sexual life styles and the sexual options of today's grandmothers. Bullough and Bullough

(1977) have published an account of the organization of "closeted" lesbian life in Salt Lake City in the 1920s and 1930s. The unfinished manuscript, dated 1938, covered 20 years of its author's experience and that of 23 lesbian friends. The study included detailed sexual histories, family histories and psychological profiles, as well as occupational data. The respondents, who were well-educated, were conversant with the theories of the day concerning the etiology of homosexuality. A dominant motivation was to remain respectable and to conceal their sexual orientations. The authors reported that the respondents viewed physical functions with repugnance, and frowned upon masturbation. They did not approve of male homosexuals of their acquaintance, particularly as these individuals violated sex-role norms to appear "feminine." They themselves tended to adopt the life style of homosexual marriage, often with one partner playing the stay-at-home wife.

These studies are as different as their research populations. Yet they do strongly contradict some of today's stereotypes concerning Victorian women, their attitudes toward sexuality, and the forms and significance of sexual expression. Echoes of these voices should accompany those who undertake research with women born in the 1890s, at the turn of the century, and in its early decades.

A historical dimension is required to understand the sexual histories of women now in their fifties and sixties as well. Thus Masters and Johnson (1968) report, and Lillian Rubin (1978), corroborates with even more recent data, that the birth cohort that had not enjoyed reliable contraception experienced a sexual liberation after menopause, finding expression in a "second honeymoon" with the long-term partner. We can assume that the same effect will be experienced by those whose major period of exposure to pregnancy preceded 1960. However, we will not necessarily expect this kind of change in what Jessie Bernard (1968) once called "the third sex": contracepted women. Moreover, we should be aware that, in the birth cohorts represented by research reported here, only 13% were ever divorced (Kovar, 1978). Among women born from 1945 to 1949, by contrast, 17% of first marriages had ended in divorce before age 30 (Bureau of the Census, 1976). No data are reported for women of younger birth cohorts, nor are statistics complete for the women now in their thirties. It is clear, however, that divorce has now become so common that long-married and single-partnered older women of these cohorts will be considerably less representative of their age groups than the married women contributing the data of these studies.

D. CONCEPTUALIZING HUMAN SEXUALITY

A number of the factors directly affecting the quality and quantity of research on the sexuality of elderly persons also exercise an indirect effect through the often unacknowledged influence on the conceptualization of what is to be studied. Sex research as a whole has been distorted by an overemphasis on exotica and neglect of the normal (Heiman, 1974b; Laws, 1973), by an emphasis on quantity to the exclusion of quality (Ehrmann, 1957), by a lack of attention to questions of sexual identity (Ehrmann, 1957; Laws & Schwartz, 1977), and by a biologistic bias that neglects the essential role of social factors in guiding human sexual behavior. The legacy of Puritan and other religious traditions defining sexuality as evil and animalistic can be seen today in taboos against the study of sex. Again, the boundaries on what is studied reveal the atherosclerotic hand of history. For adults of both sexes, but especially for women, only certain parts of the sexual history "count." Sexual accountants tally occasions of coitus but neglect other parts of the sexual spectrum. Important dimensions of sexual history and sexual identity are obscured when researchers fail to think seriously about different forms of sexual expression in the context of the life span.

Another unnecessary limitation is imposed upon our understanding of human sexuality by the custom of treating sex as discontinuous with self. Elsewhere, I have commented upon the disproportionate emphasis on the study of sexual exotica and the consequential maximization of social and psychological distance between the researcher and the "object of study" (Laws, 1973). Treating sexuality as a discrete topic, discontinuous with other areas in social and behavioral science, blocks the application of what we know about basic social and psychological processes to sexual situations. One example will suffice: Studying processes of development, stability, and change has been an abiding concern of sociologist and psychologists, to say nothing of historians. Yet these issues have been little addressed in the context of normal sexuality.

The foregoing suggests a need for a bold and integrative conceptualization of human sexuality, capable of subsuming existing empiricial findings and guiding future research. It should lend itself to applications over the life span. It should be sufficiently general to hold across situations and variations in, for example, sexual orientation. It should specify a role for experience and for personal and cultural significance of sexuality. It should be consistent with the following principles based upon current sex research:

1. Human sexuality is as flexible as is human intelligence.
2. Sexuality is an attribute of the person, not of a relationship or of a status, or of a period or periods in the life cycle.
3. Individual experience limits and forms the ways in which, and the extent to which, sexual capacity is developed.
4. There are individual differences in the level of sexual motivation and preferred frequency of sexual contact.
5. Growth and change in sexuality are normal and to be expected.

6. Factors militating toward stasis or stability in sexual identity and sexual behavior can be identified.
7. Sexual identity is formed in encounters with sexual scripts, with partners, and through reflection, evaluation, and volition.

The definition of sexuality offered at the outset provides a starting point. The individual's capacity for pleasure from intimate physical contact provides the focus for a flexible approach. Forms of "contact" correspond to observable forms of sexual behavior. Such contact may sometimes involve other individuals, may involve a range of behaviors, may be undertaken for instrumental ends such as orgasm, profit, conception, or interpersonal power. A host of contingent factors can modify the form, frequency, and rewardingness of sexual expression, the relationships among forms of sexual expression at a point in time and over the life span, and the interrelationships between sexual behaviors and sexual identity.

There is little justification for restricting the study of human sexuality, at any age, to coitus. Hence, in this chapter, we propose to organize existing research in such a way as to shed light upon the status and vicissitudes of three major categories of sexual expression among the elderly: autoerotic activity, homosexual activity, and heterosexual activity. Although each may subsume a wealth of specific behaviors, they are most commonly indexed by counts of masturbation, homosexual contact, and coitus, respectively. We will observe this convention, making a particular effort to place the current picture in a life-span developmental context organized in terms of sexual identity.

E. REPRESENTATION OF WOMEN IN SEX RESEARCH ON THE ELDERLY

Sex research has repeatedly been critiqued for bias in its treatment (or neglect) of women (Heiman, 1974; Hite, 1974; Laws, 1973; Laws & Schwartz, 1977). If sex research may be indicted for "sexism," it is also vulnerable to charges of "ageism." Regrettably, the gerontological research shares both these limitations.

In addition to skittishness about the propriety and feasibility of studying human sexuality in general, a double standard persists. Men are considered "more sexual" and in fact are more studied by sex researchers than are women. It appears that male sexuality is more readily conceptualized as an attribute of the person and hence is more likely to be studied transitationally. There appears to be a tendency to assume that only married women are sexually active. The sexuality of nonmarried women tends to be neglected, in comparison with that of their married peers. This is not to say, however, that the sexuality of married women is not neglected. It appears that marital coitus is implicitly assumed to exhaust or define the sexuality of married women: Other forms of sexual expression and other partners are generally not explored by researchers.

The study of female sexuality is particularly distorted by three traditional perspectives. First of these is the tendency to think of sex primarily in terms of procreation. This in turn leads to an overemphasis on marriage as the primary context for sexual activity and hence for the study of sex. The identification of female sexuality with fertility leads to two further errors: Women at or beyond menopause are thought of as "old" women, perhaps 20 years before their male age-mates are considered "old" men; and the sexuality of postmenopausal women is not investigated.

Women's sexuality is too often defined with reference to that of men. Men are assumed to initiate, women to respond; men to be active, women to be passive. Women without men are assumed to be nonsexual and are understudied, whereas married women are overstudied. Lesbians are thought to be "less sexual" than women involved with men (Gagnon & Simon, 1973) because their sexual union is less phallic. In general, the forms of sexual expression and the dimensions of sexuality that are researched are derived from and reflect the experience of men. Items of considerable importance to women are overlooked altogether. Thus, for example, researchers commonly confound acts of intercourse with orgasms, failing to consider the implications of their distinctness for women.

In the majority of discussions by gerontologists, the sexuality of the female is eclipsed by the contingencies of her presumed marriage. As in the conventional marriage and family literature, the wife is held responsible for her marriage, so in the gerontological literature, she is held responsible for "her" sex life. A wife who suffers from her husband's impotence is subjected to a "blame the victim" kind of logic. There is a tendency to ascribe decline in male sexual performance to attributes of the wife (Rubin, 1965, p. 146). The wife is assigned responsibility for restoring a husband's sexual capacity by whatever means necessary (including some rather disfiguring ones). There is no corresponding concern with the wife's opportunities, and no mention of the quality of her sex life. Botwinick's (1973, p. 44) discussion of the effect of boredom on coital frequency is limited to *men's* boredom.

There are instances of unwitting irony, as in Masters' and Johnson's (1968) discussion of sexual regimens for cardiac patients. Sexual contact of the most minimal and routine sort is recommended for the cardiac patient (presumed male). However, the female cardiac patient may be at risk even if her muscular involvement is minimal, *if* her pulse rate and blood pressure are affected (Masters & Johnson, 1968, p. 46). If her sexual opportunities follow the guidelines provided for the cardiac patient, she may run little risk. The lesson of this example is not, however, a medical one. Rather, it illustrates the general tendency to regard women's sexuality solely as instrumental for the attainment of men's ends. The distortion inherent in this approach pervades the available literature on elderly women.

II.   A Life-Span Approach to Human Sexuality

The study of human sexuality has not, to date, utilized a life-course perspective, with its related ecological emphasis (Elder & Rockwell, 1979). Without such a framework, development cannot be seen in relation to the individual's changing and enduring environments. The symbolic environment, which offers definitions of sexual actors, sexual contexts, and sexual activity is particularly critical. More specifically, individuals are situated within sexual communities, distinguished by a sexual life style, toward which individuals are trained. Individuals are provided with *sexual scripts that define who are sexual actors and what are sexual acts and feelings; scripts that provide scenarios of how sexual encounters may be managed and sexual communication effected.*

Sex researchers have sometimes been sensitive to time and the changes in sexual norms and contraceptive technology that the last 3 decades have brought. Some researchers have documented a generation gap or warp (LoPiccolo, 1973; Reiss, 1960). However, locating individuals in cohorts is insufficient; we need ways of taking into account the demographic shape of the population in which one "is" a certain age, and we need to identify the perspective through which we are studying identifiable age groups. The "social accounting" approach of a Kinsey, crucial though it has been, cannot inform us regarding these dimensions of sexual history and sexual status.

To be sure, current attempts to define a life-course perspective remain preliminary and programmatic. This is particularly true of methodology and research strategies, which lag behind conceptualization. A goal of the present chapter will be to point the way to approaches and issues by means of which a life-span perspective may be brought to bear upon research on the sexuality of older individuals.

A.   DEVELOPMENT OF FEMALE SEXUAL IDENTITY OVER THE LIFE SPAN

The first component of a life-course approach to female sexuality is a developmental model that specifies socially recognized stages or sexual statuses. Social (and hence personal) significance of individual events and sexual histories reflect the content of such stages. The content, however, can be expected to vary over historical time; consequently the meanings of a comparable sexual history will differ for women of different cohorts. The developmental model thus provides a normative (but historically specific) dimension to the analysis of sexual histories.

Elder and Rockwell (1979) identify three strands in a life-course analysis. First, individuals are located in a birth cohort and thus in history. Socially shared life patterns (such as age-graded sexual scripts) are depicted against this background. The individual sexual history illustrates the continual interplay between the social course of lives and individual development.

A life-course approach to the study of female sexuality, then, would need to exploit fully the sparse historical research to form a backdrop for current generations. Individual sexual histories must be viewed in the dual context of birth cohorts and social scripts. Of particular interest is the sexual identity formed as a product of individual experience and sexual scripts. Sexual identity may be defined as *the sense of self as a sexual being and awareness of the attributes that make up one's femaleness–maleness.*

The Laws model (Laws, 1970; Laws & Schwartz, 1977) of sexual identity defines six stages over the life cycle (see Table I). Each represents a concatenation of factors influencing sexual identity for a specific stage. Transitions

TABLE I

Developmental Model for Sexual Identity

Stage I Prenatal	Stage 2 Birth and Childhood	Stage 3 Puberty	Stage 4 Sexual Intimacy	Stage 5 Fertility/ Parenthood	Stage 6 Loss of Sexual Powers
Biological events					
Conception Fetal development	Birth Normal sexual morphology	Development of secondary sex characteristics Menarche	Sexual initiation Frigidity/impotence	Conception Pregnancy Parturition Lactation	Menopause Surgical loss Aging
Social events					
None	Sex assignment Sex-role socialization Sex rearing Sexual exploration	Dating Popularity Sexual experimentation Sexual morality	Role conflict Assumption of marital role Resocialization regarding sexual behavior	Marital role Parental role	Freedom from fertility Wound to self-esteem Change in sex identity
Significant others					
None	Parents Peers Physician	Peers	Partner(s) Peers	Spouse Parents Peers Community	Spouse

Source: Laws and Schwartz, *The Social Construction of Female Sexuality Sexual Scripts* (Hinsdale: Dryden Press, 1977), p. 23.

from one stage to the next are marked by biological events that are accorded social significance in the culture. It should be noted that it is the expectation of biological changes, and the social significance accorded them that define changes in sexual status rather than any effect of the biological events themselves. For each stage, significant others can be specified, who monitor the individual's developing sexuality, evaluate it, communicate about it (not always to the focal person), and mobilize expectations and sanctions regarding the scripted sexual status appropriate to that particular stage. Sexual scripts, in other words, are mediated by specific others in the face-to-face interactions of everyday life. Variations in sexual scripts, of major or minor degree, exist for different subgroups within society (e.g., for social classes). The sexual career is itself scripted. Sexual identity is age-graded; hence a woman is expected to be a different kind of sexual being at different ages.

The first stage in the Laws model is concerned with prenatal events. It is of minor importance to this discussion, except that some components of sexual identity (chromosomal gender or gender anomaly, fetal development, and hormonal history) originate in this stage.

The transition to Stage 2 is birth (the biological event) and its associated social event, sex assignment.

Stage 2, of greater interest for the present purposes, concerns childhood. Sex-role socialization and sexual exploration are major social processes during this period. Leah Schaefer (1973) has identified the sexual script of early childhood as the "Big Lie." Among the many consequences of this script is that sexuality is not a topic of shared communication in the home. A related feature is the training girls receive in passivity: Self-exploration is discouraged, and sex education is neglected. Gagnon and Simon (1973) have asserted that most female children do not develop a vigorous and competent orientation toward their own bodies, and this has implications not only for later sex with partners, but also for taking responsibility for bodily health and bodily functions throughout the life cycle.

The Kinsey *et al.* studies (1948, 1953) revealed sex differences in behavior and meaning associated with masturbation in the prepubertal period, which have been replicated in more recent research. Although the official script (or Big Lie) defines masturbation as antisocial behavior, in the actual experience of boy children it is emphatically social. The vast majority of males first learned about masturbation in the presence of other boys; group masturbation continues as an activity during preadolescence. Almost all the females in the Kinsey *et al.* study learned about masturbation "on their own." Moreover, reported rates of masturbation by children in their mid-teens are dramatically different by sex: 88% of males; less than 20% of females. Not only the social setting, but the social meaning of masturbation differs for girls and boys. The boys experience a peer group for validation of genital sexuality; other boys are both peers and partners for sexual activity. The behavior that is established and supported in this setting is the individual's actively seeking and obtaining sexual satisfaction. The expectation of social support for active sexual behavior appears to carry through to young adulthood: Kaats and Davis (1970) found that both female and male college students perceived more social support for various levels of sexual activity by males than by females. Among males, masturbation provides continuity between child and adult sexual statuses, as adolescents learn to masturbate with pictures or other stimuli that anticipate female partners.

In terming this stage, "latency," Freud inadvertently echoed the scripted Big Lie. In a sense, however, he was symbolically, if not literally, correct. Current research indicates that for girls, if not for boys, sexual activity in childhood becomes "lost data" in the sexual history. Autoerotic and same-sex physical contact "don't count" toward the scripted adult sexual status of a heterosexual married lady. These components of sexual experience are discontinuous with the projected adult identity, whereas for males, prepubertal experiences appear to have more continuity with the adult identity.

In capsule, male sexual experience in childhood already exhibits the characteristics of sexual agency and of peer group support for sexual activity.[2] Girls receive neither the social support nor the coaching for sexual agency. They may be punished if they are caught in sexual exploration, and they may learn negative labels for their body parts and for sexual activities. At the same time, however, sex-role socialization processes actively enhance the development of cultural femininity, which has utility for the female life script. Femininity includes being pleasing (but not discriminating), responsive (but not initiating). It involves vicariousness, objectivity, and narcissism.[3] It involves training for love and commitment. Together, these attributes constitute a stage of readiness for puberty and nubility when the curtain officially rises on female sexuality, in the inescapable context of courtship and marriage.

The biological events associated with puberty usher in Stage 3. The sexual status of the woman in this stage is that of the nubile female; courtship is the focus of activity, with marriage the intended destination. Sexual ac-

[2] Sexual agency is defined as the capacity to choose and control one's own sexual life (Laws, 1978; Laws & Schwartz, 1977). It implies awareness of sexual options, and the exercise of choice. It implies, too, reflection upon one's sexual experience and evaluation of that experience in the light of its consequences for self-enhancement or alienation.

[3] For an extended treatment of these dimensions of "feminine personality" see J. L. Laws, *The Second X,* Chapter 3. New York: Elsevier North Holland, 1979.

tivity, though not officially condoned, as incidental (and perhaps instrumental) to mate selection.

Sexual initiation marks the beginning of Stage 4 in the Laws model. Because of the taboos on sexuality in our culture, the first relationship consensually defined as sexual is tremendously significant for sexual identity. This may well be the first opportunity the individual has for bodily parts and bodily experiences to be verbally labeled. What is shared in the early encounters can be critical for sexual self-definition, particularly in a society that defines sexuality with a narrow genital focus. Differences in the sexual and social statuses assigned by our society to coitally active unmarried women and men persist. Social labeling of heterosexually and homosexually active young people also differs, in large part, because of the social importance attached to marriage and family formation.

The occurrence of fertility marks a change in sexual status, and inaugurates Stage 5 in the Laws model. Although the social statuses of wife and mother occupy a long time period in the individual's life span, they will be discussed only briefly here. The specifically sexual experiences associated with labor and nursing have been underlabeled or mislabeled and generally ignored by researchers. The major social significance of this stage is the accession to the sexual status of mother. Subcultural variations in the definition and experience of this status have not yet been adequately researched. It is often stated in the literature, however, that motherhood reduces the degree to which a woman is regarded as sexual. In some traditions, religious and cultural imagery of the madonna is applied to all mothers. A shift in a wife's attention coincident with taking responsibility for an infant may well change her attributes as a sexual partner. The degree of distraction and overwork that routinely accompany motherhood may depress a woman's sexual interest. Privacy and personal freedom that, for many women enhance both sexual interest and sexual opportunity, are curtailed for the duration of the child-intensive phase of the family life cycle. Thus, although many women report an increase in sexual responsivity following childbearing, the quality and quantity of their sexual activities may not reflect gains until other material conditions change (Rubin, 1978).

For women, transition to the sexual status of non-person (Stage 6) is scripted, and is associated with the cultural complex of menopause. Insofar as women's sexual validity consists in their instrumentality for men's sexual purposes, loss of capacity for childbearing is consequential. Insofar as women's sexual validity is defined in terms of the ability to attract men, it is circumscribed by the conventions confining sex objects to a restricted age range. Insofar as women's access to sexual partners is tied to the institution of marriage, it is constrained by the marriage pool, with sex ratios increasingly discrepant in the higher age groups.

In terms of sexual scripts, no positive sexual status or behavior is prescribed for the postmenopausal woman. The popular culture does provide images of inappropriate behavior. One source is *Playboy* magazine, which occupies a unique place as a cultural institution unto itself. *Playboy* has been an authoritative voice commenting on the sexual scene for more than a decade and has (arguably) formed the sexual consciousness of several generations of young adults. *Playboy* does not neglect the sexuality of older persons; however, the imagery of sexually active older women and men are dramatically different. A long-running series of cartoons portrays a concupiscent white-haired gentleman who is sleek, plump and plutocratic, resembling nothing so much as jolly old St. Nicholas in mufti. Another series portrays cartoonist Buck Brown's "Grandma," a revolting and ridiculous crone avidly pursuing normal young men who avidly flee her. She is not above using trickery and bribery to obtain sexual attention and sexual stimulation. Grandma is a parody of feminine seductiveness: When she appears in the regulation diaphanous nighty, we see the pendulous breasts and scrawny legs of an old woman.

Grandma is played for laughs; not so the sinister and enigmatic Mrs. Robinson of the much-discussed film "The Graduate." Mrs. Robinson is portrayed with a degree of female glamour, but with many witch–bitch attributes. Her affair with the lumpish Benjamin could have been presented as a peccadillo, a variation on the old theme of the irrationality of love and lust (What does she see in him?). However, this is a morality play of sorts. A virginal daughter provides a counterpoint to Mrs. Robinson, whose lust appears slightly perverted, if not downright incestuous. Her indiscretion brings about her downfall, the ruin of her sexual status as a respectable matron. Her partner, however, enjoys a happy ending (with the daughter). He is not responsible for the violation of the age and sex taboos; after all, he was raped.

Folklore provides a third cautionary image of the sexuality of older women, no less negative for being jocular. Young men are advised to seek out older women as sexual partners because:

> They don't tell
> They don't swell
> And they're grateful as hell.

These elements of sexual scripting define a rather dismal set of options for sexual expression in older women. An equally negative image of sexual identities of older women can be inferred from the same sources. Sex ratios obtaining at the later ages put further constraints upon older women's sexual options.

Nevertheless, older women's sexual experiences may show considerable variation around the scripted norm.

B. RELATIONSHIP BETWEEN SEXUALITY AND AGING IN WOMEN

The term sexuality is sometimes used in reference to the individual's sexual behavior or sexual expression, and sometimes to sexual motivation or "sex drive." Sometimes sexual interest (or lack of it) is inferred from sexual expression of lack of it, without empiricial justification. Here we wish to distinguish sexual expression and capacity from sexual motivation.

Although relationship between physical aging and sexual functioning has been observed in men, no parallel trend has been observed for women. Whereas men experience some loss of erectile efficacy beginning in their forties, women's orgasmic capacity appears unaffected by physical aging. Masters and Johnson (1968) found that women's orgasmic outlet remained stable until their sixties. Older women in their sample showed a lower incidence of sexual expression.

Great caution should be observed in interpreting the results of the cross-sectional samples that constitute the bulk of the available research. Rarely is there any basis for making comparisons among cohorts. The sexual histories of women now in their eighties will not be paralleled by those of women now in their sixties. As gerontologists well know, the meaning of a given chronological age varies by cohort. Sex ratios, too, vary by age categories, sometimes dramatically. Discontinuities in incidence and frequency of sexual expression (particularly coitus) in adjacent cohorts may have more to do with opportunity factors than with level of sexual motivation.

Physical changes can, of course, play a role in women's sexual functioning. The atrophy of genital tissues and decrease in vaginal secretions after cessation of ovarian functioning can reduce the ease or pleasurability of coitus. We might expect that, as a result, some women's preference among different forms of sexual expression might change. However, the effect on incidence or frequency of any form of sexual expression, including coitus, could be quite variable.

The complexity of factors affecting sexual expression is now acknowledged in discussions of menopause. Social expectations (varying dramatically with birth cohorts) and the elements of an individual's history appear to outweigh the physiological processes in determining the effect of menopause on a woman's sex life. For this reason, research on menopause is discussed in the context of women's sexual motivation, in the following section.

A full picture of the relationship between sexuality and aging must, of course, distinguish between sexual interest and sexual activity, among the forms of sexual expression, and must take into account opportunity factors, including the level of functioning of the usual partner. Moreover, individual differences appear to persist over long periods. Additional longitudinal and life history studies are needed to permit researchers to assess the relative effects of these factors on sexual interest and sexual expression in the later years.

Virtually the only longitudinal perspective currently available is provided by the series of studies undertaken by a research team at Duke University, beginning in 1954. At the outset, their panel included 131 women and 123 men aged 60 and above. The Duke studies do not permit any conclusive inference regarding the distinctive patterning of sexuality over the female life cycle. However, Verwoerdt *et al.* (1969) reported that sexual interest and sexual expression (coitus only) follow divergent curves over time for women. In the oldest respondents (78 or older) sexual interest increased, although the familiar pattern of decline in coitus was observed. Similarly, Christenson and Gagnon (1965) reported that a fantasy measure of sexual interest (dreams) did not decline with sexual expression in coitus in their sample. Clearly, an attempt must be made here to distinguish sexual motivation from sexual activity and the several antecedents of each.

III. Sexual Motivation in Older Women

From the empirical evidence, it is apparent that sexual expression is an outcome mediated by many aspects of sexual scripting, opportunity, and personal history. Too often, an estimate of individual differences in "sex drive" or level of sexual motivation is inferred from reports of sexual expression, without careful consideration of the constraints under which the latter occurs.

At a theoretical level, it is not difficult to conceptualize sexual motivation as *the individual's tendency to be interested in sexual occasions, sexual materials, and sexual contact; to seek to approach occasions for sexual stimulation, to persist in such approaches and stimulation; to choose sexual over other sorts of occasions or rewards; to value and dwell upon sexual experiences,* and so on. Whether such tendencies are innate or learned, and whether observable individual differences are innate or learned are ostensibly empirical questions, but ones that probably cannot be resolved with current research techniques. Early research on motivation informed us that sexual motivation is not a deprivation-based tendency resembling the tissue needs, but has more in common with social motives such as the need for achievement (Atkinson, 1958). Sexual interest, as indexed by self-report and by sexual activity, appears to operate in a cyclical fashion affected by feedback. In general, the less sexual activity, the less sexual motivation; conversely, the more sexual activity, the more interest, *if* the activity is satisfying (Spanier, 1972). There is some controversy about whether or not sexual desire satiates in humans. The role of cognitive factors is not well understood. Indeed, the role of cognitive factors has been little researched, though it is clearly important to the understanding of many facets of sexual motivation, including individual's preferences among forms of sexual expression and choices among sexual life styles (including celibacy).

Incontestably, experience plays a major role in human sexual motivation. Social learning affects expectations and the incentive value of anticipated events; expectation and incentive affect effort and overt behavior in general; and satisfaction with outcome is relative to expectations. A general model of sexual motivation might be developed that is consistent with the well-known formula for predicting achievement behavior (Atkinson, 1958; Atkinson & Raynor, 1974; Vroom, 1964). We would expect that value (or incentive) and expectancy would, over time, modify each other, although it is traditional to think of them as independent variables. Effort, in the achievement model, is thought of as the outcome of the multiplicative effect of expectancy and value, but it might enter the equation as a factor modifying success. Success (or satisfaction) must be included in a model that seeks to predict ongoing cycles of behavior such as achievement or sexual expression.

For each of the four terms in the proposed model, social determinants can be specified. These are particularly important if we bear in mind that, in comparing cohorts, we are comparing groups that may well have different values for these variables. The historical studies cited earlier suggest, for example, that sex might have been assigned a lower rank in an overall hierarchy of values for individuals who came of age before World War II. In our terms, the incentive value of sex would be lower than it would be for persons now in their thirties and forties. Expectation, as we have suggested, mediates satisfaction. If women of certain cohorts did not expect regular orgasm as part of their conjugal relations, they might well report higher levels of satisfaction overall than women with greater expectations. Clearly, cohort differences on these factors will affect the empirical relationships with the research variables to be discussed. Put another way, experience may vary systematically over birth cohorts within any study of sexuality in older persons.

By far the preponderance of research studies on the sexuality of older persons has utilized a cross-sectional strategy. Such a strategy impedes the assessment of effects of experience (unless an author ill-advisedly equates chronological age with experience). However, if differences between contiguous birth cohorts are as substantial as we suspect, comparisons between them are misleading at best.

A. FACTORS AFFECTING WOMEN'S SEXUAL MOTIVATION

Existing research provides little basis for inference concerning an individual's level of sexual motivation, net of social factors. Complexity is multiplied by the common tendency to compare levels of reported interest across gender lines. A persistent disparity in level of sexual interest of women and men has been noted by a number of researchers.

Pfeiffer's (1969) data show a lack of synchrony in sexual interest between women and men aged 60–94. Over a 10-year longitudinal study, two sorts of disparity were evident. A much larger proportion of men retained their sexual interest than that of women (80% as compared with 30%). However, the activity level of the men declined, whereas that of the women did not. The effects of gender and age are here melded with those of the effects of physical aging on sexual performance. Sex differences in the effects of aging on sexual interest and on sexual activity, and the relationship between the two, need further research.

1. Menopause

Social custom and folklore have traditionally held that sexual interest and/or sexual expression declines or disappears in women following menopause. Much of this folklore has been challenged by the empirical research on menopausal women (Neugarten, Wood, Kraines, & Loomis, 1968). Christenson and Johnson (1973) reported that for the majority of the never-married women in their sample, the termination of sexual activity coincided with menopause.[4] Research on more recent birth cohorts assigns a much less significant role to menopause. In particular, some authors noted a renascence of sexual interest in women freed of the fear of unwanted pregnancy (Masters & Johnson, 1968; Rubin, 1978). The redefinition of age categories, as well as improvement in general health of the younger age groups would predict a very different effect of menopause on

[4] Christenson and Johnson's (1973, p. 88) data do not entirely bear out this interpretation. In their group of women aged 60 ($N = 14$), 28% were still sexually active. In respondents' self-reports concerning their degree of sexual interest after menopause, about 50% experienced no change and equal proportions experienced an increase and a decrease.

the sexual life of women in birth cohorts now approaching and experiencing menopause.

Marital status appears to moderate the relationship between menopausal status and sexual interest. Christenson and Johnson (1973) found only a quarter of the never-married women reported a decrease in sexual interest following menopause. This contrasts with the findings of Pfeiffer, Verwoerdt, and Wang (1967) studying a married sample, that only 22% reported no decline, and Kinsey *et al.*'s (1953) finding that 48% reported a decline in sexual interest or activity. Kinsey *et al.* interpreted their findings in light of the effects of aging on the *male* sexual response.

Kinsey *et al.*'s interpretation serves to underscore the ambiguity in comparing data on sexual interest and activity of married women with those of single women. The indication for future research is that much greater care must be taken to elicit women's subjective responses to the joint (husband–wife) events that are commonly tallied, and to investigate issues on which only the wives can report. These data are limited further in that they refer only to interest in coitus, and tell us nothing about the respondents' motivation for other forms of sexual expression.

2. Orgasm

The theoretical model sketched in the previous discussion suggests that sexual interest (and resulting sexual activity) is affected by past experiences with sexual activity as satisfying or unsatisfying. The occurrence of orgasm is a clear-cut instance of a satisfying sexual experience for a woman, and would seem to offer a sound basis for predicting the individual's desire to repeat the experience. Regrettably, sex researchers have rarely asked women how regularly they experience orgasm, and this is particularly true of research on older persons. The Christenson and Gagnon (1965) study, an exception to this generalization, fails to exploit the data on orgasm and reports no extended analysis on either antecedents or consequents of orgasmic efficacy.

Christenson and Johnson (1973) noted the solecism implied in male sex researchers' neglect of degree of responsiveness in women: Occasions of coitus are, without apparent justification, equated with frequency of sexual satisfaction (or orgasm). Masturbation, sexual fantasy, and homosexual relations are overlooked—as though coitus constituted the extent of female sexual expression.

Christenson and Johnson (1973) did not fail to note the incentive effect of orgasmic efficacy on the persistence of sexual expression. They noted that their sample of never-married women had a high rate of success in attaining orgasm in coitus. Clearly, rate of attaining orgasm is an important intervening variable in the study of women's sexual interest and preference for different forms of sexual expression. It is regrettable that the authors neglected to report orgasmic efficacy for other forms of sexual expression that were also studied.

Quality of marriage appeared to mediate sexual adjustment in a study by Clark and Wallin (1965). Lowest rates of sexual unresponsiveness were found among women whose marriages began and continued high in "quality," whereas highest rates appeared among women whose "quality" of marriage was persistently low.

Clark and Wallin's disinhibition thesis received some support in the data on early marriage in their longitudinal study. Wives with high "quality" marriages increased substantially in orgasmic responsiveness during the first 5 years of marriage (from 65% orgasmic to 91% orgasmic), whereas wives with low "quality" marriages showed little and unstable change.

However, marital quality did not consistently effect orgasmic capability: The rate of unresponsiveness in the middle years for one group of women who were unresponsive early in marriage remain very close to 50% even though the marriage was reported as positive in quality at both points in time. Clearly, individual differences that antedated marriage affected marital responsiveness. Unfortunately, Clark and Wallin did not report any elements of premarital sexual history that could illuminate these differences.

Christenson and Gagnon (1965) investigated the frequency with which women experienced orgasm in marital coitus. They reported a relationship between the husband's age relative to that of his wife and the frequency of marital orgasm. The proportion never experiencing orgasm in coitus was higher among 50-year-old women who had older husbands (20%, as compared with 3% and 4%, respectively, for women with same age, and younger husbands). Similarly, incidence of wives reporting orgasm at least two-thirds of the time is highest for women with same-age husbands (72.7% of women aged 50; 69.2% of women aged 55), with incidence for wives with younger and older husbands lower (50% and 51.8%, respectively, for wives of 50; 46.2% and 35% for wives of 55). No interpretation is offered for these findings.

The study of orgasm has importance for predicting behavior. In the research on sexual expression among the elderly, a relationship between orgasmic efficacy and persistence of sexual interest and activity appears (Christenson & Johnson, 1973). Clearly, experience of orgasm is a significant component of individual differences observed in sexual motivation.

Orgasm has significance, as well, for sexual identity over the life span. Orgasmic efficacy or success is one component of the sense of sexual agency.

Conversely, lack of orgasm can produce sexual alienation. These concepts, to be discussed more fully in the Conclusion, can be thought of as general directions in an individual sexual history.

Complementary to the study of regularity of orgasm is the investigation of self-reported satisfaction with one's sex life. Questioning along this line is even more rare in sex research than questioning about orgasm. One recent exception indicates that this is a worthwhile area for study.

Wilson (1975) queried a representative national sample concerning their satisfaction with sex life. Women were less satisfied than men: Among women over 60, 34% reported their sex life as "very satisfactory" and 13% "somewhat satisfactory," as compared with 34% and 29% for men in the same age category. Interestingly, proportions of women and men who were dissatisfied with their sex lives were quite comparable, and this held for all age groups. Between 6 and 15% of respondents deemed their sex lives unsatisfactory to some degree. Equally significant were the nonresponses; 35% of the women over 60 did not answer this question, as compared with only 9% of the men. Unfortunately, failure to include an "inapplicable" category made interpretation of this response difficult. Moreover, to the extent that researchers neglected some forms of sexual expression in their inquiries, respondents may have found a question such as this one ambiguous. What "counts"? Can a person who is not having sexual relations with any partner be "satisfied"? Is a contented celibate "satisfied" for the purposes of this question?

3. Marital Status

Marital status may mediate sexual interest in women, although the direction of the effect can be contested. One line of argument presumes that married women have greater opportunity for sexual expression (coitus) and that, compared with unmarried women, they will be more sexually satisfied. Conversely, it can be argued that married women suffer from a lack of novelty and possibly skill in their partners, and may withdraw from sexual interaction, in spirit if not in the flesh. Marital status appears as a variable in analyses of sexual expression but not in studies of sexual motivation. The conceptualization of marriage in most research is inadequate and hence the utility of marital status as an explanatory variable is limited. Two well-known examples illustrate the kinds of paradigms of female sexuality that underlie the research to date.

A study by Christenson and Gagnon (1965) is frequently cited for a "finding" that remains an inadequately tested hypothesis. They sought to test the thesis that husbands set the lower limit on marital coitus and wives the upper limit by examining incidence data by relative ages of the spouses. No data on marital negotiation are presented, but incidence of coitus is assumed to be the outcome of such a process. The data do not exhibit the predicted linear relationship between husband age and incidence of marital coitus; indeed, the data could be interpreted to support the converse of the Christenson–Gagnon thesis. The "factualization" of the nonfinding in this study suggests that readers have found the thesis more plausible than the data.

Clark and Wallin's (1965) study of wives' responsiveness and "quality" of marriage is based upon the disinhibition thesis: Women can experience sexual arousal and orgasm only under conditions of mutuality, love, and sensitivity. This thesis received only partial support among women who are now, on the average, 65 years of age. The implicit paradigm of female sexuality is historically and culturally specific. Its applicability for the future is doubtful, in view of the early age of sexual initiation and extensive premarital experience of today's young women, who are the future elderly.

B. MEASURING SEXUAL MOTIVATION IN WOMEN

In view of the social constraints on sexual expression of women, the study of sexual interest is vital. Inferring sexual interest or motivation from sexual expression is clearly not defensible, yet the direct measurement of interest poses problems. The most commonly used measures of sexual interest—self-report and fantasy—are subject to the same effects of personal experience, social scripting, and opportunity as is sexual expression. In the case of women, most of these factors will militate toward underreporting of sexual interest. Nonetheless, investigating the "subjectively felt strength of the sexual urge" (Newman & Nichols, 1960) uncovers individual differences that predict the frequency and persistence of sexual expression.

Newman and Nichols (1960) initiated the convention of classifying women according to their degree of early sexual experience—an inexact operationalization of their definition, but one that has been followed by other researchers. They found that women classified as "high" on the basis of early sexual experience reported lower incidence and frequency of coitus at age 50 than did other groups. However, their rates of postmarital coitus exceeded those of the other groups. For women over 50, high status on the early experience variable predicted higher incidence of coitus than was observed in the other groups. The same held true for masturbation, even with marital status held constant.

Christenson and Johnson (1973) were interested in individual differences in sexual interest and sexual history among their never-married sample. They partitioned their respondents into three groups on the basis of sexual experience prior to age 30. Individuals in the high group were those who reported masturbating 12 times in any one year, coitus, or homosexual activity with 5 or more partners (or 21 or more times), masturbation to orgasm, plus any degree of coital experience, or petting to orgasm 12 or more times. Lesser levels of any of these activities, and also dreams resulting in orgasm were used to assign respondents to an intermediate level. Women assigned to the "low" category did not report orgasm from coitus, dreams, petting, or masturbation or engage in homosexual relations before age 30. Of 33 women classified as low, 23 reported no sexual activity beyond petting at any age, and most reported no experience of sexual arousal at any time.

The most common measure of sexual interest through fantasy is the reporting of night dreams about sexual contact or acts. Christenson and Gagnon (1965) found comparable rates of nocturnal sex dreams for married and postmarried women, with incidence declining with age. Of the married women, 27% reported sex dreams at age 50, as did 34% of the formerly married women. Frequency was low for both groups: Median frequency was 3.1 dreams annually for the 50-year-old married women, and 8.6 dreams for the formerly married, declining with increasing age. In the most recent of these studies, Wilson (1975) found that 57% of women 60 years old said they never had sex dreams, 38% seldom, 8% occasionally, and 2% frequently. In another measure of fantasy activity, respondents were asked whether or not they ever imagined that their partner in sex was someone other than the person he was. Only 4% of women 60 years old reported that ever happening.

Low incidence seems to characterize the self-reporting of sexual behavior in women across the range of forms of sexual expression. A general trend toward underreporting has been suggested as a result of two factors: (*a*) a cultural pattern of holding women responsible for sexual events (even rape); and (*b*) the persistence of a double standard that judges most sexual expression in women negatively. Nevertheless, fantasy measures have several features that may, in part, neutralize these factors. Material or individuals can be disguised, particularly in dreams. Methods of data collection can minimize embarassment by insuring anonymity and impersonality.

Waking fantasy should not be overlooked as a measure of sexual interest. As research has shown, interest persists independent of opportunity. Maslow's (1942) work suggests that sexual interest measured through waking fantasy may be a sensitive index of individual differences. In his interview study with female graduate students, Maslow included a self-report of the number of everyday stimuli the respondent viewed as sexual. Other components of his sex-drive measure included frequency and intensity of genital feeling, self-rated ease of excitation, frequency and ease of attaining orgasm, and actual and preferred sexual outlet. Of these, the fantasy measure may be the most independent of contemporaneous opportunity effects. If such a measure can be shown to index an individual attribute that persists over the life span, it could have great value for studying sexuality in older people.

Certainly fantasy measures are not free of cultural scripting. Wilson's (1942, p. 56) data show age differences in incidence, suggesting the influence of changing cultural mores. Imagining that one's partner is someone else was rare among women and men of 60 and above; it was more common among younger persons: 15% of women aged 21–29 and 30% of men in that age group reported such fantasies. Similarly, Sigush, Schmidt, Reinfeld, and Wiedman-Sutor (1970) discovered that sex differences in sexual arousal to visual stimuli, reported by earlier researchers, had disappeared for college students they tested in the 1970s. The conditioning of sexual response by exposure to visual images is a lively topic in sex research; its obvious relevance to older persons has not yet been exploited by gerontologists. One may hypothesize that different birth cohorts have had substantially different exposure to sexual imagery, and that such exposure will be reflected in sexual fantasy. The symbolic environment of younger age cohorts has been saturated with sexual imagery to a degree that could not be imagined by their grandparents, or even parents. To what extent different birth cohorts are affected by this factor, in both incidence, frequency, and content of sexual fantasy has not been investigated. A further research question, of great interest in the general study of sexual identity over the life cycle, is whether the individual's level of sexual fantasy reflects the prevailing saturation of sexual imagery in available media, or is more closely related to that of her formative years. A number of considerations thus lead to the recommendation of future research on sexual fantasy.

IV. Forms of Sexual Expression in Older Women

Sexual expression can take the familiar forms of masturbation, heterosexual contact, and homsexual contact, as well as less mundane forms that, to date, have not been studied among the elderly. Indeed, as we have noted, masturbation and homosexual activity are rarely covered in research on the sexuality of older persons. This reflects the social fact that sexual motivation is differentially channeled into forms of sexual expression consistent with sexual scripts. Researchers are, in this regard, mimicking the dominant social constructions of reality (Laws & Schwartz, 1977), which overlook the side trips en route to exclusive adult heterosexuality.

Quite a different approach to forms of sexual expression is implied by a life-span approach. From a life-span perspective, one might imagine that the sexual history (and its shadow, sexual identity) could involve a sequence: early autoerotic experience, followed by later homosexual contacts, heterosexual activity, and still later by coital experience. One might expect that each form of sexual expression would contribute to a cumulative sense of sexual identity and remain as a component of the individual's repertoire throughout the sexual history. In evaluating the place of each form of sexual expression in the sexual lives of older women, a life-span perspective will be helpful.

A. MASTURBATION

Research has consistently shown that women report lower rates of masturbation than do men, from the early years (Kinsey *et al.,* 1948, 1953; Simon, Gagnon, & Berger, 1972; Sorenson, 1973; Wilson, 1975). This finding directs our attention back to the origins and persistence of this form of sexual expression, which differ, as we have seen, by sex. Although masturbation is censured in childhood, its status in the adult sexual repertoire may be improved. Of the forms of sexual expression, masturbation is the most autonomous; the least vulnerable to another's rejection and the vagaries of opportunity. It is the most private of sexual acts, potentially protecting dignity and privacy. Futhermore, its effectiveness as a means to sexual pleasure or release argues for its persistence once it enters the sexual repertoire.

The place of masturbation in the sexual career is clearly differentiated by sex. Kinsey *et al.* (1948, 1953) found that 95% of males had experienced orgasm through masturbation by age 20, as compared with 40% of females. Among women, the proportion continued to increase until age 40, where it leveled off at 62%. Women and men also differed in the age at which their frequency of masturbation peaked, and in the variance of frequency. Wilson (1975) found that women tended to begin masturbating at a later age than did men. Simon, Gagnon, and Berger (1972) found that a sizable proportion of college women took up masturbation only after experiencing orgasm through coitus.

Although the initiation of masturbation in women may be fraught with prohibition, this form of sexual expression appears to persist into the later years. Masters and Johnson (1968) reported that, in their sample of older women (and men), masturbation is sustained into the sixties in women who have masturbated regularly in their twenties and thirties. They suggest that the "need for this relief" declines after 60. Riley and Foner (1968) reported that rates of masturbation are consistent in the individual, and in women they appear to be insensitive to age. Rates of masturbation in males diminish, as do rates of other forms of sexual expression. In the forties, women's rates of masturbation converge with those of men.

Christenson and Johnson analyzed 71 never-married white women from the Kinsey *et al.* files. Respondents were aged 50–69; most of them were born before the turn of the century. This sample corresponds to roughly 9% of the population, according to the 1950 census. It may be of particular interest for the present, as the proportion of young women who express the intention never to marry continues to rise. The Christenson and Johnson sample consisted of highly educated career women. Marriage had appeared as an option at one point or another in the lives of all but 10 of the 71; half reported that, at one point, they had wanted to marry, and 30% had been engaged at some time.

At age 45, 49% of Christenson and Johnson's respondents were masturbating to orgasm, with similar incidence among the 50-year-olds. Thirty-five percent of the 55-year-olds and 23% of the 60-year-olds reported masturbating to orgasm. Decline of incidence with age was least for this form of sexual expression, as compared with coitus and dreams to orgasm. Although frequencies were low for the various forms of sexual expression, rates of orgasm nearly doubled for some age categories (1973, p. 88).

Existing research does not provide a clear picture of the role of masturbation during periods when women are partnered. This is particularly true of the older cohorts, who, as we have seen, are researched mainly when yoked. Not only is masturbation in married women ignored by researchers; it is often overlooked in postmarried women as well. Moreover, few comparisons of sexual behavior by marital status are available. In one exception, Christenson and Gagnon (1965) found that incidence of masturbation for formerly married women was nearly 200% that of married women (58.8% versus 31.2%) at age 50. These rates remained nearly constant with age. Sexual fantasy and masturbation rates did not show the same decline as coitus. Riley and Foner (1968) found that masturbation became a more important form of sexual expression in later life among women who had previously been married.

It remains for future research to explore the potential of masturbation as a means of sexual self-sufficiency for older and unpartnered women. The gerontological research already contains suggestions that older women can be trained to orgasmic efficacy through learning masturbation, even where this has not been an active part of their sexual repertoire (Yeaworth & Friedeman, 1975).

B. COITUS

Verwoerdt *et al.* (1969) reported on three data-collection waves of a longitudinal study based at Duke University. The 1955–1957 study included 131 women and 123 men over age 60. Sixty-seven percent of the sample was white and 33% black. Men were more than twice as likely to be married

(82% as compared with 39% of the women). Attrition and nonresponse reduced the sample size to 190 in 1959–1961 and to 126 in 1964; item nonresponse reduced available data for some analyses still further. Questions on sexual expression and interest were embedded in a medical history schedule. Coitus was the only form of sexual expression studied.

Verwoerdt *et al.* (1969) classified respondents by their pattern of sexual activity over the three data collection points: continuously absent (A); decreased activity (D); rising activity (R); and sustained activity (C). An initial sex difference was sustained throughout the study; 53% of the men and 20% of the women were sexually active at Time I. A decline for men was linear with age, with a substantial drop after age 77. No such pattern was observed among the women: Indeed, within the period 1955–1961, 14% of the women aged 60–65 and 14% of the women aged 66–71 reported rising activity (p. 144).

A comparison between Phases I and II, shown in Table II, revealed the following distribution for sexual activity:

Respondents' reported degree of sexual interest in coitus was analyzed separately. The major findings can be summarized as follows:

1. A weak degree of sexual interest was the mode at each phase.
2. Strong interest was not reported after age 75.
3. Individual differences seemed strong at each stage.
4. No uniform or linear effects were observed.
5. The degree of interest at Phase III exceeded the mean at Phase II, suggesting a possible survival value of sexual interest.

A sex difference in sexual interest paralleled that observed for sexual activity; with 69% of the men and 29% of the women reporting interest at the initial phase. Over the three phases, women's interest declined more than did men's. A comparison of Phases I and II showed that women's sexual interest was less affected by marital status than was their sexual expression (p. 148). There were no clear-cut age differences.

TABLE II

Patterns of Sexual Activity in Older Women and Men[a]

	Percentage		
	Women	Men	Total
Continuously absent (A)	74	27	48
Decreased activity (D)	10	31	21
Sustained activity (C)	10	22	17
Rising activity (R)	6	20	14

[a] From the Duke Longitudinal Study; Verwoerdt *et al.* (1969, p. 143).

Wilson's (1975) data do not support a simple picture of clear-cut sex differences in coital activity (see Table III). Among respondents aged 60 and up, 25% of the men and 50% of the women were not having coitus at all. Fifteen percent of women, but 34% of men in this age category reported coitus less than once a month. When frequencies were compared, women over 60 showed more differences from women 30–59 years of age than was the case for men; in the middle ranges of coital frequency, men 30–59 and men over 60 resembled each other more than did the comparable groups of women. At the high frequencies, however, the women and men more closely resembled each other. Though incidence was low, 6% of the men and 5% of the women reported having coitus once or twice a week; and 3% and 1%, respectively, more than two times per week (Wilson, 1975, Table 4, p. 55). The persistence of high levels of sexual expression in older people is indicative of some sort of individual difference variable that is clearly worthy of further study.

Christenson and Gagnon's (1965) study involved 241 ever-married females aged 50 and above from the Kinsey *et al.* files. At age 50, 66% were currently married, and 75% of the total sample had married only once. Christenson and Gagnon studied self-reported coitus, masturbation, and sex dreams. Incidence of coitus declined with age, and varied by marital status. Among currently married women, incidence of coitus was 87.5% for the 50-year-olds, 89.2% at 55; and 69.7% at 60. Data for women over 60 were not reported.

In the Christenson and Johnson (1973) study, incidence of coitus showed the greatest decay with age, perhaps reflecting opportunity factors: This form of sexual expression was reported by 32% of the 45-year-olds, 25% of the 50-year-olds, 15% of the 55-year-olds, and 8% of 60-year-olds. Christenson and Gagnon were able to compare the reported sexual behavior of married and postmarried women in their sample for coitus, masturbation, and sex dreams. Incidence and frequency of these forms of sexual expression varied between the two groups. Incidence of coitus was greater for the married women, decreasing with age; showing 87.5% of the 50-year-olds and 89.2% of the 55-year-olds, but only 69.7% of the 60-year-olds to be coitally active. Data for women over 60 were not reported. Incidence rates for formerly married women were, respectively, 37%, 29.3%, and 12.5%. Frequency of coitus was higher for the married women, and frequency of masturbation, for the formerly married. The third form of sexual expression, nocturnal sex dreams, showed only minor differences between the two groups in either incidence or frequency. Twenty-seven percent of the married women reported sex dreams at age 50, and this declined somewhat with age. Thirty-four percent of the formerly married women reported sex dreams at age 50, with a comparable decline with age.

TABLE III

Frequency of Intercourse by Gender, Present Age, and Education[a] (Percent Reporting a Given Frequency Category)

Frequency of intercourse	Males (N=911)							Females (N=1370)						
		Age			Education				Age			Education		
	Total	21–29	30–59	60+	Coll.	H.S.	Elem.	Total	21–29	30–59	60+	Coll.	H.S.	Elem.
Not at all	8	8	3	25	8	6	17	20	12	13	50	21	14	38
Some, but less than 1 per month	16	10	12	34	14	14	21	11	4	11	15	9	10	16
1 or 2 times per month	17	8	20	18	17	16	16	12	10	15	6	13	13	8
1 or 2 times per week	35	34	45	6	35	39	25	30	34	37	5	29	34	17
More than 2 times per week	16	35	14	3	20	18	8	13	30	12	1	16	14	6
No answer	8	5	6	14	6	7	13	14	10	12	23	12	15	15
	100	100	100	100	100	100	100	100	100	100	100	100	100	100

Note: The exact wording of the item is, "in the past six months how often, on the average, did you engage in sexual intercourse?"

[a] From Wilson, W. C. The Distribution of Selected Sexual Attitudes and Behaviors among the Adult Population of the United States. *Journal of Sex Research*, 1975, *11*.

C. HOMOSEXUAL CONTACT

Of the major forms of sexual expression, homosexual contact is the most understudied in older samples. Kinsey *et al.*'s (1948, 1953) studies placed the incidence of homosexual experience in men at 37%, and at 13% in women. Rates of self-reported exclusive homosexual orientation were 4% for the male sample and 2% among the female subjects. However, it is the place of homosexual relations in the repertoire of the older person that is of interest here. Some authors have suggested that interest in or preference for this form of sexual expression may vary over the life span, particularly as opportunities or capacity for coitus decline. Indeed, McCary's (1973) finding is interpreted in just this way. McCary found, in a sample of 1700 men in their sixties, that 6% engaged in homosexual relations after becoming impotent with women.

In light of the flexibility of human sexual capacity and the presumed place of homosexual contact in the sexual repertoire, it is regrettable that researchers have avoided this topic in studying the elderly. Kimmel (1978) has pointed out that only five studies of aging in homosexuals had appeared in the past decade, none of them on women. In the studies reported in this chapter, *none* of those that studied couples inquired into homosexual behavior.

In the Christenson and Johnson (1973) study, homosexual activity was studied but was not reported in tabulated rates of incidence and frequency of sexual expression. Eight individuals were reported as having "extensively homosexual" histories but these reported some heterosexual coital experience as well. By inference, other respondents, whose history was predominantly heterosexual, also had some homosexual experience; this is not reported. The histories of at least some of the women considered homosexual by Christenson and Johnson afford additional information of major change in the sexual career and presumably in sexual identity for women in late adulthood. In two cases, the sexual history was initiated by intense homosexual attachments before the age of 30, followed by a rather long hiatus and the initiation of a heterosexual career. Homosexual activity declined in frequency, for these women, in their forties and did not persist into the fifties, although seven of the eight continued heterosexual activity into the fifth decade. For two of these women, masturbation was continued after the cessation of coitus. Sexual dreams to orgasm in this group followed a pattern quite similar to that of the sample as a whole.

In Bell and Weinberg's (1978) study of homosexuals, only 21% of the white females and only 8% of the black females were 46 or older. The sample was biased toward highly educated professionals. Some of the findings were indicative of the kinds of information that could be sought on older women, although the validity for women of older age groups is uncertain. Bell and Weinberg found a correlation between age and current sexual involvement, although two measures of frequency of sexual activity correlated inversely with age. Age also correlated inversely with breadth of sexual repertoire and with certain sexual practices. In comparison with the men in the study, the women tended to be less exclusively homosexual. This may be related to the female script of reacting to male initiative, or to the finding that females in that study did not use public places or facilities for cruising. Women and men in the study differed in the degree of acquaintance and persistence of sexual contacts: Whereas, among men, large percentages reported more than half of their sexual partners were strangers, among women, only 6% reported this pattern. The majority reported no partner was a stranger (as compared with 1% and 5% of white and black male homosexuals, respectively). A similar sex difference was found regarding duration of sexual relationships. Women were considerably less likely to report taking underage individuals for partners than were men. Taken together, these variables suggest a pattern of parity in sexual relationships among female homosexuals in this study.

D.   RELATIONSHIPS AMONG FORMS OF SEXUAL EXPRESSION

The foregoing clearly indicates that researchers have not systematically investigated the vicissitudes and interrelationships among forms of sexual expression over the life span. By implication, coitus is the preferred form of sexual contact. Other forms tend to be investigated when, in the researcher's view, coitus is unavailable.

As might be expected from the general failure to study the different forms of sexual expression, we know very little about women's preference among them. Marital status seems to effect a degree of specialization in sexual expression, with married women reporting higher incidence of coitus and postmarried women higher incidence of masturbation. It is probably equally premature to attribute these differences either to opportunity or to preference. The significance of coitus as a form of sexual expression in women is obscured by the failure to investigate the issues of initiation and orgasm. This is particularly true with respect to married women. The option of masturbation (like other options) is understudied for married women, but findings of research on younger age groups suggest some considerations. Both Hite (1974) and Schaefer (1973) found that women with partners inhibit masturbation, even in solitude. Both afford evidence that women feel guilty about masturbating when they have a partner. The focus of the guilt is not the behavior itself but rather its implication of "disloyalty'' to the phallic partner and to the institution of sexual intercourse. Such a finding suggests a trade-off process in choice of sexual expression: Other things being equal, the individual may pursue the most socially respectable form available.

Opportunity appeared to be a factor in reported rates of sexual expression for women in the Duke studies: Sexual activity was negligible for the unmarried women. Sexual scripts appeared to be differentiated by gender: Unmarried men reported higher rates of sexual activity than did married men in the second two phases of the research. At Phase III, however, the incidence of sexual activity in the married women exceeded that of the married men.

Clearly, opportunity (as indexed by marital status) is not the only factor. Christenson and Johnson (1973) compared incidence rates for three forms of sexual expression for the never-married sample and a previously married sample (Christenson & Gagnon, 1965; see Table IV). Incidence rates did not differ as strikingly as might have been expected: At age 50, rates for masturbation were 59% for the formerly married and 49% for the never-married; coitus rates were 37% and 25%, respectively; and incidence of dreams to orgasm were 35% and 20% respectively. The previously married women's incidence rates were more comparable across age categories, but this cannot be interpreted as indicating greater persistence of sexual expression. Rather, it may well be that previously married women have different social networks or occupy different sexual statuses affecting opportunity, particularly for coitus. It is, indeed, in incidence of coitus (at all ages) in which the two samples differ most. Comparison of the frequency data lends further support to the opportunity thesis. Formerly married women reported a frequency of coitus almost double that of the never-married (1973, p. 89). Conversely, the frequency of masturbation was almost double for the never-married as compared with the previously married after age 50.

Christenson and Johnson's sample showed a dropping-off of incidence for each type of sexual expression studied. Once again, however, these were cross-sectional comparisons and the published report provided no way of assessing the degree to which the different birth cohorts shared divergent sexual histories.

In the Christenson and Johnson study, decreases in incidence varied according to the form of sexual expression. At age 45, 49% of respondents were masturbating to orgasm; this varied little for respondents who were 50; 35% of the 55-year-olds, and 23% of the 60-year-olds reported masturbating to orgasm.

In addition to providing comparative data on incidence of sexual expression by marital status, the Christenson and Johnson (1973) study afforded

TABLE IV

Incidence and Active Median Frequencies for Three Sexual Activities for Married and Postmarital Females[b]

Activities	Age 50		Age 55		Age 60		Age 65		Age 70	
	Incidence (%)	Median frequency per year	Incidence (%)	Median frequency per year	Incidence (%)	Median frequency per year	Incidence (%)	Median frequency per year	Incidence (%)	Median frequency per year
Married										
Coitus	87.5	69.4	89.2	57.9	69.7	40.7	50.0	—[a]	—	—
Masturbation	31.2	13.3	29.7	3.7	27.3	—	25.0	—	—	—
Sex dreams	27.0	3.1	26.0	3.0	18.2	—	18.8	—	3	
N	160		74		33		16			
Postmarital										
Coitus	37.0	44.8	29.3	27.2	12.5	—	0.0	—	0.0	—
Masturbation	58.8	15.0	46.6	11.3	43.8	8.0	33.3	—	25.0	—
Sex dreams	34.6	8.6	27.6	4.0	18.8	—	11.1	—	16.7	—
N	81		58		32		18		12	

[a] Number of errors is less than ten.

[b] From Christenson, H., & Gagnon, J. Sexual Behavior in a Group of Older Women. *Journal of Gerontology*, 1965, 20.

evidence of the impact of individual differences in sexual interest or motivation, independent of marital status. Differences in incidence of masturbation, sexual dreams, and coitus were pronounced when the respondents classified as low and high on sexual experience prior to age 30 were compared (Tables 4 and 5). Although these data cannot answer the question of whether degree of early sexual interest determined the extent of early sexual experience or the reverse, they do provide impressive evidence of stability and predictive power of such individual differences over a long time period. Interestingly, the earlier study of married and formerly married women showed a weaker effect of this individual difference variable, perhaps a reflection of the fact that marital coitus rates are an unreliable indicator of women's sexual preferences (Christenson & Gagnon, 1965).

To gain an understanding of the patterning of sexual behavior in older women, detailed information on the range of forms of sexual expression must be collected over a sustained period. A long perspective is needed, which calls for retrospective and longitudinal research to complement increased efforts with cross-sectional approaches.

Taking the long perspective redirects our attention to larger questions of theoretical import. With all due humility appropriate to the inadequate basis in empirical research, we can still sketch some major issues in the later decades of women's sexual lives.

In a stimulating and original paper, Glenn (1978) has applied an opportunity-structure approach to the three forms of sexual expression of interest here. In discussing sex differences in modal sexual careers, Glenn hypothesized that sex-differentiated sexual opportunity structures shape women's and men's sexuality in ways consistent with the roles assigned them in society. Glenn pointed out that when opportunity structures are equalized by sex, as in the prison situation, sex differences in rates of homosexual expression disappear.

Glenn (1978, p. 23) emphasized the role of sexual scripting in the opportunity structures provided for women and for men in each of the forms of sexual expression discussed here. Furthermore, Glenn argued, the respective opportunity structures determine the relationships among the forms of sexual expression, which may be substitutes for each other.

The opportunity approach is a powerful perspective for interpreting reported incidence of sexual behavior. Contemporaneous social norms defining sexual acts and sexual actors are major constraints on sexual expression, particularly as norms are anchored in and mediated by specific sexual communities. However, the subtleties in the opportunity concept have not been plumbed in existing research. Various proxies for this factor are found to bear different relationships with measures of the various forms of sexual expression. Thus as we have seen, Christenson and

Gagnon (1965, p. 356) found some degree of specialization in sexual expression by marital status. Yet husband's age, another indicator of opportunity, had no effect on masturbatory or fantasy activity of these women.

A complementary and, in some sense, competing perspective has been urged in these pages. Whereas the opportunity approach implies that sexual interest remains constant in the individual, with opportunity acting as a filter for sexual expression, I think it more realistic to assume that desire for sexual contact varies over the life cycle as a function of sexual experience.[5] The incentive approach is more consistent with the possibility of substantial change in sexual life style and in sexual expression late in life, whereas the opportunity approach may be conducive to a more static approach. Future research will be enhanced by incorporating and testing both these hypotheses.

V.   Themes of the Sexual Career

The developmental understanding delineated in this chapter emphasizes the formation and transformation of sexual identity over the life span. This is conceptualized as a continuing process. Part of the process is a dialectic between individual experience and cultural sexual scripts. Sexual identity is powerfully mediated by partners and by sexual communities, which, for the most part, communicate and reinforce one sexual script and discredit alternative ones. Early in the development of sexual identity, we can assume that the process is one of accommodation of the individual to the dominant sexual script. Later, as sexual identity attains a degree of autonomy, conformity may become less automatic; a degree of selectivity and assessment may be introduced. Although the topic of formation and transformation of sexual identity cannot be treated at length in these pages, the role of sexual communities and partners in the process of change is great. Radical transformation of sexual identity (e.g., from heterosexual to homosexual or from homosexual to bisexual) is most often accompanied by a change in sexual community or reference group (see Kimmel, 1978; Ponse, 1978). These concepts are important for counteracting the assumption of stasis in sexual careers, and for dealing with issues of change, considered in the final sections.

Because of the intimate relationship between sexuality and overall iden-

[5] Dowd's (1975) analysis of the position and options of older persons in social exchange might also be applied to sexual contacts. Dowd's general thesis is that as the resources (hence, bargaining position) of older persons decline with age, many social exchanges become "too costly" and are foregone. This explanation of social disengagement might well account for low incidence of sexual activity in many older persons.

tity, long-term directions or trends in the sexual career assume significance. Although adequate sexual history data are not yet available, two important themes in the sexual careers of women can be discerned. The overall tendency of the individual's sexual history at a given point can be assessed in terms of degree of sexual alienation or sexual agency.

A. SEXUAL ALIENATION

Sexual alienation refers to a withdrawal of feeling (or cathexis) from, or repudiation of, one's sexual self, sexual contact, and sexual partners. Each of the stages of development of sexual identity contains the potential for alienation; these may cumulate over the life span and constitute a distinctive direction for the sexual career. Antecedents may include trauma, violation, frustration, or despair associated with sexual experiences. Elsewhere (Laws, 1979), I have argued that bodily experience provides a fundamental image of self and capability, as well as an association between the body and pain or pleasure. Concrete negative consequences of sexual activity—unwanted pregnancy; the symptoms of sexually transmitted diseases—can make the individual feel bad about her body, her sexual functioning, and sexual contact.

Events in the individual sexual history may produce sexual alienation. At the social level, the content of sexual scripts may militate toward sexual alienation. Cultural practices involved in dating and the marriage market objectify and commodify women's bodies. Women are bombarded with images of female bodies that are enhanced, controlled, mystified, commercialized, and tabooed. The commercial use of women's bodies serves to insure that the image of the young, nubile woman remains the standard against which changing and aging women are judged. For most women, the privileges and gratifications of the role of sex object (deBeauvoir, 1953; Laws, 1979) are lost in the later decades.

Domination and powerlessness also are conducive to alienation in sexual life. Current research on such phenomena as father–daughter incest (Herman & Hirschman, 1977) and rape (Griffin, 1975) emphasizes the role of power discrepancies between women and men. Rape illustrates one way that unequal power between women and men affects sexuality, as do female frigidity and the practice of faking orgasm. Denial of one's sexual response via dissimulation or repression illustrates what is meant by sexual alienation.

Current research on the vicissitudes of sex in marriage is not reassuring regarding the degree of sexual satisfaction experienced by wives. Future research may reveal the extent to which sustained sexual contact unrelieved by orgasm produces a history of sexual alienation in long-married women.

Sexual alienation may well be the missing link that explains sex differences in level of sexual motivation.

For the older woman, it can be argued, accepting the structures of the sexual script for postmenopausal women is an indication of sexual alienation, as well as a force toward further alienation.

B. SEXUAL AGENCY

Individual experience in each stage of the development of sexual identity has the potential for sexual agency as much as for sexual alienation. If sexual alienation involves powerlessness, sexual agency may be thought of as empowering. *Sexual agency* involves a *capacity to choose and control one's sexual life,* and more. It incorporates one's unique sexual identity, for it is rooted in the individual's experience and evaluation of that experience. It implies self-awareness; it involves a continuous process of owning and disowning. It involves a concern with authenticity, using the evolved personal sexual identity as the standard for assessing options.

It is clear that experience and *hence age* should facilitate the development of sexual agency. Awareness, discrimination, and skill should all develop with accumulated experience. Thus older women, with a lifetime of accumulated experience, should be an appropriate population for the study of sexual agency. Further, a posture of affirmation of one's sexual self and sexual history can go far to contradict the script of the sexual has-been or the sexless older years.

Clearly, sex education has a great deal to do with the development of sexual agency or its failure to develop. The way one learns to label and evaluate sexual options, bodily capacities, and sexual feelings and responses can enhance or impede the development of sexual agency. This is as true of late-life sexual learning as it is of early sex education.[6] Learning skills in sexual communication may be even more vital in later life, particularly as partner, physical condition, or preferences change.

C. CHANGE AND THE SEXUAL CAREER

The developmental approach proposed in this chapter argues against a static view of women's sexuality. Change in sexual interest, sexual identity, and sexual expression are to be expected, and need not be experienced as

---

[6] Both should involve validation of the body, its features, functioning, and capabilities. The integrity of the body and the individual's right to control it should be established early on, rather than being introduced after puberty in reaction to incursions on that integrity. Others should foster a posture of in-chargeness in the young and in the old woman. She should "own" her sexual history and understand that it will continue to develop throughout life.

disruptions or discontinuities. At the individual level, factors conducive to change include (*a*) following the age-graded sexual script; (*b*) outliving the script; (*c*) normal life crises and role transitions; (*d*) exercise of individual choice; (*e*) changes in or of partner; and (*f*) changes in sexual motivation. Intersecting with these are two factors operating at the social level: (*g*) the plurality of sexual communities and life styles coexisting at any point in time, and (*h*) changes in sexual scripts and sexual climates over time.

The interplay among these factors can be illustrated by two accounts. Lillian Rubin (1978), in a study of 160 midlife women (median age 46), found that husbands and wives were changing but not in synchrony. As their husbands' sexual initiatives decreased with age, the wives discovered their own sexual desires and sexual rhythms. Initiating sexual contact with their husbands, the women often found them uninterested or incapable. These confrontations had ramifications for sexual scripts and sexual identities that the partners had never examined.

A second account reflected an individual's active process of adaptation to some of the common effects of aging. In a history reported by Hill (1979), a woman in her seventies reflected upon her sexual history and current activity. The history included a sexually unsatisfactory first marriage and psychotherapy. At the age of 62, the respondent met the first great love of her life. Much of the report is an account of solving the sexual problems of this particular relationship, with humor, dignity, persistence, and enduring desire. After the death of this loved partner, the respondent continued to seek and select among sexual relationships. In the account, there is a sense of continuing discovery of the sexual self, and a strong trend toward sexual agency which increased substantially in the individual's sixties and seventies.[7]

These histories suggest that the reorganization of life following normal life crises may expose the individual to new opportunities, including new sexual life styles and new sexual communities. The possibility of a lateral transfer from one sexual script to another may have potential gains for women whose sexual options have been foreclosed in a sexual script centered on marriage and coitus. An alternative sexual script is found in much feminist writing (e.g., Hite, 1974, 1976; Kerr, 1977). In this view, masturbation is seen as the cornerstone of female sexuality. It was Kinsey *et al.* (1953) who commented upon the efficacy of masturbation for reaching orgasm. Current indications are that it is more efficacious for this goal than other forms of sexual contact. The emphasis on masturbation

---

[7] Christenson and Johnson (1973) found significant change in the later-life sexuality of some of their respondents. Ten individuals classified as low in sexual motivation on the basis of their early history were anything but sexless in their later years. For 8 of the 10, masturbation to orgasm was initiated for the first time in their thirties or forties.

carries the implication that every woman, whatever her sexual preferences or opportunities, should become orgasmically self-sufficient. I have referred to this state as orgasmic efficacy. For many older women, this emphasis may require learning to masturbate effectively (and perhaps unlearning disapproving definitions of this behavior). Sex education for older women might well start with such training (Yeaworth & Friedeman, 1975). Learning to masturbate to orgasm might have a number of consequences that would enhance sexuality in older women. Attaining orgasmic efficacy might well entail extending one's knowledge of her own sexual rhythms and responses. This learning could be communicated to partners, and increase the orgasmic efficacy of other forms of sexual expression as well. Further, expectation of dependable orgasm might well raise anyone's interest in sexual contact, and enhance adventuresomeness. Overall feelings of well-being should increase with increased sexual satisfaction. In short, being or becoming a capable provider of pleasure to oneself should enhance sexual agency.

VI. Conclusion

It is customary to close a discussion such as this with a call for more research. In the present case, this conventional plea can be made with unusual fervor. Existing research fails to map either the domain of late-life sexuality or the elderly population. Available studies are, with few exceptions, dated and superficial. They are conspicuously free of theory, relating neither to theories of the life cycle nor to theories of human sexuality. The life-span perspective remains undeveloped.

Certainly improvements in research design and methodology are immediately within our reach. Christenson and Johnson (1973) commented on the reciprocal difficulties male interviewers and maiden ladies might have in discussing the latter's sexual life, but did not suggest the use of female interviewers. Wilson reported higher nonresponse rates among women as compared with men, and older women as compared with younger ones. The matching of interviewers with respondents in terms of age, race, and sex, a routine procedure in survey research, has not been practiced in investigations of sexuality in older people. It can be anticipated that the use of female interviewers will reduce item nonresponse among older female respondents.

A. CROSS–SECTIONAL RESEARCH STRATEGIES

The limitations of cross-sectional research strategies have repeatedly been mentioned in this review. However, this tradition has not been fully exploited in existing research. Researchers have been too humble in their research aims to date. The variables studied have been too few and they have been underanalyzed. In particular, little effort has been made to explore the relationships among variables. No study published to date simultaneously controlled for health, age, opportunity, and interest in assessing sexual expression. Many additional variables—for example, form of residence—could shed light on sexual expression in older people, and clarify cross-sectional comparisons. However, we should go further. The multivariate research strategy and representative sampling characteristic of survey research is ideal for constructing causal models. With adequate sampling, an argument could be made for cross-validating models derived from one cohort on others. The information thus gained could be of substantive as well as methodological value, in shedding light on the continuities and discontinuities between birth cohorts.

Researchers have shown little ingenuity in trying to counteract the problem of low baseline incidence for many measures of sexual interest and expression. Utilizing a two-tiered sampling procedure, with greater emphasis given to those respondents in each age cohort who are sexually active, will add more to our understanding of the persistence and patterning of sexuality. Frequency data will prove more informative than incidence data for these purposes.

B. LIFE–HISTORY STRATEGIES

Approaches presently in use merely scratch the surface of sexuality among the elderly. Sexual expression is too often limited only to coitus; sexual interest is rarely studied at all. Moreover, incidence and frequency measures are not only ahistorical but rather inhuman. Little is to be learned about human sexuality—and especially about the issues raised here—from sexual accounting. It is possible that cross-sectional research designs exaggerate the discontinuities, not only between cohorts, but between age statuses within the sexual history. The use of longitudinal and retrospective techniques is essential to the extension of our knowledge of human sexuality through the life span. Only through a continuous account will we gather information about development and transformation of sexual identity. Very different information will be obtained when we elicit marital history and when we classify respondents by marital status. This difference may become particularly critical as the incidence of divorce increases and the duration of marriage decreases.

C. FOCI FOR FUTURE RESEARCH

The approach developed in this chapter suggests a program of research focused around sexual identity, sexual motivation, and sexual expression. The study of sexual behavior will need to be expanded to include the different forms of sexual expression, their interrelationships and the vicissitudes of each over the life span. Encounters with and definitions of the various forms of sexual expression must be a part of this focus. Sexual partners and sexual communities will form the context within which sexual expression is intelligible. Investigating the sexual history will require collecting information on the effective context of each form of sexual expression at each stage of development.

The focus on sexual identity implies a progression of sexual contexts and partners, while at the same time emphasizing the subjective and integrative dimensions of sexual experience. The emphasis on sexual history allows the individual to recount the critical incidents that exemplify an experience or mark a turning point. Self-reports will also be necessary to ascertain the subjective significance and impact of the specific social and intellectual history of the time, within which individuals' sexual history is anchored. Research published to date provides no way of assessing the effects of trends in divorce rates, family size, contraceptive technology, or media events such as the "sexual revolution."

An emphasis on the sexual history will permit researchers to deal with marriage in a more discriminating way. Too often, in the past, researchers have slipped into the assumption that sexual history began at, and is coterminous with, marriage. A static classification of individuals by marital status is no substitute for a sexual history, in which marital episodes (if any) appear in their singularity, in the context of the life stream in which they occur.

Focusing on the life history encourages us to ask whether there might not be a sexual life cycle, its different phases characterized by varying forms of sexual expression. As in the family life cycle there is a child-intensive phase, so in the sexual life cycle there may be a coitus-intensive phase. Adapting to the capacities of postreproductive physiology might induce women and men to alter their sexual practices, changing the emphasis from coitus to other forms of sexual expression (see Hill, 1979; Yeaworth & Friedeman, 1975).

Clearly, developing a reliable measure of sexual motivation is a high priority. Testing the model proposed here will require measuring incentive value, expectancy, and satisfaction or success in the component forms of sexual expression. The opportunity thesis also needs to be developed and tested.

In addition to the programmatic foci for research on sexuality in older persons, there are a number of intriguing lacunae in the existing research. The scope of this chapter did not permit us to take up the question of the role of intimacy in the sexuality of older persons. Another sexual option remains completely unresearched: celibacy, the last taboo. Withdrawal from sexual activity at a given moment in time might well represent sexual agency *or* sexual alienation. It may represent choice or accident; at present we have no means of interpreting or even estimating this sexual option.

The approach urged in this chapter emphasizes continuities in the individual's experience over the sexual history. It also emphasizes continuities between self and sexuality, and between sexuality and other aspects of life. One theme that bridges these spheres is that of power and powerlessness. Issues of power and powerlessness pervade the topic of female sexuality. These tend to be overlooked by researchers, particularly when the research population is older women. The notions of sexual agency and sexual alienation, however, directly address these issues. Clearly, research is needed that focuses upon sexual agency and sexual alienation, and their antecedents.

VII. Summary

The focus of this chapter is on human sexuality, broadly defined as the individual's capacity for pleasure from intimate physical contact. The approach emphasizes sexual identity as it is formed and transformed by experience. The sexual history is a major source of data. Both unique and common (cultural and historical) events influence not only sexual expression but sexual desire and sexual identity.

A life-span approach to human sexuality requires an adequate developmental model. Such a model should be general enough to include differences in sexual orientation; should account for the development of sexual identity and the sexual history; should permit change and development; should cover the life span. A common flaw in the treatment of women's sexuality is to confound the female sexual history with the family life cycle and female sexual expression with conjugal coitus.

The appropriate focus of a life-span study of female sexuality should include the spectrum of sexual activities and should examine the vicissitudes of sexual motivation over the life span. The problem of sexual motivation (or sex drive) is little researched, and often obscured by the practice of assuming that orgasm coincides with coitus. Thoughtful attention to the issue of sexual motivation is a high priority for future research.

The importance of social definitions of permitted sexual expression (sexual scripts) is documented in current sex research. The historical dimension is particularly critical for interpreting the sexual histories of women now in their seventies, eighties, and nineties. Stereotypes of older women are not borne out by historical studies reviewed here. The issue of comparison between age cohorts in cross-sectional studies is of concern.

Existing research is so sparse and overlaps so little in terms of variables employed that sexual expression of older women cannot be characterized with certainty. Incidence data are inadequate for estimating degree of sexual activity or interest. Coitus, masturbation, and homosexual activity are affected differentially by marital status. It is not clear at present whether level of sexual interest predicts level of total sexual outlet or frequency of preferred form of sexual expression. Existing data lend some support to an opportunity thesis as well as to an individual differences thesis.

Sexual expression and sexual interest may reflect the individual's status with respect to sexual agency and sexual alienation. Development and investigation of these themes of the sexual career is recommended. Other research foci and methodological improvements are urged in the concluding section.

References

Atkinson, J. W. (Ed.) *Motives in fantasy, action and society.* Princeton, N. J.: Van Nostrand, 1958.

Atkinson, J. W., & Raynor, J. O. *Motivation and achievement.* Washington, D. C.: V. H. Winston & Sons, 1974.

Bell, A., & Weinberg, M. *Homosexualities.* New York: Simon & Schuster, 1978.

Bernard, J. *The sex game.* Englewood Cliffs, N. J.: Prentice-Hall, 1968.

Botwinick, J. *Aging and behavior: A comprehensive integration of research findings.* New York: Springer-Verlag, 1973.

Bullough, V., & Bullough, B. Lesbianism in the 1920s and 1930s: Newfound study. *Signs,* 1977, **2**(4), 895–905.

Bureau of the Census. The number, timing, and duration of marriages and divorces in the United States: June, 1975. In *Current population reports,* October 1976 (Series P–20, #297).

Christenson, C. V., & Gagnon, J. H. Sexual behavior in a group of older women. *Journal of Gerontology,* 1965, **20**, 351–357.

Christenson, C. V., & Johnson, A. B. Sexual patterns in a group of never-married women. *Journal of Geriatric Psychiatry,* 1973, **7**, 80–98.

Clark, A. L., & Wallin, P. Women's sexual responsiveness and the duration and quality of their marriages. *American Journal of Sociology,* 1965, **71**(2), 187–196.

deBeauvoir, S. *The second sex.* New York: Knopf, 1953.

Davis, K. B. *Factors in the sex life of twenty-two hundred women.* New York: Harper, 1929. [Reprinted New York: Arno, 1972.]

Dowd, J. J. Aging as exchange: A preface to theory. *Journal of Gerontology,* 1975, **30**(5), 584–594.

Ehrmann, W. Some knowns and unknowns in research into human sex behavior. *Marriage & Family Living,* 1957, **19**, 16–24.

Elder, G., & Rockwell, R. C. The life course and human development: An ecological perspective. *International Journal of Behavioral Development,* 1979, **2**, 1–37.

Gagnon, J. H., Simon, W., & Berger, A. J. Some aspects of sexual adjustment in early and later adolescence. In J. Zubin & A. M. Freedman (Eds.), *The psychopathology of adolescence.* New York: Grune & Stratton, 1970.

Gagnon, J. H., & Simon, W. *Sexual conduct: The social sources of human sexuality*. Chicago: Aldine, 1973.

Glenn, E. N. Differential opportunity structures in male and female sexual careers. Paper presented at the annual meeting of the American Sociological Association, 1978.

Golde, P., & Kogan, N. A sentence completion procedure for assessing attitudes toward old people. *Journal of Gerontology*, 1959, **14**, 355–363.

Goldfarb, A. Introduction. In I. Rubin (Ed.), *Sexual life after 60*. New York: Basic Books, 1965.

Griffin, S. Rape: The all American crime. In Freeman, J. O. (Ed.), *Women: A feminist perspective*. Palo Alto: Mayfield, 1975.

Heiman, J. Facilitating erotic arousal: Toward sex-positive research. Paper delivered at the annual meeting of the American Psychological Association, 1974.

Herman, J., & Hirschman, L. Father–daughter incest. *Signs*, 1977, **7**(4), 735–757.

Hill, J. Sexually speaking at seventy. *Sexology*, May 1979, 47–51.

Hite, S. *Sexual honesty by and for women*. New York: Warner Paperback Library, 1974.

Hite, S. *The Hite report*. New York: Macmillan, 1976.

Jacob, K. A. Clelia Duel Mosher. *Johns Hopkins Magazine*, 1979, **30**(3), 8–16.

Kaats, G., & Davis, K. The dynamics of sexual behavior of college students. *Journal of Marriage and the Family*, 1970, **32**(3), 390–399.

Kerr, C. *Sex for women*. New York: Grove Press, 1977.

Kimmel, D. C. Adult development and aging: A gay perspective. *Journal of Social Issues*, 1978, **34**(3), 113–131.

Kinsey, A. C., Pomeroy, W. B., & Martin, C. E. *Sexual behavior in the human male*. Philadelphia: W. B. Saunders, 1948.

Kinsey, A. C., Pomeroy, W. B., Martin, C. E., & Gebhard, P. H. *Sexual behavior in the human female*. New York: W. B. Saunders, 1953.

Kogan, N., & Shelton, F. C. Images of "old people" and "people in general" in an older sample. *Journal of Genetic Psychology*, 1962, **100**, 3–21.

Kovar, M. G. Demography and epidemiology of the older woman. Paper presented at the Conference on Older Woman, National Institute on Aging, September 1978.

Laws, J. L. Toward a model of female sexual identity. *Midway*, 1970, **11**(1), 39–75.

Laws, J. L. Exotica ≠ erotica: A plea for continuities in the study of human behavior and social behavior. Paper presented at the annual meeting of the American Psychological Association, 1973.

Laws, J. L. Human sexual relationships: A life-span perspective. Invited lecture, Division 35, American Psychological Association meeting: Montreal, August 1978.

Laws, J. L. *The second X: Sex role and social role*. New York: Elsevier North Holland, 1979.

Laws, J. L., & Schwartz, P. *Sexual scripts: The social construction of female sexuality*. Hinsdale, Ill.: Dryden Press, 1977.

LoPiccolo, J. Mothers and daughters: Perceived and real differences in sexual values. *Journal of Sex Research*, 1973, **9**(2), 171–177.

Maslow, A. Self-esteem (dominance feeling) and sexuality in women. *Journal of Social Psychology*, 1942, **16**, 259–294.

Masters, W., & Johnson, V. Human sexual response: The aging female and male. In B. L. Neugarten (Ed.), *Middle age and aging*. Chicago: University of Chicago Press, 1968.

McCary, J. L. *Human sexuality*. Cincinnati: Van Nostrand Reinhold, 1973.

Neugarten, B., Wood, V., Kraines, R. J., & Loomis, B. Women's attitudes toward menopause. In B. L. Neugarten (Ed.), *Middle age and aging*. Chicago: University of Chicago Press, 1968.

Newman, G., & Nichols, C. R. Sexual activities and attitudes in older persons. *Journal of the American Medical Association*, 1960, **173**, 33–35.

Pfeiffer, E. Sexual behavior in old age. In E. W. Busse & E. Pfeiffer (Eds.), *Behavior and adaptation in late life*. Boston: Little, Brown, 1969.

Pfeiffer, E., Verwoerdt, A., & Wang, H. S. Sexual behavior in aged men and women, I. *Archives of General Psychiatry,* 1967, **19**, 753–758.

Ponse, B. *Identities in the lesbian world*. Westport, Conn: Greenwood Press, 1978.

Reiss, I. *Premarital sexual standards in America*. New York: The Free Press, 1960.

Riley, M. W., & Foner, A. *Aging and society*. New York: Russell Sage Foundation, 1968.

Rubin, L. *Sex life after sixty*. New York: Basic Books, 1965.

Rubin, L. Sex and sexuality: Women at midlife. Paper presented at the annual meeting of the American Sociological Association, 1978.

Schaefer, L. C. *Women and sex*. New York: Pantheon Books, 1973.

Sigush, V., Schmidt, G., Reinfeld, A., & Wiedman-Sutor, I. Psychosexual stimulation: Sex differences. *Journal of Sex Research,* 1970, **6**(1), 10–24.

Simon, W., Gagnon, J., & Berger, A. Beyond anxiety and fantasy: The coital experiences of college youth. *Journal of Youth and Adolescence,* 1972, **1**(3), 203–222.

Sorenson, R. C. *Adolescent sexuality in contemporary America*. New York: World, 1973.

Spanier, G. Romanticism and marital adjustment. *Journal of Marriage and the Family,* 1972, **34**, 481–486.

Stein, P., & Etzkowitz, H. Life shifts in the adult life spiral: An alternative model of the life cycle. Paper presented at the annual meeting of the American Sociological Association, 1978.

Udry, J. R., & Morris, N. M. A method for validation of reported sexual data. *Journal of Marriage and the Family,* 1967, **29**, 442–446.

Verwoerdt, A., Pfeiffer, E., & Wang, H. S. Sexual behavior in senescence, II. Patterns of sexual activity and interest. *Geriatrics,* 1969, **24**, 137–154.

Vroom, V. *Work and motivation*. New York: Wiley, 1964.

Wilson, W. C. The distribution of selected sexual attitudes and behaviors among the adult population of the United States. *Journal of Sex Research,* 1975, **11**, 46–64.

Yeaworth, R. C., & Friedeman, J. S. Sexuality in later life. *Nursing Clinics of North America,* 1975, **10**(3), 565–574.

Convoys over the Life Course:
Attachment, Roles, and Social Support

Robert L. Kahn and Toni C. Antonucci

INSTITUTE FOR SOCIAL RESEARCH
UNIVERSITY OF MICHIGAN
ANN ARBOR, MICHIGAN

Abstract

This chapter is concerned with the determinants of *individual well-being* through the life course. The central proposition of the chapter is that *social support* is an important determinant of well-being, both for its direct contribution and for its ability to moderate the effects of stress. The concept of the *convoy* or *personal network* is proposed as the structure within which social support is given and received.

Research on social support is reviewed in terms that integrate two long-established theoretical areas, theories of *attachment* and theories of *role*. Attachment in the relatively uncompartmentalized life of the infant is seen as analogous to more diverse forms of social support in various adult role settings. These constructive aspects of adult roles have been little studied; the research emphasis has been on the demand and expectational attributes of role, and on the stresses thus generated.

The function of social support as intervening between the imposition of an external stress and its consequences for individual well-being is described in terms of the buffering hypothesis, an interaction effect. This effect is most likely to be observed when any of a person's major life roles undergoes change, especially unwanted and unpredicted change.

LIFE-SPAN DEVELOPMENT
AND BEHAVIOR, VOL. 3

Evidence for the buffering effect is presented, mainly from research on morbidity and mortality.

The explanatory framework linking social support and well-being throughout the life cycle is summarized in terms of five propositions:

1. A person's requirements for support at any given time are determined jointly by properties of the person and of the situation.
2. The structure of a person's convoy is determined jointly by these enduring properties of the person, the situation, and the person's requirements for social support.
3. The adequacy of social support is determined by properties of the convoy, and by personal and situational properties.
4. Well-being and performance in major life roles are determined by adequacy of social support, and by personal and situational properties.
5. The influence of personal and situational factors on performance and well-being is moderated by convoy properties and by the adequacy of social support thus provided.

I. Introduction

The attempt to deal with interpersonal relationships from a life-course perspective encounters two difficult and complementary obstacles: Research on interpersonal attachments and events has tended to ignore the life course, and traditional work on the adult life course has given too little weight to contemporaneous events.

Brim and Kagan (in press) present convincing evidence for the latter point. They argue that in a number of diverse areas of study—physical health, psychopathology, cognitive development, criminality, and "worldly success"—recent work points up past tendencies to overestimate constancies and continuities in the life course. They conclude that the view of human nature now emerging "sees a capacity for change across the entire life span and questions the traditional idea that the experiences of the early years . . . necessarily constrain the characteristics of adolescence and adulthood."

This is an exciting and encouraging conclusion, but one that imposes particular tasks for research and theory. To the extent that the present behavior and well-being of men and women are not so strongly predicted by the past, we must pay more attention to contemporaneous factors. That requirement leads to others more specific: the conceptualization and identification of significant recent events (Holmes & Rahe, 1967); the recognition of common adult crises and transitions (Levinson, 1977); discovery of factors that facilitate successful coping (Caplan, in press; Lazarus & Launier, 1978); and the development of models that incorporate such elements and describe the structure of social relations within which they occur. This chapter proposes a model that addresses one aspect of social relations throughout the life course: the giving and receiving of social support.

Our central proposition is that *social support* is important to individual well-being throughout the life course, both for its direct contributions and for its ability to moderate the effects of stress, including stresses often ascribed to the process of aging. We further propose that the concept of social support as it has developed in recent research on adult populations can be related to two long-established bodies of theory: theories of *attachment,* because they deal with social support in infancy and childhood, and theories of *role,* because they often deal with the stressful demands and expectations for which social support is a resource. Finally, we suggest the concept of the *convoy*[1] or personal network as the structure within which social support is given and received. The convoy structure is illustrated at different life stages; some measurement issues are discussed, and the chapter concludes with proposals for research and policy.

Research on these topics—stress, social support, and role—illustrates the other shortcoming to which we have referred; it has tended to ignore the contextual relevance of the life course. Indeed, research on stress has tended to neglect the dimension of time generally and the phenomenon of aging in particular. Both in the laboratory and in the field, stress research has concentrated on the immediate effects of task content, physical conditions, and social–psychological context. Some field studies have inquired into the correlates of chronic stress—for example, in particular occupations—but few of these researches have included age as a variable and none has, to our knowledge, treated a current stress in the context of the life course. This static or episodic approach is no less characteristic of most intervention strategies for dealing with stress; they have tended to be developed and prescribed as unaffected by age or previous life experience.

Much the same can be said of research on role. It has concentrated on the demand properties of different roles and on individual responses, psychological and behavioral, to those demands. Differences in personality have sometimes been introduced as moderating factors in the relationship between role demands and individual responses, but age and life stage generally have not.

Some studies of social support have been age specific, concerned for the most part with the importance of support for adolescents facing the stress and strain of puberty or for older people coming to terms with altered capacities and needs. And some studies of social support have concentrated on events or transitions that are characteristic of certain sectors of the life course—marriage, parenthood, retirement, and widowhood, for example. Changing patterns of social support and of the need for it throughout the

The use of the term *convoy* in social science came to our attention in the work of David Plath (1975), who, in turn, credits Loki Madan for his use of the term in an ethnographic study of Kashmir.

life course have not been studied, however, nor have current theories of social support called for such studies.

Attachment theories have been more time-oriented; attachment is a developmental concept. The time frame of such theories, however, has in most cases been limited to infancy and childhood. They have not included the adult life course, and research on attachment has been more constrained than theory.

II. The Life-Course Perspective

We consider the life-course perspective important to the understanding of social support for several reasons. First, people's needs and circumstances change as they move through the life course. Some roles are relinquished and others assumed; one shifts from dependent to provider and caretaker; changes in job and in residence are common. Second, the form and amount of social support appropriate at a given time and place depend on such changing needs and circumstances; there is no single lifelong recipe. Third, with regard to social support, as with everything else, the past affects the future; to understand individual differences among adults, some systematic way of including their earlier experiences is needed. Finally, the interpretation of individual differences as age, period, or cohort effects must refer to different experiences during the life course.

Consider only a few of the factors that create differences among individuals and age cohorts, and that may well influence their needs for support in the future. The infants and children of today are much more likely than their parents were to have the experiences of day care by people outside the family. Their mothers are more likely to be working outside the home; their grandparents are more likely to be living in separate dwelling units, and the chances of divorce and single-parent upbringing are much greater. Legislation to take account of these changes, although relatively slow, adds to the cohort differences in life course. Laws making the day care of children a tax-deductible expense under some circumstances have already been passed; minimal federal standards for day-care centers have been set, and legislation has been proposed that would make day-care facilities available in sufficient quantity to meet the needs of employed parents who have no preferred alternative arrangement.

The long-term effects of these changes are not predictable, but it is plausible that they will extend throughout the life course of the children involved. Moreover, their life course is likely to be longer than that of their parents and grandparents; cohorts differ in longevity even beyond the effects of reduced infant mortality. An increasing life span makes it increasingly inappropriate to treat the elderly as a single demographic group, and gerontologists already speak of the young–old (50–65), the middle–old (65–80), and the old–old (80 and over).

Individual differences among people already old are also becoming more visible because their range of choice is increasing. A combination of improved social benefits (medical care, social security, private pension plans, and the like) enables many people to retire from work if they choose, at the same time that legislation extends the right of elderly people to continue working if they choose. The decline in family size and the geographical mobility of families make the networks of nearby relatives smaller, but gains in longevity are at the same time increasing the number of four-generation families. Today's young adults have grown up accustomed to travel and to the long-distance telephone as means of maintaining family and friendship relations. The combination of technology, relative affluence, and increased leisure has given many people a wider range of choice about the circle of their continuing relationships. That pattern may be much altered in the future by the growing costs and diminishing supplies of fossil fuels, two tendencies that will have their own period and cohort effects.

To the extent that the life-course perspective informs our theories and research, the kinds of factors described in the preceding paragraphs enter as variables rather than as error variance. Advocating a life-course perspective, however, is by no means sufficient; the broad notion of the life course is too general to guide research. To be researchable, it must be disaggregated, but in ways that reflect actual ontogenetic development.

III. Attachment and Support: Childhood

For the earliest part of the life course, life is relatively uncompartmentalized and the concept of attachment occupies a central place. The term attachment is derived from the literature of early childhood (Bowlby, 1969). Originally construed and operationally defined as seeking proximity to the primary caretaker (usually the mother) in times of stress or danger, attachment has come to be regarded more broadly and recent empirical evidence has demonstrated its far-reaching implications for infant growth and development (Ainsworth, 1973; Gewirtz, 1972). Ainsworth suggested that well-adjusted, "attached" babies have a secure base from which to explore, interact, and discover the world. Others (Antonucci, 1976; Kalish & Knudtson, 1976; Lerner & Ryff, 1978) have begun to apply the concept of attachment to interpersonal activities throughout the life span, in terms that suggest its near equivalence to social support in adult relationships.

It is a plausible connection. Psychoanalytic, ethological, and social-learning theories, each for different reasons and utilizing different mechanisms, emphasize the importance of the dyadic relationship between infant and primary caregiver. The terminology varies—early object–person cathexis, evolutionary instinct, reinforcement history—but the net effect is to assert the importance of this early relationship. In recent years, the bidirectionality of the relationship has been emphasized. Infants are coming to be regarded as active partners in the dyadic relationship, bringing to it variations in temperament, cognitive development, and experience that may be as wide-ranging as those of the adult caregivers. Consequently, it is important to think of this early relationship as a developing one in which the participants may be either well or poorly matched. For example, the combination of an active, energetic child with a quiet, passive mother suggests a different developmental sequence than that of an active, energetic child with an equally active, energetic mother.

Such ideas about individual differences have proceeded along two lines in the literature of infant development. Several researchers have discussed the importance of contingent interaction in early development. Ainsworth (1972), Gewirtz (1972), Watson and Ramey (1972), and Levitt (1978) all have noted the dramatic effects of contingent interactive experiences on the child. Lewis and Goldberg (1969) have taken this point further and suggested that mothers who are responsive to their infants develop in these infants a feeling or sense of control that is generalized to their relationships with others during infancy and becomes the basis for internal locus of control in adulthood. They argue that infants whose mothers respond contingently to them develop a sense of perceived control that in turn affects their basic interactions with the world. Such infants also develop a belief in their personal competency and are less likely to develop feelings of helplessness about their effect on the world. Empirical evidence indicates that infants who, in Ainsworth's terms, are securely attached are much more likely to explore their environment and to use their attachment person as a secure base from which to explore. Had they been adults, it might have been said that those with a strong supportive relationship coped better with the stresses of their environment.

Thus the attachment relationship in infancy may be both a prototype and a precursor of supportive interactions in adulthood. If such ideas are to become more than interesting analogies, however, they must meet the test of longitudinal research over a subtantial span of years. Although attachment research with infants has been a blossoming field for the last 10 years, longitudinal evidence for the long-term effects of attachment is sparse. There are data suggesting constancy in attachment behaviors over the first year of life (Ainsworth, 1972) and from 7 to 13 months (Antonucci &

Levitt, 1978), in attachment classification from 12 to 18 years (Waters, 1978), and in the relationship between attachment behaviors at 18 months and competence at 2 years (Matas, Arend, & Sroufe, 1978).

In addition, several longitudinal studies of children, including the Berkeley Growth Study (Bayley, 1949), the Terman Study of Gifted Children (Terman & Oden, 1947), and the Thomas, Birch, and Chess (with Hertzig and Korn) Study of Temperament (1963), have documented the consistency in such interpersonal behaviors without documenting the mechanisms of their development. It seems reasonable, therefore, to entertain the hypothesis that the early dyadic interaction between primary caregiver and infant may provide the infant with a prototype for future relationships, both in the actual receipt of support and in developing an interactive style in which information and gratification are acquired actively, not passively.

Negative experiences in early life may be especially influential. Children who fail to thrive in infancy—that is, who exhibit the symptoms of social withdrawal, listlessness, poor growth, and development sometimes associated with "maternal deprivation"—seem especially vulnerable. There appears to be a critical period for optimal socioemotional development beyond which damage may be almost irreparable. The adult behavior of Harlow's monkeys (Harlow, 1965), reared in isolation, and studies of infants reared in institutions (Provence & Lipton, 1962; Yarrow, 1967) suggest that the normal developmental course may be permanently damaged if diverted too severely in infancy. Harlow found that monkeys reared in isolation had subsequent difficulty in social interactions with other monkeys, difficulty mating, and, in turn, parenting. Somewhat similar findings have been reported with human infants. Provence and Lipton (1962) reported that infants who were institutionalized for the first 18 to 24 months of life had difficulty forming attachments when later placed in foster care homes. Yarrow (1967) reported that although babies under 6 months showed minimal disruption when provided with substitute primary caregivers, infants over 8 months seemed to have much more difficulty and expressed both protest and withdrawal at the substitution. Thus, there seems to be evidence that, for optimal development, some primary attachment relationship must be formed within the first year of life. This statement implies a minimal basis for future development that nevertheless remains flexible. Later experiences, either enriching or depriving, also affect the child and thus contribute to continuity or discontinuity, stability or change in the developmental sequence.

This hypothesis assumes a developmental sequence along the following lines: The infant does not passively accept the interactive experience with the primary caregiver, but responds actively to that relationship and, in so doing, affects it. During early childhood, this dyadic relationship is further altered as the child increasingly incorporates other members into his or her small social world (Weinraub, Brooks, & Lewis, 1977). Such relationships—with mother, father, siblings, grandparents, and others—may be shaped in part by the strengths and weaknesses of the initial attachment. The child whose initial interpersonal experience was warm, responsive, and encouraging may have acquired behavior patterns and beliefs that extend to the world of playmates, school friends, and other peers. Such a child would appear to have an expanded universe from which to seek support in coping with the increasing problems and challenges of maturation. As these developmental tasks are mastered, the child enters the adults' world in which both the need for support and its availability are likely to be affected by organizational roles and their characteristics.

IV.   Attachment and Support: Adulthood

We wish to take the concept of attachment as it has been developed in the literature of early childhood and extend it to the world of the adult. Research and theory on the adult life course have no concept that corresponds to attachment in infancy, and no functional relationship so inclusive as that of primary caregiver or parent in the early months of life. Nevertheless, research on the role of spouse, family, and friends certainly suggests the importance of these supportive relationships to adult well-being (see, for example, Candy, 1979; Caplan & Killilea, 1976). In infancy and childhood, dual forces seem to operate: maturational and experiential. In adulthood, the contribution of maturation becomes minimal but the experiential effects of the roles an individual occupies become crucial.

A.   ROLES IN ADULTHOOD

Adult life, perhaps especially in industrial societies, is more compartmentalized than the life of children. It is also dominated to a greater extent by formalized expectations and obligations. These aspects of adult life are well captured by the concept of role; there is a need to be sensitive to the changes that occur within adult roles. The changes in emotional bonding between spouses with the birth of a new child, the onset of grandparenthood, and the special bonding that occurs within a newly formed generational triad are examples of attachment and supportive relations that develop within the context of adult roles. The nurturant and supportive aspects of adult relationships, however, are not fully comprehended in terms of role, for reasons that are bound up with the meaning of the concept itself, especially as it has been developed in organizational settings. Other concepts are therefore needed; studies of adult behavior must deal with social support as well as with expectation and demand, and with relationships that cut across roles as well as those that are contained within roles. We will first discuss the concept of role and then turn to the question of social support.

The concept of role is well established in social science—in anthropology, sociology, and psychology. Its adoption in these several disciplines, each of which tends otherwise to be addicted to its own conceptual terminology, is remarkable in itself. That convergence reflects the unique quality of the role concept as a link between the social and individual levels. Communities, organizations, groups, and extended families are all structures of roles, and the life of the individual can also be conceptualized in terms of the roles that he or she holds and enacts. The sequential pattern of those roles over the years in large part defines the adult life course.

Role is a behavioral concept, and its defining components are position and expectation (expected activities). Thus, a role is defined as a set of activities that are expected of a person by virtue of his or her occupancy of a particular position in social space. Positions are interdependent, and any given position is defined in terms of its relationship to some set of others. The dominant content of roles is prescriptive, and consists of activities that the role occupant is expected to perform. Roles also contain proscriptive aspects, consisting of activities that the occupant or focal person is expected to refrain from engaging in. And there is to many roles a stylistic component; the expectations not only stipulate *what* is to be done, but also *how* it shall be done—costume, demeanor, tone of voice, and the like. The voice of command, the ministerial inflection, the quiet acquiescence of the subordinate in a hierarchical organization are all part of role behavior.

Research on roles has concentrated on their demand aspect, especially in the context of work and especially under conditions such that the role demands constitute stresses on the individual. The nature and origins of such role stresses—conflict, ambiguity, overload, underutilization, responsibility for others, and the like—have been described elsewhere in some detail (Cobb, 1974; Coelho, Hamburg, & Adams, 1974; French, 1974; House & Wells, 1977; Kahn, 1974; McGrath, 1976). The literature on the effects of role stress is also extensive, and includes alterations in physiology and performance as well as in subjective states (Lazarus & Launier, 1978; Levi, 1972).

The constructive aspects of roles have been less studied, although there is agreement that roles sometimes provide opportunities for the acquisition of skills and abilities, and for the use of valued skills and abilities already acquired. They also provide the settings in which relationships with others develop, often in ways that supersede the formal requirements of the roles themselves. Research on work illustrates these points. Until they are past 60 years of age, most people who are employed say that they would prefer to continue working rather than quit, even if they had the means to do so. They explain that the things they would miss most about relinquishing the work role are the structuring of time and the interaction with others in the work setting.

Role properties, both positive and negative, have relevance for understanding the movement of individuals through the life course. We have said that, as the life of the individual at any moment in time can be thought of as the array of roles that he or she enacts, so can the person's life course be conceptualized as the sequence of roles enacted. Throughout a lifetime, each person occupies a variety of roles. Some are explicitly age-related; for example, most people are students (in the formal sense of being enrolled in an educational institution) during their youth, relinquish the student role in early adulthood, and do not resume it in any formal sense. Worker, spouse, and parent are all age-connected roles. Moreover, many roles change in content and style with age, even though they remain nominally unchanged. The role of parent, for example, assumes very different content as children become adults.

Thus, the experience of aging inevitably involves role change. Certain roles, or valued aspects of them, must be relinquished; others are acquired. There is a dynamic aspect to roles that has to do with their continuities and discontinuities in the life of the individual rather than their content at any given moment.

B. SOCIAL SUPPORT AND ROLE RELATIONS

A crucial problem, both for research and social intervention, is the coordination of roles and role changes with individual needs. We have yet to learn how to build into the major life roles enough flexibility so that they can be responsive to changing individual requirements, rather than imposing on some people the strains of overload and on others those of underutilization. That will require more knowledge of roles than we yet have, expecially of their positive and stress-relieving aspects.

When we search for factors that reduce stress or that buffer the effects of stress, we must look both for alleviating factors in chronically stressful roles and for factors that moderate the more acute stresses of role crises or transitions. Relatively little research has been done on such buffering or moderating factors, and still less on the conditions under which different factors are effective in reducing or buffering stress. Almost all the research on work roles and most research on other roles has concentrated on their demand properties—demand for quantity of performance, for quality, style, timing, and the like. But in addition to demanding that we do certain things, roles typically provide the opportunity to do them—access to the places where they are to be done, to the people with whom they are to be done, and to the tools and equipment for doing them. Roles involve opportunities and resources as well as expectations and demands.

Roles also require proximity and interaction, often around some group or organizational outcome. In such circumstances, people of like mind tend to come together, and people who have come together tend to become of like mind. Common goals and interests develop, and matters held in common become matters discussed and shared. Relationships developed in such role-defined settings, given the time and resources, often grow beyond the boundaries of roles in several ways. They may endure after the roles are relinquished, as the friendship of coworkers may extend into retirement. They may cut across the boundaries of roles still active, for example, as marriage partners help each other manage the stresses of their work roles or as coworkers join together in community or leisure activities away from the job. And they can be expressed in the role setting itself, as the supportive and caring behavior of a supervisor or coworker goes beyond the formal requirements and expectations of role.

Among the many aspects of such relationships, social support is exceptional; it has been studied and it has been shown to be widely beneficial in moderating the effects of both chronic and acute stress. The convergence of such findings is less than perfect, but it is persuasive, partly because the findings appear in the work of many investigators whose research includes a considerable range of conceptual definitions and methods.

C. SOCIAL SUPPORT IN THE WORK SITUATION

Early studies in work settings established correlations between supportive supervisory behavior and worker or group performance. Likert (1961, 1967) summarized the results of a number of such studies in terms of three principles, the first of which was that each interaction with the supervisor be seen by the subordinate as "one which builds and maintains his sense of personal worth and importance" (1967, p. 103). A long series of studies, initiated at Ohio State University and replicated elsewhere, identified consideration (measured in terms of demonstrated concern for members of the group) as one of the main predictors of effective leadership (Stogdill, 1974). Measures of supportive behavior were generally predictive of individual satisfaction and, to a lesser extent, of performance.

More recent research at the Institute for Social Research (Michigan) has concentrated primarily on the moderating effects of social support in the presence of work-related stresses. French (1974) and his colleagues, in a comparative study of scientists, engineers, and administrators at two government scientific centers, found the administrators to be under greater stress and to be showing more symptoms of strain. Their demands were more urgent, their work more often interrupted, and their telephone calls more numerous; they scored higher than their research and engineering colleagues on scales of work load and of role ambiguity. In all three groups, however, the effects of these stresses were altered by social support on the part of supervisors, colleagues, and subordinates. Among men in the low social support condition (reported poor relations with these others), work load was positively correlated with such risk factors as high blood pressure and serum glucose levels; among those reporting good relations with others, these correlations did not hold. Similarly, a correlation was found between role ambiguity and serum cortisol, an indicator of physiological arousal tentatively linked to coronary heart disease, but this correlation did not exist among those in the high social support condition (reported good relations with subordinates).

Findings consistent with these are reported by House and Wells (1977), from a study of some 2000 hourly workers employed in manufacturing rubber, chemicals, and plastics. His analysis involved seven measures of stress in the work role (work load, role conflict, responsibility, conflict between work and nonwork life, concern over quality of performance, lack of job satisfaction, and lack of occupational self-esteem); five health outcomes (angina pectoris, ulcer, skin rash, persistent cough and phlegm, and neurotic symptoms); and social support as provided from four sources (supervisors, spouse, coworkers, friends, and relatives). Of the 35 relationships between stress and strain (7 × 5), 19 were significantly reduced by one or more of the sources of social support. As House and Wells (1977) summarize the findings, "under maxium levels of social support, marked symptoms of self-reported ill health increase only slightly, if at all, as stress increases. In contrast . . . when social support is minimal, marked symptoms of ill health increase dramatically as stress increases" (p. 15).

A study of workers in 23 occupations (Pinneau, 1975) showed consistent inverse relationships between social support and measures of psychological strain (33 of 34 significant effects in the predicted direction). Findings within occupational groups were similar; social support was negatively related to symptoms of depression, for example, in 15 of the 16 occupational groups large enough to permit such analysis.

In all these studies of stress at work, much remains to be explained. Not all relationships between stress and strain are reduced by social support; not all symptoms of strain seem equally responsive to support, and not all sources of support seem equally effective. Moreover, the pattern of such findings from study to study is neither completely consistent nor completely explained. The effects are sufficiently large and the replications sufficiently numerous, however, to encourage the search.

D. SOCIAL SUPPORT AND TRANSITIONS

One possible explanation for irregularities in the relationships among role stresses, strain, and social support involves the concept of change. The need for social support may be heightened when any of a person's major life roles undergoes change, especially unwanted and unpredicted change. Under those circumstances, the buffering effect of social support on the relationship between an acute stress and strain might also be heightened.

Cobb (1976) pursued the idea that support might have its major effects during periods of acute stress and role change, by reviewing research on such episodes at different times throughout the life course, from infancy to old age. For example, women encountering stressful life changes during pregnancy were more likely to have complications in delivery, but not if they were strongly supported by others (Nuckolls, Cassel, & Kaplan; 1972). Surgical patients in a double-blind experiment who were given special supportive care by the anesthetist required less medication for postoperative pain and were discharged an average of 2.7 days earlier than patients in the control group (Egbert, Battit, Welch, & Bartlett, 1964). Adult asthmatics hospitalized for steroid therapy after significant life changes of various kinds required a lower steroid dosage to alleviate symptoms if they received high social support than if they did not (de Araujo, van Arsdel, Holmes, & Dudley, 1973).

A statewide study of the elderly in Texas (Stephens, Blau, Oser, & Miller, 1978) found that "as informal social support increases, so does planned engagement, zestful engagement, child-centered participation, leisure activity, and activity with friends" (pp. 37–38). Moreover, depression and alienation decrease monotonically as social support increases.

A 10-year study of mortality in Alameda County, California found that the highest rates of death from all causes occurred among people with fewest social contacts (Berkman, 1977). Moreover, this pattern is independent of self-reported health, socioeconomic status, life satisfaction, and preventive health behavior. Lally, Black, Thornock, and Hawkins (1979) reporting similar data for older women in SRP (single-room-occupant) hotels, suggest that "restrictive networks are easily exhausted by prolonged or multiple crises because they do not provide a 'cushion' of potential support which a more extensive network can provide" (p. 71).

A recent longitudinal study of the effects of job loss (Cobb & Kasl, 1977) was designed around the closing of two manufacturing plants, thus incorporating both preceding themes—the effects of support in the work situation and during periods of significant personal transition. A sample of 100 blue-collar workers who lost their jobs in these plants was followed over a 2-year period, with physiological and self-reported measurement at five intervals during that time. Data for these workers were compared also with data for control subjects from similar plants that did not shut down. The main effects of job loss were substantial: "In the mental health sphere changes were noted in sense of deprivation, affective states, and self identity. In the physical health area . . . physiological changes suggesting an increased likelihood of coronary disease took place as did changes in blood sugar, pepsinogen, and uric acid suggesting increased risk of diabetes, peptic ulcer, and gout. There was an increase in arthritis and hypertension . . ." (p. vi).

Social support from spouse, relatives, and friends reduced many of these relationships between stress and strain. Such buffering effects occurred for all of the deprivation measures and six of the nine measures of affective states (depression, anomie, anxiety–tension, physical symptoms, anger–irritation, and suspicion). Social support also buffered the negative effects of job loss on self-identity, on the maintenance of other activities, and on social interaction. The buffering effect was less with respect to the physiological impact of job loss, although "the effect of social support in protecting against arthritis (swollen joints observed by nurse interviewers) was notable" (Cobb & Kasl, 1977, p. 179).

Other research (Conner, Powers, & Bultena, 1979) suggests that the quality of the supportive interaction is more important than its frequency. The well-being of some 218 noninstitutionalized men and women aged 70 or more was not predictable from frequency of interaction or from the number of people with whom interaction occurred, but was explainable in terms of quality of interaction.

This interpretation is consistent with the finding that the crucial quantitative difference in the number of supportive relationships is between zero and one—between those who must face stressful events with no close relationship and those who are supported by at least one such relationship. Lowenthal and Haven (1968), in a widely quoted study of elderly people, found that the reported availability of a confidant, someone to confide in and to share one's troubles with, was the single strongest indicator that an elderly person would not eventually require institutionalization. Among single and divorced men, the likelihood of suicide was nine times higher for those whose mothers had died during the preceding year, but among married men the death of the mother was not associated with subsequent higher suicide rates (Burch, 1972). The health status of women whose husbands had died during the preceding 13 months tended to worsen, but mainly among those who lacked a confidant (Raphael, 1977).

Complementary to this research are studies in which support is lost, and there is ample evidence that such loss can have negative effects on well-being. Loss of a loved one through death, divorce, or separation has been found to induce clinical depression (Myers, Lindenthal, & Pepper, 1971), to increase the overall risk of death for the surviving (male) partner (Parkes, Benjamin, & Fitzgerald, 1969), and to increase the incidence of angina pectoris—when the work supervisor is not supportive (Medalie, Snyder, Groen, Neufeld, Goldbourt, & Riss, 1973).

V.   Networks and Convoys: The Structure of Support

The preceding research, with its emphasis on sources and patterns of social support at various points in the life course, suggests extension of the support concept in three main ways: (*a*) *substantive,* so that the defining properties of supportive transactions are stated in explicit and measurable terms; (*b*) *spatial,* so that the entire structure of support-relevant relationships for a given person can be represented and analyzed; and (*c*) *temporal,* so that the support structure is seen in dynamic terms, changing through the life course.

In other words, we propose to think of support as coming from a personal network of family, friends, and others—a network that is no less structured and tangible than roles and role sets but that often cuts across their boundaries in its interpersonal relationships and interactions. Such networks, seen in the perspective of the life-course, we have called *convoys.* We regard the concept of convoy as complementary to that of role, and we propose to use these concepts jointly to understand the way in which patterns of stress and coping change with age, in individual cases and in general.

Our first proposal for extending the concept of support to that of convoy calls for an explicit substantive definition of social support, and is perhaps more properly regarded as a corrective measure than an addition. Social support is one of those terms that carries considerable colloquial meaning and has therefore been more often used than defined. We propose that it be defined as interpersonal transactions that include one or more of the following key elements: *affect, affirmation,* and *aid.*

By affective transactions we mean expressions of liking, admiration, respect, or love. By transactions of affirmation we mean expressions of agreement or acknowledgment of the appropriateness or rightness of some act or statement of another person. Finally, we include as social support those transactions in which direct aid or assistance is given, including things, money, information, time, and entitlements. The operations for measuring support in these terms are available in tentative forms, and their adequacy is being assessed in current research. By making our definitions and measures explicit, we hope to contribute to the process of methodological refinement among investigators concerned with social support.

Second, the representation of interpersonal relationships as networks—that is, in spatial terms—has a considerable history. References to sociometry date from Moreno (1934) and continue; more recently there has been a surge of methodological interest in social networks and their analysis (Barnes, 1972; Fischer, 1978; Wellman, 1979). Some specialists in graph theory, that branch of mathematics concerned with structures consisting of points and paths between them, also have become interested in the application of their discipline to the analysis of social networks (Harary, 1969).

This body of work is highly relevant for specifying the formal properties of such networks. For our purpose, these properties can be regarded as consisting of two subsets, properties of the network as a whole, and properties of the separate dyadic links between the focal person and each of the network members.

Major network properties include size, stability, homogeneity, symmetry, and connectedness. These can be defined respectively as number of network members, average duration of membership, proportion of relationships that are both support-giving and support-receiving, and proportion of network members who are acquainted with each other. Properties of dyadic links within networks include interaction frequency, type, magnitude, initiative, range, duration, and capacity. These can be defined as the number of interactions during some stipulated period of time, the substantive category of such interactions (affect, affirmation, aid), the importance of the interactions initiated by the focal person, the number of life domains included in the interactions, the time elapsed since the relationship began, and the maximum potential support under specified hypothetical circumstances. These listings and definitions are partial, and both owe much to Barnes' (1972) work on network analysis.

As the mathematics of networks develops, especially in application to social structure, we may hope that a logically complete set of network properties will be specified. For the present, any list of such properties must be open-ended, generated in part from formal sources, but in part also from intuitive notions about the giving and receiving of social support, and the relationships within which such transactions occur.

Third, the life-course perspective, our interest in transitions, and the concept of aging itself call for the temporal extension of the network concept to include changes over the life course. The methodological implications of such an extension include an emphasis on longitudinal studies, with comparison of network properties for the same individuals at different points in time—before and after entering the labor force or leaving it, for example—or at different ages.

The conceptual implications are that each network property or variable shall be thought of both in terms of its magnitude at a given time and in terms of its rate and direction of change. Each network property, in other words, would be regarded both as a "state variable" and as a "delta variable." Thus, the property of network size would be treated both as present size (number of people) and as a rate of change in size (net rate at which people are being added to or lost from the network).

It seems useful to designate these dynamic networks of social support with a unique term. Following Plath (1975), we suggest convoy as an appropriate term, and propose its use for studying the process of aging and other life-course changes. By choosing this metaphorical label we imply that each person can be thought of as moving through the life cycle surrounded by a set of other people to whom he or she is related by the giving or receiving of social support. An individual's convoy at any point in time thus consists of the set of persons on whom he or she relies for support and those who rely on him or her for support. These two subsets may overlap, of course; there are relationships in which one both gives and receives support, although all relationships are not symmetrical in this sense.

The convoy is a structural concept, shaped by the interaction of situational factors and enduring properties of the person, and in turn determining in part the person's well-being and ability to perform successfully his or her life roles. It is thus the central concept in an explanatory framework (Fig. 1) that can be summarized in terms of five general propositions, each of which identifies a category of more specific hypotheses:

1. A person's requirements for support at any given time are determined jointly by enduring properties of the person (age, other demographic characteristics, personality, etc.) and by properties of the situation (expectations and demands of work, family, and other roles) (Arrows 1a and 1b, Fig. 1).
2. The structure of a person's convoy (size, connectedness, stability, etc.) is determined jointly by enduring properties of the person, by the person's requirements for social support, and by properties of the situation (Arrows 2a, 2b, and 2c, Fig. 1).
3. The adequacy of social support received by a person is determined by the properties of the convoy, and by personal and situational properties (Arrow 3a, 3b, and 3c, Fig. 1).

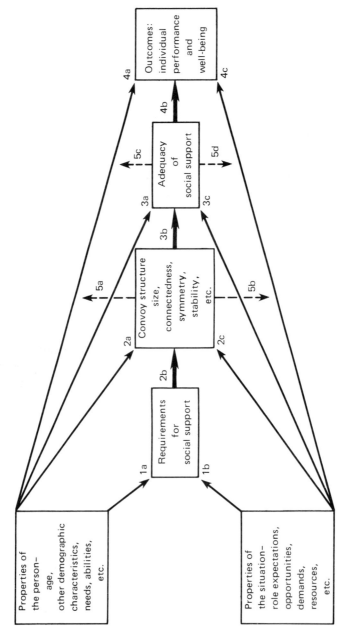

Fig. 1. Hypothetical determinants and affects of convoy properties.

4. Life outcomes, including measures of well-being and performance in major roles, are determined jointly by enduring properties of the person, adequacy of social support, and properties of the situation (Arrows 4a, 4b, and 4c, Fig. 1).
5. The influence of personal and situational factors on criteria of performance and well-being is moderated by convoy structures and by the adequacy of social support (Arrows 5a, 5b, 5c, and 5d, Fig. 1).

If we regard the convoy as the core of this model, the remainder of it consists of the hypothesized causes and consequences of convoy structure, including its moderating or interactive effects as well as its direct outcomes. The model emphasizes interactions. For example, a person's requirements for social support at any given time are jointly determined by properties of the situation (performance demand, resources, etc.) and of the person (abilities, experience, personality etc.). The structure of the convoy and the adequacy of the support it provides are also affected by these personal and situational factors as well as by the causal sequence that constitutes the major part of the model.

A necessary though not obvious implication of this interactional schema is that the model allows for the possibility of too much support as well as too little, and for support of inappropriate or unwanted kinds as well as for that appropriate and wanted. It is, to that extent, a goodness-of-fit model, although goodness of fit is not its primary focus. French, Rodgers, and Cobb (1974) have developed a model of personal adjustment in which goodness of fit is the central concept, and research done in terms of that model suggests that the relationships between supportive behavior and various positive outcomes are frequently curvilinear. They are not always so, and even the curvilinear relationships tend to be asymmetrical; too much is usually better than too little.

For example, in studies of white-collar and blue-collar workers, person–environment fit explained an additional amount of variance in mental well-being, in comparison to that accounted for by measures either of the person's needs and abilities or of the environment's supplies and demands (Caplan, Cobb, French, Harrison, & Pinneau, 1975; Harrison, 1977).

What leads a person to evaluate certain actions of others as supportive or not is a question that has only begun to be answered. It requires, among other things, measures that distinguish objective social support from subjective social support (that is, support as perceived by the person who receives it). There is some evidence that the extent to which objective support is perceived as supportive may depend on whether it is experienced as threatening one's needs for control or as interfering with one's ability to make choices (Bem, 1974; Nisbett & Valins, 1972).

Social support may be ineffective even when it is accurately perceived by the target person. Caplan (in press) emphasized the importance of equity in predicting the effects of social support. If the target person sees himself or herself as receiving support beyond what is deserved or can be repaid, the positive effects may be dampened or eliminated. Evidence for the importance of equity in social relations generally is considerable (Adams, 1965), and there is at least some evidence for the importance of reciprocity in supportive relations (Caplan & Killilea, 1976; Cobb, 1976).

VI. Convoys over the Life Course

The framework represented in Fig. 1 is a summary of concepts and hypotheses, each of which requires elaboration and specification. The concept of the convoy is central to our propositions about the functions of social support over an individual's lifetime. We turn, therefore, to an elaboration of the center box in Fig. 1, which represents convoy structure. Specifically, we shall consider the internal structure of a convoy and the manner in which it is likely to change, chronologically and developmentally. In addition, we shall provide an example of the changing convoy of a single individual over 35 years.

To understand the development of convoys, we return to the concept of roles as discussed earlier in this chapter. All individuals enter and leave a variety of roles over their life course (e.g., spouse, parent, worker, supervisor, neighbor, friend). These roles are the bases for contact and interaction with others. Indeed, most role expectations and requirements consist of specifications for interpersonal behavior. In many cases, the actual behavior of individuals in related roles will differ little from these expectations. In other cases, the role behavior may be considerably elaborated, in ways that add to the interest and satisfaction of the participants.

Convoy membership develops in this way. Although informal origins of convoy membership are certainly possible, it seems likely that most members of a person's convoy are initially connected to that person through the performance of related roles. The supportive relations of convoy membership will in some cases continue to be role constrained; the support of a co-worker may become very important on the job, go far beyond the formal requirements of the work role, and yet not extend beyond the boundaries of the work situation. In other cases, the relationship grows beyond the role structure in which it originated and comes to be valued for other reasons and active in other contexts.

Figure 2 represents an example of a convoy, with indications of the role origins of the various relationships. The smallest circle (P) represents the person in question, the focal person. The three larger concentric circles

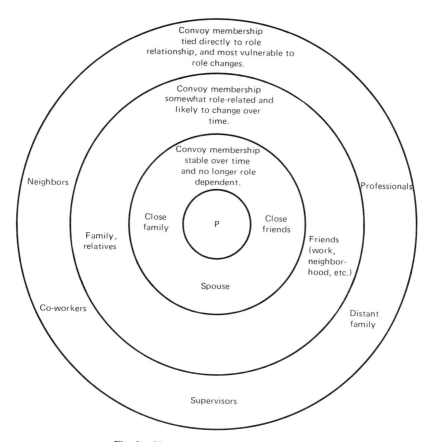

· **Fig. 2.** Hypothetical example of a convoy.

represent that person's convoy. Membership in a person's convoy is limited to people who are important to him or her in terms of social support, and does not include all the people known to P or who merely function in some role in relation to P. The outermost (third) concentric circle represents convoy members who are least close to P, but have nevertheless been identified as sources of support. People in this tertiary convoy circle are very likely to relate to P on the basis of role. Membership is likely to consist of supervisors, co-workers, and neighbors whose relationship to P has achieved some level of importance beyond the formal role requirements. Membership in this third concentric circle tends to remain role-dependent; it is not stable in itself and is extremely vulnerable to role changes. These are people to whom P feels generally less close and with whom the domain of relationship is likely to be limited. For example, a person in this circle might be a co-worker or supervisor with whom P shares work goals and whose interactions with P are very supportive at work but do not go beyond the work setting.

The second concentric circle consists of people who may be family, friends, or co-workers of the person. Membership in this circle constitutes some additional degree of closeness, in that P perceives support from these persons to be less dependent on the roles that they fill in his or her life. Times, places, and subjects of interaction are outside the boundaries of the role. However, the relationship is not wholly independent of the role and may not be maintained if either member loses the role. Such relationships are therefore likely to be less stable over adulthood, and substitutions may be readily made as new people fill the roles vacated by others. For example, a supportive relationship with the husband of a close friend may not survive a divorce, but may be replaced after divorce and remarriage by the new husband of the friend. Or a neighbor whom P saw daily and depended upon when they lived in adjacent houses may nevertheless be replaced as friend and convoy member by a new neighbor when P moves into a new house and a new neighborhood.

The first concentric circle consists of people who are very close to P. They are perceived as the important support givers. Spouse and some family members are likely to be included here, but their location in this first circle is determined by the supportive quality of their relationship to P and not the role or familial relationship. Because it is so highly valued, membership in this inner circle is likely to remain fairly stable through the years, in spite of changes in job or residence. Indeed, geographical proximity or frequency of direct contact may not be a good indicator of membership in this closest of convoy circles. An old friend who now lives far away and is seen only rarely may nevertheless be the person to whom P turns in a crisis.

People differ in the number of persons with whom they have supportive relationships and in the degree of closeness that characterizes those relationships. We defined support as consisting of certain kinds of transactions: expressions of positive affect and affirmation, and the giving of aid or assistance. Inclusion anywhere in a person's convoy implies such transactions, and the degrees of support (closeness) represented by the successive circles are also defined transactionally. People differ, of course, not only in the closeness of their relationships but also in their frame of reference for assessing closeness. Some relativity in response is probably unavoidable, and minimizing it is likely to be a persistent methodological problem. The explanatory power of this approach, however, is greater when the dimension of closeness is absolute, and we are attempting to develop measures that will have this quality.

Thus, to qualify for the first concentric circle of a convoy, something like the special relationship of confidant or "best friend" must be achieved. Such relationships are capable of providing support in a variety of situations. Their support is specific to the person's needs rather than to situational formalities. These are the kinds of relationships that kept Lowenthal and Haven's (1968) older respondents from requiring institutionalization. Individuals differ with respect to such relationships. For some, the inner circle does not exist at all; for others it includes only one person, and for still others it may be quite large. We regard both its existence and its size as predictors of well-being and of the ability to cope successfully with stress. Even the loss of support may be better managed by people who have had such relationships. There is some evidence (Bowlby, 1969) that they are better able to adjust to loss of various kinds and to find substitutes for the lost relationships.

Losses and gains in any circle of the convoy can occur in several ways. Loss in the innermost circle during the adult years is likely to be the result of death or the kind of break experienced as a major betrayal. Changes in the second and third circle, as we suggested, may simply reflect changes in role or location. Moreover, the boundaries between these circles are permeable, and flow between them is possible, as is flow into and out of the convoy as a whole.

The magnitude of such flows and the conditions that affect it are not known; indeed, the patterns of consistency and change in convoy structure throughout the life course remain to be discovered. Consistency at the individual level would consist in the repetition of certain qualities in the successive relationships of the same person as infant to primary caregiver, child to peers, adolescent to boy- or girlfriends, adult to spouse or partner, and again parent to child. Consistency at the aggregate level would consist in similarities of convoy structure among people at the same stage or of the same cohort.

Some age-linked changes in convoy structure are readily predictable and a few are already well documented. The transition from school to work, for example, or from one job to another involves almost certain loss of some convoy members and opportunity to acquire others. The relationship of new convoy members to old ones, and the stance of old members toward potential new additions are important determinants of convoy structure and of its net supportiveness for the focal person.

Of all such age-connected changes in convoy properties, recurring loss is probably the most researched, perhaps because certain role losses are almost universal. To take only the most obvious example, almost all workers relinquish the work role with age. For a person wholly dependent on role membership for convoy support, these role losses will be devastating. For a person with a well-developed inner circle of close rela-

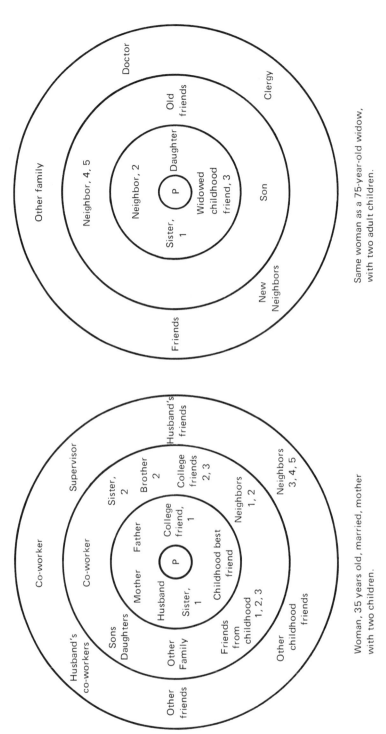

Fig. 3. Changing convoy composition over the life course: one woman's convoy at two different points in her life cycle.

Woman, 35 years old, married, mother with two children.

Same woman as a 75-year-old widow, with two adult children.

tionships, the loss of roles does not imply the loss of these relationships. People whose convoy relationships remain role-linked are thus at greatest risk with increasing age.

To illustrate some changes in convoys over the life course, Fig. 3 presents hypothetical convoys of the same individual at two different points in her life cycle. The diagram on the left represents the convoy of a married woman, approximately 35 years of age, with two young children. The diagram on the right presents the convoy of this same woman (P) at the age of 75, as a widow with two adult children. The convoy on the left includes considerably more members than that on the right. Moreover, although membership in the inner circle is hypothesized to be relatively stable, over the 40-year interval there have been several major changes. Parents and spouse have died and remain in some very real sense unreplaced. However, this elderly woman feels particularly close to her daughter, who is now an adult and a major support giver. In addition, P still maintains a close relationship to one of her sisters. Other losses have been compensated for in some degree by a neighbor to whom P feels very close, and by an old friend who is now also widowed. The second and third concentric circles have also changed over the years. Convoy membership in these categories has decreased. Relationships with neighbors, friends, and family members remain. Major categorical losses are co-workers, supervisors, and husband's friends and co-workers. These losses are replaced, in part, by a minister and physician who now play an important role in this woman's life.

These representations of convoy patterns are illustrative, rather than drawn directly from data. They illustrate unavoidably some of the complexities of the convoy concept; we hope that they illustrate as well some of its potentialities for the study of social support and the life-course changes in support patterns.

VII. Methods and Measurement

The preceding discussion of social support through the life course, and the concept of the convoy as a personal network of social support, involves two main methodological issues—the analysis of network data and the measurement of social support. If the analysis of networks is to be widely practiced, there should be agreed-upon procedures for characterizing networks in quantitative terms. Such procedures should be applicable in principle to any network—that is, to any set of points and connections between them: communities and roads, sociometric preferences, the authority structure of organizations, and so on through an infinite list.

In recent years, a good deal of work has been done along these lines, and with encouraging results. The development of the computer has been a prime facilitating factor in this work; one has only to look at the laborious precomputer efforts to deal with large aggregations of network data (Jacobson & Seashore, 1951; Weiss, 1956) to realize the importance of computer technology for such analyses. Moreover, there has been a concomitant development of the mathematics of networks (Burt, in press) and of network sampling (Granovetter, 1976). As a result, procedures for casting the data of social networks as graphs or matrices and for quantitative analysis of those structures are now available and effective.

Many of these developments are summarized in *Sociological Methods and Research* (November 1978), the entire issue of which is devoted to applied network analysis. Burt (1978), in commenting editorially on the various articles, noted the variety of analytic modes, the simultaneous but not closely related work on networks by mathematical theorists and substantive researchers, and the considerable progress of recent years. In his introduction he pointed out two issues common to all modes of network research but undiscussed in the articles that followed: how systems are to be operationalized and how relations can be operationalized. Both these problems are relevant to research on convoys, but the relational question is primary; it deals with the nature of the bond.

Network analysts, even those who concentrate on person-centered networks, are not agreed on the relationship or bond that they are studying. Most of them use sociometric citations (expressed preference) as the basis for network relations, but the scatter of other measures is wide and still increasing. The problem is not only methodological; prior to it—logically first and first in importance—is the matter of conceptual definition: What is the relationship of interest? What theory is it a part of? How specific is the conceptual definition of this relationship? Answering these questions does not solve all the operational problems, but it increases the probability of solution.

The convoy is explicit about the relationship of interest: That relationship consists of transactions of social support, both given and received. The convoy is a person-centered network; each convoy is a personal network of social support, defined around a focal person whose activities and well-being we wish to understand. The boundaries of the network are thus defined by the relations to that person. There is no "snowballing"; the network stops with that set of other persons with whom the focal person has a direct relationship of support-receiving or giving. With this definition, some things are of course lost; every concept "defines things out" as well as in. But our primary interest is in social support, and the convoy structure is the delivery system.

The next problem is to define and devise measures for social support. As

McCallister and Fischer (1978) state, after describing their own network measures: "it is important that network researchers consciously and clearly specify what they need to know about networks and what they mean theoretically by 'relation.' The findings of network research can be strongly influenced by the measures of 'relation' used to define the network. Therefore, researchers should pay as much attention to the methods they use to identify network memberships as they do to the analysis of data describing those networks" (p. 146).

Several approaches have been developed for the measurement of social support as the network relationship of interest, all of them treating support as a multidimensional concept and all treating supportiveness as a continuum rather than as a dichotomous present-or-absent quality. Sociometric nomination is thus inappropriate for measuring support and defining networks of support, despite the fact that it is the most widely used method of network measurement and analysis. Kinship is also inappropriate for our purposes, although network theories and measurements for analyzing kinship structures have been instructive for all those who work with network concepts (see Nadel, 1957, for example).

Among social scientists who are concerned with social support (or analogous concepts) and who have done empirical network research, the most common approach has been to depend on a single basic question to identify network members. Thus, Laumann (1973) asks each individual to name his or her best friends (and restricts the number of possible mentions to three). Wellman (1979) asks each respondent to name "the people you feel closest to." Kleiner and Parker (1976) ask respondents to name people who occupy certain related roles—friend, co-worker, and the like.

More complex procedures for identifying network members have been used by other research workers. Fischer (1978), Fischer, Jackson, Stueve, Gerson, and Jones (1977), and McCallister and Fischer (1978) have illustrated the multi-item approach to network identification. Their underlying concept is that of "valued interactions or rewarding exchanges," and they begin by asking respondents to name people that they talk to "when you are concerned about a personal matter." They then ask 10 name-eliciting questions that are primarily behavioral—caring for your home in your absence, helping you with household tasks, being asked for and giving you advice on important decisions, lending you a large sum of money, and so on.

Other questions in the set of 10 refer to social and recreational activities shared, topics of conversation, and the like; these imply supportive transactions but are less specific in a behavioral sense. Following this, the interviewer and the respondent review the list of names generated, to eliminate redundancies. The resulting network obviously goes beyond relations of social support, but so do the research objectives of the investigators; they want to describe the "social worlds" of their respondents and the relative "bondedness" of neighbors and communities.

Kahn and Quinn (1976), in a community-based survey, used a procedure that allowed respondents to name as many people as they wished as members of their personal networks. The interviewer introduced the subject by explaining that it involved "talking about people you know, in terms of what they can do for you and what you can do for them." The interviewer then asked the respondent to "think about all the people toward whom you feel particularly close these days" in six categories: family and relatives, co-workers, other organizational members, neighbors, professionals, and friends. These people were listed individually and the social support they provided was measured by means of a 12-item sequence, with subscales for each of three categories of support—affect, affirmation, and aid.

People found the questions meaningful, and their responses provided some evidence for the proposed categories of social support. Affective or emotional support emerged as a distinct category in factor analysis; the differentiation of affirmation from more concrete forms of aid and assistance, however, was less clear. The size of the convoy increased during the years of early adulthood and appeared to be quite stable during the years from 35 to 55. The pattern of affective expression did not decrease significantly within this age range, but the receiving of aid and assistance in various forms increased with age.

Kahn and Antonucci, in a current study of social support among new teachers, have adapted this interview procedure for paper and pencil questionnaires. Respondents are asked to list "people who are important to you or to whom you are important," in each of six role categories: spouse or partner, family and relatives, co-workers, supervisors, professionals, and friends. Social support is measured separately, as before, for the three categories of affect, affirmation, and aid.

In another recent study of social support, Kahn (1978) utilized the diagram of concentric circles as a way of obtaining an initial listing of network members. Interviewers gave a copy of the unlabeled diagram to respondents and asked them to enter the initials of "people who are important in your life right now, in terms of what they do for you and what you do for them." The interviewer explained, pointing to the diagram, that "this is you in the middle" and then asked the respondent to put the initials of "those you feel closest to, nearer to you on the diagram." In the remainder of the interview, the respondent was asked to identify the network members by category (neighbor, co-worker, and the like), and to describe their supportive behavior in various situations of stress.

All these procedures involve compromises between the goal of generating complete and valid network data about social support and the constraint of making the data collection acceptable to the respondent. What measurement operations will best meet these requirements remains to be learned. Support and attachment deserve better measures than they have yet had, and only methodological research can provide them. That work has scarcely begun. Active methodological research on networks is underway in a number of places, however, and the results are encouraging.

VIII.   Priorities and Implications

In addition to the methodological issues discussed, two areas of work seem particularly important for the future: the identification of age-related patterns of support, both successful and unsuccessful; and the development of modes of intervention that supplement and encourage natural support patterns.

A.   AGE-RELATED PATTERNS OF SOCIAL SUPPORT

As is frequently the case with life-span questions, the best test of convoy structure and function over the life course would be provided by a cross-sequential design. Many research questions can be explored, however, before committing the time and resources necessary for such designs. As Fig. 3 suggests, patterns of convoy structure are likely to differ both interindividually and intraindividually. One research priority is to explore differences in convoy membership among people of different ages, with special attention to distribution of membership in the first, second, and third concentric circles. The relationship between these convoy patterns and criteria of overall well-being could then be analyzed within age groups, and should permit the tentative delineation of convoys that are most able to maintain support through the life course.

Such research should also illuminate the relationship between convoy structure and forms of support. For example, it seems likely that the dimension of distance (the radial dimension in Figs. 2 and 3) is associated with generality or specificity in the forms of support provided. A member of the innermost circle of an individual's convoy is more likely to provide support of several kinds—aid, affect, and affirmation. A member of the third convoy circle is more likely to provide only one of these; the relationship is more specified.

As information on convoys is accumulated for representative populations, it becomes possible to describe "normal" conditions of social support and also to identify individuals who, because of their circumstances or convoy composition, are at unusual risk. The delineation of a population "at risk" will be useful both for research and application. Short-term longitudinal research designed around stressful life events (birth of siblings, divorce of parents, leaving the parental home, first job, compelled residential relocation, strenuous medical treatment, and the like) could reveal the effects of support under conditions of acute need.

The eventual use of cross-sequential design (which combines the strengths of longitudinal and cross-sectional design) will permit an examination of convoy structure as it affects various criteria of well-being over the life course, distinguishing aging from cohort and period effects. Such a design will also provide an assessment of the effectiveness of different convoy patterns for coping with particular life crises and transitions.

B. MODES OF INTERVENTION

Knowledge of convoys and their functions could have several direct applications. In the case of people who do not have convoys that are conducive to successful aging, intervention programs could be devised that specifically address the development of a more supportive convoy pattern. The success of programs such as Widow-to-Widow, Alcoholics Anonymous, and Parents without Partners suggest that people can be helped through major crises for which they have had no preparation, and that the proper support can be effective despite a history of past failures.

For people who have had successful convoys throughout their lifetime, knowledge of the composition and functions of convoys may lead to more enlightened behavior, official and familial, and thus prevent the unnecessary disruptions of these networks by government actions or the decisions of relatives. Among the convoy-disruptive aspects of present policies are: greater government support for the institutionalization of an elderly or handicapped person than for family members who wish to keep that person at home; nursing home regulations that separate married couples from each other and enforce other forms of segregation of men and women; regulations that discourage remarriage among the elderly by reducing or eliminating social security benefits upon remarriage; and social security regulations (recently revised) that prevent willing older people from continuing to work and thereby maintaining important supportive relationships.

These examples suggest a history of social policy interfering with natural support networks. This can be remedied. In addition, supportive services probably can be invented that will not only provide formal support to people at risk or in crisis but will do so in ways that strengthen the development of natural support networks. Current research (Durlak, 1979) indicates that informal and nonprofessional helpers are no less effective than professionals. It is a challenge for research and for application to invent professional modes of support that develop and then give way wherever possible to natural networks.

Acknowledgments

This chapter represents a collaborative effort, with both authors sharing equally in all phases of the work. We wish to acknowledge the support of the National Institute of Aging (Grant #R01 AG 01532-01), which greatly facilitated this work. This paper incorporates and extends a paper by the same authors, prepared for the National Academy of Sciences.

References

Adams, J. S. Injustice in social exchange. In L. Berkowitz (Ed.), *Advances in experimental social psychology* (Vol. 2). New York: Academic Press, 1965.

Ainsworth, M. Attachment and dependency: A comparison. In J. L. Gewirtz (Ed.), *Attachment and dependency*. Washington: Winston, 1972.

Ainsworth, M. The development of infant mother attachment. In B. M. Caldwell & H. N. Riciuti (Eds.), *Review of Child Development Research III*. Chicago: University of Chicago Press, 1973.

Antonucci, T. Attachment: A life-span concept. *Human Development,* 1976, **19**(3), 135–142.

Antonucci, T., & Levitt, M. Separation and reunion behaviors as indices of attachment: A short-term longitudinal study of infants from seven to thirteen months. Presented at the International Infancy Conference, Providence, Rhode Island, 1978.

Barnes, J. A. *Social networks.* New York: Addison-Wesley Reprints, 1972.

Bayley, N. Consistency and variability in the growth of intelligence from birth to eighteen years. *Journal of Genetic Psychology,* 1949, **75**, 165–196.

Bem, S. L. The measurement of psychological androgyny. *Journal of Consulting and Clinical Psychology,* 1974, **42**, 155–162.

Berkman, L. F. Social networks, host resistance, and mortality: a follow-up study of Alameda County residents. Doctoral Dissertation, University of California, Berkeley, 1977.

Bowlby, J. *Attachment and loss, Vol. 1. Attachment.* New York: Basic Books, 1969.

Brim, O. G., Jr., & Kagan, J. *Constancy and change in human development.* Cambridge: Harvard University Press, in press.

Burch, J. Recent bereavement in relation to suicide. *Journal of Psychosomatic Research,* 1972, **16**, 361–366.

Burt, R. S. Editorial comments. *Sociological Methods and Research,* 1978.

Burt, R. S. Models of network structure. *Annual Review of Sociology* (Vol. 6). Palo Alto: Annual Reviews, (in press).

Candy, S. Comparative analysis of friendship functions through the adult years. *Psychology of Women,* 1979.

Caplan, G., & Killilea, M. *Support systems and mutual help.* New York: Grune & Stratton, 1976.

Caplan, R. D. Social support, person–environment fit, and coping. In L. Furman & J. Gordis (Eds.), *Mental health and the economy.* Kalamazoo: Upjohn Foundation, (in press).

Caplan, R. D., Cobb, S., French, J.R.P., Jr., Harrison, R. V., & Pinneau, S. R., Jr. *Job demands and worker health: Main effects and occupational differences.* (USGPO #HE 7111-J57, USPO Stock 1733-0083), Washington, DC: United States Government Printing Office, 1975.

Cobb, S. Role responsibility: The differentiation of a concept. In A. McLean (Ed.), *Occupational stress.* Springfield, Ill.: Charles C Thomas, 1974.

Cobb, S. Social support as a moderator of life stress. *Psychosomatic Medicine,* 1976, **38**(5), 300–314.

Cobb, S., Kasl, S. *Termination: The consequences of job loss.* (Publication No. 77–224). Washington, D.C.: DHEW (NIOSH), 1977.

Coelho, G. V., Hamburg, D. A., & Adams, J. E. *Coping and adaptation.* New York: Basic Books, 1974.

Conner, K. A., Powers, E. A., & Bultena, G. L. Social interaction and life satisfaction: An empirical assessment of late-life patterns. *Journal of Gerontology,* 1979, **34**(1), 116–121.

de Araujo, G., van Arsdel, P. P., Holmes, T. H., & Dudley, D. L. Life change, coping ability and chronic intensive asthma. *Journal of Psychosomatic Research,* 1973, **17**, 359–363.

Durlak, J. A. Comparative effectiveness of paraprofessional and professional helpers. *Psychological Bulletin,* 1979, **86** (1), 80–92.

Egbert, I. D., Battit, G. E., Welch, C. E., & Bartlett, M. K. Reduction of postoperative pain by encouragement and instruction of patients. *New England Journal of Medicine,* 1964, **270**, 825–827.

Fischer, C. S. The social contexts of personal relations: An exploratory network analysis. Working Paper No. 281. Institute of Urban and Regional Development, University of California, Berkeley, 1978.

Fischer, C. S., Jackson, R. M. Stueve, C. A., Gerson, K., & Jones, L. M. (with M. Baldassare). *Networks and places: Social relations in the urban setting.* New York: The Free Press, 1977.

French, J.R.P., Jr. Person-role fit. In A. McLean (Ed.), *Occupational stress.* Springfield, Ill.: Charles C Thomas, 1974.

French, J.R.P., Jr., Rodgers, W. L., & Cobb, S. Adjustment as person–environment fit. In G. Coelho, D. Hamburg, & J. Adams (Eds.), *Coping and adaptation.* New York: Basic Books, 1974.

Gerwitz, J. L. *Attachment and dependency.* New York: Wiley, 1972.

Granovetter, M. S. Network sampling: Some first steps. *American Journal of Sociology,* 1976, **81**, 1287–1303.

Harary, F. *Graph theory.* New York: Addison-Wesley, 1969.

Harlow, H. F. Total social isolation: Effects on Macaque monkey behavior. *Science,* 1965, **148** (Whole No. 3670), 666.

Harrison, R. V. Person–environment fit and job stress. In C. L. Cooper & R. Payne (Eds.), *Stress at work.* New York: Wiley, 1977.

Holmes, T. H., & Rahe, R. H. The social readjustment scale. *Journal of Psychosomatic Research,* 1967, **11**, 213–218.

House, J., & Wells, J. A. Occupational stress, social support, and health. Paper presented at the Conference on Reducing Occupational Stress. Sponsored by Center for Occupational Mental Health, Cornell University and the National Institute of Occupational Safety and Health, White Plains, New York, 1977.

Jacobson, E., & Seashore, S. E. Communication practices in complex organizations. *Journal of Social Issues,* 1951, **7**, 28–40.

Kahn, R. L. Conflict, ambiguity, and overload: Three elements in job stress. In A. McLean (Ed.), *Occupational stress.* Springfield, Ill.: Charles C Thomas, 1974.

Kahn, R. L. Social support networks among students. Unpublished manuscript. Ann Arbor: Survey Research Center, The University of Michigan, 1978.

Kahn, R. L., & Antonucci, T. Social support networks among new teachers. Research study at the Survey Research Center, The University of Michigan, Ann Arbor, 1979–1980.

Kahn, R. L., & Quinn, R. P. Mental health, social support, and metropolitan problems: A research proposal. Ann Arbor: Survey Research Center, The University of Michigan, 1976.

Kalish, R., & Knudtson, F. W. Attachment versus disengagement: A life span conceptualization. *Human Development,* 1976, **19**, 171–182.

Kleiner, R. J., & Parker, S. Network participation and psychological impairment in an urban environment. In P. Meadows & E. H. Mizruchi, (Eds.), *Urbanism, urbanization, and change* (2nd ed.) Reading, Mass.: Addison-Wesley, 1976.

Lally, M., Black, E., Thornock, M., & Hawkins, J. D. Older women in single room occupant (SRO) hotels: A Seattle profile. *The Gerontologist,* 1979, **19**, No. 1

Laumann, E. *Bonds of pluralism.* New York: Wiley, 1973.

Lazarus, R., & Launier, R. Stress-related transactions between persons and environment. In L. A. Pervin & M. Lewis (Eds.), *Perspectives in interactional psychology.* New York: Plenum, 1978.

Lerner, R., & Ryff, C. Implementation of the life-span view of human development: The sample case of attachment. In P. B. Baltes (Ed.), *Life-span development and behavior* (Vol. 1). New York: Academic Press, 1978.

Lewis, M., & Goldberg, S. Perceptual–cognitive development in infancy: A generalized expectancy model as a function of mother–infant interaction. *Merrill-Palmer Quarterly,* 1969, **15**, 81–100.

Levi, L. *Stress and distress in response to psycho-social stimuli.* Oxford: Pergamon, 1972.

Levinson, D. *The Seasons of a man's life.* New York: Knopf, 1977.

Levitt, M. The effect of response contingent feedback on infants' reactions to a stranger. Presented at the biennial meetings of the Society for Research in Child Development, San Francisco, 1978.

Likert, R. *New patterns of management.* New York: McGraw-Hill, 1961.

Likert, R. *The human organization.* New York: McGraw-Hill, 1967.

Lowenthal, M. P., & Haven, C. Interaction and adaptation: Intimacy as a critical variable. *American Sociological Review,* 1968, **33**, 20–30.

Matas, L., Arend, R. A., & Sroufe, L. A. Continuity of adaptation in the second year: The relationship between quality of attachment and later competence. *Child Development,* 1978, **49**, 547–556.

Medalie, J. H., Snyder, M., Groen, J. J., Neufeld, H. N., Goldbourt, U., & Riss, E. Angina pectoris among 10,000 men: 5-year incidence and univariate analysis. *American Journal of Medicine,* 1973, **55**, 583.

McCallister, L., & Fischer, C. S. A procedure for surveying personal networks. *Sociological Methods and Research,* 1978, **7**, 2.

McGrath, J. E. Stress and behavior in organizations. In M. D. Dunnette (Ed.), *Handbook of industrial and organizational psychology.* Chicago: Rand McNally, 1976.

Moreno, J. L. *Who shall survive?* Washington, D.C.: Nervous and Mental Disease Publishing Co., 1934.

Myers, J. K., Lindenthal, J. L., & Pepper, M. P. Life events and psychiatric symptomatology. *Journal of Nervous & Mental Disease,* 1971, **152**, 149–157.

Nadel, S. *The theory of social structure.* Glencoe, Ill.: The Free Press, 1957.

Nisbett, R. E., & Valins, S. Perceiving the causes of one's own behavior. In E. E. Jones, D. E. Kanouse, H. H. Kelley, R. E. Nisbett, S. Valins, & R. Weiner (Eds.), *Attribution: Perceiving the causes of behavior.* Morristown, New Jersey: General Learning Press, 1972.

Nuckolls, K. B., Cassel, J., & Kaplan, B. H. Psychosocial assets, life crisis, and the prognosis of pregnancy. *American Journal of Epidemiology,* 1972, **95**, 431–441.

Parks, C. M., Benjamin, B., & Fitzgerald, R. G. Broken heart: A statistical study of increased mortality among widowers. *British Medical Journal,* 1969, **1**, 740–743.

Pinneau, S. R. *Effects of social support on psychological and physiological strains.* Unpublished Doctoral Dissertation, The University of Michigan, 1975.

Plath, D. Aging and social support. A presentation to the Committee on Work and Personality in the Middle Years, Social Science Research Council, 1975.

Provence, S., & Lipton, R. C. *Infants in institutions.* New York: International Universities Press, 1962.

Raphael, B. Preventive intervention with the recently bereaved. *Archives of General Psychiatry,* 1977, **34**, 1450–1454.

Stephens, R. C., Blau, Z. S., Oser, G. T., & Miller, M. D. Aging, social support systems, and social policy. *Journal of Gerontological Social Work,* 1978, **1**.

Stoghill, R. *Handbook of leadership.* New York: The Free Press, 1974.

Terman, L. M., & Oden, M. *The gifted child grows up.* Stanford, Calif.: Stanford University Press, 1947.

Thomas, A., Birch, H. G., Chess, S., Hertzig, M. E., & Korin, S. *Behavioral individuality in early childhood.* New York: New York University Press, 1963.

Waters, E. The reliability and stability of individual differences in infant–mother attachment. *Child Development,* 1978, **49**, 483–494.

Watson, J. B., & Ramey, C. T. Reactions to response-contingency stimulation in early infancy. *Merrill-Palmer Quarterly,* 1972, **18**, 219–227.

Weinraub, M., Brooks, J., & Lewis, M. The social network: A reconsideration of the concept of attachment. *Human Development,* 1977, **20**, 31–47.

Wellman, B. The community question: The intimate networks of East Yorkers. *American Journal of Sociology,* 1979, **84**.

Weiss, R. S. *Processes of organization.* Ann Arbor: Institute for Social Research, The University of Michigan, 1956.

Yarrow, L. J. The development of focused relationships in infancy. In J. Hellmuth (Ed.), *Exceptional infant.* Seattle, Wash.: Special Child Publications, 1967.

Contours of Consociation:
Lessons from a Japanese Narrative

David W. Plath

THE UNIVERSITY OF ILLINOIS

URBANA, ILLINOIS

Abstract

"Entity" models of development build upon the individual as an isolate. But a person as a social being only emerges from within a collective shaping of growth. This process can be viewed as a form of social discourse among those who grow older together (consociates), and who mutually define and redefine the meaning of each other's maturing and aging. The process is examined as it appears in the Japanese novel *Sasameyuki*. The implications are that by studying the interaction of consocial currents we may discover higher-level orderings of orders of development as human relationship. And that by scrutinizing consocial engagements we may mentally grasp the transformations of self-awareness as they emerge from within longterm human communion.

I. Introduction

I was reminded of a remark of Willa Cather's, that you can't paint sunlight, you can only paint what it does with shadows on a wall. If you examine a life, as Socrates has been tediously advising us to do for so many centuries, do you really examine the life, or do you examine the shadows it casts on other lives? Entity or relationships?

—Wallace Stegner, The Spectator Bird

A. LIGHT AND SHADOWS

The idea of looking at human development from a life-span perspective has a subversive charm. It asks us to set aside the usual ballistic-missile image of maturity and aging, and not assume that we can predict the later curve of the life course just from knowing what takes place on the launching pads of childhood. Instead it invites us to take up a guided-missile image, and allow for drastic changes in direction or speed at any point along the trajectory of years. It tempts us to search for the guidance systems that steer the course of development. And in so doing it may lure us into modifying our habits of thinking about the time-warped nature of personal experience.

To put the point in a slogan: Human development has been thought of as a problem of biography, it may need to be rethought as a problem of cobiography. In the former model, maturity and aging are properties attributed to the individual as monad entity. This entity is tracked across a sequence of stages and transitions that are triggered either externally by social norms or internally by an "epigenetic" mental clock that is supposed to inhere in our species. By contrast, a cobiographical approach would take maturity and aging to be properties of a person as embedded in an ongoing convoy of human relationships. His or her growth and self-realization will be shaped by theirs, and development is seen as the outcome of mutual human cultivation, of the "shadows" we cast upon each other's lives.

In studying the adult life course as revealed in Japanese narratives, I have come to view development as a form of extended discourse among consociates (Plath, 1980). A matured human sensibility is one of the most remarkable products that any society can bring forth. He or she is a living cathedral, the handiwork of generations. "If you want to reform a man," wrote Victor Hugo, "begin with his grandmother." No Rubicon divides those who are mature from those who are not. To know if we are mature we must convince people—and ourselves—that we own the right history of experience. And this propels us into long engagements with the cultural symbols that identify experience, and with those persons around us who control the meaning of the symbols. Discourse is the process of making such continuing identifications and reidentifications, of construing the meaning of personal change.

In this chapter, I want to sketch a consocial point of view and illustrate it with examples drawn from a Japanese fictional narrative. With the case before us, I then will discuss some key dimensions of consocial action. The root ideas in this will be familiar to anyone versed in the concepts of interactionist social psychology and cultural phenomenology. To offer a general review of such concepts here seems gratuitous. It could even distract from my main purpose, and that is to indicate how we might revamp current lines of thinking and so bring them to bear on the elements of cumulative coexperience that are the heart of human development as a mutual endeavor.

B. CONSOCIATION

We are born alone and we die alone, each an organism genetically unique. But we are born incomplete: In the company of others we must mutually domesticate the wild genetic pulse as we shape ourselves into persons after the vision of our group's heritage. Perhaps the growth of an organism can be described well enough in terms of trends and stages within the individual entity. But the growth of a social animal must be described in terms of a collective fabricating of selves, a joint building of biographies. And this is all the more so for the symbol-stuffed animal that is *Homo sapiens*. Maybe our every human encounter, however trivial, contributes its traces, however feathery, to our cumulative realization. But our biographies are formed most of all by our repeated encounters with those around us whose lives run close, and parallel, to ours, by those who grow older with us. These are our consociates.

As a technical term, "consociates" originates in the work of Alfred Schutz (1970). If "associates" are people I relate to in the moment-to-moment of daily behavior, "consociates" are those intimates whom I engage and reengage across long chains of interaction. Consociation implies depth in time and in attachment. The bonds are personal, many sided, not confined merely to the execution of some particular set of role duties. My consociates know the "real me," not just some of my role masks.

My convoy of consociates, then, will consist of an array of kin, friends lovers, colleagues, classmates, and so on. Some of them already were shaping my life course, beginning to define the meaning of my existence, long before I was born. Others may continue to redefine that meaning long after I have died. My biography will be one-dimensional if it omits them. I am, like any person, answerable for the conduct of my life, obliged to "author" my behavioral biography. But my consociates have the power to certify which version of that life's narrative is "authoritative."

Some notion of this power that consociates hold is probably standard equipment in any culture—American popular tradition, for one, speaks of "life's companions" and "fellow travellers." And the modern social science lexicon offers a number of terms that refer loosely to the phenomenon. Charles H. Cooley's "primary group" is the earliest and most widely known, with Harry Stack Sullivan's "significant others" perhaps running second. But one also comes across terms such as "ambience" (Caplow, 1955), "entourage" (Hanks, 1975), "personal community" (Henry, 1958), or "vital role others" (Perlman, 1968). And during the last few years an explosive radiation of changes has been rung upon the concept of "social networks."

All of these terms suggest a self-and-others unit of human process. Held against the sweep of the life span, however, such concepts pale. If not time-blind they are at least time-dim. They tend to pull our attention down to the immediate, forensic features of a human encounter or else out to the formal characteristics of social ties. A life-span perspective challenges us instead to look up from momentary events, episodes and behavior strings. It asks us to examine the longer-running currents of social process that lend maturity a direction and give experience its ramifying frameworks of significance.

Perhaps every little personal identification has an implicit pathway of further development. In a consocial approach we need not, it seems to me, attempt to deal with all of these little changes, with every shift in the presentations of self. The Goffmanites already can do that rather well. We will want to examine a person's passage into a new role, for this is likely to alter the pattern of consocial conduct. But here again the study of the well-known normative features of role socialization might be left to the heirs of Van Gennep. Instead the goal is to uncover those larger self–other transformations that arise from within the stream of social discourse itself. The focus is not on forensic presentations of self but rather on the *preservations* of self in continuity and change across extended engagements.

This only restates the usual assumption of human interdependence. If the identity of one partner is to change, there must be compensating changes in the others. My successes and failures "shadow" the life options of my consociates. They and I have a "developmental stake" (Bengtson & Kuypers, 1971) in each other's continuing integrity and continuing growth. They have the power to ratify, even to compel, changes in my portfolio of identities. This is beautifully portrayed in one of the foremost narratives in modern Japanese literature, Jun'ichirō Tanzaki's novel *Sasameyuki*.

II. A Japanese Narrative

A. THE MAKIOKA SISTERS

The novel has been masterfully translated into English by Edward Seidensticker, and published under the title *The Makioka Sisters* (Tanizaki, 1957). The English title may have been coined to invite comparison with landmarks of world literature such as *The Brothers Karamazov*, but it drops nuances that are important in the Japanese title. The book is, to be sure, the story of all four sisters in the Makioka family. But the chief problem that they all face is to find a husband for the third daughter, Yukiko ("Snow"). The phrase *sasameyuki* is old poetic diction for "a delicate snowfall." To enjoy the beauty of such a scene, one has to refrain from trampling down the delicate snow.

The Makiokas were an old-line merchant household in downtown Osaka, but ever since the death of the girls' parents the family's wealth and prestige have been slipping. Of the four daughters, the two youngest remain unmarried, although Yukiko already is 30 and Taeko, the youngest, is 25. With the parents dead, responsibility for finding mates for these two sisters officially devolves upon Tsuruko, the eldest daughter, and her husband Tatsuo, as successors to the Makioka line.

But Yukiko and Taeko long have felt put off by Tsuruko's stuffiness. So rather than live with her in the main house in Osaka they connive to spend much of their time in suburban Ashiya with their more sympathetic second sister, Sachiko. And thus it comes about that de facto responsibility for the two younger women is taken over by Sachiko and her husband, Teinosuke. If Sachiko's affection for her younger sisters is deep, warm, and sororal, her duty towards then becomes maternal. She and they are, furthermore, caught up in a lifelong community of shared experiences and interests. How Sachiko manages these conflicting pulls of affection, duty and comradeship is one of the central story lines across the more than 500 pages and 5 years of narration time in the book.

To focus upon Sachiko as I do here is to assault the greater architecture of symbols that Tanizaki has built into *Sasameyuki*. He characterizes all four sisters in depth, and this is only slightly less true of Sachiko's husband or of their daughter, Etsuko. However, if the author occasionally takes us into the minds of others in the family he consistently makes us privy to Sachiko's feelings and reactions. She does not narrate the story, nor do we see events unfold only through her eyes. But the action revolves primarily around her position in this commune of fate. Sachiko does not dominate this human galaxy, but the others in it gravitate about her, relying upon her to mediate their conflicts and to hold the system in balance.

A delicate and complex sensuality toward the drifting flow of time permeates the book. "It is the interior time that passes within humans that is the central concern of this novel," Tanizaki was to write some years later (Noguchi, 1977, p. 6). Symbolically the author plays off men's time against women's tempo. Men's time is seen as "artificial" in its concern with a man's rise or fall in commerce or politics or war; women's tempo is more "natural." But, if more natural, it also is more difficult to control or influence, with its repetitive outbursts of menstruation and childbirth, its imperatives of bodily aging and the stages of the life cycle. By preserving the Osaka bourgeois life style, Sachiko provides her menage with a channel of continuity in which to tame the wild currents of time so that they can be esthetically savored. Since the book is neither pornographic nor manifestly unpatriotic, a foreign reader may find it curious that portions of the novel were banned during the Pacific War. Perhaps its very celebration of the voluptuousness latent in modern middle-class life ways—a favorite theme of Tanizaki's—was sufficient to arouse the censorial impulse.

More important for our purposes, Tanizaki conveys this artistry of time with a technique that is close to cinema verite. The Makioka women are, in fact, modeled closely on his second wife (who becomes Sachiko in the novel) and her three sisters. Events in the narrative replicate events in their actual lives, even to taking place at the same dates and times in the late 1930s. People confront just the right range and balance of improbabilities that they remain credible.

B.   PROBLEM PERFORMERS

Sachiko has no towering compulsion or supercharged interest by which to plot her course of life. She has no career separable from her family. She finds the root meaning of existence in the Osaka bourgeois life style. In the novel, this is symbolized by her appreciation for traditional dances performed in the Osaka manner. She herself is a spectator, not a dancer; the dancers in the family are Yukiko and Taeko—destined by the norms of the life cycle to marry and leave. If Sachiko is to sustain the richness of her involvement in the bourgeois life style she must somehow remain close to her younger sisters while, at the same time, help them into life's next phase. Her challenge thus is to preserve these other selves through change, to preserve the integrity of her own life's pattern.

When we first meet her, Sachiko is not sure that she can rise to that challenge. Back when the Makioka family had thrived in its merchant glory she had been her father's pet; at 35, she retains traces of the spoiled daughter she once was. Her defenses still are shaky. She is prey to minor colds and indispositions.

However, in 12 years of married life, she has built a stable menage. She and her husband still exchange poems, take second-honeymoon trips, and can erupt in marital tiffs in public without having bitter afterattacks. Daughter Etsuko is more troublesome, a coltish and wilful child. At times she seems neurotic, and is more attached to Yukiko than to her mother. Yukiko responds by fussing over Etsuko more than would a devoted nanny. The household also contains one or more maids who require correcting and supervising. In recent years, domestic service has become a commercial trade, but at the time of the novel the household "helper" usually was a teenage girl sent for training as an apprentice housewife. Her services were rewarded with lessons in the household and marital arts, and with help in finding a husband.

Husband, daughter, maids—all require Sachiko's attention. But if it were only a matter of looking after them, she reflects, the Ashiya house might be terribly dull. The problem performers who add zest to her situation are Yukiko and Taeko.

> Not that they were a bother to her: she was delighted at the color they gave the life of the family. Sachiko among the four sisters had in largest measure inherited her father's love of excitement. She disliked too quiet a house. Out of deference to her married sister and her brother-in-law she could not purposely lure her younger sisters away. Still she rejoiced in the fact that they preferred her house to the main house, and it seemed natural that they should be where there was more room and where children were less of a problem. (Tanizaki, 1957, p. 256)

The younger sisters are by no means unsought in the marriage market. Like Sachiko herself, both are cheerful, stunning women who look a decade younger than their years. They take lessons in French conversation as well as in Osaka dance. They combine East and West, traditional and modern, in appealing blends, each with her own accent—Taeko being the bold modern woman, Yukiko the demure maiden of old.

If the Makioka fortune is gone, the family name remains respected across mercantile Osaka. Kin, friends, and Sachiko's helpful hairdresser, Mrs. Itani, staff a distant early warning line that detects the approach of potential husbands. But Yukiko is in danger of superannuation. During the span of the novel she even enters the "danger year" [*yakudoshi*] traditionally thought to be most inauspicious for a woman, 33. She and her supporters are pressed by that most scarce of natural resources, time.

Taeko affirms that she will not marry out of sequence, not before Yukiko has been married. Partly this is from regard for family honor, partly from personal affection for Yukiko. The difficulty is that Taeko has had a steady boyfriend for some years. He is the pampered son of a merchant family, socially appropriate for the Makiokas, though personally they think him crude. And he and the impulsive Taeko are feisty. They even try to elope, and both families are obliged to suppress the affair.

Taeko is the sort who, once she has made up her mind, will go ahead "quite without hesitation—sometimes even to the point of making herself a little unpleasant" (Tanizaki, 1957, p. 189). She is as socially adept as Yukiko is socially inept, so worldly wise that now and then her more housebound sisters feel that she is condescending to them. She develops a following as a maker of Japanese style dolls and an instructress in the craft. From there she wants to go on to become a modiste, designing and making

Western clothes. She demands that the family finance her plan to go study in Paris and then open a salon in Kobe. But, if the Osaka main house will tolerate her dollmaking "hobby," it flatly rejects her ambition to become a "working woman" in the pedestrian trade of "seamstress."

Yukiko, on the other hand, is a fragile snowflake, beautiful but so shy that she cannot at times even articulate her feelings or wants to others in the family. Outside the house she almost never speaks even in situations where common courtesy expects it. She will plead with others to accompany her when she leaves the house on a trivial errand. One of her suitors loses heart when she can only mumble an incoherent reply to his telephoned invitation to join him for a cup of tea. Sachiko, Teinosuke, and the marital go-betweens must take pains to convince prospects that first impressions of Yukiko can be in error. Her intimates know that within the protecting walls of home she can be a treasure.

> With Yukiko back the Ashiya house was gay and noisy again. Yukiko, so inarticulate that one hardly knew she was about, added little to the noise, but one could see from the difference she made that something bright was hidden behind that apparent melancholy and reserve. (Tanizaki, 1957, p. 288)

Physically Yukiko is the sturdiest of all the Makioka women, never prey to colds or aches. But she has a blemish that erupts prominently on her forehead during menstrual periods. Physicians assure them that this is common in young women and that it will disappear permanently soon after she marries. But it means anxious moments for Sachiko and the go-betweens whenever they must schedule a "viewing" for her. Eventually they pressure Yukiko until she submits to a series of inoculations that will erase the spot.

C. SUSTAINING AND STEERING

Sachiko finds herself in a polygon of conflicting interests—between Taeko and Yukiko, between each of them and the main house, between her duty to find mates for them and her delight in what they add to the Ashiya menage. They are her sisters and yet they are more like daughters. They also are her best friends.

> Everything considered, then, her feelings for the two had not been what one usually understands by the affection of sister for sister. She was sometimes startled at the thought that she spent more time worrying about her sisters than about her husband and daughter, but they were like daughters—they were on a level with Etsuko in her affections, and at the same time they were her only friends. Left alone, she was surprised to note that she had no friends worthy of the name. Her relations with other housewives had for the most part been cool and formal. Because of her sisters she had not needed friends. (Tanizaki, 1957, p. 256)

When they were girls in the Osaka house, the three of them always slept in the same room, down to the night before Sachiko was married. Tsuruko slept in a room of her own. Even now the three of them freely borrow and wear each other's kimono, obi, undergarments. No one in the Ashiya house can muster interest in a suitor who, though otherwise acceptable, would take Yukiko away to rusticate in a distant country town. And when negotiations turn serious with another man (whom Yukiko eventually marries) Sachiko is chilled because he is from Tokyo—until he remarks that he plans to come live in Osaka. The sisters must marry, Sachiko allows, but if they move far away the Ashiya house will go humdrum. "It was like a spring breeze to have all the sisters under one roof. The mood would be broken if one of them were to go" (Tanizaki, 1959, p. 288).

Sachiko has heard that people accuse her of holding Yukiko in the Ashiya house as a cheap nanny for Etsuko. That may not be entirely untrue, Sachiko admits, but it is a minor motive. Far more prepotent is her appreciation of Yukiko's rare beauty, beauty which can be achieved, like the beauty of a bonsai, only by careful cultivation along traditional lines. Sachiko could not push her sister into marriage to any philistine incapable of cherishing such beauty.

Her involvement in the arts inclines Sachiko to favor Yukiko. Still, Sachiko also is partial to the "Japanese maiden" who appears in Taeko when she dresses in kimono and performs, as she does with great skill, Osaka dances. After all, Sachiko reasons to herself, Taeko never enjoyed her fair share of parental affection. Sachiko would like to make amends for that.

> There were reasons why Taeko should be different from the rest of them. It was not entirely fair to reprove her. She alone of the four sisters had known almost nothing of their father's prosperous days, and she had but the dimmest memories of her mother, who had died just as the youngest daughter was starting school. Their pleasure-loving father gave the daughters everything they wanted, and yet Taeko had never really known—had never had an immediate sense of—what had been done for her. . . . She remembered chiefly how her father would describe her as the darkest and plainest of all, and indeed she must have been a most untidy girl, with her face quite uncared for and her clothes so shapeless that she could have passed for a boy. She liked to say that some day she too would finish school and dress up and go out as her sisters did. She would buy pretty clothes. But before she had her wish, her father died, and the good days were over for the Makioka family. (Tanizaki, 1957, p. 266)

Taeko is more complex than Yukiko, is even capable of deceiving her sisters. Rumors of Taeko's misconduct—which she denies—rebound to harm Yukiko's marital prospects and reflect back upon Sachiko herself for not being more firm about supervising this flamboyant sister. Sachiko is inclined to blame herself more than Taeko, blame herself for not having judged her sister's character more accurately. But a time comes when Sachiko must act decisively, or else Yukiko and Taeko will be summoned back to the main house to live.

D. CRISIS MANAGEMENT

Sachiko expels Taeko from the Ashiya house—at least for appearance's sake—and reports to the main house that from now on Taeko will live alone. Perhaps Sachiko is not deliberately conning the main house, but she is more and more discouraged by Tsuruko's lack of sympathy. Tsuruko always had been somewhat distant from her sisters. Her actions now, however, alienate her further: When the Makiokas of Ashiya next call at the main house it is only to transact official business.

Sachiko's trials reach a climax when at long last Yukiko is betrothed—and Taeko announces that she is pregnant. It is too late to risk an abortion, and her condition will soon be visible. Sachiko activates the entire Ashiya household. Teinosuke talks to the bartender–lover Miyoshi, who appears to be a decent man more than willing to marry Taeko, once Yukiko has safely been married. Taeko is sent to a resort, where she registers as "Mrs. Abe." She is tended, but also policed, by the maid Oharu. Once a blabbermouth country girl, in her years under Sachiko's tutelage, Oharu has grown into a cool-headed young woman who can be trusted to guard the family's reputation, even to the point of bossing Taeko around.

> Sachiko purposely called a cab from a stand some distance away, and had her sister change to another cab in Kobe for the trip across the mountains. She gave Oharu detailed instructions: Taeko was to be in Arima for several months, under the name Abe; Oharu was to call her Mrs. Abe and not Koi-san [the family's pet name for her]; for liaison a messenger would be sent from Ashiya, or Oharu herself would come back, and no one was to use the telephone; Oharu was to understand that Miyoshi and Taeko were not to see each other and that Miyoshi was not to be told where Taeko was staying; and Oharu was moreover to watch for strange letters, or telephone calls or visitors. (Tanizaki, 1957, p. 504)

But when Taeko's labor proves troublesome, a breech presentation, it is Sachiko herself who "breaks cover" and rushes to the hospital. Waving her husband's business card she demands that "Mrs. Abe" be treated with the German pharmaceuticals that she is sure the hospital has in reserve for its favored patients. In what seems a melodramatic tribute to propriety, however, the child is stillborn.

Perhaps the sisters do not live on happily ever after—for the shadow of war is over the nation—but they will be living not far from Ashiya. Sachiko has held her convoy together, seen them through illness and tragedy, covered their failures and helped salvage their self-respect. Teinosuke offers to pay the expenses of Yukiko's wedding and to repay Taeko's debts to a former boyfriend, even though the main house should be responsible for such matters. Etsuko is shedding her neurotic habits and becoming a sassy but likable teenager. Oharu has become discreet and competent, ready to be sent as a bride herself. Taeko will live with Miyoshi until it is time for them to be married. Yukiko can finish packing her trousseau, the bride of a man who will nourish her fragile charm. And yet, "At the thought of how still the house would be, Sachiko felt like a mother who had just seen her daughter married" (Tanizaki, 1957, p. 530).

III. Consocial Action

A. CODEVELOPMENT

From a consocial point of view, the singularity of the term life span is misleading. We need to think of spans, courses, and cycles of life in their copresent plurality. What matters most in cobiography are the contours of maturity and aging of persons as shaped by the careers of relationships; and these occur in heaps and clusters. Their plurality is fused and flattened in an "entity" model to project a single linear sequence of stages. However, at any moment my developmental tasks or crises may be set, and surely will be "shadowed," by the developmental tasks that my intimates face on their life trajectories. As I act jointly with each of them I may have to march to a different drumbeat of growth. Alexander Moore (1973), introducing his study of the multiple linkages of life cycles in a Guatemalan village, remarks that:

> These various ages of man spin off from the meshing—as of gears—of a number of differently timed human life cycles coexisting within particular communities. The ages of man spin off from the intricate cycling of three generations at once. [For example] the coming into existence of a generation also creates generational statuses and life crises further up the line. Birth and the various ceremonies that mark it, such as baptism, must bear the weight of at least two higher generations, whose status is thereby changed. (p. 3)

Furthermore, I can engage each consocial partner in multiple idioms; we can play a whole repertory of roles to one another. Each role has its own implicit career futures. So I may stand concurrently at different stages, may move at different tempos across the same interval, in relating to every person growing older with me. Julius Roth (1963, p. 113), in his pathbreaking analysis of the timing of careers, comments that: "If one wishes to apply a timetable analysis to the whole of a person's life, he must realize that each person is operating on a number of timetables simultaneously. . . . If the focus is on individual development, the interactions between timetables may be of more interest than the separately analyzed career timetables."

Consocial action, then, has the task of "reconciling" at least two types of "contradictions": that one's partners are in different seasons of life, and that one is moving simultaneously on several career pathways with each of these partners. Both types can be seen in *Sasameyuki*.

If we take one of the linear models—Erik Erikson's for example—and apply it to the Makioka sisters we are obliged to deal with separate cases of life stage crisis: crises of generativity for Tsuruko and Sachiko, of intimacy for Yukiko and Taeko. This is of course a useful way to account for some of the developmental trends in each of these women. Sachiko, for example, as we come to know her, already has surmounted the crisis of intimacy. Her ties with her husband and younger sisters are strong, trusting, affectionate, healthy. However her generative capacity—for Erikson the ability to nurture one's juniors—remains uncertain. Her child is neurotic, the maids underdisciplined. Five years later, however, Sachiko has shown that she can act like a mother toward her younger sisters, helping each of them into a marriage with long-term potential. Under Sachiko's nurturing, Yukiko has become a little more talkative, Taeko a little more tractable. Etsuko and Oharu have become more self-possessed, and now can be trusted with family secrets. When there are sensitive matters to be discussed, Sachiko no longer walks out to use a public telephone so that Etsuko and Oharu will not overhear.

But the crisis of generativity erupted "early" in Sachiko's life because of her younger sisters. They triggered it by moving into her Ashiya house. In a more "typical" career tempo Sachiko need not have faced the emptying of the nest for another decade, the time when daughter Etsuko will enter the marriage market. And by then Sachiko would have had pretests, experience gained by marrying off Oharu and the other maids.

However, the younger sisters moved to Ashiya because the Osaka main house was failing them in their crises of intimacy. Tsuruko was unable to deal effectively with Yukiko's reluctance or with Taeko's self-assertiveness. Tanizaki invites us to feel sympathy for Tsuruko: As the eldest child she bears the dual burden of legal responsibility for her sisters' marriages and of social responsibility for preserving the family's good name. But she values status consistency too much, and her bonds with Yukiko and Taeko shrivel in richness. If only Yukiko would get married to somebody, snaps Tsuruko in exasperation, marry somebody, anybody, even if it ends in divorce. And when she hears that Taeko almost died from an attack of dysentery at the home of a lover, Tsuruko murmurs that it would have been only fit punishment for all the trouble that Taeko has been causing.

Sachiko is, in a sense, usurping Tsuruko's responsibilities. So she has to be careful to maintain the impression that the Osaka house still is in control of the marriage negotiations. Using an "entity" model here, we might want to postulate that an unconscious sibling rivalry has erupted—except that, we are told, in childhood it was Sachiko who was father's favorite. And in any event Tanizaki explains the matter instead by consocial history. As he depicts them, the three younger sisters have accumulated a battery of roles they perform for one another. (The very opening lines of the narrative express this in a deceptively mundane way. Sachiko is seated in front of a mirror powdering the back of her neck and shoulders, when Taeko approaches from behind and completes the task for her, as they talk about Yukiko's newest prospect.) The three younger sisters share clothing, jewelry, secrets. They echo one another's tastes in food, dance, drama, and the many particulars that make up the rich texture of the Osaka bourgeois life style. When any of the three is away, that texture goes soggy.

This is why Yukiko, who seems to be such a wallflower, is such a charm. For she reflects light into the lives of the others, just by moving softly among them, the way a gentle snowfall brightens the interior of a dark room. Marry she must, and the sooner the better, since her market value is dwindling, and Taeko is impatient in the wings. But Sachiko never could force Yukiko to marry a man incapable of savoring her gentleness, of preserving the "real Yukiko" that the Ashiya menage knows so well.

Even as she assumes maternal responsibility for her younger sisters, pushing them away into marriage, Sachiko is at pains to keep them close to her for yet another reason. She hopes to continue their mutual careers as friends. One day an epiphany comes to her: Sachiko discovers that she has no friends "worthy of the name." She already is beyond the season when it is easiest to cultivate life-span friendships—Japanese folk wisdom says that this can be done best in the secondary school years. So she *must* hold on to her younger sisters as a matter of sensible life-course insurance. Theirs may be the only friendships she will ever know.

Here again for Tanizaki the explanation does not lie in an "entity" notion of personality but rather in cobiography. Sachiko always has been gregarious, cheerful, the sort of person who can make friends easily if she chooses to. But she did not trouble herself to do so in the seedtime years of girlhood because she was "friends" with her father, sharing his enthusiasm for the theater, for restaurants, for the urban good life. He didn't care if his daughters skipped school or ignored their studies. If anything, he would entice them away from school to spend the day at the theater with him. So Sachiko had her father and sisters as steady companions during her school years and never made friends with her classmates.

In the years of the novel, then, Sachiko is not just being tested for maternal talent. She is under the equally difficult developmental test of evolving a new format for her bonds with her two most promising lifelong friends. Perhaps we should not be surprised that more than 4 years of consocial action are needed to transform such a tangled cluster of timetables of codevelopment that are at once maternal, sororal, and amical.

B. DISCOURSE

Said figuratively, we grow as social persons by feeding upon nurturant others and nourishing symbols: social psychology's "significant others" and cultural anthropology's "life-giving myths." My consociates are those whose lives very literally "mean a lot" to me, as mine does to them. They and I repeatedly rewrite our cobiographies during our engagements of discourse. And, although our discourse can be about anything under the sun, the meanings of space and time and the universe as well as our lives in it, the consocial part of all this has to do with how we evaluate our joint progress in life's journey. A consocial approach aims at elucidating how intimates come not only to mean something to each other, but how over time they may come to mean *more* to each other.

Yukiko and Taeko, for example, have become friends and daughters to Sachiko, as well as sisters. Therein lie powerful measures of Sachiko's own human maturing. Japanese commonsense concepts define the mature woman as one who has become a "good wife and wise mother" (*ryosai kembō*). Such a women has shucked the lesser shell of self she knew as a "spoiled daughter." No adult Japanese woman is likely in my experience to openly proclaim herself to be a good wife and wise mother. To do so, except in jest, would strain the limits of modesty. Instead, women I have interviewed, and asked, "Do you think of yourself as mature now?" responded by biographical indirection. "Well," they said, "I used to be such a spoiled daughter. . . ." In *Sasameyuki* we find Sachiko musing to herself in the same vein.

There is, after all, no graduation ceremony to single out those who have passed their examinations in human generativity. Recognition must come by reflected glory, as when your child marries or when you successfully have negotiated a marriage for someone else's child. (Some Japanese tell me that their personal measure is three betrothals: Only when they have arranged three marriages will they think themselves fulfilled as adults.) Your own life-course progress thus hinges on the uncertain progress of others in their life-stage tasks. And this is particularly so for a woman like Sachiko, who has no crafts, hobbies, or avocations, much less a working career, by which her maturity and mastery might be gauged. The very measure of her own maturity, is what Yukiko's and Taeko's lives have come to mean for her.

In addition, if Yukiko and Taeko as daughters are evidence for Sachiko's expanding mastery, as friends they also are key witnesses to it. Remember that Sachiko has no childhood friends who might otherwise perform this witness for her. When one's progress is judged by kin, by colleagues, by neighbors, there are likely to be overtones of social control, hidden agendas of self-interest in the evaluation. Friendship—at least in Japanese conception—is not muddied by the demands of institutional solidarity. If anyone can be trusted to judge you frankly, it is a true friend.

The importance of friends as witnesses came out, for example, in interviews I had with a woman I will call Goryōhan. (For her life narrative see Plath, 1980, Chap. 5.) Now a vivacious, self-confident woman of 42, Goryōhan for 20 years has been the junior wife in a stem family household. When I asked her if she considered herself mature, she at first said no. After all, she pointed out, *she* is still around—the senior wife, her husband's mother. So long as mother-in-law remains alive and well, Goryōhan by definition is in juniority.

Then Goryōhan commented that she used to be such a spoiled daughter—and at once added that her friends remind her of that. They tell her they once doubted whether she could make a go of it as a junior wife, but now they are impressed by her success. Their testimony is particularly valuable because, in contrast to her husband or children or senior wife, these friends actually knew Goryōhan in the days when she may have been a spoiled daughter. They can confirm, as no one in the household can, her memory of what she used to be. They can validate in a special way her claim to have grown into something more. *Kyūyū ni masaru kagami nashi* runs a Japanese saying: "There is no better mirror than an old friend."

Goryōhan's life offers a second example of how consociates may come to mean more to one another, in this instance in her 20-year engagement with her senior wife. Goryōhan never spoke to me of the woman as "mother-in-law" or used any other distance-putting locution. Always it was "Granny." After two decades in the house, Goryōhan, for all practical purposes, holds power over the domestic arena. She might openly claim the baton of household command if she chose, particularly now that her father-in-law is dead and her husband has assumed public headship of the family. But rather than thrust her senior wife crudely into retirement, Goryōhan continues to thrust "Granny" forward as the woman nominally in charge.

As a relational strategy, this requires interim trade offs. A rambling old house must be kept up, someone must always be left to guard it from burglars and fires. Goryōhan serves Granny as a social secretary, taking dictation and answering letters for her. For many years Granny was a teacher of the Japanese aesthetic of tea. And although Goryōhan dislikes the bitter taste of the tea used in the aesthetic, she joins her senior for a bowl of it every morning after breakfast. "Three hundred and sixty-five danged days a year she has to have that tea," she said to me with some asperity one day.

Goryōhan's obligations toward the woman are defined by their roles in the household and their relative positions along the life cycle. But 2 decades of migrating together through time have personalized their bond and enlarged its repertoire of idioms of expression. Given her selfish wishes, Goryōhan would sell the house and move into a modern apartment or condominium. But to do so while Granny is alive would put an end to her garden and her formal tea chamber. It probably would break her heart.

Goryōhan hesitates to do that. For what has happened between them is this: "Other people are surprised by how freely Granny and I can talk to each other," says Goryōhan, contrasting theirs with the cold and ugly pattern that in popular stereotype is assumed to obtain between a senior and a junior wife. "It's just as though we are mother and daughter." Her husband even protests, if jokingly, that the relationship has become too free and open. The neighbors may begin to get the idea that Goryōhan actually is the blood-line daughter of the household and that he is only a hapless male who had to marry in and take his wife's family name. And who, by implication, must be henpecked.

So Granny's taste for tea may amount to an addiction. Nevertheless, Goryōhan prepares it every single morning in a daily ritual of private duet. Into their cups they pour 20 shared years of growing and aging together as senior and junior wife in this house that each of them entered, in turn, as bride and stranger. Tea is the wine of their communion of maturity.

It is possible that in her younger years Goryōhan never was, in truth, a spoiled daughter. I have no reason to doubt her self-report, but neither do I have any outside evidence to corroborate it. Even her friends, were they pressed about the issue, might turn out to say that in the school years she really wasn't much of a brat. The point is that "spoiled daughter" can serve as a symbol of consensus about the evaluation of Goryōhan's development. She and her friends agree that she has matured, and one way to express this is to identify her as no longer being a spoiled daughter.

Such identifications and agreements, such mutual buildings of biographies, are the heart of consocial discourse, of determining the meaning of who we are as we grow and age. In the lingo of role analysis this could be called role making: not simply living up to the norms of a role but making the relationship into something more. As to what that something more might be, Sachiko and Goryōhan verbalize it as the adding of other role idioms to a relationship. By the end of *Sasameyuki* Sachiko is able to feel toward Yukiko like a mother who has just lost a daughter. After 20 years together, Goryōhan and Granny can treat each other as if they were a real mother and daughter. It is not just a making of roles in the singular but a making of whole anthologies of them, cultivating the potential we have for cumulatively coming to mean even more to one another.

C. ENGAGEMENTS

I have been referring to persons as "engaged" in consocial interplay with nurturing others and nourishing symbols. Such engagements may vary widely in time span when measured by the clock or calendar. They are marked off instead by internal signs of closure, of redefinition, of a "reconciliation of contradictions" in the development of a person as a cluster of human relationships. Partners in an engagement may or may not be able to verbalize this sense of closure or change to an outsider, nor always even to each other. I assume that they do communicate it in some form, however, and that these forms of discourse are open to an outsider to discover and state.

In following an engagement analytically we watch the currents of experience and the contours of discourse about the meaning of that experience, as they move across a sequence of encounters and episodes. (In *Sasameyuki,* for example, the Makiokas go through five successive rounds of negotiations before they conclude a betrothal for Yukiko.) We note how selves are identified and ratified (e.g., "a spoiled daughter"). We trace these identifications as they become transformed, redefined, outgrown in favor of larger—or of course sometimes smaller—integrities (e.g., "a selfless mother"). We search for the orderings of orders of growth and aging that emerge from, and are guided by, this mutual processing of lives.

Events on wider levels can rough-hew the course of consocial possibilities. An analysis of engagements is no substitute for investigating the trends of demography or the family cycle or cohort history, or drifts in the local pattern of values and world views. But conversely these macrophenomena do not predict the finer tunings of guidance that the partners to an engagement effectuate as they direct their mutual impulses to self-completion. If "entity" approaches reveal modal personality, the mental integration typical of each later stage of the life trajectory, a consocial approach may reveal "nodal" personality: the kind of human who evolves at each node in a web of cojourners.

Yukiko, for example, suffers from a kind of interpersonal disease; her shyness leaves her developmentally disadvantaged. So the Makiokas must mobilize again and again to bring about a betrothal for her. And yet the very delicacy of her condition is the product of her consocial history. The Makiokas may not have deliberately set out to create it but they have come to treasure it—to the point where they are ambivalent about sending her into any betrothal. This is the irony of human cultivation, that we nurture one another only, in time, to have to let go.

IV. Conclusion

"There may be wide differences in what is conceived as possible," writes Helen Merrill Lynd (1958) in *On Shame and the Search for Identity,* "according to whether one starts with the assumption of separate individuals and then considers how they may be linked together or starts with the assumption of related persons and then considers how they may develop individuality within the group" (p. 159). If "entity" approaches begin with the assumption of separate individuals, a consocial approach starts with engagements and seeks to discover the dynamic of personal cultivation within them.

Consociates may advance or retard each other's spark of life. They can help one another sustain the uncertain promise of maturity against the certainties of eventual change, loss, and death. They can help each other complete themselves as social animals, not just in averages and typicalities but in the concreteness of "nodal" experience.

I have tried to show how that occurred across a 5-year engagement among a cluster of fictional persons in a Japanese setting. I can think of no reason why, in principle, the perspective should be any less useful when applied to other settings or to longer spans of human development.

Clifford Geertz (1973) remarks that, "We all begin with the natural equipment to live a thousand kinds of lives but end in the end having lived only one" (p. 45). Perhaps the chief office that consociates perform for us, amid all the support and guidance they give, is to help us come to terms with the meaning of the time-warped singularity of human experience.

References

Bengtson, V. L., & Kuypers, J. A. Generational differences and the developmental stake. *Aging and Human Development,* 1971, **2**, 249–260.
Caplow, T. The definition and measurement of ambiences. *Social Forces,* 1955, **34**, 28–33.
Geertz, C. *The interpretation of cultures.* New York: Basic Books, 1973.

Hanks, L. M. The Thai social order as entourage and circle. In G. W. Skinner & A. T. Kirsch (Eds.), *Change and persistance in Thai society*. Ithaca, New York: Cornell University Press, 1975.

Henry, J. The personal community and its invariant properties. *American Anthropologist,* 1958, **60**, 827–831.

Lynd, H. M. *On shame and the search for identity*. New York: Harcourt Brace, 1958.

Moore, A. *Life cycles in Atchalán: On the diverse careers of certain Guatemalans*. New York: Teachers College Press, 1973.

Noguchi, T. Time in the world of *Sasameyuki. Journal of Japanese studies,* 1977, **3**, 1–36.

Perlman, H. H. *Persona: Social role and personality*. Chicago: University of Chicago Press, 1968.

Plath, D. W. *Long engagements: Maturity in modern Japan*. Stanford, Calif.: Stanford University Press, 1980.

Roth, J. A. *Timetables: Structuring the passage of time in hospital treatment and other careers*. Indianapolis: Bobbs-Merrill, 1963.

Schutz, A. *On phenomenology and social relations*. Chicago: University of Chicago Press, 1970.

Stegner, W. *The spectator bird*. New York: Doubleday, 1976.

Tanizaki, J. *The Makioka sisters*. New York: Random House, 1957.

Patterns and Implications of Life-Course Organization: Studies from Project TALENT

Ronald P. Abeles[1]
Lauri Steel
Lauress L. Wise

AMERICAN INSTITUTES FOR RESEARCH

PALO ALTO, CALIFORNIA

Abstract

Longitudinal data from Project TALENT were used in investigations of how people's adult lives are patterned and how these patterns are related to occupational achievement (job prestige and earnings). In conceptualizing life patterns, an expanded version of the concept of "career" from occupational sociology was employed, where *career* was defined as a sequence of roles and associated activities that a person enacts within a particular life domain. The pattern of a person's life emerges through the simultaneous consideration of his or her educational, occupational, marital, and procreational careers.

Data presented on people's career patterns during late adolescence and early adulthood revealed differences not only in the particular roles people occupy but also in the temporal patterning of those roles. Three dimensions of temporality were distinguished (comparative timing, ordering, and continuity), and their predicted relations to occupational achievement were derived from a consideration of the perspectives of human capital and social age norms. Empirical examination of these relationships showed that temporal aspects of careers were, in general, only weakly related to occupational prestige and earnings, when various background

[1]Present address: Social and Behavioral Research, National Institute on Aging, Bethesda, Maryland 20205.

LIFE-SPAN DEVELOPMENT
AND BEHAVIOR, VOL. 3

307

and ability measures were controlled. However, a number of significant sex interactions with temporality were found. For the most part, the results were more consistent with human capital predictions than with predictions from the normative perspective.

I. Introduction

A decade of accumulated research findings has established that the processes of development continue throughout the life span and can be influenced by a host of subtly interacting environmental and social conditions (Binstock & Shanas, 1976; Birren & Schaie, 1977; Finch & Hayflick, 1977). However, researchers have only begun to specify the nature of these conditions; the interactions among biological, psychological, and social processes of aging, and the ways in which people's earlier lives may affect their later years. During the past decade, there has been increasing convergence between certain theoretical work in life-span developmental psychology (Baltes & Schaie, 1973; Datan & Ginsberg, 1975; Datan & Reese, 1977; Goulet & Baltes, 1970; Nesselroade & Reese, 1973) and the sociological analysis of age (Cain, 1964; Clausen, 1972; Elder, 1975; Neugarten & Hagestad, 1976; Riley, Johnson, & Foner, 1972). Out of this convergence, a broad perspective is emerging for the study of human development throughout the entire life course (Abeles & Riley, 1976–1977). As a perspective—as opposed to a theory—it provides a general orientation for posing research questions, analyzing data, and interpreting findings. It does not present a rigorous set of postulates as explanations for relationships between variables, but it does represent a step toward such explanations.

In this chapter, we employ the emerging life-course perspective and data from Project TALENT in a consideration of how people's adult lives are patterned, and how these patterns are related to their occupational achievement. In using the terms "patterned" and "pattern" we mean to draw attention to the varying paths of people's lives and to the timing and the sequencing of the various roles and role transitions that comprise people's lives. Such a focus on patterns of roles and role transitions reflects the basic assumptions of the life-course perspective (Elder, 1977). It emphasizes that change in one's life is continuous and possible throughout the life span and it recognizes that change is multidirectional and multidetermined. Moreover, it emphasizes the possibility of preventive and corrective intervention efforts aimed at optimizing aging processes or at correcting dysfunctional aspects of aging. That is, to the extent that life-course patterns are subject to modifications, it may be possible to design and implement prospective social intervention programs that may prevent some of the dysfunctional consequences of aging (Baltes, 1977; Danish, 1977; Harshbarger, 1973).

A. AN OVERVIEW

The chapter begins with an introduction of Project TALENT, the data base used in the research to be described. Following this, the major life paths pursued by TALENT respondents during the first 11 years following high school are reviewed. This section illustrates, through a few examples, how early decisions can have long-range consequences in people's lives. That is, many decisions to engage in particular activities, which are often unintended or unrecognized as decisions, close off or open up the possibility of pursuing other activities later in one's life (cf. Spilerman, 1977). Once a life path is embarked upon, it is often difficult to change one's direction, with the consequence that certain opportunities (e.g., obtaining a college education) become more or less likely.

The remainder of the chapter examines the implications of different life paths for later occupational attainment. Emphasis is given to the chronological patterning of roles and role transitions in early adulthood. The major premise of this section is that it is not only important to attend to the particular roles that people occupy, but also to the patterning of those roles (Elder, 1975; Hogan, 1978, 1979; Modell, Furstenberg, & Hershberg, 1976; Neugarten & Datan, 1973). Various temporal aspects of role transitions are considered as possible contributors to subsequent occupational achievements.

B. PROJECT TALENT

Ongoing research studies based on Project TALENT data have provided an opportunity to examine empirically the patterning of individuals' lives during the early adult years. The Project TALENT data base contains extensive information collected over a 15-year period from a sample initially of 400,000 men and women who are now in their mid-thirties. The overall design for TALENT called for the comprehensive assessment of individuals' cognitive skills and other characteristics while in high school (Grades 9–12) with periodic follow-ups on a variety of topics to be conducted following graduation from high school.

1. The TALENT Samples[1]

The initial Project TALENT samples were chosen to be representative of the national population of American high school students and also to be

---

[1] A description of the original design and the development of the 1960 test battery may be found in Flanagan, Dailey, Shaycoft, Gorham, Orr, and Goldberg (1962). Wise, McLaughlin, and Steel (1977) provide the most complete description of the TALENT samples, the available data, and procedures for accessing the TALENT data base.

large enough to enable the study of TALENT participants pursuing various occupations (e.g., physicians, engineers, teachers) and following various educational and familial paths. To achieve these goals, a stratified random sample of all secondary schools in the United States was drawn, consisting of 1225 schools—987 senior high schools and 238 associated junior high schools; and all students in grades 9–12 in these schools were tested by Project TALENT in 1960.

2. The TALENT Data

All TALENT participants answered a battery of tests and inventories, which were designed to provide baseline data on the aptitudes and abilities of these individuals, as well as to assess their backgrounds, interests, aspirations, and various other personal characteristics. At the same time, information was also collected on the characteristics of each of the schools in the TALENT sample.

Since 1960, mail follow-up surveys have been conducted 1, 5, and 11 years following each class's graduation from high school. These surveys have focused on postsecondary educational experiences, early career choices and experiences, marital and childbearing status, plans for the future, and the participants' evaluations of and satisfactions with their educational and occupational careers to date and with other aspects of their lives.

The response rates to these mail follow-ups varied from over 60% for 1960 twelfth graders followed up one year after high school (1961) to about 20% for 1960 ninth graders followed up 11 years after high school (1974). To overcome the problem of potential nonresponse bias, special surveys of representative samples of nonrespondents to each follow-up were conducted (generally about 2500 individuals for each grade cohort). Members of the special samples selected for intensive follow-up were contacted by telephone or in person to secure their answers to the questionnaire items. By developing special case weighting procedures for the regular and special sample survey respondents, data from the TALENT original and follow-up samples can be used to derive essentially unbiased estimates of nationally representative population parameters (McLaughlin, Fulscher, & Yen, 1974; Wise, 1977). For example, those who responded to the initial 11-year follow-up mail survey had 1960 academic aptitude scores that averaged .30 of a standard deviation higher than the mean of the entire 1960 sample. Applying the case weight corrections based on the special survey of nonrespondents resulted in the mean academic aptitude score being only .06 of a standard deviation greater than the original 1960 mean, which is less than the potential error due to sampling alone (Abeles & Wise, 1980).

Tests such as this demonstrate a sufficient correction for attrition biases to permit analyses such as those presented in this chapter.

II. Careers and Patterns of Life

In thinking about life patterns, it may be useful to borrow and expand upon the concept of career from occupational sociology. For our purposes, a *career* can be defined as the sequence of roles and associated activities that a person enacts within a particular domain of life. Our use of the term is purely descriptive, and its application is *not* limited to any particular frequently occurring or normatively prescribed sequence of roles (cf. Brim, 1975; Slocum, 1966; Spilerman, 1977). Moreover, we are applying career to other life domains beside the occupational. Thus, we can refer to a person's sequence of moving in and out of educational roles as his or her educational career and, in a similar manner, we can speak of a person's procreational and marital careers. The pattern of a person's life emerges through the simultaneous consideration of educational, occupational, marital, and procreational careers (cf. Elder, 1975, 1977; Hill, 1970; Neugarten & Hagestad, 1976).

Individuals' careers become increasingly differentiated as they move from childhood through adolescence to adulthood, developing particular interests and abilities and making more and more choices regarding schooling, work, and family-related activities. The various career paths followed by the men and women in the Project TALENT ninth grade cohort (the high school class of 1963) between ages 15 and 30 are depicted in Figs. 1 and 2. These paths reflect the individuals' status in high school (in terms of curriculum type as well as whether or not they completed high school with their class) and their primary activities at each of four subsequent points. A major early branching point for these individuals appears to have occurred following high school graduation, with many individuals electing to continue their schooling (50% of the males and 40% of the females) and many others (45% of all males and females) directly entering the labor force. The general course of study pursued in high school sharply differentiated the students pursuing each of these major paths. The career paths of those who went on to college showed further major divisions in the 5 years following high school, as some students dropped out of college (27% of all males and 21% of all females), whereas others graduated and did not seek further education (roughly 15% of all members of the population) or went on to graduate school (roughly 6% of the population).

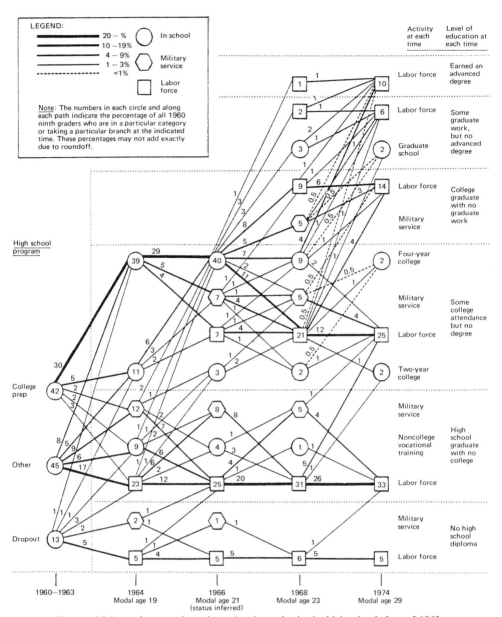

Fig. 1. Major early career branches taken by males in the high school class of 1963.

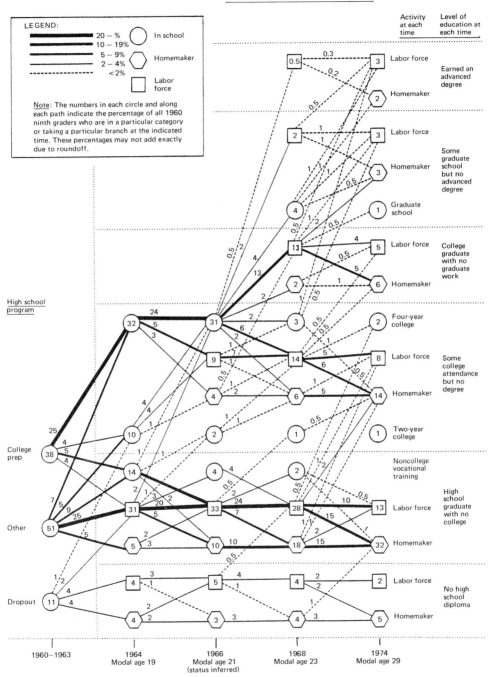

Education and work status at each follow-up

Fig. 2. Major early career branches taken by females in the high school class of 1963.

Figures 1 and 2 also indicate a wide variety of less frequent patterns of education, work, and other major roles in early adulthood. Many of the lower frequency paths indicate possible transpositions of the modal ordering of these early roles. For example, for both sexes, 20 to 23% had earned college degrees within 5 years of high school graduation, indicating a more-or-less continuous educational career. However, an additional 13% of the males received a college degree at some point more than 5 years following high school (see Fig.1), indicating some combinations of their educational careers with other activities. This option was less available to, or at least less frequently exercised by, women. Only 2.5% of the women in this population completed college more than 5 years after high school graduation. The greater frequency with which males successfully intermixed education and other activities may have resulted from a greater degree of support for their education associated with their other activities (e.g., military benefits or employers' tuition aid programs) compared to the common alternative activities pursued by the women—childbearing and homemaking. At any rate, this difference warrants further study as we strive to maximize the flexibility to pursue alternative career paths. The results would undoubtedly have implications for assessing the benefits of national youth service programs such as those currently under congressional consideration.

As career paths diverge during the transition to adulthood, it becomes increasingly likely that individuals will make choices that effectively lock them into or out of particular career lines for the remainder of their lives. Moreover, such choices may frequently be made with no realization of their consequences. Two recent Project TALENT studies illustrate potentially far-reaching career-path limitations resulting from choices made as early as the high school years.

The first study (Card, 1979; Card & Wise, 1978) examined the consequences of adolescent childbearing for individuals' subsequent achievement. Both women and men who became parents as adolescents were much less likely than their peers to have obtained a bachelor's degree by age 29, even after prior differences in individuals' backgrounds, abilities, and aspirations were controlled. Fewer than 2% of the teenage mothers went on to complete college by age 29 compared to more than 22% of a matched sample of women who had identical aptitudes, aspirations, and socio-economic backgrounds in ninth grade but delayed childbearing until after age 24. Not surprisingly, the impact of early childbearing appears to be most pronounced for women. Nearly 10% of the men who became parents as teenagers were eventually able to get a college degree compared to the 2% rate for women. The effect of teenage parenthood was quite significant for males as well. This 10% college completion rate for teenage fathers was dramatically less than the 27% rate for the matched sample of males who waited until at least age 24 to begin child rearing. Apparently, because of their relatively low educational attainment, adolescent parents were also much more likely than their classmates to have low-prestige occupations. For the adolescent mothers, reduced occupational attainment also meant lower income and greater job dissatisfaction than was experienced by their classmates (cf. Furstenberg, 1976).

A second study, investigating the origins of sex differences in the pursuit of mathematics-related careers (Steel & Wise, 1979; Wise, 1979), examined the linkages between high school course selection, achievement, and career outcomes. Math achievement was found to be a potent determinant of the realization of math-related career plans for both women and men. Overall, those with math-related career plans in the twelfth grade had mathematics achievement scores *averaging* at the 75th percentile. Among these students, the average mathematics achievement score of those who persisted in their career plans and who actually entered a math-related career by age 29 was at the 90th percentile. Whereas men and women in this sample did not differ appreciably in math achievement at the beginning of high school, pronounced sex differences in math achievement had developed by twelfth grade. Virtually all of the observed sex difference in twelfth-grade math achievement, however, could be explained by sex differences in the number of math courses taken in high school. The seemingly routine decisions regarding whether or not to take a third or fourth year of math in high school led to such large differences in twelfth-grade math achievement for students of equal initial abilities that students who decided against high school mathematics beyond the second year were effectively closing out any option that they might have had to pursue a wide range of math-related careers.

These examples illustrate how the trajectories of one's various careers can be interconnected, with early decisions and actions having major implications for subsequent career options and accomplishments. As examples, they are suggestive of the kinds of consequences that major decisions—such as whether and when to get married, whether or not to divorce, whether to take some time off from one's work—may have in terms of opening up or foreclosing various opportunity structures to individuals. Often without knowing it, individuals make or fall into decisions that can shape the future course of their lives, and it can be extremely difficult to change one's direction at a later time in one's life.

In the next section, we focus in greater depth on the temporal patterning of careers during early adulthood and examine the extent to which variations in patterns have implications for subsequent occupational achievement.

III. Temporal Aspects of Careers

Historically, there has been great variation in life patterns from one cohort to the next (Modell, Furstenberg, & Hershberg, 1976; Uhlenberg, 1969; Winsborough, 1979). For example, in the United States, the ages at which people leave their parental homes and/or complete schooling have been steadily increasing, whereas the ages of marriage and childbearing have been decreasing over at least the past 100 years[2] (Neugarten & Hagestad, 1976; Riley & Foner, 1968). There also appears to be a tendency in recent cohorts to intersperse education, work, childbearing, and leisure over the life course, as is evidenced in particular by the growing number of adult women electing to return to school and/or work following a period devoted to homemaking and childbearing (Hayghe, 1978; Young, 1977). Similarly, there is great variation within an age cohort in the patterning of lives, as is suggested by social class differences in the ages of completion of education, of first marriage, and of childbearing (Neugarten & Hagestad, 1976).

Such variations in the sequencing and timing of roles raise the question as to the consequences that such temporal aspects of careers might have for individuals. In this section, we pursue this general question first by defining a few temporal dimensions of careers, then by considering some leads available from economic and sociological theories as to the possible relationships between temporal variations and life outcomes (e.g., annual income and job prestige), and finally by briefly summarizing some data from Project TALENT.

A. TEMPORAL PATTERNS

In conceptualizing the temporal patterning of careers, we have drawn heavily upon the work of others (e.g., Elder, 1975, 1977; Hogan, 1978; Modell, Furstenberg & Hershberg, 1976; Neugarten & Datan, 1973) and have arrived at three different temporal dimensions of the sequencing of roles. The first is *order*, which simply refers to which roles precede or follow which other roles. Order is relevant to sequences both within as well as across life domains. For instance, within the occupational life domain, order would refer to whether one was a policeman before or after being a lawyer. Across life domains, order would mean whether one assumed the role of spouse before or after that of parent.

The second dimension is *discontinuity*, which denotes whether or not there have been breaks in the period(s) of performance of a role. For instance, 10 years of experience as a spouse may be achieved either through

---

[2] However, since 1960, the age of marriage has been increasing (Sweet, 1977).

10 consecutive years or over 20 years, where 10 years of marriage are interspersed among 10 years of being divorced or widowed.

The *comparative timing* of role transitions is the final temporal dimension, which refers to whether a person experiences a role transition at the "usual age" for the peer group. Put another way, comparative timing is whether a person is "early," "on time," or "late" in comparison to the age that similar others undergo that role transition (Neugarten & Datan, 1973).

B. PERSPECTIVES FROM ECONOMICS AND SOCIOLOGY

Although there is a general belief among life-span researchers that the temporal aspects of lives are important, there is a paucity of theoretical rationales indicating what the occupational consequences of different temporal sequences might be and how temporality is supposed to have any impact. Although rarely stated in explicit terms, there appear to be at least two general theoretical orientations that have been called upon to direct the few existing studies of temporality: human capital and normative perspectives.[3]

1. Human Capital Perspective

Some economists and sociologists have drawn on the human capital perspective in the examination of temporal patterns of careers (Becker, 1962, 1964; Mincer, 1958; Schultz, 1971). The major assumptions of this perspective may be summarized as follows:

1. Individuals' achievements are determined by their personal resources or "human capital," which include their abilities, skills, and knowledge.
2. Individuals may increase their stock of human capital by investing their time and energy in activities that improve their skills, abilities, or knowledge.
3. The greater a person's capital, the greater the return (e.g., higher salary).

Within this perspective, particular life-course patterns may facilitate or inhibit the growth of one's capital, and thereby influence one's occupational attainments. Given the interest of economists, this theoretical orientation

---

[3] A third perspective, stress, has been used to guide a significant body of research on the life course under the rubric of "life events" (e.g., Dohrenwend & Dohrenwend, 1974; Glass, 1977; Holmes & Rahe, 1967; Hultsch & Plemons, 1979; Pearlin & Lieberman, 1979). However, its relevance seems to be more for health-related consequences than for occupational consequences of life patterns. Hence, we are not considering it in the present discussion.

has usually been limited to the monetary consequences of temporal patterns in occupational careers. Temporal aspects of transitions in other life domains (e.g., educational) are considered only to the degree that they influence the accumulation of human capital.

Discontinuity is a temporal aspect of career patterns that is commonly investigated under the rubric of human capital. It is assumed that the longer a person enacts a role, the greater the opportunities for gaining and perfecting skills, knowledge, and social assets (e.g., seniority), and, hence, the greater one's financial returns. Discontinuities in enacting a role (educational or occupational) are assumed to have negative consequences by interfering with the accumulation of human capital or by resulting in the obsolescence of one's human capital (e.g., a person's skills or knowledge may fall behind the state-of-the-art through lack of practice and of exposure to new knowledge and skills). Discontinuity has been employed frequently as an explanation of differences in men's and women's salaries, where the cause of women's lower salaries is sought in their shorter duration of work experience and in the discontinuities in their occupational careers (Brown, 1976; Hudis, 1976; Huttner, 1977; Jusenius, 1976; Kahne, 1978; Mincer & Polacheck, 1974; Polachek, 1975; Stevens & Herriot, 1975).

Although there would seem to be theoretical reasons for also studying the *order* and *comparative timing* of role transitions from a human capital viewpoint, they have not received the same degree of attention. It is conceivable that the assumption of some roles before other roles might interfere with the acquisition of the requisite cognitive, physical, and social skills and capabilities for high-paying occupations. For example, assuming the role of parent before completing school might mean that a person was less able to devote time and energy to schooling and thereby not be able to obtain as much benefit from his or her education. Similarly, it is possible that early entry into a role (in comparison to other similar people) might put one at a competitive advantage by providing an earlier or longer opportunity to obtain skills, knowledge, or abilities associated with the role (e.g., early entrance into an occupation). However, in other instances, being late may be advantageous, if the tardiness resulted from time spent increasing human capital in preparation for the role. A few studies do suggest the utility of considering order and comparative timing. Featherman and Carter (1976) found that delays in entering postsecondary programs cost individuals approximately 1 year in educational achievement and over $1000 in annual earnings. In a study of Detroit women, Freedman and Coombs (1966) reported that early marriage and parenthood, a short interval between marriage and parenthood, and close spacing of the births of children were all detrimental to the accumulation of goods and assets. Similarly, Card and Wise (1978) in their study of Project TALENT participants found that adolescent parenthood resulted in low levels of educational and occupational attainment.

2. Normative Perspective

The basic premises of a normative perspective are that there are social norms governing the order, continuity, and timing of role transitions and that deviations from the prescribed patterns result in the application of social sanctions (Elder, 1977; Neugarten & Datan, 1973). People are presumed to be aware of these norms and to be attempting to pattern their lives accordingly. If role transitions take place at the "wrong" time (either too early or too late) or out of sequence (e.g., childbirth before marriage), then various social sanctions may be brought to bear against the transgressor. As a result of these social sanctions, deviants may face barriers that hinder their educational and occupational advancements. For example, until recently, adolescent mothers have been treated as social deviants and segregated from their contemporaries, which interfered with their ability to complete their schooling.

There is some evidence that people are aware of the appropriate ages for such role transitions as marriage, completing school, and getting a job (Neugarten, More, & Lowe, 1965), and there are probably norms concerning the order in which transitions are supposed to occur (e.g., career lines in Slocum's [1966] sense). Most likely, there are normative expectations associated with discontinuity of roles as well. "Too much" discontinuity in the enactment of a role is probably interpreted as evidence of lack of commitment to the role, or inability to perform the role, or of indecisiveness. Conversely, "too much" continuity (i.e., a long duration) in performing a role may also result in negative reactions (e.g., "He is in a rut, and it is high time he did something new").

However, the presumed links between awareness of appropriate ages for role transitions, the application of social sanctions, and the resulting negative consequences for individuals have not been sufficiently tested (Elder, 1977). Recent steps in this direction are two studies by Hogan (1978, 1979) in which he has shown that those experiencing the presumed normative pattern of school, job, and marriage had more stable marriages and earned higher incomes than those who experienced deviant orderings. Hogan's studies can only be construed as an indirect test of the normative perspective, since there were no measures of either the presumed normativeness of particular patterns of roles or the presumed processes leading to marital dissolutions and higher incomes. This points out one difficulty in applying the normative perspective: The norms surrounding life-course patterns probably differ from one social category to the next and probably change from one cohort to the next (Neugarten & Peterson, 1957; Riley, Johnson, & Foner, 1972). Thus, it cannot be safely assumed—without some confirming evidence—that particular patterns are normatively held by the population being studied. In other words, to invoke norms as explanations, one must first show that they are operative.

C. A STUDY OF TEMPORALITY AND OCCUPATIONAL ACHIEVEMENT

Although these theoretical models do not always lead to unequivocal predictions, they do suggest that the temporal aspects of life-course organization can affect individuals' occupational achievement. Using data from a sample of the Project TALENT ninth grade cohort, we operationalized these dimensions of the temporal patterning of four role transitions (i.e., completion of school, start of first job, first marriage, and birth of first child). From the human capital and normative perspectives, we anticipated the following relationships to occupational attainment.

Order. Those experiencing the role transitions in order of completion of school, start of first job, marriage, and childbirth would do better than those experiencing other orderings (especially in comparison to those for whom marriage and childbirth preceded school and job). This expectation is based on the assumption that this is the preferred or normative ordering of events (cf. Hogan, 1978) and that marriage and childbirth can interfere with the development of capital by forcing the person to invest less time and energy in education and/or occupation.

Comparative Timing. The normative perspective leads us to anticipate that those who are on time will, in general, be more successful in their occupations than those who are off time. The human capital perspective suggests that those who are early in starting their first job may have a greater opportunity to develop their capital through on-the-job experiences than those who are late or on time, all things being equal. However, being early in marriage and in the birth of one's first child may result in the investment of time and energy in "nonproductive" activities that do not increase a person's capital and thereby lead to lower occupational attainment.

Discontinuity. Although there may well be norms associated with how much continuity people should have in a given career, it is difficult to arrive at predictions based on the normative perspective. However, the human capital perspective clearly predicts that those with no discontinuities should achieve higher job prestige and greater income than those with discontinuities in their education and/or work experience.

1. Operationalization of Variables

Comparative Timing. The measures of comparative timing of role transitions were based upon the ages at which an individual experienced each role transition. The person's age (to the nearest year) at the time of the first marriage and at the birth of the first child had been asked directly in the 11-year follow-up survey. However, it was necessary to estimate the ages at completion of schooling and at the start of one's first job. The latter was calculated by subtracting the number of years of full-time work experience from the person's age, both measured at the 11-year follow-up survey. Age at completion of schooling was calculated by subtracting the birthdate from the date at which the participant's highest educational degree had been obtained. For those participants who had additional schooling beyond their highest degree, it was not possible to estimate accurately the date of completion of schooling, so all such cases (about 49%) were combined into a single category of "incomplete data" in the analyses.

Two further steps were involved in the calculation of comparative timing after establishing the respondent's age at each role transition. First, the age at which the person experienced a role transition was subtracted from the mean age at which the sex-by-SES group experienced that transition. Second, the distribution of resulting difference scores was categorized into early, on time, and late, depending on whether the person's score was, respectively, more than 1 standard deviation below the mean, between 1 standard deviation below and above the mean, or greater than 1 standard deviation above the mean difference score. For the measures of comparative timing of marriage and of birth of first child, a category was included for those who had never been married or who had not had children as of the 11-year follow-up study, similar to the category of cases for which the age at completion of schooling could not be accurately estimated.

Order. The order of the role transitions was indexed by noting for each pair of role transitions whether the age at one transition was less than, the same as, or greater than the age for the other transition. As in the case of comparative timing, categories were included as appropriate for unknown timing and for not having experienced a role transition.

Discontinuity. Two dichotomous variables were created to indicate whether a person had interrupted his or her schooling or work. These measures were derived from the respondents' reported activities at the time of each follow-up survey and their reports of the amount of schooling received and of work experience obtained.

Occupational attainment. Two measures of occupational attainment were employed. *Annual earnings* were derived from answers to the question of "How much was your pay or other earnings (before deductions) **on this**

job [i.e., current job] as of September 30, 1974?'' The mean and standard deviation for annual earnings were $11,181 and $5284, respectively, for full-time workers. *Occupational prestige* was based on an adapted version of the NORC Occupational Prestige Scale (Hodge, Siegel, & Rossi, 1964), which ranged from 15 (lunch counter attendant) to 82 (medical doctor), with a mean of 45 and a standard deviation of 13 for this sample.

2. The Sample

A sample of 2010 men and 2025 women was drawn from those members of the TALENT ninth-grade cohort who had responded to all three of the follow-up surveys. Because of the use of case weights, however, it was necessary to use the so-called "effective sample size" (effective N) in calculating tests of statistical significance. Effective N refers to the size of a sample of uniformly weighted individuals that would have the same power and stability as the actual weighted sample.[4] Because the Effective N is smaller, and usually much smaller than the raw N, it results in more conservative tests of statistical significance than those based on the raw N (Wise, McLaughlin, & Steel, 1977). The Effective N for the analyses discussed herein was 755 males and 694 females.

As noted earlier, TALENT data cover only the period from high school through early adulthood (to the approximate age of 29). Consequently, they pose a potential difficulty in analyzing life patterns: A sizable minority of respondents will not have undergone some of the role transitions in question by the time of the most recent follow-up survey. For example, 14% of the ninth-grade cohort had not married and 22% had not had children by 11 years after high school graduation. To some unknown degree, our calculations of the mean ages at various role transitions will be underestimates, as those experiencing the transitions at later ages will pull the mean upward. This has particular relevance for our measures of comparative timing in that some of those now considered on time might eventually be categorized as early.

However, because we are interested in the relationships between variables and are willing to restrict their generalizability to the period covered by the TALENT surveys, this limitation should not cause us undue concern. Furthermore, we can assess the occupational achievement of the group of people who are still at risk in terms of experiencing transitions at a later age by simply including a category in our analyses for those who, for example, were never married or had no children at the time of the 11-year follow-up. In effect, we can consider such individuals as having a different

---

[4] The effective N is equal to the square of the sum of the weights divided by the sum of the squared weights or, alternatively, it is equal to the sum of the weights divided by the weighted mean weight.

life pattern from those, for example, who were early, on time, or late in their marriages as of age 29.

3. Results

The analyses of the relationships between life-course patterns and occupational attainment were performed in two steps. First, 24 one-way analyses of variance were carried out with the 12 temporal patterns as the single factor (four measures of comparative timing, two of discontinuity, and six of ordering) and the two measures of occupational attainment as the criterion variables (occupational prestige and annual income). Then, 17 covariate analyses of variance were undertaken *for those relationships shown to be significant in the first step.* Because of the longitudinal aspects of the data base, it was possible to control for known antecedents of occupational attainment and thereby to assess the *independent* contribution of the temporal patterns to occupational attainment. Five variables were thus included as covariates: sex, general academic aptitude, the prestige rating of the respondent's expected post-high-school occupation (all measured while the respondent was in high school in 1960), educational attainment, and number of years of work experience (both obtained at the 11-year follow-up).[5] Because previous studies have demonstrated sex differences in life-course patterns and have focused upon these as potential explanations of sex differences in occupational achievement, the significance of the interaction between sex and life-course patterns was tested. The results of these covariate ANOVAs are presented in Tables I and II as multiple classification analyses. That is, the values of the criterion variables for each category of the predictor variable(s) are represented as mean deviations from the unadjusted and adjusted (for covariates) grand means of occupational prestige and annual income.

As was just noted, nearly 75% of the bivariate relationships proved to be significant (17 out of 24) before the introduction of control variables, with

[5] The covariates were defined as follows: (*a*) *Sex* was a dichotomous variable coded 1, if male, and 2, if female; (*b*) *General academic aptitude* is a continuous variable with a mean of 454 and a standard deviation of 101; (*c*) *Prestige of expected post high school occupation* is a continuous variable in which the NORC occupational prestige score was assigned to the person's expected occupation; (*d*) *Educational attainment* refers to a 13-category variable, ranging from "high school dropout" to "doctoral degree"; and (*e*) Number of years of full-time work experience was measured by a self-report item ranging from 0 to 11 years. All five of these variables were used as covariates, except when the temporal pattern variables involved "age of school completion" and/or "age at first job." In the former case, educational attainment was omitted, since age at school completion is highly dependent (almost by definition) on the respondent's level of educational attainment. In the latter instance, number of years of full-time work experience was excluded because of its inclusion in the calculation of age at first job.

the majority of these being for job prestige. For example, those who were early in all four role transitions consistently held jobs with lower prestige ratings than those who were on time or late, and those who experienced interruptions in their work careers suffered in both their job prestige and in their annual income. (See Table I, "unadjusted" column.) The relationships involving the ordering of transitions are difficult to summarize, and it is probably not fruitful to attempt such a summary until the effects of the control variables have been removed. At this time, the important point is merely that some orderings are related to higher levels of earnings and prestige. Before turning to the "adjusted" results, we should realize that these relationships are not very strong when compared to the standard deviations for job prestige and annual income (13 and $5284, respectively). In terms of the percentage of variance accounted for (η^2), they range from 1.4% to 11.6% with an average of about 4%.

After the introduction of control variables, 8 of these 17 relationships became nonsignificant, although two of these analyses showed significant interaction effects between life-course patterns and sex (as did four of those with significant main effects). As the column labeled "adjusted" indicates, the form of the relationship between life-course pattern and occupational attainment was not changed, but the strength of relationships was reduced (compare size of unadjusted to adjusted deviation scores). After removing the effects of the covariates, the temporal patterns contributed from 1.6% to 6.25% (with an average contribution of 2.1%) to the variance in annual earnings and/or occupational prestige.

Order. Turning our attention solely to the adjusted column of Table I, we note that the results are not entirely consistent with our expectations in regard to the order of role transitions. Starting one's job before or at the same time as marriage was associated with higher earnings, but starting one's job before or at the same time as completing school was also related to higher job prestige and earnings. In addition, those getting married or having children before completing school were more likely than others to have higher occupational prestige. The latter two results are contrary to predictions. Perhaps the last two findings reflect the higher educational attainment of those who complete school after marriage or the birth of their first child. That is, obtaining more education required individuals to stay in school longer, but did not necessarily result in postponements of marriage or having children, which occurred while they were still obtaining an education. From the human capital perspective, this could be interpreted as meaning that the process of developing capital through further education was not impeded by the additional responsibilities associated with marriage or childbirth.

Comparative Timing. Contrary to expectations based on the normative perspective, being on time was *not* associated with higher occupational at-

TABLE I

Multiple Classification Analyses of Relationships between Life-Course Patterns and Occupational Attainment[a]

Life-course patterns	N	Job prestige[b]		N	Annual income[c]	
		Unadjusted	Adjusted		Unadjusted	Adjusted
Comparative timing						
Marriage						
Early	112	−4.56	0.40		ns[d]	
On time	570	0.48	−0.03			
Late	145	0.97	0.70			
Never married	155	0.61	−0.84			
F-tests		5.129**	0.571 #			
Child						
Early	124	−4.15	0.44		ns	
On time	402	−1.45	−1.09			
Late	101	1.82	0.93			
No children	248	3.68	1.17			
F-tests		13.463***	2.776* #			
First Job						
Early	168	−2.77	−0.32	138	−1384	34
On time	695	−0.16	−0.08	569	228	33
Late	129	4.45	0.84	92	290	−253
F-tests		11.288***	0.471 #		5.838**	0.076
Completion of School						
Early	86	−7.75	−5.02		ns	
On time	391	2.98	1.18			
Late	91	9.45	7.17			
Incomplete[e]	447	−3.05	−1.53			
F-tests		45.457***	18.196***			

(Continues)

TABLE I (cont.)

Life-course patterns	N	Job prestige[b]		N	Annual income[c]	
		Unadjusted	Adjusted		Unadjusted	Adjusted
			Order of Role Transitions[f]			
Job and marriage						
Job < marriage	514	−0.93	−0.13	436	613	426
Job = marriage	84	3.36	2.23	69	1123	789
Job > marriage	225	0.34	−0.03	150	−1044	−387
Never married	157	0.75	−0.71	120	−1578	−1527
F-tests		2.895*	1.480		9.066***	6.177***#
Job and school						
Job < school	233	8.23	4.92	192	1544	682
Job = school	155	1.10	1.74	133	159	284
Job > school	124	−6.91	−5.58	86	−2390	−1372
Incomplete	499	−2.47	−1.45	387	−290	−131
F-tests		55.689***	24.265***		12.386***	3.406*
Job and child						
Job < child	458	−0.68	−0.25	377	640	162
Job = child	45	0.21	1.26	39	596	564
Job > child	124	−4.76	−1.68	74	−3202	−1003
No children	246	3.61	1.08	202	−134	−43
F-tests		12.543***	2.099		11.373***	1.222
Marriage and child						
Marriage < child	445	−0.09	0.17		ns	
Marriage = child	137	−5.55	−2.24			
Marriage > child	35	−2.35	0.30			
No children or never married	334	2.65	0.67			
F-tests		13.404***	2.384			
Marriage and school						
Marriage < school	162	6.95	3.14	130	1426	752
Marriage = school	66	3.59	1.28	47	688	547
Marriage > school	193	−2.30	−1.04	166	−220	6
Never married	87	3.46	1.71	63	−1275	−1301

Incomplete	500	−2.44	−1.08	387	−260	−110
F-tests		21.456***	4.287**#		3.887**	2.099
School and child					ns	
School < child	201	−0.26	−0.37			
School = child	35	−4.44	−4.86			
School > child	61	5.20	2.11			
No children	156	6.08	3.32			
Incomplete	500	−2.11	−0.80			
F-tests		16.409***	5.849***#			
Interruptions						
Work						
Interrupted	323	−3.39	−2.83	220	−1913	−863
Not interrupted	610	1.79	1.50	522	805	363
F-tests		33.442***	26.689***		45.272***	8.590**

a Entries are unadjusted and adjusted deviation scores from the grand mean, where the latter refers to adjustments in scores for the relations among covariates, predictors, and criterion variables. That is, they result from a covariate analysis of variance. The covariates (control variables) used were sex, general academic aptitude, prestige of expected post-high-school job, parental socioeconomic status (all three measured in 1960), educational attainment, and number of years of work experience (both measured at age 29). Whenever a life-course pattern was based upon the age of completion of schooling (e.g., on-off-time school), educational attainment was *not* employed as a covariate. Similarly, whenever a life-course pattern was based on the age of first job (e.g., order of marriage and job), then the number of years of work experience was omitted as a covariate. These covariates were excluded from these analyses because of their use in the definition of the life-course patterns.

b Job prestige is measured on a scale ranging from 15 to 82, with a mean of 45 for this cohort.

c Annual income is restricted to full-time workers only.

d Indicates that the bivariate relationship between life-course pattern and occupational attainment is nonsignificant and, therefore, that no multiple classification analysis was performed.

e Category for those individuals who could not be classified because of missing information as to their age of completion of their education.

f The symbols have the following meanings:

    < the event to the left occurred *before* the event to the right.

    = the two events occurred at the same age.

    > the event to the left occurred *after* the event to the right.

    # indicates a significant life-course pattern by sex interaction.

* $p < .05$.

** $p < .01$.

*** $p < .001$.

TABLE II

Multiple Classification Analyses: Interactions between Life-Course Patterns and Sex for Occupational Prestige or Annual Income[a]

Life-course pattern (LCP)	Males			Females			F-test (LCP × Sex)
	N	Unadjusted	Adjusted	N	Unadjusted	Adjusted	
Comparative Timing							
First marriage							2.784*
Early	65	-3.57	2.27	46	-5.79	-1.47	
On time	386	0.64	0.27	184	0.01	-0.37	
Late	88	0.07	-0.60	59	2.47	2.10	
Never married	90	-0.23	-2.21	65	1.95	0.26	
First child							3.520*
Early	82	-2.93	1.55	42	-6.60	-0.72	
On time	267	-0.99	-0.34	135	-2.47	-2.27	
Late	74	0.43	-0.68	28	5.02	4.24	
No children	137	3.45	0.10	111	4.24	1.97	
First job							6.651***
Early	52	-4.32	-1.58	116	-1.47	0.16	
On time	495	-1.15	-0.41	200	2.00	0.63	
Late	94	8.42	3.04	35	-6.51	-4.10	

Order of Role Transitions[b]

Job and marriage							3.949**
Job < marriage	346	$ 149	$ 346	89	$507	$574	
Job = marriage	52	$1424	$1319	17	− $688	− $997	
Job > marriage	70	$ 498	− $ 92	80	− $671	− $447	
Never married	72	− $2252	$2251	48	$416	$ 29	
Marriage and school							3.253*
Marriage < school	113	8.65	4.30	48	2.79	0.03	
Marriage = school	39	4.64	1.59	27	2.22	1.79	
Marriage > school	52	−2.54	−0.76	70	− 1.86	− 1.79	
Never married	52	3.70	0.84	34	3.19	1.24	
Incomplete	318	−3.28	− 1.57	182	− 0.97	0.17	
School and child							5.354***
School < child	137	0.06	0.33	64	− 1.08	− 1.50	
School = child	23	0.48	− 1.39	12	− 14.17	− 11.05	
School > child	40	8.39	5.05	22	− 0.69	− 2.61	
No children	89	6.64	2.21	66	5.51	3.30	
Incomplete	318	−2.97	− 1.29	182	− 0.62	0.36	

[a] In all but one instance, entries are unadjusted and adjusted deviation scores from the grand mean for job prestige. For job and marriage, the dependent variable is annual income of full-time workers. Adjusted scores are corrected for the relationships among covariates, predictors, and criterion variables. That is, these scores result from a covariate analysis of variance. See notes to Table I for listing of covariates.

[b] See Table I for meaning of symbols.

* $p < .05$.
** $p < .01$.
*** $p < .001$.

tainment. Indeed, being on time for the birth of one's first child was associated with lower job prestige, whereas being late or having no children went with higher job prestige. An early completion of schooling, however, led to lower than average job prestige, and a late completion was associated with much higher than average job prestige. To the extent that later completion of schooling reflected more schooling, these results are compatible with the human capital perspective.

Discontinuity. The one relationship that was stable and consistent with a prediction, both before and after the introduction of controls, was that between job discontinuities and occupational attainment. Those with interrupted work careers tended to have both lower incomes and lower job prestige in comparison to those with uninterrupted careers.

Interaction effects. Perhaps the most interesting results from these analyses are the life-course patterns by sex interactions shown in Table II. Being early for either marriage or childbirth tended to have negative consequences for women but beneficial effects for men in terms of their job prestige. Just the reverse was the case regarding the comparative timing of the start of one's first job: Men gained in prestige, whereas women lost prestige when they started late. These results are consistent with what one might have anticipated on the basis of the human capital perspective. Early marriage or childbirth tends to remove women from labor-market work and to prevent them from continuing their education, either of which leads to a lesser development of their human capital. A late start in work for women is likely to reflect time out for marriage or child rearing, whereas, for men, it is more likely to result from higher educational attainment. Thus, for women, the time is spent unproductively (in terms of building capital), and, for men, it is passed productively.

The order of marriage and job appears to have been more important for women than for men, although the shape of the relationship is the same for both: Starting work before marriage was associated with higher job prestige. This is, of course, consistent with both theoretical perspectives. However, the ordering of marriage and school was more crucial for men than for women, with marrying before completing school related to higher job prestige. It is likely that many of the men who married before completing school attended graduate school, which would contribute to higher job prestige and earnings when they entered the labor force.

In regard to the final sex by life-course pattern interaction, the significant relationship between the order of school completion and birth of first child stems more from the consequences of having a child versus not having one than from the ordering of school and childbirth. That is, women who do not have a child are better off in regard to job prestige than those who do (regardless of the order of school and childbirth), and this seems to be less so for men. Women are more likely to take time out from their occupational careers to care for children, and childcare is unlikely to improve women's labor market skills, abilities, and knowledge.

In closing, we should note once again that all of these interaction relationships were weak in terms of the percentage of variance accounted for.

Unclassified. Earlier, we drew attention to the fact that some individuals who had not yet been married or had children would do so at a later date and that this might introduce a bias into our analyses. In examining the "never married" or "no children" categories in Tables I and II, it appears that, in some instances, a shift from those categories would strengthen relationships, whereas in other cases they would probably weaken them. Only time will tell how many marry and/or have children and with what consequences. However, so long as we do not attempt to generalize the results beyond early adulthood, we may consider not marrying and/or not having children as an additional life pattern and consider the present results as informative of the relationship between temporal patterns and occupational attainment during early adulthood.

Of more importance is our inability to categorize many individuals in terms of the timing of their school completion. The pattern of results of these cases seems to be similar to those of individuals with lower educational attainment (i.e., more like high school graduates than college graduates). Although it cannot be said with any certainty, this may mean that if we were able to categorize them in terms of comparative timing and order of role transitions, the shape of the observed relationships would not change.

IV. Conclusions

Considerable variation in the patterning of educational, occupational, and familial careers was observed for both men and women in the high school class of 1963. Although modal career paths could be identified for each sex, high proportions of women and of men appeared to have interspersed education, work, military service or homemaking, and perhaps other activities during the years between high school and age 29. This is, perhaps, not surprising given the social and historical context in which these individuals made the transition from youth to adulthood. Certainly the Vietnam War and military service (or the avoidance thereof) had a profound impact on the educational and occupational careers of the men in this cohort. It is likely that Vietnam and military service also influenced couples' decisions regarding marriage and childbearing.

Moreover, the TALENT cohorts participated in the trend toward greater and greater amounts of education for both men and women. Not only were men and women staying in school longer, but many were returning for additional schooling after a period of time spent working, in the military, or raising children. Changes in social values, including values regarding work, family size, and sex roles, are also likely to have influenced the career decisions of these individuals. The true significance of the career patterns observed for these women and men, then, can only be assessed in comparison to the career patterns of chronologically older and younger cohorts.

There is some evidence that early career decisions, particularly educational and familial decisions, can have far-reaching, and perhaps irreversible, consequences for the nature and trajectories of individuals' subsequent careers. In an attempt to delineate more precisely the consequences of variations in the patterning of careers, we examined the impact of particular career patterns on occupational attainment. Drawing on the so-called human capital and normative perspectives, we identified three aspects of the temporal patterning of careers to study: The comparative timing and ordering of key role transitions into and out of particular roles and the continuity of those roles. In general, these temporal aspects of the patterning of careers were found not to be major determinants of either occupational prestige or annual income.

Several possible reasons for these weak relationships come to mind. First, it may not be the patterns of careers per se but rather the events or experiences that result in these patterns that influence one's occupational attainment. For example, perhaps being comparatively late in completing school is not as important as that those who are late tend to be late because they have obtained more education. Similarly, it may be that those who marry late have spent the intervening years in school and/or gaining work experience that in turn contributes to higher occupational prestige and earnings. Clearly, more effort needs to be devoted to specifying the mechanisms by which particular patterns of careers contribute to occupational attainment.

Second, it is possible that the consequences of variations in the patterning of careers may be cumulative, and the full impact of particular career patterns may not be apparent this early in one's occupational career. Recent work reported by Hogan (1979) suggests that not only is there a significant relationship between the ordering of role transitions and occupational attainment (at least for men) but that relationships appear to grow stronger with increasing age. Third, variations in the patterning of careers may possibly have consequences for other aspects of individuals' lives than their occupational attainment. For example, the literature on life events and stress suggests that temporal patterns may be relevant to physical and mental health over the life course (Dohrenwend & Dohrenwend, 1974; Glass, 1977; Holmes & Rahe, 1967; Hultsch & Plemons, 1979; Pearlin & Lieberman, 1979).

Fourth, the number of significant sex interactions also suggests that the consequences of variations in the temporal patterning of careers may be more pronounced for women than for men. Society is structured to process cohorts through particular roles at particular times and in particular sequences. For example, educational institutions often have regulations regarding full- versus part-time attendance or maximum age at entrance. Employers, too, may place such restrictions on their employees. Unfortunately, in contemporary America, women are less likely than men to conform to these normative career patterns, and are thus likely to be at a considerable disadvantage in terms of reaping societal rewards. It is likely that other societal subgroups (e.g., members of ethnic minority groups) may also be differentially affected by the impact of career patterns on occupational attainment.

Further research into the implications of the patterning of careers, then, should focus on two objectives. First, the consequences of variations in the patterning of educational, occupational, marital, and procreational careers should be assessed with different cohorts, and the scope of the careers examined should be broadened to cover as much of the life span as possible. In this way, it will be possible to examine both inter- and intracohort differences in the patterning of careers. In addition, it will be possible to investigate the implications of such important developmental patterns as midcareer change or the interweaving of education, work, and leisure over the life span.

Second, further research on the processes by which various career patterns affect occupational achievement needs to be carried out. The results reported here lend some credence to the human capital perspective, and further specification of this theoretical model would be helpful. For example, the nature of human capital needs to be more precisely defined, in order that changes in capital as a result of various experiences can be assessed. Our results were not as supportive of the normative perspective. It may be that the effects of norms and social sanctions are more pronounced in other areas than in occupational attainment or that different norms exist for different subgroups. Further specification of the norms that do exist and whether and when sanctions are perceived by or applied to individuals deviating from these norms would help clarify the relevance of this perspective for the temporal patterning of roles.

The conditions under which particular career patterns might affect occupational achievement also require further investigation. For example, it might be fruitful to develop a classification of occupational careers in terms of their "orderliness" and then to examine the consequences of various temporal patterns within orderly versus disorderly careers (e.g., military officer versus manual laborer). Through such a classification, it may be possible to develop a better understanding of the processes underlying relationships between temporal patterns and occupational attainment.

Acknowledgments

We would like to express our appreciation to Orville G. Brim, Jr., Richard T. Campbell, Glen H. Elder, Jr., and to David L. Featherman for their advice and recommendations regarding an earlier version of this chapter. The research reported in this chapter was carried out under grants from the National Institute of Mental Health (1-R01-MH29509-01), the National Institute of Education (NIE-G-78-0001) and under a contract from the National Institute of Child Health and Human Development (HD-62831).

References

Abeles, R. P., & Riley, M. W. A life-course perspective on the later years of life: Some implications for research. *Social Science Research Council Annual Report,* New York, 1976–1977.

Abeles, R. P., & Wise, L. L. Coping with attrition in a longitudinal study: The case of Project TALENT. *Journal of Economics and Business,* Winter 1980, **32**(2), 170–181.

Baltes, P. B. Functional age and social policy in aging: Perspectives from the behavioral sciences. Paper presented at the Conference on Aging and Social Policy, Vichy, France, April, 1977.

Baltes, P. B., & Schaie, K. W. (Eds.). *Life-span developmental psychology: Personality and socialization.* New York: Academic Press, 1973.

Becker, G. S. Investment in human capital: A theoretical analysis. *The Journal of Political Economy* (Supplement), October 1962, **70**, 9–49.

Becker, G. S. *Human capital.* New York: National Bureau of Economic Research, 1964.

Best, F., & Stern, B. Education, work, and leisure: Must they come in that order? *Monthly Labor Review,* 1977, **100**(7), 3–10.

Binstock, R. H., & Shanas, E. (Eds.). *Handbook of aging and the social sciences.* New York: Van Nostrand Reinhold, 1976.

Birren, J. E., & Schaie, K. W. (Eds.). *Handbook of the psychology of aging.* New York: Van Nostrand Reinhold, 1977.

Brim, O. G., Jr. Career paths and personality consequences: A memorandum for discussion. Paper presented at the Social Science Research Council Conference on Occupational Career Analysis, Greensboro, N. C., March 26–28, 1975.

Brown, G. D. How type of unemployment affects earnings differences by sex. *Monthly Labor Review,* 1976, **99**(7), 25–30.

Cain, L. D., Jr. Life course and social structure. In R.E.L. Faris (Ed.), *Handbook of modern sociology.* Chicago: Rand McNally, 1964.

Card, J. J. *Consequences of adolescent childbearing for the young parent's future personal and professional life* (Final report). Palo Alto, Calif.: American Institutes for Research, 1979.

Card, J. J., & Wise, L. L. Teenage mothers and teenage fathers: The impact of early child-bearing on the parents' personal and professional lives. *Family Planning Perspectives,* July–August 1978, **10**(4), 199–204.

Clausen, J. A. The life course of individuals. In M. W. Riley, M. Johnson, & A. Foner (Eds.), *Aging and society:* Vol. 3, *A sociology of age stratification.* New York: Russell Sage Foundation, 1972. Pp. 457–514.

Danish, S. J. Human development and human services: A marriage proposal. In I. Iscoe, B. L. Bloom, & C. D. Spielberger (Eds.), *Community psychology in transition.* New York: Hemisphere Press, 1977.

Datan, N., & Ginsberg, L. H. (Eds.). *Life-span developmental psychology: Normative life crises.* New York: Academic Press, 1975.

Datan, N., & Reese, H. W. *Life-span developmental psychology: Dialectical perspectives on experimental research.* New York: Academic Press, 1977.

Dohrenwend, B. S., & Dohrenwend, B. P. (Eds.). *Stressful life events: Their nature and effects.* New York: Wiley, 1974.

Elder, G. H., Jr. Age differentiation and the life course. In A. Inkeles, J. Coleman, & N. Smelser (Eds.), *Annual Review of Sociology* (Vol. I). Palo Alto, Calif.: Annual Reviews, 1975.

Elder, G. H., Jr. Family history and the life course. *Journal of Family History,* 1977, **2**, 279–304.

Featherman, D. L., & Carter, T. M. Discontinuities in schooling and the socioeconomic life cycle. In W. H. Sewell, R. M. Hauser, & D. L. Featherman (Eds.), *Schooling and achievement in American society.* New York: Academic Press, 1976.

Finch, C. E., & Hayflick, L. (Eds.). *Handbook of the biology of aging.* New York: Van Nostrand Reinhold, 1977.

Flanagan, J. C., Dailey, J. T., Shaycoft, M. F., Gorham, W. A., Orr, D. B., & Goldberg, I. *Design for a study of American youth.* Boston: Houghton-Mifflin, 1962.

Freedman, R., & Coombs, L. Childspacing and family economic position. *American Sociological Review,* 1966, **31**, 631–648.

Furstenberg, F. F., Jr. *Unplanned parenthood: The social consequences of teenage childbearing.* New York: Free Press, 1976.

Glass, D. C. *Behavior patterns, stress, and coronary disease.* Hillsdale, N. J.: Erlbaum, 1977.

Goulet, L. R., & Baltes, P. B. (Eds.). *Life-span developmental psychology: Research and theory.* New York: Academic Press, 1970.

Harshbarger, D. Some ecological implications for the organization of human intervention throughout the life span. In P. B. Baltes & K. W. Schaie (Eds.), *Life-span developmental psychology: Personality and socialization.* New York: Academic Press, 1973.

Hayghe, H. Special labor force reports—summaries. *Monthly Labor Review,* February 1978, 51–54.

Hill, R. *Family development in three generations.* Cambridge, Mass.: Schenkman, 1970.

Hodge, R.W., Siegel, P. M., & Rossi, P. Occupational prestige in the United States. *American Journal of Sociology,* 1964, **70**, 286–302.

Hogan, D. P. Order of events in the life course. *American Sociological Review,* 1978, **48**, 573–586.

Hogan, D. P. The transition to adulthood as a career contingency. Paper presented at the meeting of the Rural Sociological Society, Burlington, Vermont, August 23–26, 1979.

Holmes, T. H., & Rahe, R. H. The social readjustment rating scale. *Journal of Psychosomatic Research,* 1967, **11**, 213–218.

Hudis, P. M. Commitment to work and to family: Marital status differences in women's earnings. *Journal of Marriage and the Family,* 1976, **38**(2), 267–278.

Hultsch, D. F., & Plemons, J. K. Life events and life-span development. In P. B. Baltes & O. G. Brim, Jr. (Eds.), *Life-span development and behavior* (Vol. 2). New York: Academic Press, 1979.

Huttner, T. The effects of discontinuous participation in the labor force. Unpublished manuscript, 1977. (Available from Sloan School, Massachusetts Institute of Technology, Cambridge, Mass. 02138.)

Jusenius, C. Economists' approaches to sex segregation in the labor market. In H. S. Parnes & A. Kohen (Eds.), *Labor market experience of noncollege youth: A longitudinal analysis.* Columbus: Ohio State University, 1976.

Kahne, H. Economic research on women and families. *Signs: Journal of Women in Culture and Society,* 1978, 3(31), 652–661.

McLaughlin, D. H., Fulscher, G. W., & Yen, W. M. *Project TALENT's Special Sample: Is it necessary?* Palo Alto, Calif.: American Institutes for Research, 1974.

Mincer, J. Investment in human capital and personal income distribution. *The Journal of Political Economy,* August 1958, **66,** 281–302.

Mincer, J., & Polachek, S. W. Family investments in human capital: Earnings of women. *Journal of Political Economy,* 1974, **82**(2), S76–S108.

Modell, J., Furstenberg, F. F., Jr., & Hershberg, T. Social change and transitions to adulthood in historical perspective. *Journal of Family History,* 1976, **1,** 7–32.

Nesselroade, J. R., & Reese, H. W. (Eds.). *Life-span developmental psychology: Methodological issues.* New York: Academic Press, 1973.

Neugarten, B. L., & Datan, N. Sociological perspectives on the life cycle. In P. B. Baltes & K. W. Schaie (Eds.), *Life-span developmental psychology: Personality and socialization.* New York: Academic Press, 1973.

Neugarten, B. L., & Hagestad, G. O. Age and the life course. In R. H. Binstock & E. Shanas (Eds.), *Handbook of aging and the social sciences.* New York: Van Nostrand Reinhold, 1976.

Neugarten, B. L., Moore, J. W., & Lowe, J. C. Age norms, age constraints, and adult socialization. *American Journal of Sociology,* 1965, **70,** 710–717.

Neugarten, B. L., & Peterson, W. A. A study of the American age–grade system. *Proceedings of the Fourth Congress of the International Association of Gerontology* (Vol. 3). 1957, pp. 497–502.

Pearlin, L. I., & Lieberman, M. A. Social sources of emotional distress. *Research in Community and Mental Health,* 1979, **1,** 217–248.

Polachek, S. W. Discontinuous labor force participation and its effect on women's market earnings. In C. Lloyd (Ed.), *Sex, discrimination, and the division of labor.* New York: Columbia University Press, 1975.

Riley, M. W., & Foner, A. *Aging and society* (Vol. I). New York: Russell Sage Foundation, 1968.

Riley, M. W., Johnson, M., & Foner, A. *Aging and society* (Vol. III). New York: Russell Sage Foundation, 1972.

Schultz, T. W. *Investment in human capital: The role of education and of research.* New York: Free Press, 1971.

Slocum, W. L. *Occupational careers.* Chicago: Aldine, 1966.

Spilerman, S. Careers, labor market structure, and socioeconomic achievement. *American Journal of Sociology,* 1977, **83,** 551–593.

Steel, L., & Wise, L. L. Origins of sex differences in high school mathematics achievement and participation. Paper presented at the Annual Meeting of the American Educational Research Association. San Francisco, Calif., April 1979.

Stevens, J. A., & Herriot, R. A. Current earnings differentials for men and women: Some exploratory regression analyses. Paper presented at Conference on Reconciliation of Survey and Administrative Income Distribution Statistics through Data Linkage, sponsored by Bureau of the Census, 1975.

Sweet, J. A. Demography and the family. In A. Inkeles, J. Coleman, & N. Smelser (Eds.), *Annual Review of Sociology* (Vol. 3). Palo Alto, Calif.: Annual Reviews, 1977.

Uhlenberg, P. A study of cohort life cycles: Cohorts of native born Massachusetts women, 1830–1920. *Population Studies,* 1969, **23**(3), 407–420.

Winsborough, H. H. Changes in the transition to adulthood. In M. W. Riley (Ed.), *Aging from birth to death: Interdisciplinary perspectives.* Boulder, Colorado: Westview Press, 1979, pp. 137–152.

Wise, L. L. The fight against attrition in longitudinal research. Paper presented at the meeting of the American Educational Research Association, New York, April 4–8, 1977.

Wise, L. L. The role of mathematics in women's career development. Paper presented at the annual convention of the American Psychological Association, Toronto, August 29, 1978.

Wise, L. L., McLaughlin, D. H., & Steel, L. *The Project TALENT data bank handbook.* Palo Alto, Calif.: American Institutes for Research, 1977.

Wise, L. L., Steel, L. & MacDonald, C. *Origins and consequences of sex differences in high school mathematics achievement* (Final Report). Palo Alto, Calif.: American Institutes for Research, 1979.

Young, A. M. Going back to school at 35 and over. *Monthly Labor Review,* 1977, **100**(7), 43–45.

Developmental Intervention:
Enhancing Life-Event Processes

Steven J. Danish
Michael A. Smyer
Carol A. Nowak

COLLEGE OF HUMAN DEVELOPMENT
THE PENNSYLVANIA STATE UNIVERSITY

Abstract

In this chapter, current trends in critical life events and intervention are considered together. It is argued that a critical life-events framework provides a conceptual focus for developing preventive strategies and enhancing interventions. A number of characteristics and types of critical life events are delineated. In addition, a variety of interventions are distinguished based on the timing of the intervention in relation to the event. It is concluded that age-related life events that have a high likelihood of occurring are most amenable to prevention and enhancement. Because such events are predictable and expected, interventions can be implemented prior to the event. Finally, an attempt is made to contrast prevention and enhancement by considering the theory of human behavior inherent in each. By linking life events to intervention strategies, we believe that more effective and efficient interventions can be developed.

LIFE-SPAN DEVELOPMENT
AND BEHAVIOR, VOL. 3

339

I. Introduction

For those who are interested in mental health intervention in the second half of life, two recent trends are important: (*a*) the increasing acceptance of the contribution of critical life events to adult development theories; and (*b*) the growing interest in the concepts of prevention and optimization in the intervention area. These conceptual perspectives complement each other; however, until now, they have been developed independently. This chapter is an initial step toward developing a critical life-event framework for preventive and enhancement programs focusing on the second half of life.

In the first section, we review the critical life-events framework. As markers for adult development, the concept of life events is popular in the human development literature (e.g., Dohrenwend & Dohrenwend, 1974; Elder, 1975; Hultsch & Plemons, 1979; Lowenthal, Thurnher, & Chiriboga, 1975; Neugarten & Hagestad, 1976). The problems most likely to occur during the second half of life (e.g., changing family situations, declining physical abilities, changing economic resources, etc.) are more than discrete "events." Each can be considered a process that begins well before the discrete event occurs and that continues beyond the actual discrete event. For example, in the case of widowhood, Neugarten (1976) has suggested that most women go through a subliminal process of anticipatory socialization to widowhood, realizing that, on the average, they will probably outlive their husbands. Widowhood is just one example of a discrete event that is actually embedded in processes occurring throughout the life span. In the first section, both the types and major dimensions of life events will be discussed.

In the second section of the chapter, we review developments in the area of intervention. In recent years, there has been an increasing interest in preventive and optimizing intervention strategies (e.g., Albee & Joffe, 1977; Caplan, 1964; Danish & D'Augelli, 1980). Mental health practitioners have borrowed the divisions of primary, secondary, and tertiary prevention from the public health area. However, when applied to the human service sector, these distinctions take on a different meaning. Primary prevention is not limited to the elimination of disease or mental illness; it also includes mental health promotion and optimization (Goldston, 1977). This emphasis upon health promotion is consistent with a human development perspective in general (Ford, 1974) and with a critical life-events framework in particular.

Interventions are based on assumptions regarding the nature of development and dysfunction. The disease and developmental conceptions of behavior are two perspectives that have influenced intervention activities.

Each perspective suggests different goals of intervention and varied roles for providers and consumers of services. Regardless of conceptual perspective, several questions must be considered in the process of developing an intervention: (*a*) what activities constitute the intervention; (*b*) what is the expected outcome of the intervention; and (*c*) with whom and under what circumstances are such interventions appropriate? These questions provide a perspective for contrasting the disease and developmental conceptions of behavior.

In the final two sections of the chapter, we present a framework for guiding the choice of intervention. Our framework assumes that life events are an appropriate focus for intervention. The type of intervention chosen will vary depending upon the properties of the event selected as the focus of intervention. Using two event properties as examples, we illustrate the links between these characteristics and intervention design especially as it relates to retirement.

The purpose of this chapter is to suggest the value of combining knowledge of life events and intervention approaches emphasizing prevention and enhancement. Although others have considered life events as targets of intervention (Dohrenwend & Dohrenwend, 1974), for the most part, their orientation has been remedial without major reference to developmental research or theory about individual development. In contrast, enhancement approaches that focus on life events offer a rare opportunity for combining knowledge of development and intervention.

II. Conceptions of Life Events

A. OVERVIEW

Recent advances in life-span developmental theory, the sociological analysis of age, and life-history methodology have contributed to the popularity of a life-events approach to the study of human development. However, no single view of life events has emerged as universally accepted. The Dohrenwends (1974) and Holmes and Rahe (1967), for example, envision life events as catalysts to physical and emotional illness. Costa and McCrae (Chapter 3, this volume) see them as potential crises for people with somewhat nonadaptive personality styles. Others acknowledge the importance of life events for personal growth, but choose to focus on single events and individual assessments of their impact (e.g., Lopata, 1973, on widowhood; Parkes, 1964, on death of a spouse; Rossi, 1968, on parenthood). Still others view life events as antecedents to behavioral change (Baltes & Willis, 1979; Hultsch & Plemons, 1979). Across these different perspectives, however, there is consensus about the pivotal role played by life events in individual development.

Events can be viewed in two ways: as markers and as processes. When events are viewed as markers, they become milestones or transition points, giving shape and direction to the various aspects of a person's life (Neugarten & Hagestad, 1976). For example, becoming pregnant is a marker in the course of one's family development. It signifies to a couple, and to those interacting with them, that a specific course of events is beginning to unfold, namely, the birth of a child, child rearing, child launching, and so on. Similarly, retirement signifies the transition from an active work career to a life of leisure. This involves changed perceptions, expectations, and priorities for the use of one's time and energies.

It is inappropriate, however, to consider events solely as markers that occur at single points in time. Events are also processes. They have histories of their own from the time they are anticipated, through their occurrences, until their aftermaths have been determined and assessed. It is this process that the marker signifies but does not describe. Viewing events only as markers underestimates the importance of the *context* of events. Events do not occur in a vacuum; they occur in a rich life space of the individual, including competing demands from a variety of areas (e.g., work, family life, physical development) and people significant to the individual.

Events also influence each other. Consider the example of pregnancy once again. Pregnancy is not solely a marker event in the family life cycle. For many individuals, it is the result of a conscious decision-making process that includes the effects of a child on the couple's marital relationship, work roles, physical health, and economic well-being (Elder & Rockwell, 1976).

When events are viewed as markers, the importance of the individual's experience of the event is ignored. For social scientists, events are viewed in the larger perspective of life-cycle development. For the individual, however, the *event and its current impact* assume an importance of its own. For the pregnant woman, pregnancy may be more the morning sickness than the anticipation of the child's sex or future occupation.

Whether an event is considered as a marker or as a process, two properties of events must be considered: structural characteristics, and types of events.

B. STRUCTURAL CHARACTERISTICS OF LIFE EVENTS

The structural characteristics of life events are properties common to all events over time regardless of history or content (Nowak, 1979). Some of these structural properties are event timing, duration, sequencing, cohort specificity, contextual purity, and probability of occurrence.

1. Event Timing

The timing of a life event refers to its congruence with either personal or societal expectations of when it *should* occur (Neugarten, 1968). Thus, retirement at 50 years of age is "off time," whereas retirement after 62 is considered "on time." The more on time an event or life transition is, the greater the likelihood that both informal and formal support networks will exist to ease or assist the change (Elder, 1977; Neugarten, 1968). For example, getting married shortly after completing college is a fairly common, expected event. People about the same age are readily at hand to serve as informal consultants, event sharers, and commiserators. In a more organized way, mass media, advertising promotions, and special services such as family and budget consultants gear their campaigns to this age group. Those individuals marrying for the first time at age 40, however, are less likely to have access to such support networks, and might therefore have a more difficult time adapting to the impact of such a major life change.

2. Duration

The duration of a life event refers to the length of time it is experienced. When events are viewed as processes, rather than as discrete occurrences, event duration includes the anticipation of the event, the event itself, and the postevent influences (Nowak, 1979). Many life events are anticipated before their actual occurrences. The birth of a child, marriage, and retirement all offer sufficient opportunity for a "preoccurrence priming" that can serve to ease the transition into postoccurrence life. Kimmel (1974) suggests that this period of anticipatory socialization can serve two useful and adaptive functions. First it can be educative, in that the role, rights, expectations, and responsibilities of the impending event can be explored and learned ahead of time. Second, it can provide rehearsal time to try out various adaptive styles and establish alternatives in case expected coping strategies should fail. Individuals who can not only anticipate, but also prepare for their major life changes are presumed to have an easier time adapting to them (Neugarten, 1968). Individuals who are victims of a nonanticipated event—for example, floods, fires, sudden death of spouse—are caught off guard and possibly overwhelmed with the simultaneous tasks of experiencing the event and figuring out how to cope with it. As a result, their adjustment may be more difficult.

3. Event Sequencing

Event sequencing refers to whether or not life events appear in personally or societally expected order. Thus, having one's first child prior to marriage would be considered an out-of-sequence event with respect to the usual life course of family development (Neugarten, Moore, & Low, 1965).

As with event timing, there are more formal and informal support networks for those individuals experiencing events in societally sanctioned order (Neugarten, 1968).

4. Cohort Specificity

Cohort specificity refers to the fact that a given event may have different meanings and effects for different cohorts or generations (Modell, Furstenberg, & Hershberg, 1976; Nowak, 1979). Cohort specificity is closely linked to the concept of transition prevalence as described by Modell and his colleagues (1976). Transition prevalence represents the proportion of the population experiencing a given life change. The cohort element is important because of its implications for the formal and informal supports of the individual experiencing the event. For example, a woman of 40 becoming a top corporate executive in 1920 was a functionally different experience from the same occurrence in 1980, in part because of the prevalence of the event.

5. Contextual Purity

Contextual purity refers to the extent to which an event interferes with the resolution of other, concurrent life events (Nowak, 1979). To the extent that an event occurs at a relatively stable, otherwise uneventful time in a person's life, it can be considered "contextually pure." Events, however, tend to change not only the domains in which they originate, but also related life courses as well (Neugarten & Hagestad, 1976). They may also occur simultaneously with major events in other life domains (Elder, 1977). Finally, they may interfere with the resolution of events occurring in the life domains of significant others (Hultsch & Plemons, 1979).

The implications of event interactions are difficult to examine. Table I illustrates a number of life domains, critical markers within them, and primary and secondary effects related to their occurrence. Examining events out of context, without consideration for the other areas of people's lives they affect, provides a myopic view of the impact of various life experiences. Interventionists must, therefore, develop strategies that consider such critical life changes in the context of other life changes.

6. Probability of Event Occurrence

The probability of life-event occurrences refers to the likelihood that certain events will be experienced by large proportions of the population over time. Events can have either high or low probability of occurrence. High probability events are those often referred to as "normative life crises" (Datan, 1975). They are usually expected, predictable, and backed-up by community support networks. Examples of such events are marriage, birth of children, job promotion, grandparenthood, and retirement. Low probability, or nonnormative (Baltes, Cornelius, & Nesselroade, 1979) events are those that affect either a great number of people at a single point in time, or small numbers of a total population over time (Nowak, 1979). Examples of events affecting many people at once are floods, earthquakes, nuclear reactor accidents, and famine. Example of events that affect smaller numbers of people over time are considerably more complex. They would include deviations from expected life experiences (Baltes & Willis, 1979; Hultsch & Plemons, 1979), event absences (Nowak, 1979), and tail-end generational shifts (Nowak, 1979).

Deviations from expected life experiences are events that occur significantly off time or out of sequence. These events throw the expected life course off track. Examples of such deviations are single parenthood, divorce, serious illness, and early widowhood. Event absence refers to the lack of experiencing a normative life event. Remaining childless once married, not launching one's children, or not becoming grandparents are examples of such nonevents within the family domain. Event absences have rarely been considered in the life-span developmental literature (Hagestad, 1979).

Tail-end generational shifts are changes in role expectations, role options, and role enactments for the youngest or oldest members of a given generation (Nowak, 1979). This concept is related to transitional spread. Modell *et al.* (1976) define transitional spread as the time required for a fixed proportion of the population to complete a given life change. Whereas Modell and his colleagues are concerned with the majority of individuals undergoing a life change, our focus is on the minority who go through the life change either very early or very late. The experience for these individuals may be qualitatively different as this group may have a range of options unavailable to the majority. These shifts are usually the result of secular trends and historical changes in priorities, and represent behavioral and attitudinal options not readily available to most members of a generation. By-products of the feminist movement such as delayed marriage, smaller families, returning to school, and increased labor-force participation by women are examples of current tail-end generational shifts. For example, a 35-year-old woman may have the opportunity to return to school while her children are young. Her 55-year-old generation-mate is unlikely to have had that option.

C. TYPES OF LIFE EVENTS

In addition to their many structural properties, life events can also be classified according to type: individual or cultural.

TABLE I

Critical Markers within Event Domains

Examples of critical markers[a]	Event domain			
	Family	Career	Biological	Psychosocial
1. EMPTY NEST	1. CHANGE IN NU-CLEAR FAMILY INTERACTION PATTERNS	1. change in employment status	1. no obvious interactions	1. change in leisure opportunities
	2. REDEFINITION OF PARENTING ROLE	2. change in commitment to work		2. change in perceptions of self, body, and age concept
	3. CHANGE IN FINANCIAL RESOURCES			
2. MENOPAUSE	1. end of childbearing stage	1. no obvious interaction	1. CHANGE IN REPRO-DUCTIVE AND RE-LATED BODY SYSTEMS	1. change in perceptions of sexuality
	2. redefinition of role of wife and mother			2. change in body image

3. RETIREMENT	1. increased time spent in family context	1. END OF ROLE AS MEMBER OF THE PAID LABOR FORCE 2. CHANGE IN FINANCIAL STATUS 3. LOSS OF SKILL FUNCTIONING 4. CHANGE IN PHYSICAL SETTING	1. changes in activity level	1. changes in perceptions of self-worth and esteem 2. changes in leisure opportunities 3. change in contact with colleagues-coworkers 4. changes in self as a result of societal value placed on work 1. CHANGE IN SOCIAL NETWORK OR REFERENCE GROUP 2. CHANGE IN PHYSICAL SETTING 3. CHANGE IN SELF-DEFINITION
4. INSTITUTION-ALIZATION	1. decreased interaction with family 2. change in financial status	1. end of postcareer work activity	1. changes in physical dependence 2. change in activity level	

a Key—All caps = Main Effects; Lowercase = potential domain interactions.
a Other examples of critical markers in the second half of life are: death of spouse or relative; death of friend or confidant; beginning of the launching phase of the family; promotion or change in jobs; acute illness; onset of chronic illness; relocation and moving; births of grandchildren.

1. Individual Life Events

Individual life events are points that demarcate a person's specific developmental domains across the life cycle. Such events can be biological, such as pregnancy, severe illness, or menopause; or socialization-related, such as marriage, job promotion, or grandparenthood (Baltes & Willis, 1979; Hultsch & Plemons, 1979). Regardless of their nature, individual life events are presumed to be age-related, having their primary impact upon the developmental histories of the persons experiencing them (Hultsch & Plemons, 1979). This is particularly true at the time of their onset, as their appearances signify milestones or turning points in people's lives that require new adjustments, behaviors, decisions, or growth (Neugarten, 1976).

2. Cultural Life Events

Cultural life events are those societal and historical happenings that shape the biocultural context in which individuals develop (Baltes & Willis, 1979; Hultsch & Plemons, 1979; Nowak, 1979). They may be of major historical magnitude and significance, such as the Great Depression (Elder, 1974); major societal assaults, such as floods, tornados, and earthquakes (Hartsough, 1975, 1976, 1977); pervasive secular trends such as the feminist movement; or matters of national, regional, or local politics, such as the election of officials or endorsement of policies. In any case, such events are responsible for the reallocation of wealth and resources in a society, the establishment of social policy, the generation of community support systems, and the creation of new roles, priorities, expectations, and options for growth and development (Ryder, 1974; Nowak, 1979).

Both individual and cultural life events can be examined with respect to the various life-event structural characteristics described earlier (e.g., timing, duration, etc.). The complex patterns of event types and event characteristics may have significant implications for the target, scope, and pur-

TABLE II

Event Types and probabilities

Types	High probability	Low probability
Individual	Marriage	Not marrying
	Retirement	Not having children
	Birth of a child	Catastrophic illness
		Windfall legacy
Cultural	Congressional elections	World wars
	Technical advances	Economic depression
	Changes in resource	Acts of God (flood)
	distribution	Tail-end generational shift
	Cohort succession	

poses of intervention. However, the development of a complete taxonomy of life events and corresponding intervention strategies is beyond the scope of this chapter. One event characteristic, the probability of occurrence, will be used to illustrate the importance of structural characteristics for intervention. In Table II, examples of event types and the probability of such events are presented. Brim and Ryff (Chapter 11, this volume), have developed independently a similar framework. After reviewing a variety of intervention approaches, we will offer suggestions for intervention strategies depending upon the type and probability of the event.

III. Innovative Directions in Intervention

A. OVERVIEW

The use of a critical life-events perspective as a framework for understanding adult development has generated considerable enthusiasm among individuals interested in life-span development, in part because of its potential relevance to intervention. While a critical life-events perspective has been developing, the view of what constitutes effective intervention has also been changing. Psychotherapy is no longer considered the only intervention for intra- and interpersonal problems. In part, this is due to the equivocal results of psychotherapy research (Parloff, 1979). However, even if psychotherapy were proven effective, the need for helping services would exceed the supply of available service providers (Rappaport, 1977). Consequently, more effective systems of intervention are required to meet the present human service needs (Albee, 1959; Smyer & Gatz, 1979).

In this section, we will examine several different intervention models designed to influence individual development. Our discussion is based partly on a schema proposed by Rappaport and Chinsky (Rappaport, 1977; Rappaport & Chinsky, 1974) for evaluating intervention models. They delineate two components: a *conceptual* component, and a *style of delivery* component. The conceptual component refers to the theory of human behavior inherent in the intervention model. The style of delivery component refers to how the conceptual component is to be delivered to the target population (Rappaport, 1977).

Rappaport (1977) suggests that a number of conceptual components are possible including a disease component, a behavioral component, a sociological component, and the like. Conceptual components are limited only by the number of theories of human behavior available. A developmental conception is especially relevant to intervention but it is usually overlooked. We will contrast a developmental conception with the disease conception most often used in intervention.

The second aspect of an intervention model focused on by Rappaport and Chinsky is the style of delivery. It is generally taken for granted in intervention that the medical model ("the doctor–patient relationship") is the accepted delivery system (Guerney, 1977). Even proponents of non-disease conceptual models, such as behaviorists, support the medical-model delivery system. In this model, termed the *waiting mode,* the expert passively waits for others to request help. An alternative to this delivery mode is the *seeking mode* in which the helper seeks out individuals needing help. In this latter mode, the professional, rather than serving as a passive expert, is more likely to provide services indirectly either by training others to deliver services (Danish, D'Augelli, Brock, Conter, & Meyer, 1978) or by assuming the role of a consultant, program developer, or evaluator (Danish, 1977; Rappaport, 1977). In the seeking mode, the style of service delivery is proactive. The helping agent seeks out potential consumers often trying to provide services in a preventive manner.

Although the style of delivery is an important aspect of intervention, the timing of intervention is a more salient element when planning interventions of life-event processes. As described earlier, life events can be considered as processes that include the anticipation of the event, the actual occurrence of the event, and the aftermath of the event. Within this perspective, interventions can be undertaken before the occurrence, during the event itself, or after the event. Table III presents examples of several intervention approaches. Each intervention strategy represents a distinct combination of conceptual assumptions and timing of interventions in relation to an event. In the following sections, we will elaborate the distinctions among the various intervention approaches.

B. DISEASE AND DEVELOPMENTAL CONCEPTIONS OF INTERVENTION

The major assumption of the disease conception is that life events are stresses or crises for the individual (Holmes & Rahe, 1967). Crises are viewed as pathological, and the goal of intervention is the elimination of stress so that the individual may return to the path of normal development (Danish, 1977).

TABLE III

Intervention Approaches Classified by Timing and Conceptual Components

Conceptual components	Timing of intervention in relation to event		
	Before	During	After
Disease	Primary prevention	Secondary prevention	Remedial services
Developmental	Enhancement efforts	Support groups	Counseling

The major assumption of the developmental approach is its emphasis on continuous growth and change. This framework has been identified as one which: (*a*) incorporates statements about desirable goals of behavior; (*b*) focuses on sequential change; (*c*) emphasizes techniques of optimization (rather than remediation); (*d*) considers that the individual or system is an integrative biopsychosocial unit (Ford, 1974) and therefore is amenable to a multidisciplinary focus; and (*e*) views individuals or systems as developing in a changing biocultural context (Baltes, 1973; Danish, 1977).

Within the developmental approach, crises are not viewed as pathological; they are considered states of imbalance that precede growth and that may make growth possible (Riegel, 1975). Crises are viewed as having either positive or negative outcomes; therefore, the goal of intervention is not the prevention of critical life events but the enhancement of the individual's ability to grow or develop as a result of the event (Danish & D'Augelli, 1980).

Within each conceptual framework, interventions can be differentiated according to their timing in relation to specific life events. In the disease conception, three types of intervention predominate: remedial intervention, secondary prevention, and primary prevention. Three illustrations of developmental approaches are counseling, support groups, and enhancement efforts.

1. Remedial Interventions

Psychotherapy is the typical mental health intervention considered when the problem has already occurred. Such interventions are designed to alleviate already existing problems. Unfortunately, the delivery of psychotherapeutic services is unevenly distributed. Preliminary estimates indicate that at least 15% of the population in our country is affected by mental disorders in one year. In 1975, only 20% of these were served by the mental health sector. About 60% were seen by the general medical sector (Regier, Goldberg, & Taube, 1978). Thus, millions of individuals in need of services do not receive help from mental health professionals. The findings of Regier and his colleagues are not new. The fact that most individuals experiencing emotional problems do not receive professional mental health services has been substantiated in several studies of urban (Ryan, 1969; Srole, Langner, Michael, Opler, & Rinnie, 1962) and rural (Young, Giles, & Plantz, 1979) residents.

Of the millions of potential clients not being served, some are not receiving services because the providers have decided that they are not good candidates for psychotherapy. Schofield (1964) described the type of client most appropriate for effective therapy from the therapists' view. Such clients are young, attractive, verbal, intelligent, and successful (YAVIS). If such a selection system is operating in choosing clients, then the aged, some of the young, and the poor will remain underserved (Butler, 1975). However, the decision not to become a client is not a decision made only by the provider. Individuals who do not meet Schofield's (1964) criteria often avoid professionals. They believe that individual therapy with its emphasis on the doctor–patient relationship and "talking," as a cure, does not meet their needs. Many behavioral scientists not directly associated with intervention consider psychotherapy to be synonymous with intervention and are unaware of any alternatives.

2. Secondary Prevention

When the problem has already been identified but may be in its most formative stages, secondary prevention efforts may be implemented. Secondary prevention is the early detection and treatment of a population "at risk" (Caplan, 1964; Rappaport, 1977).

Most of the examples of secondary prevention have been carried out with young children in school settings. The Primary Mental Health Project developed by Cowen, Trost, Lorion, Dorr, Izzo, and Issacson (1975) to detect young high-risk school children and provide services to prevent maladaptive school behavior is an oustanding example of secondary prevention.

Two observations reflected the need for the project: (*a*) teachers spend a large percentage of their time dealing with relatively few youngsters; and (*b*) school mental health personnel find that referrals increase markedly during transitions from elementary schools to junior high schools and from junior high to high schools and that, during these transitions, the helping resources are inadequate. Furthermore, school records of many youngsters who are referred often indicate that early signs of school maladjustment were overlooked. Consequently, a program of early detection and intervention was developed using school personnel, parents, and nonprofessional manpower.

3. Primary Prevention

When the intervention approach is implemented prior to the occurrence of the problem, it is primary prevention. Primary prevention involves counteracting harmful circumstances before they have a chance to produce illness. The intervention is generally directed at the total population or community, not at a single individual. The main tools of primary prevention are education and social engineering, not therapy or rehabilitation (Bryant, 1978).

Although the concept of prevention is both intriguing and attractive, successful primary prevention interventions are infrequent. Again, most, if not all, of the examples have been with young children. The work of Spivack and his colleagues (e.g., Spivack & Shure, 1974) is a good example of primary prevention. They have identified a group of skills known as interpersonal cognitive problem skills that facilitate the adjustment of children and adolescents. Those who are deficient in these skills are often seen as maladjusted. Spivack and his associates have taught these skills to a variety of populations as a means of preventing psychopathology. In one such study, Spivack and Schure (1974) developed 46 lessons given over a 10-week period for Head Start children. The children both learned the skills and improved their behavioral adjustment to school. In addition, these changes were maintained a year later.

Both the primary prevention program developed by Spivack & Shure (1974) and the secondary prevention program developed by Cowen *et al.* (1975) are examples of proactive attempts to prevent psychopathology. Such programs deliver services via a mass teaching or educational model. Unfortunately, few preventive efforts of this type have been conducted (Cowen, 1977b). Cowen (1977b) and Danish and D'Augelli (1980) have suggested that the infrequency of successful prevention activities, especially primary prevention, is due to the definitional confusion of what constitutes prevention. Additionally, Broskowski and Baker (1974) and Bryant (1978) have identified personnel, administrative, and research barriers to primary prevention efforts.

4. Counseling

The Committee on Counselor Training, Division of Counseling and Guidance of APA identified the professional goal of a counseling psychologist as fostering the psychological development of the individual. The focus was on stimulation of personal development to maximize one's effectiveness through life (APA, 1952). Hurst and Parker (1977), Super (1977), and Wrenn (1977) have reiterated this position. Counseling, then, is designed to facilitate development. As it is most often practiced, it is implemented after problems have been experienced.

When counselors work with individuals experiencing critical life events (Bocknek, 1976; Schlossberg, 1976), their goal is to help the individual grow from the experience. In contrast, the psychotherapist might focus on alleviating a crisis or reducing stress. Despite the acknowledgment that a developmental counseling perspective is essential, little detail has been provided on what such an intervention entails. Perhaps the most explicit intervention strategy is described by Farmer (1976); however, she fails to clarify the relationship between the intervention process and the developmental conception. Thus, although counseling has the potential for a developmental emphasis, much of counselor training and practice at the present time seems to parallel that of psychotherapy.

5. Support

When individuals seek help from a counselor, they often feel incapable of overcoming the consequences of the event. However, during the time of the event's occurrence, individuals often seek support and solace from friends, neighbors, and/or individuals experiencing similar events. Self-help groups and mutual helping (Caplan & Killilea, 1976), designed to facilitate the widowhood experience, single parenthood, the empty nest, retirement, various illnesses and other critical life events, have proliferated rapidly. The goal of these groups seems to be to ease the adjustment to the event and to help the participants avoid the potential stress of the events, allowing them to use the event as an opportunity to restructure their lives (Danish, 1977).

The impact of critical life events may be altered by the quality of the support system available to the individual. A number of studies have pointed out the importance of supportive networks and interpersonal resources for individuals experiencing critical life events. For example, in a study of life events and complications during pregnancy by Nuckolls, Cassel, and Kaplan (1972), support measures such as the quality of the marriage relationship, quality of interaction with extended family, and adjustment within the community were found, in conjunction with past history of events, to reduce the complications of pregnancy. Similarly, Gore (1973) found that men with highly supportive spouses and friends had fewer negative consequences as a result of unexpected unemployment than did men with fewer supports. The value of social support is recognized as a positive force in the successful encounter with critical life events. As pointed out earlier, social supports are likely to be more available when the event is on time and in sequence because one's support system is expecting such events.

6. Enhancement

If one can anticipate an event prior to its occurrence, an intervention designed to promote the individual's growth as a result of the event can be developed. Unfortunately, to date, few such interventions have been developed.

An example of an enhancement intervention is a project proposed by the first two authors to disseminate self-help information about life events for adults living in rural areas who are entering the second half of life. The objective of these materials is to enable individuals to prepare more effectively for the critical life events that occur after age 40 and to decrease the need for traditional human services among older adults.

Three sets of self-help materials will be developed: life event brochures, 'Cooperative Extension Minute" public service television announcements, and TEL–MED tapes. Each brochure will describe a specific critical life event that adults are likely to experience after 40. The brochure topics will also serve as the themes for the "Cooperative Extension Minute" announcements and the TEL–MED tapes. The brochure format will include not only descriptive information about the event but also specific self-help suggestions for the reader. Examples of such events are: menopause, retirement, widowhood, institutionalization, and onset of chronic illness (Danish & Smyer, 1979).

We believe that we can help prepare individuals for these events by developing self-help materials for knowledge dissemination. If the self-help suggestions involve skills that the project participants do not possess, professional and neighborhood resources will be required for skill teaching and/or support.

In this section, we have identified six intervention approaches varying in conceptual assumptions and the timing of the intervention in relation to the event. The interventions based on the developmental concepts are less well delineated and have been tried less frequently. In the next section, we will examine different approaches to one class of events: high probability, individual life events.

IV. Applying Interventions to Life Events:
The Example of Individual High-Probability Life Events

A. OVERVIEW

As pointed out earlier, life events can be differentiated by their structural characteristics and type. Table II presented four classes of life events using individual and cultural types and focusing on the structural characteristic of the probability of the event. At the present time, there is no clear treatment of choice for each particular class of life events. The development of treatments of choice for various classes of events is essential, however, if intervention is to become systematic.

In this section, we will focus on two intervention approaches to high probability, individual life events: primary prevention and enhancement. These two types of intervention differ in their assumptions regarding the nature of events and individual development. They share, however, a commitment to intervention before the occurrence of the critical life event.

We have chosen to focus on individual, high probability life events for two reasons. First, within this class of events, the differences between disease and developmental conceptions of intervention can be seen most clearly. In addition, this class of events can be categorized as normative for individual development. As such, policymakers and the general public are likely to support general intervention strategies focusing on this class of events. The report of the President's Commission on Mental Health (Bryant, 1978) reflects a concern with critical periods of development (e.g., old age, childhood) as well as with intervention strategies linked to critical life events. Thus, for conceptual and pragmatic purposes, high probability, individual life events are important.

B.   DISTINGUISHING ENHANCEMENT FROM PRIMARY PREVENTION

Although both primary prevention and enhancement efforts are appropriate for this class of events, considerable confusion about the distinction between these two intervention approaches has existed. Goldston's (1977) definition of primary prevention reflects the ambiguity: "Primary prevention encompasses activities directed toward specifically identified vulnerable high risk groups within the community who have not been labeled psychiatrically ill and for whom measures can be undertaken to avoid the onset of emotional disturbance and/or to enhance their level of positive mental health" (p. 20).

To Goldston, primary prevention refers to both *protection* and *promotion*. In explicating this definition, Goldston (1977) stated: "The goals of primary prevention are twofold: first to prevent needless psychopathology and symptoms, maladjustment, maladaption, and misery regardless of whether an end point might be mental illness; and second, to promote mental health by increasing levels of 'wellness' among various defined populations" (p. 21). Although the philosophical underpinnings are well defined, the activities that might be undertaken under the name of primary prevention are not (Cowen, 1977a, 1977b). When primary prevention interventions can have two such distinct goals, their implementation and evaluation are difficult. For this reason, the concept of enhancement or enriching interventions (Baltes, 1973; Danish & D'Augelli, 1980) has been proposed to label efforts aimed at promoting development. Until now, however, the distinction between enhancement and primary prevention has been more theoretical than substantive (Cowen, personal communication, 1979).

It is our belief that the distinction is a meaningful one that has significant implications for the expected outcomes and interventions, the implementation of interventions, and their acceptance by the public and by policymakers.

If prevention is defined as the promotion of health, problems arise regarding the expected outcomes of the intervention. For example, mental health is usually defined as the absence of mental illness. Few behavioral referents of mental health exist that hold up over the life span and across cultures even within our own country. How does one know, then, that an intervention has promoted health except by the inference that there is an absence of illness? When one attempts to evaluate the success of the intervention and finds no incidences of the disease, should one conclude that the primary prevention intervention that was implemented *prior* to the onset of the illness has succeeded, or that there was no illness to begin with? If the intervention does not succeed in eliminating the illness, should one conclude that the intervention has failed, and that health has not been promoted? Either conclusion seems indefensible. Until health is viewed as a *process* and not the *state* of disease absence, primary prevention will continue to be a confusing enterprise.

Adler, Levinson, and Astrachan (1978) have raised similar questions about the meaning of prevention as it relates to the implementation of preventive interventions. They contend that preventive inteventions should be classified according to (*a*) specificity of aim; (*b*) specificity of method; (*c*) direction; and (*d*) risk. Specificity of aim refers to the extent that the intervention is designed to affect a clearly identified condition. The method refers to the activities; the direction relates to the target population. Finally, identifying the risk involves assessing any unintended consequence of the intervention. Adler *et al.* (1978) concluded that preventive activities are most appropriate when they are specific in aim and method, when the target population is clearly identified, and when the risks are limited.

As noted earlier, the aim of primary prevention is problem reduction. Interventions focusing on enhancement, however, are directed toward aiding individuals or groups to encounter the future so that events provide opportunities for growth. Initially, our view was that the end state was not a specific outcome for each event but the ability to plan for a variety of future life events (Danish & D'Augelli, 1980). Whereas we still believe preparing individuals to plan for their future is essential, we now recognize that specific outcomes for specific events may be identified as well. The identification of specific outcomes is a recognition of the interrelationship between intervention efforts and life-span theory and research (Baltes & Danish, 1980). The specification of intended outcomes requires a careful delineation of the potential intervention effects and a willingness to do time series, longitudinal research, and evaluation. Interventions based on an enhancement framework, then, require a solid background in life-span human development.

An enhancement-oriented model of intervention has the following attributes:(*a*) a central focus on life events;(*b*) a developmental as opposed to a disease conception; and (*c*) a belief that experiencing past life events helps one prepare for future life events. The framework is summarized here. A more complete description of such a model has been presented elsewhere (Danish & D'Augelli, 1980).

Although the consideration of life events as markers for development is an integral part of our model, individual interventions are not necessary for each life event. In fact, we begin with the assumption that there is significant similarity across life events. While the *content* or *knowledge* one needs to encounter the events differs, the *skills, risks,* and *attitudes* necessary for a successful outcome generally overlap. For example, the life events of marriage and retirement differ in the content of events, but require related skills—decision making, risk taking, and so on. When a life event is encountered, one's history and life style influence the impact of the event and one's response to it. For example, Lawton and Nahemow (1973) proposed that an individual's response to an external stress is, in part, dependent on the individual's past history with similar phenomena. They suggested that experiences with similar events increase one's competence, thus providing the capacity to cope successfully with a wider range of environmental demands.

The ability to respond effectively to events because of past successes, can be explained, in part, as the development of an expanded repertoire of behaviors or social reinforcement. Although these explanations can account for the behavior once the individual encounters the event, it does not explain the initial appraisal of the situation. Part of the reason why individuals with a past history of effective responses to events are able to respond to present events effectively is *intraindividual similarity.* Individuals who respond effectively may recognize the similarity between the event they are presently experiencing and both past and future events in their lives. They understand that they have experienced similar situations. At a cognitive level, they know they *can* deal with the event. At the behavioral level, they employ a behavioral sequence that has been successful in the past. Therefore, the psychological uniqueness of the event becomes deemphasized and similarities are highlighted (Danish & D'Augelli, 1980).

In summary, the distinctions between prevention and enhancement are important, as the two types of intervention embody different assumptions regarding aims and outcomes. Neither approach has been adequately evaluated because the bulk of individual and social interventions have been designed to be implemented after an event or crisis arises. Some have suggested, however, that interventions in anticipation of life events may reduce the economic and emotional costs of life events. If this is the case, primary prevention and enhancement interventions should be viewed as good investments for the future.

V. Individual High-Probability Life Events: The Case of Retirement

A. OVERVIEW

As indicated earlier, for both pragmatic and conceptual purposes, individual, high probability life events are important targets for intervention. This class of events has an intuitive appeal because most people will experience these events. Both policymakers and citizens can identify the events and their expected characteristics. If one is interested in combining developmental theory with intervention, the class of individual, high probability events is a good place to start. In this section, one individual high probability event, retirement, will be used as an example. Many of the issues arising in the design and implementation of interventions can be clarified by considering retirement.

B. DIFFERENT INTERVENTION APPROACHES TO RETIREMENT

Both disease and developmental conceptions of intervention have been used as frameworks for helping adults with retirement. Holmes and Rahe (1967) suggested that retirement presents a considerable adjustment problem; they listed retirement as the tenth most stressful life event. Recent findings, however, offer another view of retirement. For example, Streib and Schneider (1971) compared a sample of men who were retiring with a sample of men continuing to work. Their purpose was to identify the effects of retirement on adjustment. They concluded that retirement was not, *in itself,* as difficult an experience as previously thought. Kasschau (1974) and Taylor (1972) have also concluded that retirement does not lead to an adjustment crisis.

Intervention approaches to retirement have varied in terms of their conceptual models and have differed in terms of the timing of the intervention. Butler and Lewis (1977) and Dorken (1962) have focused on *remedial* interventions that treat individuals who have developed psychiatric symptoms as a result of retirement. Sinick (1977) has described *counseling* interventions to assist individuals to accept retirement "as another positive phase of life" (p. 45). Glamser (1974) described *secondary prevention* programs that focus on "easing the transition to retirement and reducing the problems which may be encountered in retirement" (p. 1). Bartlett (1974) described the value of a retiree association, a telephone hotline, a newsletter, and other forms of *support* for retirees. Hunter (1974), in describing the objectives of his *primary prevention,* preretirement program, includes "helping older adults take steps to prevent retirement problems from arising in the first place" (p. 4). Finally, Boyack (1978) has described the need for *enhancing* the life-planning skills of individuals at time of employment.

Boyack (1978) suggested that the following questions may be important for individuals to ask themselves:

> Will I have sufficient annual income to provide for the type of lifestyle I want in retirement? What are some of the questions I need to ask in regard to my legal affairs? Have I established a long-range health maintenance plan? Have I reviewed my lifestyle and relationships in preparation for transition into retirement? What are my current interests and activities? What gives my life a sense of fulfillment? What concerns do I have about my own aging process? And have I developed a viable plan for my future? (p. 18)

She concludes that exposure to such a life-planning process acts as a motivational force to seek additional information, change attitudes about life planning, and change behavior toward a positive future life style. Garrison and England (1979) have described a program designed to make retirement a positive experience by stimulating early life planning.

C. THE COMPARATIVE ADVANTAGES OF AN ENHANCEMENT APPROACH

Although we have categorized many of the intervention efforts in the retirement area, most researchers and program developers have adopted a combination of disease and developmental conceptions in their retirement interventions. In addition, many have not clearly delineated the timing element of their interventions. Thus, they have focused on problems associated with preretirement, the retirement itself, and postretirement. In summary, previous efforts have not clearly identified the goals of intervention (crisis resolution, prevention, or growth) or when the intervention should be implemented.

We believe that those interested in retirement intervention should adopt an enhancement, life-planning approach for several reasons. First, proponents of enhancement interventions recognize that retirement must be considered as a process. Retirement is not simply the day at age 65 or 70 when one stops working; it is a process that can and should begin with one's entrance into the job market. As such, the popular expression "Today is the first day of the rest of your life" takes on real meaning. Second, enhancement interventions make specific assumptions regarding the competencies of individuals. Such interventions assume that individuals have both skills and deficits, and that they are active problem solvers and participants in intervention (Kahn, 1975; Smyer & Gatz, 1979). In contrast to the social services approach outlined by Moody (1976) that requires service recipients to be passive and dependent upon professionals (Estes, 1979), an enhancement approach encourages self-reliance and life planning. This assumes a self-definition by the adult as competent, in contrast to the learned helplessness that may be induced by professionalized, reactive services (Schultz, 1980).

A third dimension of the enhancement orientation relates to the development of professional personnel. Several years ago, Albee (1959) pointed out the impossibility of training enough direct service personnel for the population in need of mental health services. A similar argument can be made for the personnel situation in the area of mental health and aging in general, and retirement in particular. As Smyer and Gatz (1979) noted, sufficient numbers of doctoral-level personnel cannot be trained to meet the direct service needs of older adults. Therefore, one strategy is to develop approaches that will reduce or minimize the reliance upon professional services.

A fourth aspect of an enhancement orientation is the potential radiation effect of life planning. In addition to making retirement a more positive experience, one's life satisfaction may improve across a number of life dimensions. Life planning takes into account that several events may impinge on an individual, and that planning skills may facilitate positive growth across several events.

VI. Summary

The major purpose of this chapter has been to describe the relationship between life events, viewed within a life-span developmental framework, and intervention. During the last few years, the concept of life events has become increasingly popular among developmental researchers, those interested in intervention, and the general public. However, there has been little agreement regarding what constitutes a life event and what are effective interventions for life events.

In this chapter, we have suggested that life events must be viewed as both markers of development and as processes. As markers, they serve as milestones and transition points for charting one's development. As processes, they require expanding one's view of intervention to include the context of the individual's experience and the relationship between the event and other aspects of the individual's life.

Whether events are viewed as markers or processes, two event properties are particularly important: the structural characteristics of an event and the type of event. In this chapter, two properties have been considered in detail: the probability of occurrence; and the type of event—individual as opposed to cultural. Probability of occurrence refers to the likelihood that an event will be experienced by a large proportion of the population. Individual life events are age-related events having their primary impact upon the individual's developmental history. In this chapter, we have focused on high probability, individual life events that are predictable and usually expected for the individual.

At the same time that the life-events concept has been increasing in popularity, there have been major changes in the conceptualization of human development intervention. In considering intervention, two elements are important: the theory of human behavior inherent in intervention; and the timing of the intervention in relation to the event process. We have focused on two conceptual frameworks that have influenced intervention: disease and developmental approaches. These two frameworks differ in their assumptions regarding the goals of intervention and the roles of service providers and consumers. The distinctions between the two conceptual perspectives is clearest when one considers the example of interventions focused on anticipation of an event—interventions occurring before the discrete event itself occurs. Primary prevention efforts and enhancement oriented interventions share the element of anticipation, but they differ in their conceptual frameworks. We have used the case of retirement to compare preventive and enhancement approaches to one life event.

This chapter is an initial attempt to link developmental conceptions of life events with intervention. At the present time, there is no clear treatment of choice for particular types of life events, or for events with different characteristics. Before a taxonomy of treatment approaches can be developed, however, it is necessary to clarify the conceptual foundations of intervention strategies. The distinctions between disease and developmental approaches and the recognition of the importance of the timing of intervention provide a context for additional consideration of the links between life events and intervention.

Acknowledgments

We appreciate the thoughtful comments of Donald Ford, Pat Piper, Rachel Pruchno, Carol Ryff, and Ellen Skinner. Craig Schweon was especially helpful in conceptualizing and writing the section on retirement.

References

Adler, D. A., Levinson, D. J., & Astrachan, B. The concept of prevention in psychiatry. *Archives of General Psychiatry,* 1978, **35,** 786–789.

Albee, G. W. *Mental health manpower needs.* New York: Basic Books, 1959.

Albee, G. W., & Joffee, J. H. (Eds.), *Primary prevention of psychopathology* (Vol. 1). Hanover, N.H.: University Press of New England, 1977.

American Psychological Association, Division of Counseling and Guidance, Committee on Counselor Training. Recommended standards for training counseling psychologists at the doctoral level. *American Psychologist,* 1952, **7,** 175–181.

Baltes, P. B. (Ed.). Strategies for psychological intervention in old age: A symposium. *The Gerontologist,* 1973, **13,** 4–38.

Baltes, P. B., Cornelius, S. W., & Nesselroade, J. R. Cohort effects in developmental psychology. In J. R. Nesselroade & P. B. Baltes (Eds.), *Longitudinal research in human development: Design and analysis.* New York: Academic Press, 1979.

Baltes, P. B., & Danish, S. J. Intervention in life-span development and aging: Issues and concepts. In R. R. Turner & H. W. Reese (Eds.), *Life-span developmental psychology: Intervention.* New York: Academic Press, 1980.

Baltes, P. B., & Willis, S. Life-span developmental psychology, cognitive functioning, and social policy. In M. W. Riley (Ed.), *Aging from birth to death.* Boulder, Colo.: Westview Press, 1979.

Bartlett, D. M. Retirement counseling: Making sure employees aren't dropouts. *Personnel,* 1974, **51,** 26–35.

Bocknek, G. A developmental approach to counseling adults. *The Counseling Psychologist,* 1976, **6,** 37–40.

Boyack, V. L. Statement before the Subcommittee on Retirement Income and Employment (Select Committee on Aging, House of Representatives Comm. Pub. 95-150). Washington, D.C.: United States Government Printing Office, 1978.

Broskowski, A., & Baker, F. Professional, organizational, and social barriers to primary prevention. *American Journal of Orthopsychiatry,* 1974, **44,** 707–719.

Bryant, T. E. *Report to the President from the President's Commission on Mental Health.* Washington, D.C.: United States Government Printing Office, 1978.

Butler, R. N. *Why Survive? Being old in America.* New York: Harper & Row, 1975.

Butler, R. N., & Lewis, M. I. *Aging and mental health* (2nd ed.). St. Louis, Mo.: C. V. Mosby, 1977.

Caplan, G. *Principles of prevention psychiatry.* New York: Basic Books, 1964.

Caplan, G., & Killilea, M. (Eds.), *Support systems and mutual help: Multidisciplinary explorations.* New York: Grune & Stratton, 1976.

Cowen, E. L. Personal communication with the author, January, 1979.

Cowen, E. L. Baby steps toward primary prevention. *American Journal of Community Psychology,* 1977, **5,** 1–22 (a).

Cowen, E. L. Psychologists and primary prevention: Blowing the cover story. *American Journal of Community Psychology,* 1977, **5,** 481–490 (b).

Cowen, E. L., Trost, M. A., Lorion, R. P., Dorr, D., Izzo, L. D., & Isaccson, R. V. *New ways in school mental health: Early detection and prevention of school maladaption.* New York: Behavioral Publications, 1975.

Danish, S. J. Human development and human services: A marriage proposal. In I. Iscoe, B. L. Bloom, & C. C. Spielberger (Eds.), *Community psychology in transition.* New York: Halsted Press, 1977.

Danish, S. J., & D'Augelli, A. R. Promoting competence and enhancing development through life development intervention. In L. A. Bond & J. C. Rosen (Eds.), *Primary Prevention of Psychopathology* (Vol. 4), Hanover, N.H.: University Press of New England, 1980.

Danish, S. J., D'Augelli, A. R., Brock, C. W., Conter, K. R., & Meyer, R. J. A symposium on skill dissemination for paraprofessionals: Models of training, supervision and utilization. *Professional Psychology,* 1978, **9,** 16–38.

Danish, S. J., & Smyer, M. A. Primary prevention, self-help and the rural elderly. Unpublished paper. The Pennsylvania State University, 1979.

Datan, N. Normative life crises: Academic perspectives. In N. Datan & L. H. Ginsberg (Eds.), *Life-span developmental psychology: Normative life crises.* New York: Academic Press, 1975.

Dohrenwend, B. S., & Dohrenwend, B. P. (Eds.), *Stressful life events: Their nature and effects.* New York: Wiley, 1974.

Dorken, H. Remarks on retirement. In *Pre-retirement counseling: The community's responsibility.* San Dimas, Calif.: The Educational Center, California State Polytechnical College, 1962.

Elder, G. H., Jr. *Children of the Great Depression.* Chicago: University of Chicago Press, 1974.

Elder, G. H., Jr. Age differentiation and the life course. *Annual Review of Sociology* (Vol. 1). Palo Alto: Annual Reviews, 1975.

Elder, G. H., Jr. Family history and the life course. *Journal of Family History,* 1977, **2,** 279–304.

Elder, G. H., Jr., & Rockwell, R. Marital timing in women's life patterns. *Journal of Family History,* 1976, **1,** 34–53.

Estes, C. L. *The aging enterprise.* San Francisco: Jossey-Bass, 1979.

Farmer, H. INQUIRY project: Computer-assisted counseling centers for adults. *The Counseling Psychologist,* 1976, **6,** 50–54.

Ford, D. H. Mental health and human development: An analysis of a dilemma. In D. Harshbarger & R. Maley (Eds.), *Behavior analysis and system analysis: An integrative approach to mental health programs.* Kalamazoo, Mich.: Behaviordelia, 1974.

Garrison, R. B., & England, C. M. *Retirement: A time for fulfillment.* Providence, Utah: Keith W. Watkins, 1979.

Glamser, F. D. The efficacy of preretirement preparation programs for industrial workers. Paper presented at the Annual Meeting of the Gerontological Society, Portland, Oregon, October, 1974.

Goldston, S. E. Defining primary prevention. In G. W. Albee & J. M. Joffee (Eds.), *Primary prevention of psychopathology* (Vol. 1). Hanover, N.H.: University Press of New England, 1977.

Gore, S. The influence of social support and related variables in ameliorating the consequences of job loss. Unpublished Doctoral Dissertation, University of Pennsylvania, 1973.

Guerney, B. G. Should teachers treat illiteracy, hypocalligraphy, and dysmathematica? *The Canadian Counselor,* 1977, **12,** 9–14.

Hagestad, G. O. Problems and promises in the social psychology of intergenerational relations. Paper presented at the Workshop on Stability and Change in the Family sponsored by the Committee on Aging, National Research Council, Annapolis, Md., March 1979.

Hartsough, D. Meddling with "Acts of God": A disaster recovery intervention. Paper presented at the American Psychological Convention, Chicago, August, 1975.

Hartsough, D. Lafayette crisis center volunteer training program. Paper presented at the Southern Psychological Convention, New Orleans, March, 1976.

Hartsough, D. Monticello in retrospect: Confessions of a mental health disaster recovery worker. Paper presented at the American Psychological Association Convention, San Francisco, August, 1977.

Holmes, T. H., & Rahe, R. H. The social readjustment rating scale. *Journal of Psychosomatic Research,* 1967, **11**, 213–218.

Hultsch, D., & Plemons, J. Life events and life-span development. In P. B. Baltes and O. G. Brim, Jr. (Eds.), *Life-span development and behavior* (Vol. 2). New York: Academic Press, 1979.

Hunter, W. W. *Preparation for retirement.* Ann Arbor, Mich.: Institute of Gerontology, 1974.

Hurst, J. C., & Parker, C. A. Counseling psychology: Tyranny of a title. *The Counseling Psychologist,* 1977, **7**, 16–19.

Kahn, R. L. The mental health system and the future aged. *Gerontologist,* 1975, **15**, 24–31.

Kassachau, P. L. Reevaluating the need for preretirement preparation programs. *Industrial Gerontology,* 1974, **1**, 42–59.

Kimmel, D. *Adults and aging.* New York: Wiley, 1974.

Lawton, M. P., & Nahemow, L. Ecology and the aging process. In C. Eisdorfer & M. P. Lawton (Eds.), *The psychology of adult development and aging.* Washington, D.C.: American Psychological Association, 1973.

Lopata, H. Z. *Widowhood in an American city.* Cambridge: Schenkman, 1973.

Lowenthal, M. F., Thurnher, M., & Chiriboga, D. *Four stages of life.* San Francisco: Jossey-Bass, 1975.

Modell, J., Furstenberg, F., & Hershberg, T. Social change and transitions to adulthood in historical perspective. *Journal of Family History,* 1976, **1**, 7–33.

Moody, H. R. Philosophical presuppositions of education for old age. *Educational Gerontology,* 1976, **1**, 1–16.

Neugarten, B. *Middle-age and aging.* Chicago: University of Chicago Press, 1968.

Neugarten, B. Adaptation and the life cycle. *The Counseling Psychologist,* 1976, **6**, 16–20.

Neugarten, B., & Hagestad, G. Age and the life course. In R. H. Binstock & E. Shanas (Eds.), *Handbook of aging and the social sciences.* New York: Van Nostrand Reinhold, 1976.

Neugarten, B., Moore, J., & Low, J. Age norms, age constraints, and adult socialization. *American Journal of Sociology,* 1965, **70**, 710–717.

Nowak, C. Life events research: Conceptual consideration. Unpublished manuscript, The Pennsylvania State University, 1979.

Nuckolls, K. B., Cassell, J., & Kaplan, B. Psychosocial assets, life crisis, and the prognosis of pregnancy. *American Journal of Epidemiology,* 1972, **95**, 431–441.

Parkes, C. M. Effects of bereavement on physical and mental health: A study of the medical records of widows. *British Medical Journal,* 1964, **2**, 274–279.

Parloff, M. B. Can psychotherapy research guide the policy maker: A little knowledge may be a dangerous thing. *American Psychologist,* 1979, **34**, 296–306.

Rappaport, J. *Community psychology: Values, research and action.* New York: Holt, Rinehart & Winston, 1977.

Rappaport, J., & Chinsky, J. M. Models for delivery of service from a historical and conceptual perspective. *Professional Psychology,* 1974, **5**, 42–50.

Regier, D. A., Goldberg, I. D., & Taube, C. A. The de facto United States mental health system. *Archives of General Psychiatry,* 1978, **35**, 685–693.

Riegel, K. Adult life crises: A dialectic interpretation of development. In N. Datan & L. Ginsberg (Eds.), *Life-span developmental psychology: Normative life crises.* New York: Academic Press, 1975.

Rossi, A. Transition to parenthood. *Journal of Marriage and the Family,* 1968, **30**, 26–39.

Ryan, W. *Distress in the city.* Cleveland: Case Western Reserve University Press, 1969.

Ryder, N. The demography of youth. In J. S. Coleman (Ed.), *Youth: Transition to adulthood.* Chicago: University of Chicago Press, 1974.

Schlossberg, N. K. The case for counseling adults. *The Counseling Psychologist,* 1976, **6,** 33–36.

Schofield, W. *Psychotherapy: The purchase of friendship.* Englewood Cliffs, N.J.: Prentice-Hall, 1964.

Schultz, R. Aging and control. In J. Garber & M. E. P. Seligman (Eds.), *Human helplessness: Theory and application.* New York: Academic Press, 1980.

Sinick, D. *Counseling older persons: Careers, retirement, dying.* New York: Human Sciences, 1977.

Smyer, M. A., & Gatz, M. Aging and mental health: Business as usual? *American Psychologist,* 1979, **34,** 240–246.

Spivack, G., & Shure, M. B. *Social adjustment of young children.* San Francisco: Jossey-Bass, 1974.

Srole, L., Langner, T. S., Michael, S. T., Opler, M. K., & Rennie, T. A. C. *Mental health in the metropolis: The midtown Manhattan study.* New York: McGraw-Hill, 1962.

Streib, G. F., & Schneider, C. J. *Retirement in American society: Impact and process.* Ithaca, N.Y.: Cornell University Press, 1971.

Super, D. E. The identity crisis of counseling psychologists. *The Counseling Psychologist,* 1977, **7,** 13–15.

Taylor, C. Developmental conception and the retirement process. In F. M. Carp (Ed.), *Retirement.* New York: Human Sciences, 1972.

Wrenn, C. G. Landmarks and the growing edge. *The Counseling Psychologist,* 1977, **7,** 10–13.

Young, C. E., Giles, D. E., & Plantz, M. Community survey: Paper number 1. Unpublished manuscript. The Pennsylvania State University, 1979.

On the Properties of Life Events[1]

Orville G. Brim, Jr.

FOUNDATION FOR CHILD DEVELOPMENT
NEW YORK, NEW YORK

and

Carol D. Ryff

FORDHAM UNIVERSITY
BRONX, NEW YORK

Abstract

The concept of life events is presented as integral to the study of life-span development. Definitional categories of life events are provided, distinguishing among biological, social, physical, and psychological events. Various event properties (e.g., correlation with chronological age, probability of occurrence, extensiveness of occurrence) are also discussed, and a typology of events based on these properties is presented. The typology is then illustrated with actual life events and the related implications for anticipatory socialization and support systems are considered. Also illustrated in the event typology is the tendency of most investigators to focus on the normative, predictable events, thereby neglecting other important event types. Thus, the typology serves to broaden the range of events under study and

[1] This chapter is drawn from research in progress by the authors on the maintenance of self-respect through the life span. Material from this chapter was included in the 1979 Kurt Lewin Memorial address by the senior author: "Types of Life Events," *Journal of Social Issues,* 1980, **36**(1), 148–157.

enhances the discovery of hidden or emerging events. Finally, prominent fallacies in using life events to explain behavioral processes are discussed.

Central to the field of life-span development is the concept of life events. As Hultsch and Plemons (1979) have observed, research on life events has examined the relationship to physical illness in general, to specific types of physical illness, to psychiatric disorders, to psychological symptoms, to self-assessed status, and to life transitions. Researchers have focused on specific events, such as combat, entrance into school, marriage, parenthood, widowhood, migrations, and institutionalization. Given this diversity, the use of the term "life events" is somewhat hazardous. Nevertheless, life events are as integral to life-span development theory as are atoms and other lesser particles to physical theory. The purpose of the present chapter is to provide a conceptual analysis of certain aspects or properties of life events to enhance their usefulness in furthering our understanding of life-span development.

I. Biological, Social, and Physical Events

Imagine that each person could look ahead from birth over the life course to be covered and envision the tens of thousands of naturalistic life events to be confronted in the passage from birth to death. Some of these events issue from within, so to speak, caused by one's growth as an organism, as in the case of puberty. Other events are the consequences of the fact that humans must live in social groups: Life thus is patterned by major social events that are customary in a given society. Life is also filled with events that are noncustomary, whether they are deviant or unregulated social acts, or the intended or unintended consequences of other individuals in society with whom one is going through life. Still other events, such as fire, storm, avalanche, and tidal wave, are results of the physical world in process. The clarity of the life-event concept is advanced by distinguishing among these definitional categories.

Biological events encompass developmental changes in body size and bone structure, in the endocrine system, in the brain and central nervous system, in susceptibility to various diseases and to organ failures, among other things. For instance, the onset of puberty is one of the best-known illustrations of changes in hormonal activity, along with the female changes in progesterone and estrogen that appear rather abruptly in midlife. Less well-known are the male changes in testosterone initiated during the midlife period and continuing over a 10–20-year period (although with great individual differences in the length of this period of decline and activity), and the decline in adrenalin and noradrenalin in the 50–70 age period and its relationship to depression.

The customary events of social life are given in the roles that people play during the life span, in family, work, community, religion, friendship, and other familiar sectors of society. Marriage, starting a family, becoming independent of parents, establishing a home, starting to work, reentering an occupation at midlife, developing friendship groups, taking on civic and social responsibilities, creating leisure-time activities, accepting retirement, caring for aging parents, dealing with separation from a spouse, or the birth of a brother or sister, starting school, beginning heterosexual activities—and so on, through the myriad of social changes that constitute social life (Havighurst, 1972). The nonnormative, noncustomary social events include, as mentioned, deviant acts, including crimes against a person, being cheated, lied about, derogated, having extramarital affairs, physical fights, automobile accidents—and the whole range of events that constitute the deviant culture, the accidents, the marginal and excluded social behavior, that is the infrequently seen underside of society.

In the physical world, the steady state of the physical world, in the diurnal cycle, the rotation of the seasons, the nature of the weather, the character of the atmosphere, even the earth's gravitational field, all provide a context of physical changes occurring slowly during one's life span. Indeed, the slowness of certain of these forces does not yield events to be reckoned with in the sense that we have used the term. The set of unpredictable events in the physical world—earthquake, fire, injury from accident (the falling rock, the misplaced step on the mountain trail, the broken collar bone from the fall on the ski slope, the loss of vision from an automobile accident, the destruction of one's apartment by gas explosion)—do, however, provide many critical life events for the person, which take their place along with the social and biological, though less predictable in their occurrence.

II. Psychological Changes as Events

Some will say that there is an obvious omission from this description of events, namely, the internal or psychological events that occur through the life span: for instance, the religious experience and conversion, the "born again" experience; the resolution to devote one's life to one's country; the decision to leave one's spouse; the recognition that one has reached the top in one's career; the confrontation with one's own mortality at midlife and the changing orientation toward time wherein one starts defining time in terms of years left to live rather than in years since birth (Neugarten, 1968) and emphasizes the importance of the immediate day; the acceptance of the fact by fathers that their sons may turn out to be stronger and more successful than themselves, and by mothers that their daughters may be more competent and attractive than they are; the realization that one has, on balance, done more harm than good to mankind; and so on through a great number of psychological experiences, named and unnamed, that are met along the course of life. One feels that these events should take their place as equals with significant events in the physical, biological, and social realms through the life span.

Obviously, internal or psychological changes can be viewed as "causes" of physical, biological, and social events that may follow. For example, if one were studying biological illnesses of a psychosomatic nature, that is, illnesses induced by a psychological event, one would take this course. In contrast, were one to study the maintenance of self-respect as a psychological process, it might be more appropriate to focus on the three nonpsychological sources of events as the causes of changes in one's level of self-respect. As the latter question has guided our thinking, we have chosen to view psychological events as the *outcome* of events in the biological, social, and physical realms. The event framework selected is, therefore, a matter of ordering events for the scientific purpose of understanding a particular phenomenon.

There are, of course, still other modes of scientific research: Some concentrate on the relationship between two biological events in the person, separated by time; others on the relationship between two social events, over time; and some concentrate on the inner psychological life of the person, linking a given inner or psychological event to a subsequent development in the personality, with little interest in some of the concurrent or intervening biological and social correlates. All of these are productive endeavors. Each contributes to our understanding of the life-span development of men and women. Our concern, again, lies with the impact of outside events (biological, social, physical) on the personality dimension of self-respect.

III. The Life Event as a Social-Science Concept

Social psychology seeks to predict, explain, and eventually to understand the contemporary behavioral responses to contemporary situations (e.g., an aggressive response to a threatening social situation). In a very similar way, life-span development seeks to predict, explain, and, it is hoped, to optimize, changes in behavioral responses as a consequence of life events as they occur over a long period of time (e.g., the expression of loss of self-respect as the result of work disability or an increase in the sense of personal control over one's life as the consequence of an occupational promotion).

There is much that life-span development can gain from keeping this parallelism in mind. Primarily, the comparison might prevent the life-span perspective from repeating the same mistakes as occurred in the evolution of the social psychological view. Lundberg (1939) once said that it seems to be the dismal fate of sociology to follow in the footsteps of psychology, making the same mistakes 25 years later. We hope the work in life-span development can avoid a similar future scenario. Of course, in social psychology there is the issue of the influence of personality traits and situational characteristics on the response, with questions about the relative weights given to each component and how these interact to produce the response. The parallel in life-span development theory is in one's view of the person and the event—the relative influence of the enduring nature of personality over the life course and of the thousands of life events, great and small, experienced across the same time. Thus, we see that the issue of traits versus situational determinism becomes, in life-span theory, the question of constancy versus change in personality as the result of various life events. A life-span perspective of human development differs from most Western contemporary thought on the subject.

> The view that emerges from this work is that humans have a capacity for change across the entire life span. It questions the traditional idea that experiences of the early years, which have a demonstrated contemporaneous effect, necessarily constrain the characteristics of adolescence and adulthood. There are important growth changes across the life span from birth to death. Many individuals retain a great capacity for change and the consequences of the events of early childhood are continually transformed by later experiences, making the course of human development more open than many have believed. (Brim & Kagan, 1980, p. 1)

Moving from social psychology to life-span theory requires the recognition that the environment is no longer a large set of similar situations "out there" confronting the person but is, instead, a great variety of successive events to be faced as time goes by; some benign, some not so benign. The concept of present life space is stretched across time and becomes the expected future environment over the life span.

IV. The Meaning of Life-Event Properties

The properties of life events, like the properties of situations in social psychology, are described in ways that are salient for the observer or investigator, the student of human behavior—salient because they help the person explain the behavior of particular interest. Life events, as Hultsch and Plemons (1979) pointed out in their review, have been studied as subjective and objective, gains and losses, controllable or uncontrollable, and so on. Drawing on our parallel to situation analysis in social psychology, one recognizes that the possible number of event properties that one might conceive is very large indeed.

Sometimes properties are assigned to events in terms of the effect the event has on behavior (e.g., one that causes a significant change in a person's life style, or produces stress; this is similar to describing situations in terms of their stimulus characteristics). At other times, properties are assigned to events in terms of the person's perception of the event, that is, whether the event is subjectively experienced as good or bad, under control or not, or as being stressful or not. Indeed, much of the work on stressful events has used a subjective appraisal rating of events with regard to their stress-producing characteristics (Dohrenwend & Dohrenwend, 1974; Holmes & Rahe, 1967; Hultsch & Plemons, 1979; Sarason, Johnson, & Siegel, 1978; Zill, 1974). It has been found that there are important differences in rankings depending on the population groups doing the rankings (e.g., rural versus urban samples, and in samples differing in cultural backgrounds). Moreover, there is wide variability found among individual respondents.

We use a third approach to event properties. The properties of the life event are seen to be in the event itself, qualities that can be appraised objectively, such as whether or not its occurrence is highly correlated with a person's chronological age, or whether the event occurs for a large number of people rather than for just a few. This approach to considering event properties is more general, less tied to research on specific behavioral questions, and therefore it permits the derivation of types of events for which consequences then can be appraised.

The third mode just mentioned brings with it certain complications that need our attention. If we say that an event has certain properties, such as being highly correlated with age, the fact is that these properties do not always hold across different groups of people, in different subcultures, and in different historical periods. This is to say that the properties of events change under different conditions of history and culture, in the same sense that the physical properties of objects change with the application of intense heat or intense cold. But, if one can say, with reference to most people in the world, or even to a society at most times in history, or even for the present, that an event has a certain property (e.g., it is experienced by many persons), then this modality is a useful characteristic, and it is similar to the state of the physical object under its natural conditions. The task then is to describe events in terms of properties of interest according to their modalities, that is, how they are for most persons, and then to study the variability in different times and places. It suffices to say that for many people, the event has these properties.

Even in the case in which an event property, such as a high correlation between its occurrence and chronological age, is generally true for a social group, there obviously remains some intragroup individual variability. At one extreme are a possible set of events that have a perfect association with chronological age (e.g., the event occurs for every member of society at age 12). At the other extreme is a similar possible class of events that have no relationship to age at all. In between are events with varying degrees of correlation with age, and it is a matter of convenience where one chooses to divide age-linked and non-age-linked events. Consider events whose occurrence has a high correlation with age, that is with little dispersion around the modal age of occurrence. We now can see that there will be individual differences in how the event property of age correlation might affect the person experiencing the event, according to whether or not it occurs for the person at the modal age. Neugarten (1968) has given us the very creative and useful concept of "on-time" and "off-time" occurrence of events in life-span development. Neugarten (1968) points out that the individual passes through a socially regulated cycle from birth to death, a succession of socially delineated age statuses. There exists a socially prescribed timetable for the ordering of major life events. Men and women are aware of the social clocks that operate in their lives and are aware also of their own timing, describing themselves as early, late, or on-time with regard to finishing school, marriage, first job, parenthood, top job, grandparenthood, and so on.

According to Neugarten (1970) predictable on-time events are not unsettling when they arrive, for "the events are anticipated and rehearsed, the grief work completed, the reconciliation accomplished without shattering this sense of continuity of the life cycle" (p. 86). She then uses her concept of on-time–off-time to formulate a new hypothesis about the status changes causing midlife crises:

> it is the unanticipated, not the anticipated, which is likely to represent the traumatic event. Major stresses are caused by events that upset the sequence and rhythm of the expected life cycle, as when death of a parent comes in adolescence rather than in middle age; when the birth of a child is too early or too late; when occupational achievement is delayed; when the empty nest, grandparenthood, retirement, major illness or widowhood occur off-time. (p. 86)

V. A Typology of Life Events

Any person confronting the future and the great range of events that might take place wants to know: Will it happen to me? If so, when will it happen? If it happens, will there be others like me, or will I be the only one? In terms of properties of events, these questions point to three fundamental properties, namely, (*a*) the probability that the event will take place for a person; (*b*) the correlation of the event with chronological age; and (*c*) whether the event will occur for many people or just one or a few persons. When events are cross-classified by these three properties, eight types of events are produced, as set forth in Table I.

We have selected these three properties from among the many that might receive attention because they seemed most useful in our current analysis of how persons try to maintain self-respect through the life span. To illustrate, *social distribution* is important because it tells us whether or not the individual has a support system to help buffer the change, and to provide new reference figures to link with new norms for behavior. *Age relatedness* matters because it usually is associated with whether or not the individual was prepared for the life event or caught unexpecting by it. The *likelihood of occurrence* for the individual is fundamentally important on the premise that individuals will only attend in advance to those events that are likely to happen to them. This line of classification is similar to that used in studies of stress mastery and coping behavior in crisis, and it is also proving useful in analyzing how individuals change their beliefs or theories about themselves, such as past, present, and future time orientation, and a sense of personal control over life. We need not repeat that the classification is designed to aid in problem solving and was established for a particular range of life-span developmental problems. There are other classifications useful for other purposes (e.g., Baltes, Cornelius, & Nesselroade, 1978; Danish, Smyer, & Nowak, Chapter 9, this volume; Hultsch & Plemons, 1979).

The properties of life events under discussion here and the typology following from them has, in our view, general value for life-span developmental research and theory by suggesting new and major strategies in this field of study. In particular, three gains can be seen for life-span development researchers in the form of imagination-stretching and seeing new lines of inquiry. These gains will be discussed in the following sections.

A. EXTENDING THE RANGE OF EVENTS

Type 1 events include the familiar status changes frequently studied in the sociological tradition. In these instances, where the event is shared by many, the probability is high, and the event is related to age, the stage is set for anticipatory socialization. The new roles that one is expected to learn when the event takes place, the new attitudes, values, and overt behaviors, and the new persons and groups who become significant, all can be worked on in advance (e.g., as in the case of children who have been prepared by

TABLE I

Life Events Typology

Correlation with age	Experienced by many		Experienced by few	
	High probability of occurrence	Low probability of occurrence	High probability of occurrence	Low probability of occurrence
	1	3	5	7
Strong	Marriage Starting to work Retirement Entering school Woman giving birth to first child Bar Mitzvah First walking Heart attack Birth of sibling	Military service draft Polio epidemic	Heirs coming into a large estate Accession to empty throne at 18	Spinal bifida First class of women at Yale Pro football injury Child's failure at school Teenage unpopularity
	2	4	6	8
Weak	Death of a father Death of a husband Male testosterone decline "Topping out" in work career Childrens' marriages Accidental pregnancy	War Great Depression Plague Earthquake Migration from South	Son succeeding father in family business	Loss of limb in auto accident Death of daughter Being raped Winning a lottery Embezzlement First black woman lawyer in South Blacklisted in Hollywood in 1940s Work disability Being fired Cured of alcoholism Changing occupations Grown children returning home to live

their parents and others for their first day of school). It is not only the role behavior that can be taught ahead of time in the prechange socialization; it is also the new social reference groups, which are easily found and entered in such familiar status changes. These events are most frequently studied in the sociological tradition, emphasizing socialization processes, transitions between major roles, age grading, family life-cycle studies, status gains or losses, and so on (Brim, 1966; Hill & Mattessich, 1979; Neugarten, 1968; Neugarten & Hagestad, 1976; Neugarten, Moore, & Lowe, 1965; Riley, 1976; Riley, Johnson, & Foner, 1972; Rosow, 1976).

These formulations are limited by the fact that they address life experiences that are largely age-related, socially recognized, well-labeled, and normative. The theorists deal only with the most obvious of social roles that follow predictable timetables and have well-established socialization patterns. The events of a person's life rarely are as orderly as the sociological study of the life span implies in emphasizing such regular status changes. A potentially large component of life experience is events of other types, e.g., work disabilities (over 10% of the heads of U.S. families); the loss of reputation, as for persons convicted or otherwise destroyed by Watergate, for John Dennis Profumo, for the former Justice Abe Fortas, for the Hollywood writers ruined by the blacklisting of the 1940s and 1950s (Kanfer, 1973); great changes in fortunes, as in Forest City, Iowa, a small corn-farming town where 25 new millionaires "got rich quick" on stock of Winnebago Industries, a local company that was unheard of a few years before, only to have 90% of these fortunes wiped out a few years later by the stock market decline and the gasoline shortage; similarly, the rise and fall of fortunes of the silver miners of the late 1880s who turned into paupers overnight as silver was debased; and so on, for professional gamblers, oil prospectors, and many others. There is no such story in the Type 1 events. A child is born, grows up, marries, has children, works, grows old, and dies. If this were all, then lives would be much the same. The Type 1 events describe a culture, constitute an ethnography of phases of lives, describe the status structure of a society, but apart from a possible interest in exotic ethnography of some other culture, there is no story here. John Cheever's (1978) collected stories, for instance, are filled with events of many other types: of child runaways, of falling in love with a younger girl, of a near fatal fight with a brother.

It is not original to call attention to this imbalance of emphasis in life-span studies, to the need to study other types of events (e.g., Pearlin & Johnson, 1977), but the point warrants reiteration. As Neugarten (1970) has clarified, the normal expectable life events do not themselves constitute crisis. Neither the menopause nor the empty nest is viewed as stressful, suggesting the possible conclusion that crisis theory has arisen from studies of clinical rather than of community samples. Retirement may be another noncrisis event. Similarly, death is perhaps a normal expectable event to old people. The same is probably true of widowhood if it occurs after 65. It is, she says, not the birth of a child but the death of a child we should be studying.

The greatest contrast to the traditional sociological events are the Type 8 events, where the events have a low chance of occurrence, where the individual does not know when they might happen, and where there are few other people with whom to share the experience. This type of event has been the province of study among scholars of stress adaptation and coping behaviors in response to varieties of loss through accident, disfigurement, and death of a loved one (Coelho, Hamburg, & Adams, 1974). Consider the Type 8 instance of a person who wins a $1 million lottery. Apart from possible transitory fantasies, it is hard to conceive that the person would have prepared in advance for the role of a millionaire before the winning lottery ticket was drawn. Similarly, few would spend much time anticipating what life would be like and how one might adjust to the loss of a leg in an automobile accident.

Although the probability of any given Type 8 event occurring for a person is small, the cumulative probability of at least one Type 8 event occurring in the life span is substantial. Even so, little anticipatory socialization is engaged in by the person. In contrast, an event that is rare and unpredictable for most persons, may be a Type 1 event for other subgroups in society, and is dealt with as such in terms of anticipatory socialization. Merlin Olsen, speaking for many professional football players, said, "I knew that on any Sunday afternoon an injury could end it all" (Freeman, 1978), and, as other ballplayers do, he developed business ventures concurrently with his playing career.

By examining the typology we can see that for Type 5 events, prior socialization and establishment of reference figures and support systems takes place, although in a highly specialized manner: The young future king or queen is trained in advance for succession to the throne. In contrast, Types 2 and 6 present life events that the person knows are likely to occur, but does not know when. Because there is no age linked to the events of these types, they are not embedded in any social context. Indeed, they frequently are not even named by society because they lack age specification. There is, as a consequence, less anticipatory socialization by society. The person is alone, and, if he or she tries to deal in advance with the event, is forced into an "advance rehearsal" on an individual basis (e.g., a wife contemplating what it would be like to get out of her marriage or a mathematician realizing that his most productive years will soon be over). Even so, Type 2 and 6 events catch most people by surprise because advance rehearsal does not occur. The motivation to deal with a future event when one does not know when it will happen cannot be very strong. The lack of immediacy, and thus lower salience, works against investment of individual time or thought in advance rehearsal.

The other classes of events, Types 3, 4, 7, and 8, have a low probability of happening and have little anticipatory socialization or advance rehearsal. For Type 4, there is an additional uncertainty that the event will come into one's life. The Type 4 events, as compared to Type 8 events, are, however, characterized by having more people who experience the event, and this greater social distribution does lead to organized attempts to provide anticipatory learning, even though the probability is low and one is uncertain when it might happen. Familiar anticipatory socialization efforts are teaching persons what to do in cases of fire (e.g., fire drills, and Red Cross first aid courses designed to help persons deal with natural disasters). Fire extinguishers, first aid kits, and more recently, smoke detectors, are standard items in many households. Also notable have been recent efforts on national network television to provide anticipatory socialization to the nation as a whole in the management of fires, earthquakes, tornadoes, and other Type 4 events. These efforts at socialization tend to be hard work in contrast to anticipatory socialization for Types 1 and 5 experiences; the fundamental difference is that the person's motivation to learn is not very high when events are improbable and non-age-related.

Consideration of event Types 3 and 7 furthers our understanding of anticipatory socialization. In both instances, as noted previously, the events have a low probability, but, if they occur, they have a strong relationship with age. It must be noted that the bulk of these types of life events may come from the biological sector because of the association with biological maturation (closely correlated with chronological age). The only difference between Types 3 and 7 is in the distribution among the population. Poliomyelitis, admittedly an event less common now than earlier in history (and a matter to be discussed later with regard to transitional forms among event types), was once a threat to many children. Urethritis, in contrast, may be encountered by 10% of the female population, with some distribution across the age span but a modal concentration in the midlife period because of hormonal changes and vaginal shrinkage. For both types of events, the human stance seems to be one of wariness and a concern to get the event behind one, recognizing that there are age periods in which the possibility of events increases substantially only to disappear as one gets older. With reference to health events, for instance, it is the case "that at any point in life, there are anywhere from a dozen to fifteen conditions which comprise the major part—about 70 percent—of the risk we face. Thousands of conditions—such as being struck by lightening—make up the remaining 30 percent. What we do is identify and quantify the major hazards'' (Chew, 1976, pp. 104–105). There is little incentive for anticipatory socialization on society's part or even for advance rehearsal by the individual. Young parents, for instance, can hardly be expected to start practicing to take care of a birth-damaged child when there is no reason to believe ahead of time that the odds are anything but remote that they will need to. Most people here trust luck and hope to get through the age categories in which they are vulnerable to this type of event. Even where the experience is more widely shared, where the concentration of the event in an age category involves larger numbers, few parents would think ahead in a systematic way about what should be done if their child is struck with polio, and few young men begin to rehearse on their own for military service, probably anticipating instead that they will not be called.

B. DISCOVERING HIDDEN EVENTS

With this topic, and the one following on the discovery of transitional or changing events, we can see that the study of life events stands at the intersection of many kinds of inquiries into the human condition. Sociologists, clinicians, poets, historians, and futurists, as well as psychologists, all have, and will have, a hand in creating our understanding of life-span events.

Each person in the course of life goes through events that are unnamed. What are these nameless experiences? In what sense do they exist? At the most general level, there are events that are unrecognized and unnamed by any member of humanity—events for which no concept has ever been invented. At a less general level, cross-cultural analyses of life-span development reveal that each culture has its own distinctive set of life-span terms. To paraphrase Ruth Benedict (1961), each culture selects from the life span some events that it chooses to identify and leaves behind a myriad of other events never recognized or named. Thus, in addition to unnamed experiences for humanity as a whole, there are some life experiences for which one's culture has no name. All of us, therefore, have passed through some life events that we could not name; and it is likely that many of us have had the same nameless experiences.

The search for as yet unnamed significant life events should be like the search for new plants, animals, elements, particles, planets, and diseases, but it has not had the systematic sustained effort that is merited. Instead, the discoveries come as by-products of work for other purposes. For instance, advances through the working career are not as well-marked as are the transitions through the family career. The event of reaching the top of one's achievement, or "plateauing," in a career has had some attention in works of fiction, but it has only been in the past decade that there has been any serious scholarly attention given to this event, associated with studies of social mobility; and we still do not have any well-accepted name for the event equivalent to, say, marriage or widowhood. Similarly, there is an increasing interest in male hormonal changes during adulthood, and some gain in understanding of the properties of this event, but, at present, it is named by analogy only as "the male menopause." Both of these can be viewed as Type 2 events, with a variable relationship to age in adulthood. Another illustration, of the Type 4 event variety, is the 1973–1974 economic depression in the United States, which still remains unnamed as such, because the economists insist on calling it something else, thereby taking it out of common discourse. As a consequence, men who suffered reversals of careers and fortunes cannot talk about the event with each other as they did about the Great Depression of the 1930s.

Unnamed events are likely scattered throughout the eight types described in our classification, but one must wonder whether there can be many Type 1 events that are not named in a society. We can think of the event of a son changing from childhood to young adulthood, becoming hostile to his father, and expressing this hostility in one or more ways; this event is age-linked, met by many persons, and highly probable. But with no anticipatory socialization and no real name except, as Freud might say, "killing the old man," the event goes unnamed and undiscussed. Certainly the home run of research on life events would be the discovery of an unnamed Type 1 event.

In the search for unnamed life events, one will come across events, the names of which are hidden, or secret, or suppressed. We need here to add another criterion: Are the events viewed as deviant or acceptable to society? There are certain life events that are viewed by society as reprehensible, as involving a threat to social norms and the stability of society and, therefore, even though the events have names that everyone knows perfectly well, no one is allowed to talk about them. Venereal disease, disfigurement, a homosexual rape, and many others, are events in the dark underworld of society. As a consequence, the experience must often be borne alone by the individual, although in general one could say that there is no event so ugly in the eyes of society that the person cannot find at least one other person, if there is a name for the experience, with whom one can identify and discuss the event. This seems to parallel the pre-Freudian, pre-sexual-revolution attitude toward various sexual experiences in the need for secrecy, secret names, and the lack of any social reference frame. We might say that a number of life events yield closet reference groups and significant others, but most people do find each other. Whether or not a life event is viewed by society as unrecognizable, reprehensible, and deviant, is, of course, another characteristic of life events that can be used to further specify the relationship between events and personal adjustment, with special reference to the facility with which new social support systems can be established.

The search for unnamed events should lead us back to reading cultural anthropology and to the study of subgroup cultures within our own society, with the expectation of recognized and named events in those other groups that can be generalized to our society as a whole. Every culture and subculture has its special life events with esoteric names that are not readily known to the outsider, and their transferability to other cultural groups has not often been tested. More systematic use should also be made of national sample surveys collecting individual subjective reports and comments on life-span events, with the expectation that members of our society may have made up their own names for experiences where society has failed to do so, so that individuals can deal with such events effectively and talk about them with their friends. In the end, though, the best means of identifying unnamed events probably remains the ear of the clinician—Horney (1937), Erikson (1950), Levinson (1978)—and the revelations of poets and other artists in their attempts to describe their own personal experiences and to provide a basis for sharing these with other human beings.

C. EMERGING AND TRANSITIONAL EVENTS

Matilda White Riley (1978) says:

> We know that death is inevitable. And we are widely led to believe that aging over the life course is also inevitable, that the process of growing up and growing old must inexorably follow an immutable pattern. Yet a principal tenet of the sociology of age, a newly emerging scientific specialty, is that aging is not inevitably prescribed, that there is no "pure" process of aging, that the ways in which children enter kindergarten, or adolescents move into adulthood, or older people retire are not preordained. In this view, the life course is not fixed, but widely flexible. It varies with social change—not only with the changing nature of the family, the school, the workplace, the community, but also with changing ideas, values, and beliefs. As each new generation (or cohort) enters the stream of history, the lives of its members are marked by the imprint of social change and in turn leave their own imprint (p. 39).

Social change brings new kinds of life experiences, not just in substance but in number and intensity, and thus changes the life-span development of a birth cohort in a given historical period in ways that we have only begun to analyze. Each birth cohort moves through a different event structure during its life span. Sometimes events may be similar in type but differ in time; successive generations confronted with World War I, the Great Depression, World War II, the Korean War, and the Vietnam War. More often, the social, physical, and biological conditions of life change and the properties of life events are not the same. For instance:

> People 55 years old today were in the labor market after the Great Depression and World War II, got secure jobs before the baby boom and the vast immigration of women into the labor market led to increased competition for jobs and slower advancement, had a chance to accumulate savings and retirement equities before inflation made it difficult, and perhaps have been getting substantial wage increases during the last 10 years even when unemployment was hitting younger, older, and less educated groups. (Barfield & Morgan, 1977, p. 31)

In earlier times, the probability was that, before a person was 20 years old, someone in the immediate family would have died, the most likely being a younger sibling. But infant mortality rates have dropped, and the death of one's child or one's younger sibling, which used to be a probable, age-linked, and widely distributed experience, has now become an accident and a tragedy.

Hill and Mattessich (1979) showed that historical changes alter the chronology of developmental sequences and the timing of life events, speeding up or slowing down the process of status transition. Glick (1977) also described how change in the demographic properties of the twentieth-century population has produced a lengthening of the family career, shorter child-rearing periods, longer times both early and late in the family life during which spouses live without children being present, families with smaller numbers of members and thus more parent–child interaction, and a change, especially among women, toward a later age for marriage and birth of the first child (see also van Dusen & Sheldon, 1976). The age distribution of events changes not just from population characteristics; they also come from transformed concepts of the nature of man in human development. The new social history includes a number of thought-provoking works on the history of childhood, adolescence, and the family. "The history of the life cycle is a flourishing research enterprise," as John Demos (1977, p. 11) notes, and he goes on to say:

> Before the start of the 19th century, youth progressed to adulthood along a smoothly surfaced path; thereafter the way become increasingly disjunctive and problematic. Teen-age boys, in particular, began to leave home for work, for education, for adventure and worldly experience; yet periodically they would return, and they remained for many years formally bound to their families of origin. As a result their conditions swung sharply back and forth between opposite poles of autonomy and dependence. Even little children were expected to participate in the lives of their elders, while still observing traditional norms of filial submission.

Lastly, increased social distribution of the event occurrence is seen in the familiar illustration of the consequence of increased longevity (e.g., the experience of retirement from a life of work and the experience of the "empty nest," the woman's life after her children are grown and gone; both being life events faced by a small part of the population with unusual longevity for that historical period).

It is through the contribution of historians that our understanding of life events has changed, both in terms of the emergence of events and in their disappearance, and also in the transition from one type of event to another as the properties are altered through time. As for the eras ahead of us, the futurists have their long lists of events, evolving biological, technological, and social inventions, many with probable dates of appearance assigned to them. And, as we all know, the rate of such change in our world, or as we would say here, in the probable event structure of one's life, is increasing.

VI. Four Fallacies in the Attribution of Cause to Life Events

When we speak about cause at this point, we realize that no event comes *de novo,* without cause or antecedents of its own. The causal chain in a person's life-span development stretches back to birth and beyond, as far back as one wishes to imagine. We select a particular point in this chain of causality that allows us to make a useful statement about the relationships between life events and subsequent behavior change. There are, nevertheless, fallacies that are typical in thinking about events as causes, and these require comment because much personal planning and many attempts to cope with events, as well as deliberate social intervention programs to ameliorate the effects of events, proceed from these fallacies of thought and are therefore likely to fail.

Most people, in thinking about events in life and their effects on behavior, tend to attribute causality to a single, large, vivid, and recent event. In part, this comes about because it simplifies the interpretation of behavioral change: An explanation is ready at hand, and thinking more carefully, spending more time in analysis, or putting one's mind to the task of understanding what really happened in all its complexity, is hard work with no apparent or immediate gain. Societies, in the main, explain changes in personality by fixing both the time of, and the reason for, the change upon some obvious, widely shared, socially labeled event. Ritual makes changes easier; latching onto a named and ritualized event that can be accepted as "the cause" provides a social label that unifies the society in a renewed commitment to its ideology and shared epistomology. Agreement on such matters knits society together. One thinks of the familiar concept of rites of passage and the analysis of discontinuities in development that

Benedict (1961) brought to our attention, thus underscoring the fact that society uses dramatic changes in social status as a reason to demand dramatic changes in personality that otherwise would be difficult to produce.

The individual alone, undergoing a change in behavior, is called upon to explain to others in a way that is readily understood; required, one might say, to describe what is happening in conventional terms rather than in some idiosyncratic and perhaps more penetrating way that others do not want to hear. Thus, a person's own explanation of changes in the self, or even one's own attempts to transform oneself, take the same line of explanation as it is used by society. In addition, a person who, in experiencing a major change in behavior, does not understand it or cannot explain to others what is going on will seize on a well-named, socially legitimate event such as an accident, a death, a promotion, a fight with a spouse, an insult at work, and attach the relatively unnamed event and personality change to this other event. Perhaps the most notable here is the function of a religious revival meeting, where it is legitimate to say that one was "possessed by God" to give a label for a transitional period. The events themselves, such as the day of retirement or marriage—viewed in custom as a point of definition, as the delineation between one segment of the life span and another—do not really mark the beginning of the personality-change process. The named event may occur midway or toward the end of the actual process of change. The four fallacies to guard against are intertwined, but each present a slightly different aspect of the general fallacy, and, as such, each will be discussed separately below.

A. VIVIDNESS

People often seize on a vivid or dramatic event, among a number of recent events, as the particular cause of resulting change (and even label a more extensive experience as a whole with that single event's particular title). In the social arena, one focuses on status changes such as marriage; or, in biology, on maturational events such as puberty. In the instance of marriage, often viewed as a key event in the life span with ensuing self-examination and personal adjustment, reflection reminds us that marriage, in fact, refers to an experience of some duration filled with many discrete events: the first meeting, the ups and downs of courtship, the wedding preparations, the rehearsals of the ceremony itself, the honeymoon period, and so on. The personal changes set in motion during this experience labeled marriage do not necessarily begin at the moment of the event when one says "I do," but more often are triggered earlier by one of the less dramatic events.

B. RECENCY

In relating life events to personality changes, people often select the most recent event as cause. Thus, one often misses the main precipitating event by not looking far enough back in time. The useful and efficient explanation of personality change, linked by theory to its occurrence, often lies in an earlier event whose influence extends over time. This can happen either through a causal chain of successive minor consequences, or the influence may, in a manner of speaking, lie dormant for a while, not being noticed, or perhaps suppressed in the person's mind, only to resurface later, in full impact, to start the person down the road of personality change.

C. SIZE

Size and power are associated in the primitive mind, and people think that big events are causes and hence miss the gradual cumulative impact of small events on personality. Consider an analogue to the way in which the human organism gradually changes into death. Gerontology has been described as "the study of the silent, gradual, cumulative changes that take place within cells, tissues, organs, and systems over time" (Chew, 1976, p. 84). The patient may "die of cancer," but what has been the role of the aging process? What indeed is the "cause" of death? So it is also with events like changing on occupation or moving to a new neighborhood. The big event viewed as cause might be the failure to gain a promotion, or a child's fight with a school classmate, but, prior to these events, there usually has been a growing number of experiences of dissatisfaction with the work or community.

This view, familiar to some as the behavior modification approach to personality change, emphasizes gradual change from adaptation to successive and cumulative learning experiences. As Ray Bortner (personal communication, 1976) has said, "It is adult socialization by the drip method." Marjorie Fiske (personal communication, 1975), in writing about changes in self-definitions as one ages says:

> We need to learn a lot more about the subtle external cues—e.g., coming upon a mirror unexpectedly and not recognizing one's self, assumed or genuine hints of deference and/or protectiveness (perhaps often in their own self-interest) from younger people (which for the old-old may shift to indifference or disgust). I am sure there are dozens of such verbal and non-verbal signals, some subliminal, but hard to pinpoint . . .

We all recognize that there may be a number of small events of which the individual is well aware, but need not deal with—for instance, little facts that one may "choose to ignore"—until the accumulation of experience forces one to deal with what is going on. The events may occur over months or perhaps even years without a subjective conscious perception but with a sudden recognition when the critical mass of the episodes explodes into awareness.

D. SIMPLICITY

The tendency to attribute cause to a single event turns attention away from the obvious interaction effects of a number of events in inducing personality change. Although, ordinarily, this caution need not be stated for scientists, as they are sensitive to interaction effects within their own areas of science, the range of events under consideration (biological, social, and physical) takes us outside the domain of any one area of science, with the consequence that the scientist might be bound by the perspectives of his or her own scientific field. In life-span event analysis one must be concerned with the interaction of these different classes of events. Several leading research investigators have pointed the way.

Holmes and Rahe (1967) and Dohrenwend and Dohrenwend (1974), have studied the amount of stress that various events produce in the individual. Various life events are assigned weights or scores according to their likely stress-inducing qualities and individual stress scores can be developed from adding the individual event scores. Because the events dealt with differ in nature, the total stress score emphasizes the combined effect of several events occurring more or less simultaneously, and includes the additive effects of social, physical, and biological events. Recent work analyzing the "midlife male crisis" (Brim, 1976; Levinson, 1978) describes the variety of difficulties from biological, social, and sometimes from physical event classes occurring more or less simultaneously for some men in the midlife period.

The research just cited is more additive than interactive, but work on adolescence deals more directly with interactive effects of different events. Exemplary is the work of Hamburg (1974, 1980) on the simultaneous rapid bone growth rate, social demands to start being interested in the opposite sex, hormonal changes, and other developments. Simmons (1979) and Blyth, Simmons, and Bush (1978) have studied the effects of interaction between the onset of puberty, a biological event, and the alternative social events of leaving elementary school to move to a junior high school after sixth grade, or staying in the same school until eighth grade before leaving for high school. Because the two possible school changes occur at different age periods during the adolescent hormonal changes, the combined social–biological effects are different than if each were experienced separately.

To sum: In examining life events as causes, we must keep in mind: (*a*) the need to look behind the attention-grabbing vivid event for the experiences that really matter in launching personality change; (*b*) the most influential event may not be the most recent; (*c*) some personality changes result from the cumulation of various minor events over a period of time rather than from one big event; and (*d*) the potential for interaction effects of biological, social, and physical classes of life events.

VII. Summary

Life events are becoming increasingly salient variables for life-span developmental researchers. To maximize the usefulness of these variables in understanding growth and development, it is important to examine a broad range of experiences covered by life events. This broadened perspective is achieved by attending to hidden or unnamed events as well as by an awareness of emerging or transitional events. Similarly, related investigations must guard against focusing only on those events that are most vivid, recent, large, or simple. Future research will benefit from linking these event perspectives to specific content areas such as the study of self-respect.

References

Baltes, P. B., Cornelius, S. W., & Nesselroade, J. R. Cohort effects in behavioral development: Theoretical and methodological perspectives. In W. A. Collins (Ed.), *Minnesota symposium on child psychology* (Vol. 11). Hillsdale, N.J.: Erlbaum, 1978.

Barfield, R. E., & Morgan, J. N. Early retirement planning. *Economic outlook U.S.A.* (Vol. 4, 2). 1977.

Benedict, R. *Patterns of culture.* New York: Houghton, 1961.

Blyth, D., Simmons, R. G., & Bush, D. The transition into early adolescence: A longitudinal comparison of youth in two educational contexts. *Sociology of Education,* 1978, **51**(3), 149–162.

Brim, O. G., Jr. Theories of the male mid-life crisis. *Counseling Psychologist,* 1976, **6**, 2–9.

Brim, O. G., Jr. Socialization through the life cycle. In O. G. Brim, Jr., & S. Wheeler (Eds.), *Socialization after childhood: Two essays.* New York: Wiley, 1966.

Brim, O. G., Jr., & Kagan, J. Constancy and change: A view of the issues. In O. G. Brim, Jr., & J. Kagan (Eds.), *Constancy and change in human development.* Cambridge: Harvard University Press, 1980.

Chew, P. *The inner world of the middle-aged man.* New York: Macmillan, 1976.

Cheever, J. *The stories of John Cheever.* New York: Knopf, 1978.

Coelho, G. V., Hamburg, D. A., & Adams, J. E. (Eds.). *Coping and adaptation.* New York: Basic Books, 1974.

Demos, J. Growing up American. *The New York Times Book Review,* April 24, 1977.

Dohrenwend, B. S., & Dohrenwend, B. P. (Eds.). *Stressful life events: Their nature and effects.* New York: Wiley, 1974.

Erikson, E. H. *Childhood and society.* New York: Norton, 1950.

Freeman, D. Merlin Olsen of Little House on the Prairie. *TV Guide,* May 31, 1978.

Glick, P. C. Updating the life cycle of family. *Journal of Marriage and the Family,* 1977, **39,** 5–13.

Hamburg, B. A. Developmental issues in school age pregnancy. In E. Purcess and S. Berenberg (Eds.), *Aspects of psychiatric problems of childhood and adolescence.* New York: Macy Foundation, 1980.

Hamburg, B. A. Coping in early adolescence: The special challenge of the junior high school period. *American Handbook of Psychiatry* (Vol. 2, 2nd ed.). G. Kaplan (Ed.), New York: Basic Books, 1974.

Havighurst, R. J. *Developmental tasks and education.* New York: McKay, 1972.

Hill, R., & Mattessich, P. Family development theory and life-span development. In P. B. Baltes & O. G. Brim, Jr. (Eds.), *Life-span development and behavior* (Vol. 2). New York: Academic Press, 1979.

Holmes, T. H. & Rahe, R. H. The social readjustment rating scale. *Journal of Psychosomatic Research,* 1967, **11,** 213–218.

Horney, K. *The Neurotic personality of our time.* New York: Norton, 1937 (paperback edition, 1965).

Hultsch, D. F., & Plemons, J. K. Life events and life-span development. In P. B. Baltes & O. G. Brim, Jr. (Eds.), *Life-span development and behavior* (Vol. 2). New York: Academic Press, 1979.

Kanfer, S. *A journal of the plague years.* New York: Atheneum, 1973.

Levinson, D. J. *The seasons of a man's life.* New York: Knopf, 1978.

Lundberg, G. *Foundations of sociology.* New York: Macmillan, 1939. (A revised and abridged paperback edition was published in 1964 by McKay.)

Neugarten, B. L. Adaptation and the life cycle. *Journal of Geriatric Psychiatry,* 1970, **4**(1).

Neugarten, B. L. Adult personality: Toward a psychology of the life cycle. In B. L. Neugarten (Ed.), *Middle age and aging.* Chicago: University of Chicago Press, 1968.

Neugarten, B. L., & Hagestad, G. O. Age and the life course. In R. H. Binstock & E. Shanas (Eds.), *Handbook of aging and the social sciences.* New York: Van Nostrand Reinhold, 1976.

Neugarten, B. L., Moore, J. W., & Lowe, J. C. Age norms, age constraints, and adult socialization. *American Journal of Sociology,* 1965, **70,** 710–717.

Pearlin, L. I., & Johnson, J. S. Marital status, life-strains and depression. *American Sociological Review,* 1977, **42**(5), 704–715.

Riley, M. W. Age strata in social systems. In R. H. Binstock & E. Shanas (Eds.), *Handbook of aging and the social sciences.* New York: Van Nostrand Reinhold, 1976.

Riley, M. W. Aging, social change, and the power of ideas. *Daedalus,* Fall 1978, 39–52.

Riley, M. W., Johnson, W., & Foner, A. (Eds.). *Aging and society: A sociology of age stratification* (Vol. 3). New York: Russell Sage Foundation, 1972.

Rosow, I. Status and role changes through the life-span. In R. H. Binstock & E. Shanas (Eds.), *Handbook of aging and the social sciences.* New York: Van Nostrand Reinhold, 1976.

Sarason, I. G., Johnson, J. H., & Siegel, J. M. Assessing the impact of life changes: Development of the life experiences survey. *Journal of Counsulting and Clinical Psychology,* 1978, **46,** 932–946.

Simmons, R. G. Entry into early adolescence: The impact of school structure, puberty, and early dating on self-esteem. *American Sociological Review,* 1979, **44**(6), 948–964.

Van Dusen, R. A., & Sheldon, E. B. The changing status of American women: A life cycle perspective. *American Psychologist,* 1976, **31,** 106–116.

Zill, N. Developing indicators of effective life management. Revision of paper delivered at Urban Regional Information Systems Association (URISA) meetings August 29–31, 1973, Atlantic City, N.J. Washington, D.C.: Social Science Research Council, 1974.

Author Index

M

Subject Index

A

Abstinence, sexual, 211
Activity, in extraversion, 94
Adolescence
  definition of, 157
  life events in, 386
  microsystems in, 16
Adolescents
  childbearing by, 314–315
  criticism of mothers by, 195
  desired age and rearing, 187–188
  "limit testing" by, 195–197
  maternal age and aging and, 194–197
  mothers' relationship with, 190
  sociability of, 195
Adult development
  Berkeley Guidance Study, 150
  cohort particularity in, 149–152
  current models of, limitations of, 149–156
  decremental view of, 104
  definition of, 82
  Oakland Growth Study, 150
Adult education, 4, 11–12
Adulthood
  attachment in, 260–267
  roles in, 260–262
  social support in, 260–267
Adult life course, in Japanese narratives, 288
Adults
  mesosystem of, 16
  problem-solving and problem-finding in, 124
Adult-specific stages, Piaget on, 123
Affective transactions, 267
Affirmation, transactions of, 267
Age, 167–188
  actual versus subjective, 168
  and attributes linked with youth, 181

behavior and, 49
best aspects of, 175–178
desired, 170–174
family roles and, 175
meanings of, 170–174
minimum death, 170–174
personality changes with, 80
sex life and, 182
subjective, 170–174
subjective versus actual, 168
wisdom and, 119
women and desired, 183–188
worst aspects of, 175–178
Age identification, 168–169, 178–181
Aging
  adaptation to, 245
  adolescent and maternal age and, 194–197
  chronological age and, 182–183
  "continuity principle" in, 73
  coping and stress and, 95–97
  Daily Exhaustion Level and, 183
  in homosexuals, 237
  National Institute of Aging longitudinal study on, 177
  personality influence on, 81–87
  physiological process of, 198
  and sexuality in women, 222–223
  stress and coping and, 95–97
  symptoms of, 181–184
  women and attitudes on, 157
Aging Symptoms Index, 183
Aid, transactions of, 268
Alcohol problems in families, 166
"Antecedent probability," 47
Anxiety, in neuroticism, 93
Aquinas, 106
Aristotle, on wisdom, 108
Arthritis, social support in, 266
Assertiveness, in extraversion, 94
Asthma, social support in, 265

O

Oakland Growth Study, 150
Occupational attainment, 321–322
Occupational role of men, 146–147
Older persons
coping styles of, 74–75
education for, 11–12
Erikson on, 76
happiness among, 84–86
homosexuality in, 231
individual differences among, 257
Jung on, 76
masturbation in, 231
mesosystem of, 16
negative stereotypes about, 119
Rorschach on, 76
sexuality of, 208–216
social support in, 265, 266
stereotyped views of, 209
wisdom in, 131
coitus in, 233–236
masturbation in, 232–233
sexual expression in, 231–242
sexual motivation in, 223–231
Olsen, Merlin, 377
Ontogenetic development, 17
Ontogenetic sex-role patterning, 36
Openness to experience, 69–72
facets of, 94
maturational effects in, 78
stressful life events and, 86–87
traits of, 72–73
Optimization in educational psychology,
10
Order, 316, 318–319, 320, 321, 324,
326–327, 329
Ordered-change template in prediction,
45
Organismic model
of developmental theory, 39
individual as participant in, 40
ordered-change account in, 40
Orgasmic efficacy, 246
Orgasm in females, 211, 222, 226–228
faking, 243
in sexual identity, 227–228
O-sort rating, in personality assessment,
75

P

"Paper-and-pencil" as term, 88
Parenthood in middle years, 137–201
adolescent stress and, 142
and difficulty of child rearing by age of
child, 191–194
economic responsibility of, 141, 151
"Establishment" cycle in, 141
family formation and 162–167
family size and, 162
financial responsibilities in, 170
and gratification in children, 189–190
historical change and, 199
life-course perspective on, 143–145
"New Parents" cycle in, 141
pleasure–worry balance in, 188–191
positive and negative experiences in,
balance of, 189
"Postparental" cycle in, 141
research on, 158–159, 199
sample characteristics in, 159–161
social stress in, 151
Parents, as path to wisdom, 106
Pattern and patterned, as terms, 308
Peers, education by, 12
Permanent education, 4–5
Personality
age and changes in, 80
aging and, 66–74, 81–87
case study method of research on, 95
clinical assessment of, 74–76
definition of, 96
interview-based assessments of, 74, 95
projective techniques in research on, 95
research on, 95
self-report measures in research on, 95
stability of, 74–81
Personality and aging, trait research in,
87–97
Personality assessment
Bernreuter Inventory, 89
Buss and Plomin's EASI-III Temperament Survey, 89
Cattell's 16 Personality Factors Questionnaire, 89
Crowne-Marlow Social Desirability Scale,
88–89
Eysenck Lie Scale, 88–89